Owen Lovejoy and the Coalition for Equality

Owen Lovejoy and the Coalition for Equality

Clergy, African Americans, and Women United for Abolition

JANE ANN MOORE AND
WILLIAM F. MOORE

**UNIVERSITY OF
ILLINOIS PRESS**
Urbana, Chicago, and Springfield

Library of Congress Control Number: 2019954094

ISBN 978-0-252-04230-0 (hardcover) |
ISBN 978-0-252-08409-6 (paperback) |
ISBN 978-0-252-05114-2 (e-book)

Contents

That which characterizes the present age above all others . . . is the
overshadowing question of human rights—of human equality.

—Owen Lovejoy, Mid-Century Sermon, 1850

You know that this nuclear thought is the equality of mankind. This is
the sun around which our political system revolves.

—Owen Lovejoy, Cooper Union Address, June 12, 1862

Acknowledgments

We want to express our gratitude to those who brought us to the story of nineteenth-century interracial collaboration in Illinois. These are the people who pointed us toward an understanding of the depth of the struggle experienced by African Americans in antebellum and Civil War times and by Owen Lovejoy and the political abolitionists included in the coalition for equality.

They include hosts and friends who, out of commitment to human equality, led us during the summers we spent in West Africa. They include the faculty and students who mentored us while we taught African studies at Howard University, as well as our black and white, male and female clergy colleagues in the Washington, D.C., area, including Rev. Ted Ledbetter and Gretchen Eick, who worked with us in the effort to end American investment in apartheid South Africa.

Some were found among the progressive citizens of Montgomery County, Maryland, led by Idamae Garrett, who invited Jane Ann to run as a candidate and serve on the County Council in the 1974 Year of the Woman. Others stood out among the black citizens of Benton Harbor, Michigan, who dared to plan a gala Martin Luther King Jr. celebration with white citizens from St. Joseph. Still others gather together today in coalitions of diversity in DeKalb, Illinois, activists in the interfaith network, the Beloved Community, the Micah Group of interracial clergy, and the Lovejoy Society, and in Oak Park, Illinois, inside Pilgrim United Church of Christ, which is working to become a multicultural congregation.

We are grateful to Edward Magdol, whose 1967 biography of Owen Lovejoy in the DeKalb Public Library captured our imagination in 1994 and never let us go. We are indebted to the black churchmen and -women of the Chicago Friends of the Amistad Research Center who have been preserving precious documents of black history in the Amistad Archives in New Orleans; to its founder, Clifton

Johnson; to Rev. Dr. Sterling Cary, former Illinois Conference Minister, UCC; to Rev. Dr. Kenneth Smith, former president of Chicago Theological Seminary; and to the Chicago Friends' current leader, Willie Lee Hart.

The Society for Historians of the Early American Republic (SHEAR), an unusual academic group that encourages young historians in research and publication, graciously included us and gave direction to our research. We especially thank Frederick J. Blue, whose own research recognized the unusual contributions of Owen Lovejoy and who opened doors for us. We remember Merton Dillon in southern Michigan: his enthusiasm for antislavery research in Illinois, his discovery of the Lovejoy family letters, and his success in finding a home for them in the archives of Texas Technological University at Lubbock. We value the professional leadership James Brewer Stewart has given to SHEAR, as well as Stewart's appreciation of the roles Christianity played during the antebellum years.

In Illinois Tom Schwartz directed us to material about Lovejoy when the state library was still squeezed under the Old Capitol and later when it relocated to the Abraham Lincoln Presidential Library and Museum, which he headed. Always ready to help was director Katherine Harris, now president of the Abraham Lincoln Association. William Furry, director of the Illinois State Historical Society, alerted us to new material, and John Hoffman hunted down sources for us at what is now the Illinois History and Lincoln Collections in the University of Illinois at Urbana-Champaign Library.

Those who coached us through reading and critiquing our successive manuscripts deserve our deep appreciation. They include especially Frederick J. Blue and also Sarah Cooper, Sarah Criner, Maylan Dunn-Kenney, Bob Hey, Clinton Jesser, Lolly Voss, Marlene Meeter, John and Carol Stoneburner, and Tony Stoneburner. We give additional thanks for technical assistance from Bill Feldman and Kyle Kent.

Research offers zestful moments. We remember the young technician at Andover-Newton Seminary who discovered online the existence of an article by Lovejoy's grandson at Cornell University. We remember the devotion of Phil and Janet Dow in Albion, Maine, who keep the spirit of the Lovejoy family alive in that town. We remember the archivist at the McLean County Historical Society who handed us the unidentified handwritten manuscript of Lovejoy's 1862 Cooper Union speech. We remember Julie P. Winch, who sent us pivotal issues of the *Christian Recorder* that opened up a new path in our research; and we will not forget Lorna Vogt and Phyllis Kelley, who gave us important resources, such as our very own copy of the 1855 *Journal of the Illinois General Assembly*. Julia Edgerley, a historian from Granville, Illinois, bequeathed her well-read 1951 microfilm copy of Dillon's dissertation, "The Antislavery Movement in Illinois," and Pam Lang acquainted us with Lovejoy papers in the Bureau County Historical Society Archives in Princeton, Illinois.

We are grateful to the peer reviewers of the University of Illinois Press, and to the perceptive and concise UIP acquisitions editor Dawn Durante and assistant director Jennifer Comeau, who helped shape and sculpt the manuscript into a book.

Finally, in the midst of everything is our family, Deborah, Bill, Kyle, Kaitlin, and Watson, who give us constant inspiration and gifts of cutting-edge books on American history, and who respond to almost every question with the rousing answer, "It must be Owen Lovejoy!"

We also acknowledge Owen Lovejoy himself. Of all the politically active pastors and laymen involved in the antislavery movement in Illinois, the Reverend Owen Lovejoy was the one elected to the United States Congress—and when he got there, he made an indispensable difference.

Abbreviations

AA	American Antiquarian, Worcester, MA.
ALP	Abraham Lincoln Papers, Library of Congress
ALPLM	Abraham Lincoln Presidential Library and Museum, Springfield, IL.
ARC	Amistad Research Center, Tulane University, New Orleans, LA.
BCGS	Bureau County Genealogical Society, Princeton, IL.
BCHS	Bureau County Historical Society, Princeton, IL.
BCR	*Bureau County Republican*
Clements	Clements Library, University of Michigan, Ann Arbor, Owen Lovejoy Papers
CC	Colby College
CG	*Congressional Globe*
CHS	Chicago Historical Society (Museum)
CTS	Chicago Theological Seminary
CW	Roy P. Basler, ed., *The Collected Works of Abraham Lincoln*, 8 vols. (New Brunswick, NJ: Rutgers University Press, 1953–55)
HBB	*Owen Lovejoy, His Brother's Blood*, by Owen Lovejoy, edited by William F. Moore and Jane Ann Moore (Urbana: University of Illinois Press, 2004)
IHLC	Illinois History and Lincoln Collections, University of Illinois at Urbana-Champaign Library

JHR   *Journal of the House of Representatives of the State of Illinois,*
                   1853, 1855

JISHS   *Journal of the Illinois State Historical Society*

LC   Library of Congress

Memoir   Joseph and Owen Lovejoy, *Memoir of the Rev. Elijah P. Lovejoy,*
                   Who Was Murdered in Defence of the Liberty of the Press at Alton,
                   Illinois, Nov. 7, 1837 (New York: John S. Taylor, 1838)

MHS   Massachusetts Historical Society, Boston

NIS   Northern Illinois Survey, Northern Illinois University, DeKalb

OHS   Ohio Historical Society

TT   Texas Tech University, Lubbock, Texas. Southwest Collection;
                   Special Collections: Wickett Wiswall Papers; Austin Wiswall
                   Papers; Lovejoy, Elijah Parish, Papers, 1804–1891

Owen Lovejoy and the Coalition for Equality

Introduction

Before the U.S. Civil War, when white supremacy was the law of the land and justifications for slavery were embedded in American culture, three political abolitionist groups in northern Illinois formed a coalition to confront slavery, the Fugitive Slave law, and Illinois Black Laws and to obtain human rights and equality in their state and nation.

This coalition was composed of antislavery white ministers and laymen who organized formal church associations and political parties in Illinois; white women who formed antislavery societies that supported political parties and invited black women to participate; and African American men and women who gathered in congregations, debating societies, and sewing circles and organized political campaigns to submit petitions for equal status to city councils, the Illinois General Assembly, the U.S. Congress, and the president. All three of these groups agreed to put abolition ahead of the many other needed reform movements of the day and decided that the constitutional political system offered the best way to break the spell of the Slave Power.

These radical activists forged a coalition that relied on racial and gender equality among participants, on local churches and religious affiliations, on pragmatic and reasoned strategic compromises, and on electoral success. Interracial, interdenominational, and mixed-gender, the coalition was motivated by its members' religious beliefs and by the radical idea that slavery could be abolished and that human rights and equality could be obtained via the democratic process.

Political abolitionists in Illinois differed in several crucial ways from many of the opponents of slavery who followed William Lloyd Garrison in the East. Members of both camps agreed that slavery was a heinous sin against the laws of God, but whereas the Garrisonian abolitionists denounced the U.S. Constitution as proslavery, western political abolitionists presented it as an antislavery document with a great flaw that needed to be corrected. In addition, unlike Garrisonians, who rejected politics as the path to abolition because it meant associating with disreputable men in an evil system, the westerners selected candidates from within their religious community and sought to work within the political system. Moreover, easterners had divided over the role of women in the movement, but western clergy urged women to participate. Finally, the Illinois group did not believe that Garrisonian persuasion would change slaveholders' behavior but rejected the use of violence except for self-defense.

Illinois's political abolitionist movement began in 1840 at an antislavery meeting at the Hampshire Colony Church in Princeton served by the Reverend Owen Lovejoy. By 1846 these activists had formed the Illinois State Liberty Party, consisting of their coalition of clergy, women, and African Americans, which brought together opponents of slavery based on the principle of equality for all. They subsequently organized the Illinois Free Soil Party in 1848, the Free Democratic Party in 1852, the early Republican Party in 1854, and the antislavery wing of the Republican Party in 1856. The coalition prepared the way for Lovejoy's election to the U.S. Congress in 1856 and for his subsequent influence in Washington, D.C., and over the next four years contributed to fellow Illinoisan Abraham Lincoln's rise to the presidency. In the nation's capital, Lovejoy expanded the coalition to include women, clergy, and African Americans from across the country, and by 1865 it had accomplished its goals—at least legally. The Fugitive Slave Law, Illinois' Black Laws, and slavery were no more.

The members of the northern Illinois coalition were committed to developing personal relationships of mutual respect and esteem in which none dominated. Putting this idea into action required reflection and adjustment, white humbleness and black empowerment. Though black and white members came from vastly different backgrounds, they shared a vision of a democratic society that was based on the same sources: the Declaration of Independence, which protected the inalienable rights of all; scripture, which affirmed that all people were equal in the sight of God; and social philosophies that valued raising people out of poverty, expanding the middle class, and modifying the despotic powers of the wealthy planter class—the Slave Power. The coalition proposed applying the principles of human rights in all their practical consequences within the interracial community and society at large.[1]

Each group in the coalition selected its own leaders, surveyed and recruited its own constituency, and used the *Western Citizen*, the *Free West*, and the *Chicago Tribune* for communication. Each group initially organized its own conventions, selected its own venues, sent emissaries on tour and delegates to conferences, and decided on its own legislative priorities. Members of one group sometimes attended other groups' conventions, and the three groups almost always endorsed the same priorities. At the 1846 Liberty Party Convention in Chicago, the three diverse constituencies decided to merge, forming a united religious and political campaign against slavery and for equality. And Owen Lovejoy became its leader.

•   •   •

Even before Illinois achieved statehood in 1818, residents of the northern and southern parts of the region had widely varying attitudes toward slavery that reflected the divisions between the U.S. South and the North. The area that is now Illinois had joined the United States as part of the Northwest Territory, created by the Continental Congress on July 13, 1787. Although slavery was prohibited under the Northwest Ordinance, it remained widespread in the territory.

Two waves of migrants composed the vast majority of citizens. The first wave originated in the slave states and settled in the southern part of the territory. Some anticipated that slavery would be permitted when the area gained statehood, and most expected enforcement of strict Black Laws.[2] In 1800 slavery existed in the territory of Illinois as completely as in any of the Southern states. Illinois's first constitution was a compromise permitting residents to keep their slaves and indentured servants. In 1824 proslavery legislators initiated a referendum to hold a second constitutional convention in hopes of making Illinois a slave state, but the referendum failed, 6,640 to 4,972.[3]

Nevertheless, African Americans did not have equal rights with white citizens, who remained firmly in control. In addition to stringent laws that regulated the lives of African Americans, the Illinois General Assembly passed an 1839 resolution disapproving the formation of antislavery societies and promulgation of their doctrines.[4] Later, legislators also instituted fines and jail sentences for anyone convicted of participating in the Underground Railroad.[5] In 1846 proslavery Illinoisans lobbied to pass a Black Exclusion Act. Although only a tiny percentage of the Illinois population was black, residents of the southern part of the state expended a great amount of political energy to control them.

A second wave of white migrants began to arrive in the early 1830s, when the city of Chicago was surveyed and mapped. Settlers from New England and New York rushed into the northern part of the state, attracted not only by the upward mobility available in the burgeoning town but also by the possibilities for agricultural success offered by the area's rich soil and clear streams. These new arrivals brought with them a highly stratified society that had accumulated considerable wealth from the African slave trade in the seventeenth and eighteenth centuries.[6] Nineteenth-century advancements in the manufacture of slave-produced cotton continued to widen the gap between the rich, the middle class, and the poor. Although northeastern state legislatures had gradually outlawed slavery, they had stopped far short of granting full equality to African Americans, and abolitionists found themselves the targets of harassment.[7] Most of the migrants from the Northeast were moderates who considered slavery a part of their ancestors' lives and who now focused on building colleges and cultural institutions on the prairies and supporting innovations in agriculture and technology.[8] They feared that the extension of slavery into the West would hinder educational institutions and technological networks that could spread prosperity.[9] Though these moderate emigrants tended to ignore Illinois's small clusters of antislavery radicals, the Illinois General Assembly's proslavery sympathies and enactment of Black Laws created increasing discomfort and, ultimately, support for abolition.

In the early years of statehood, Illinois also received a trickle of free and fugitive African Americans. In 1820, the state's 55,211 residents included 457 free blacks as well as a few slaves, indentured servants, and runaways.[10] Some lived and worked in the southern and central parts of the state, while others traveled north to Chicago, where the less restrictive urban environment offered refuge and, if necessary, a quick exit to Canada via railroad or ship.[11] As of 1840, the state's population of 476,183 included 3,598 black people, 68 of them in Chicago. By 1850, 5,436 of Illinois's 851,470 residents were black, and ten years later, on the eve of the Civil War, those numbers were 7,628 and 1,711,951, respectively. Only in 1870, after the end of the Civil War and the abolition of slavery, did the black population top 1 percent—28,762 of 2,539,891 residents.[12]

Antebellum African Americans came with a mixture of anxiety and relief, despair and hope.[13] Once on Illinois soil, they were technically free, but they carried with them memories of trauma and the scars of slavery.[14] Because the state's borders were porous, fleeing slaves often entered clandestinely and hid until they found allies who could lead them to relative safety.[15] Small African American communities along the Mississippi and Illinois Rivers tried to protect them on their journey.[16] But federal commissioners, civilian vigilantes, entrepreneurial kidnappers, and angry slave masters also entered the state and pursued, captured, and re-enslaved fugitives. In addition, state and county sheriffs stood ready to arrest violators of the Black Laws.[17] Blacks struggled to distinguish proslavery white men, ready to arrest them, from antislavery men they could trust. They often felt unsettled until they could bring family members to the relative safety of Illinois. Many of these African Americans not only lacked knowledge of the white folkways and northern laws but also were illiterate and had little money and few belongings.[18] Yet they brought extensive agricultural and artisan skills, religious strength, fresh energy, and a fierce commitment to democracy.

A fourth emigration to the northern Illinois prairie consisted of small groups of white antislavery radicals who arrived between 1830 and 1860, often by wagon. Many came as part of religious groups converted during the Second Great Awakening, who had covenanted to build productive, educated Christian communities in the West. These migrants, generally from the educated middle class, brought with them enough money to buy land and build a cottage. They were also radical abolitionists who envisioned building humanitarian communities, churches, schools, and families that replaced authoritarianism and patriarchy with relationships of equality. Historian Hermann Muelder identified twenty-eight such colonies that settled in Illinois between 1830 and 1837 with Congregational, Presbyterian, Baptist, and Quaker stakeholders.[19] When they arrived, these churchmen learned that Illinois was not a free state but harbored slaves.[20]

As these tiny groups settled in Illinois, they began to develop their own kind of organization. They established antislavery churches.[21] White abolitionist clergy and laity, motivated by forward-looking religious belief, were the first to organize with the intention of changing the political structure of Illinois and the nation. They formed the Illinois State Anti-Slavery Society in 1837, created several associations of Congregational churches over the next decade, and united with the nondenominational Christian Anti-Slavery Society in the late 1840s and 1850s and with the interracial, nondenominational American Missionary Association when it was organized in 1846. They fought against missionary societies that threatened to take away their livelihood unless they were silent about slavery. When they met resistance, they formally adopted political abolitionism; state officials responded by arresting, fining, and prosecuting churchmen who aided runaways. From Southern whites, the abolitionists' attempts to alter the status quo provoked physical violence against ministers, riotous interruptions of meetings, public ostracism, and expulsion from the community.

But instead of withdrawing to the confines of their colonies, retaliating against their harassers, or accommodating to those in mainstream life, these radicals responded with political activism, building a succession of political parties that envisioned practical and progressive legislation on behalf of African Americans, ultimately becoming the operative radical core of the Republican Party. They worked to control their own political destiny, maintaining their religious principles while broadening the party's base to include conservatives who had condoned slavery but were now ready to press Congress and the White House to exclude slavery from the U.S. territories as a step to abolition. They also united with blacks, who alone could authenticate radical whites' right to speak publicly on behalf of African Americans and to demand black and white equality.

In New England and New York, women had been the conscience and prime movers of the abolitionist movements despite many clergy members who discouraged them from speaking in public or taking action outside their own homes. Social constraints often forced these women to lead under the cover of men. Despite being unable to vote, women organized petition drives and frequently influenced men around them to vote for antislavery candidates. Although men in the House of Representatives took credit for the December 1844 repeal of the gag rule forbidding discussions of slavery, the thousands of eastern urban women who signed and gathered hundreds of thousands of petitions brought the issue before the nation.[22]

In Illinois, white women from various colonies began establishing community and regional antislavery societies from 1842 through 1844.[23] In 1843 women from various northern Illinois societies joined to form the Illinois State Female Anti-Slavery Society. They protested the indictment of church leaders prosecuted for disobeying the state's Fugitive Slave law by writing dissenting letters, gathering signatures for petitions, and flooding the courtrooms of those on trial.[24] White and black women also illegally aided runaways on the Underground Railroad. Black women were especially vulnerable for their work with the Underground Railroad, yet leaders like Mary Jones and "Aunt Charlotte" were ready to help when runaways appeared.[25] The women realized that these acts of helping a few runaways was not enough; they must also campaign for each antislavery political party, spreading the news, influencing the vote, and preparing food for the rallies. The formal Female Antislavery Societies in Illinois lasted only a few years, but the political skills and community networks they developed were of great use in antislavery political campaigns from 1852 through 1862.[26]

From before the American Revolution, African Americans had been the prime instigators of the antislavery movement along the eastern coast and waterways of the United States. Slaves had always run away. By the 1830s, scattered supporters along escape routes in Illinois began to work together to help runaways reach northern Illinois and continue on to Canada. Once the Civil War began, thousands of slaves in Missouri and Kentucky emancipated themselves. The army sent some former slaves, labeled "contraband" by whites, to Illinois. Those who decided to settle in the state began to organize churches and societies to repeal discriminatory laws and change racist attitudes.

Black abolitionists in Chicago developed a political consensus by 1846. That same year, white and black radical communities in Chicago consolidated. John and Mary Jones arrived in Chicago in 1845 and immediately joined the black political activity taking place there.[27] Abraham T. Hall organized a prayer group from the small black population that pressed for the 1847 formation of Quinn Chapel, later an African Methodist Episcopal Church where African Americans could meet for sorrow, recovery, celebration, and political action.[28] John Jones, Henry O. Wagoner, Joseph H. Barquet, James D. Bonner, and others developed strategies for responding to the harsh state and national laws.[29] These abolitionists organized surveys, petitions, newspaper articles, and letters to the editor; held statewide Colored Conventions and provided leadership for national ones; appointed delegations to confront white state legislators; and joined the national network of black abolitionists. Jones informed white associates in the antislavery coalition when they needed to express their views to Congress and the White House.[30]

• • •

Religion was prominent among the factors that bound the coalition together. All three groups rejected proslavery forms of Christianity. African Americans wanted to be free of the perversions of Christianity instilled by slaveholders. Churchmen from New England wanted to escape the despair and predestination of Calvinism, which denied preachers and parishioners the free will to protest, change, and reform society. Antislavery women wanted a God who would free them from authoritarian religious denominations and from patriarchal clergy who denied them the opportunity to preach and to lead antislavery political work. These activists were developing new religious-political roles for themselves, coached and encouraged by black and white radical clergy and religious politicians in northern Illinois.

White planters had encouraged their slaves to convert to Christianity but had promoted a specific doctrine that interpreted scripture to demand obedience to the master and acceptance of torture. By firing any minister who dared question slavery, slaveholders had established a theology of personal submission in order to deny the human rights of both slaves and poor whites. Black political abolitionists wanted to destroy all remnants of this proslavery Christianity preached by southern clergy, favoring instead a message of rescue and deliverance. Black pastors told the story of the Hebrew slaves fleeing from unbearable bondage in Egypt through the Red Sea to the Promised Land. In this message, African Americans were God's chosen people, born of God's creation, fully belonging to the human family, liberated from slavery, free and equal.[31] The African Methodist Episcopal Church and other black churches sought to aid in the radical transformation of persons moving from slavery to freedom. The interracial and interdenominational American Missionary Society worked to prepare whites to support and participate in this transition. In an open-air campaign speech in 1860 in Freeport, Illinois, Owen Lovejoy shouted to the predominantly white crowd, "Such a radical was Christ. He was a Negro equality man, for his divine precepts belong to ALL men."[32]

Working with the Underground Railroad was a second vital experience that united the coalition. Collaborating with strangers across racial lines to establish escape routes for runaway slaves built solid friendships. The abolitionists could not free slaves in the South, but they could rescue those who got as far as Illinois. The coalition considered the Fugitive Slave Law unconstitutional, and members had pleaded with city councilmen and state legislators to repeal it. Ignored by lawmakers, they formed night patrols to deter federal agents and provided mechanisms for escape. Participants did not engage in violence; they considered their actions to be civil disobedience, even holy acts. The act of rescuing human beings escaping oppression became a universal symbol of resistance to immoral laws and protection of human life.

The Underground Railroad provided many kinds of rescues and deliverances to slaves who were seeking freedom. Often facing close calls, black and white participants were vulnerable to arrest by officials and violence from slaveholders. These traumatic experiences were transformative for both whites and blacks.[33] Black abolitionists who were looking for an entry into the dominant society discovered radical whites who were looking just as fervently for black comrades with whom they could share an ideal integrated community.

A third factor that united political abolitionists was their daily confrontation with the pervasive pseudoscientific theory that people of color were inferior, mere things, pieces of property available for purchase and sale. White pastors such as Lovejoy, Ichabod Codding, and William T. Allan and black pastors and intellectuals such as Henry Highland Garnet, Charles B. Ray, and Samuel Ringgold Ward quoted scriptures that claimed all people to be of one blood and one race. Scientist Charles Darwin had come to the same conclusion as a result of his long voyage around the world, but pseudoscientists—Harvard professor Louis Agassiz among them—procured the national spotlight. Agassiz pronounced that God had developed separate races in different climates and that the races were hierarchically arranged, with whites at the top and blacks at the bottom.[34] In the nineteenth century Agassiz's theory was used to justify slavery and racism in law and custom.[35] In the twenty-first century, physical and social scientists consider the concept of race to be an artificial, ideological construct that perpetuates unscientific misconceptions. As historian Dana Weiner has described, this outdated concept of race is the product of deliberate efforts to shore up white supremacy. When an unscientific theory is applied to groups of people as a justification for discriminatory policies and coercive power, it is racism at work.[36]

Uniting the three groups in the coalition required a leader with an unusual personality. Owen Lovejoy was a gregarious man with persuasive speaking skills, a gentle sense of humor and irony, probing analytical abilities, and profound religious convictions. Within the coalition he was viewed as a man of character and courage. He showed no interest in the trappings of fame or wealth, and he shared leadership with others easily. He was elected to office and acquired power with the support of white ministers, antislavery women, and African Americans, first in Illinois and later across the nation.

Lovejoy's career continued for twenty-five years. He was considered the leader of the Illinois antislavery movement from 1846 to 1857, and he promulgated the political approach of containment—that is, containing slavery to the South by prohibiting it in the territories. As a master strategist, he weighed public opinion and altered approaches to achieve his goals, such as pursuing a "bob-sled" strategy to achieve fusion among all who were outraged by the Kansas-Nebraska Act, regardless of party affiliation, and promising state offices to conservative Republicans in exchange for placing antislavery Republicans in congressional offices. Elected to the U.S. House of Representatives in 1856, Lovejoy immediately became a major antislavery figure, delivering momentous speeches using religious and political arguments to awaken listeners' consciences. Once the Civil War had begun, he urged the Congress and President Lincoln to free the slaves by means of military emancipation. As a member of the inner circle in the House, Lovejoy successfully chaired three committees during his years in Congress. He was regarded as an innovative, problem-solving legislator and was a confidante of President Lincoln.[37]

Lovejoy formulated an antislavery Christianity that brought together scripture, Joseph Bellamy's moral government theology, and William Ellery Channing's Unitarian concept of equality. Although he grew up in Maine, he was not a Calvinist, as many New Englanders were. He was not a fiery camp meeting revivalist nor an Oberlin perfectionist. When asked to describe his theology prior to his ordination, he answered simply that he was orthodox, but his views were more complicated than that term implies. Family letters show that Lovejoy was strongly influenced by Bellamy's book *True Religion Delineated, or Experimental Religion.*[38] Bellamy posits that moral beings are governed by the laws of divine authority. In 1842 Bellamy preached that "human government is a part of God's moral government, and of course, human laws are to be in accordance with the Divine Law."[39] This moral government approach was further developed by several theologians in the New Divinity school of thought, including Samuel Hopkins and Jonathan Edwards Jr. In this view, divine power is limited by the freedom God has given to people, who can choose to obey or disobey divine imperatives. God does not save societies but gives people the ability to act for the betterment of society. Individuals have the free will to choose whether to work toward God's kingdom on earth.[40] Lovejoy reflected Bellamy's thinking when in 1837 he pleaded with the citizens of Alton, where his brother Elijah had been assassinated, to repent "before that power which can pardon the penitent and still maintain the majesty of the law."[41] He believed that individuals and societies suffered consequences when divine laws were broken. He saw evil in slaveholding. He saw it in the actions of the rioters in Alton and in the silence of Alton citizens.

Although Lovejoy preached a serious theology, his friends said that he was by nature an optimist. He was drawn to the writings of Channing, who focused on the human capacity for goodness. While all were capable of goodness, Channing especially applied it to African Americans. He believed that each person manifested the divine likeness and therefore must be treated with equality and respect. This concept became a cornerstone of Lovejoy's antislavery thesis: "A spark of the divine is in every person," therefore "Abolition is a religious cause." Channing believed that in view of society's grievous injustices, redistribution of wealth would help lift up all classes.[42]

Lovejoy despised slaveholders' deliberate misuse of religion to fabricate a proslavery Christianity. One of the ways he confronted internal contradictions in the Bible as well as historic perversions of biblical interpretation was to consider four authorities when making an important decision: what does the Bible say about it; how does reason analyze it; what does humanity say about it; and where does justice stand on it? Proslavery Christianity used distorted interpretations of biblical passages as its sole authority and taught standardized sets of distortions to their slaves. Lovejoy preached that God never made a human being into a thing.[43] God never advocated torture. Historical criticism, developed by German scholars and slowly reaching American pastors,[44] held that the Bible was not the voice of God alone but a compilation of sometimes conflicting, divinely inspired texts by human authors.[45] Antislavery Christianity was a powerful influence, advocating the freeing of all people. By the end of his life, Lovejoy seemed to be moving in the direction of a proto-progressive liberal Protestantism.

After Owen Lovejoy's death in 1864, twenty-six colleagues in Congress presented tributes to him—more colleagues than had spoken on behalf of any other congressman who had died in office since John Quincy Adams.[46] Members of the coalition also paid tribute to him. Representing the radical western clergymen who were planning a monument to Lovejoy, Rev. Ichabod Codding spoke in Princeton, Illinois. Ministers of the African Methodist Episcopal Church in Washington, D.C., held a special memorial service, at which they affirmed Lovejoy as the successor to the great antislavery heroes John Quincy Adams and Joshua Giddings.[47] Gail Hamilton (pen name of Mary Abigail Dodge, a white woman journalist who had watched Lovejoy in action in Washington), spoke for other women as well when she wrote a two-page eulogy printed in the *Congregational Herald.*[48]

In 1909 Lovejoy received a posthumous honor when Evarts B. Greene, dean and history professor at the University of Illinois, was asked to identify twenty contemporaries of Lincoln who had made significant contributions to the state and nation. Greene championed Owen Lovejoy as the best representative of "the radical abolitionist attitude" of the state. Lovejoy was then portrayed on a medallion set in terra cotta on the outside of Lincoln Hall.[49]

Black historians must correct what John Ernest calls the white supremacist construction of history, a construction that pervades public culture and that, even when corrected, reappears in each generation. In addition to doing new research, these scholars must re-educate the public about slavery, slave protest, racism in the North, the cause and purpose of the Civil War, the self-emancipation of black abolitionists, and their victories in battle as Union Army soldiers.[50] In view of this necessity, writing about white abolitionists is hardly a priority.

Yet although black scholars do not need to write about Owen Lovejoy, they remember him. They have mentioned him in ways that suggest that his memory has remained in African American minds longer and more deeply than it has in white minds. Frederick Douglass, speaking in 1870, said that Lovejoy, among others, could "never be forgotten."[51] W. E. B. DuBois, who was born after Lovejoy died, was well aware of Lovejoy also. He wrote in 1937 that Lovejoy's essence was in the pure joy he expressed upon hearing, in December 1863, that Lincoln promised to emancipate the slaves still in bondage. Another time, Du Bois commented that Lovejoy's conversational style was to relate biblical allusions to contemporary political events in surprising ways.[52] In *The Negro in Illinois: The WPA Papers*, which presents research completed during the 1930s Black Chicago Renaissance, a black Chicagoan spoke familiarly about Lovejoy's work, exclaiming, "To Owen Lovejoy fell the honor of proposing the bill which abolished slavery forever."[53] In 1953 Benjamin Quarles described the adulation African Americans showered upon Lovejoy at the Union Bethel Church in 1862 as the clock struck midnight and the District of Columbia Emancipation Act went into effect.[54]

Although Lerone Bennett Jr.'s 2007 *Forced into Glory* ignores Lovejoy's prediction that Lincoln would become the Great Emancipator (evaluating the president as only a reluctant emancipator), he praises Lovejoy for being one of a small set of radical white political abolitionists in Congress who were the prime movers for emancipation. "These men, especially Sumner and Owen Lovejoy, were leaders of vision and the word."[55]

1. Becoming a Political Abolitionist

1811–1842

Life in Maine

In 1820 a distressing event took place that seared the memory of citizens of what is now the state of Maine. The Southern states, led by Kentucky senator Henry Clay, were pressing the five representatives from the District of Maine (then part of Massachusetts) to cast their votes in the U.S. Congress to legalize slavery in Missouri; in return they would be granted statehood for Maine.

The people around Waterville, Maine, heard about this proposition when their newly elected congressman, the Reverend Joshua Cushman, returned from Washington to his home in Winslow. He hastily informed his constituents that he was disgusted with this Devil's bargain. The Slave Power was admitting new states always in pairs—one free, one slave—to guarantee the South continued control over enough senators to prevent any future constitutional amendment that would abolish slavery. Cushman did not want to commit the "crime" of allowing slavery in Missouri in exchange for Maine becoming a state. Abhorring bondage, he preached the universality of equality as stated in the Declaration of Independence. He was an advocate of the proposed constitution for the new State of Maine that granted suffrage to all men, white and black.[1]

Cushman carefully wrote "An Address to the People of Maine" denouncing the compromise. Three of the other four representatives from the District of Maine signed it with him, but they failed in their efforts to persuade all other northern congressmen to vote against Clay's compromise. The Missouri Compromise of 1820 seemed to settle the matter: Missouri would become a slave state, and slavery would be prohibited in western territories north of Missouri's southern border. From then on, Mainers considered prohibiting slavery in the territories to be a "sacred trust" made by the federal government, a promise that would not be broken.[2]

Among Cushman's constituents was his ministerial colleague Rev. Daniel Lovejoy and his family, living on a farm in central Maine. The remarkable thing about the Lovejoy family was that despite repeated disappointments and even tragedies, their concern for each other kept them together. Their response to suffering was grounded in a strong religious ethos. Each faced God's judgments squarely; each tried his or her best to bring about the Kingdom of God on earth. This religious bonding as a family seemed to provide them with the capacity to relate to marginalized groups on the basis of equality.

The parents, Daniel and Betsey Lovejoy, started each day by leading their children in religious conversation in front of the kitchen hearth. They called their home altar the "throne of Grace." A descendant said that twice a day they shared their apprehensions and hopes for each of their seven children with the family and with God.[3]

No special attention went to Owen, the fifth child, who grew up with four brothers and two sisters. The sibling Owen felt closest to was Elijah, the oldest son. Elijah, who was nine years older than Owen, helped care for Owen as a small child, introducing him to the outdoors, helping him discover birds' nests in the meadows and hiking along old Indian trails with him. He also opened the world of ideas to Owen, tutoring him as a youth and mentoring him as a young adult.

Owen's father, Daniel, was an intelligent, well-read man who was subject to emotional highs and lows. In 1795 he began several years of intense study at the renowned Byfield Academy under the direction of Rev. Elijah Parish, reputed for his Calvinistic theology and his Federalist political views.[4] After Daniel was ordained, the Massachusetts Missionary Society assigned him to work among the clusters of white pioneers living at the edge of the frontier of the District of Maine and to minister to Indian communities still residing in the area. Lovejoy relished the assignment and for years faithfully cultivated small new congregations.[5]

Owen's mother, born Betsey Pattee, was also highly gifted. She was raised in Vassalboro, Massachusetts (now Maine), on the Kennebec River. In 1793, at age twenty-one, she moved with her parents to the unbroken forests surrounding the new village of Unity. Although she had objected to leaving civilization behind in the form of Vassalboro's library and Presbyterian church,[6] later she stated in her handwritten autobiography that it was a blessing to be in the pristine wilderness. There she met several evangelists from the Free Will Baptists, and they introduced her to a more expressive style of Protestantism, one that encouraged women to offer leadership and allowed black men to be ordained.[7]

Betsey was strongly influenced by *True Religion Delineated, or Experimental Religion*, a 1750 book by Dr. Joseph Bellamy, a colleague of theologian Jonathan Edwards.[8] She urged all young people to read it, including her own children.[9]

Bellamy's theology exposed Betsey to a Divine Spirit that was not hostile but gracious and to a belief that the Calvinist doctrine of election was a dishonor to God's love and goodness. Suddenly she felt freed from the terrors of predestined hell and guided toward a purposeful life. Human beings were free (within limits) to act for good under the umbrella of God's moral government; failure to do so would bring admonition and judgment. In Bellamy's view, God was as concerned for the soul of institutions as for the souls of individuals, and prayer led to human action on behalf of both neighbor and society. Betsey's religious life was not creedal but covenantal and experiential. Her husband, Daniel, remained Calvinistic in his thinking.

Daniel and Betsey married in 1801 and moved into a cottage a mile from Albion, Maine, that his father, Francis Lovejoy, had built, shaded by oak trees and edged with rose bushes.[10] A chaplain in the Revolutionary War, Francis was the family historian and a storyteller, regaling the grandchildren with tales of resisting autocratic English kings and bishops as well of describing greeting neighbors as equals made in the image of God.

When Owen was eleven, in 1822, the people in the nearby village of China opened an academy and asked Rev. Daniel Lovejoy to be a trustee. Owen and his siblings studied at this school, and brother Elijah taught there one year. China was a Quaker settlement that provided schooling for the children of a half-dozen free black families living there.[11]

As Owen finished his studies at China Academy in the spring of 1829, his older brother Joseph, a student at Bowdoin College, wrote to his parents that he had decided to become a minister. Daniel Lovejoy expressed relief and great joy to hear that one of his sons would join the institution to which he had given his life. His other sons, Elijah, Danny, Owen, and John, had not had a religious experience that led them to join the church, and until they did, Daniel expressed anxiety for their eternal souls.

Owen entered Bowdoin College in Brunswick, Maine, in 1830. In February 1831, his mother wrote to inform him that his older brother Danny had died of alcoholism. Addressing her letter to "My Dear Child," she urged Owen to "love and fear God all the day long, for the fear of the lord is the beginning of wisdom."[12] She admitted that she did not feel reconciled to God, criticizing herself for what she regarded as vile ingratitude. She also expressed her hope that Danny was now rejoicing in the presence of a forgiving God. She encouraged Owen to think about his eternal life, echoing Danny's earlier exhortation to his younger brother. She also told Owen that he was talented at expressing himself in abstractions but slow to take responsible action. Owen kept this letter for the rest of his life.

Elijah graduated from Maine's Waterville College (now Colby College) in 1826 and settled in St. Louis a year later, first running a school but subsequently becoming a journalist. In 1832, Elijah suddenly decided to become a minister and returned east, enrolling at New Jersey's Princeton Theological Seminary. After only thirteen months, he graduated with honors.

In the spring of 1833, Owen, aware that his emotionally ill father was unable to pay his tuition, abruptly left college without telling anyone and sailed to New York City to meet Elijah. When Owen arrived, Elijah was preaching for a month at the prestigious Spring Street Congregational Church in New York City.[13] Owen, who loved Greek, Roman, British, French, and American literature, told Elijah that he wanted to open a bookstore in Manhattan. That same week, however, Elijah received an offer from several well-to-do men in St. Louis who had been converted by the Reverend David Nelson with him at the First Presbyterian Church. They wanted to start the *St. Louis Observer*, the first Presbyterian newspaper west of the Mississippi River, with Elijah as editor. He was thrilled and was eager to leave for Missouri.[14]

Owen returned to Maine and learned that his father, who had suffered increasingly from severe depression, had just committed suicide. This tragedy affected all members of the Lovejoy family. After soul-searching for God's forgiveness, they set out on individual journeys. Joseph returned to Bangor, Maine, to finish seminary. Sibyl, two years older than Owen, found a teaching assistantship. Lizzie, four years younger, entered Mary Lyon's Ipswich Female Seminary, an innovative experimental school in Byfield, Massachusetts, that was one of the first to offer formal advanced education for women.[15] Owen's youngest brother, seventeen-year-old John, went to live with Elijah in Missouri. While his siblings scattered, Owen remained at the family's cottage with Betsey and worked on the farm by Lovejoy Pond. A few weeks later, on August 26, 1833, Elijah wrote to Owen from St. Louis, urging him to face his "hardness of heart" and turn to God. On February 6, 1834, Owen answered that a "miracle of grace" had come upon him. That autumn, he entered the seminary at Bangor.

Elijah's Ordeal

Over the next year, Elijah frequently published strong antislavery editorials in the *Observer*, provoking violent reprisals from defenders of slavery. Fearing for his safety, in 1836 he moved his press across the Mississippi River to Alton, Illinois, and renamed the newspaper the *Alton Observer*.

As a teenager, after Elijah had left Maine for St. Louis, Owen expressed his affection for Elijah in a poem, "To Our Absent Brother," which began, "By thy side, and by thy hand supported, I've wandered oft in that wide extended meadow," and ended, "For one short moment, would I give a whole eternity of manhood years."[16]

In November 1836, twenty-five-year-old Owen and his younger sister, Lizzie, joined Elijah and John in Illinois. Elijah would tutor Owen for the ministry, and Lizzie would help Elijah's wife, Celia, care for their toddler and cope with the controversy surrounding the *Observer*, which had not abated with the move to Illinois. Rioters had already twice thrown the paper's printing presses into the Mississippi River. After Owen and Lizzie's arrival, rioters destroyed a third press and repeatedly threatened Elijah's life. Alton citizens were unable to offer protection. Tension increased on October 26, 1837, when the statewide Anti-Slavery Society organized at the Upper Alton Presbyterian Church. Antiabolitionists disrupted the meeting, forcing the new society's formalization to take place on the following day in the home of Elijah's associate editor, Rev. Thaddeus Hurlbut. On November 7, 1837, four local men, three of whom were physicians, murdered Elijah in public view as he was trying to save yet another printing press.

A devastated Owen Lovejoy had lost his dearest brother. At first he was hardly aware of Celia or John or Lizzie, or the black and white staff members of the *Alton Observer*. Nor had his mind yet focused on Betsey. On his knees before God, he vowed never to forsake the cause for which his brother's blood was sprinkled.[17]

Alton citizens were afraid to come to a public funeral, so Elijah was buried in secret. A black friend crafted the coffin and a black youth drove the wagon to a bluff overlooking the Mississippi River, where Owen's Presbyterian minister friend, Rev. Thomas Lippincott, gave a prayer, and Elijah was buried.

News of Elijah Lovejoy's death spread rapidly throughout the nation. Black and white abolitionists were horrified. Memorial services were held in many locations. New antislavery societies sprang up.

On December 9, Owen wrote to James Gillespie Birney, the president of the American Anti-Slavery Society, that his brother had done more for the antislavery cause in dying than he could in living. "I advised him in a conversation we had a short time before his death to stand firm at his post although I did not think that these tragical results would follow." Owen wrote that Elijah had done his duty in remaining in Alton. "I trust in God, if called upon I shall be willing to follow the same course, even though it leads to the same end."[18] Owen had learned from the experience of his father's suicide to look beyond the devastating death to new possibilities. Looking into the future, he could see how Elijah's death would strengthen the antislavery movement.

Antislavery newspapers pointed out that Elijah, the first white man killed on northern soil by proslavery men, had become a symbol of the Slave Power's encroachment upon the constitutional rights of citizens in the free states of the North.[19] Southern-leaning papers blamed Elijah, saying that he caused his own death. The *Missouri Republican* editorialized that those who obstinately persisted in the attempt to establish an abolitionist press bore the guilt.[20] Usher Linder, the antiabolitionist Illinois attorney general, prosecuted twelve of Elijah's supporters for inciting the riot. When the jury found the first one not guilty, the state quickly dropped charges against the rest. Linder then defended those who had killed Lovejoy. All were found not guilty. Biographer Paul Simon wrote that "Not one person paid a penny fine and not one person went to prison for a single day" for the murder of Elijah Lovejoy.[21]

Immediately after Elijah's burial, Owen chronicled the sequence of events that led to the murder, sending a copy to his family in Maine. He attempted to explain what had happened, and why, to a defiant southern public and a bewildered northern press, at first trying to correct the many mistaken characterizations of Elijah that were appearing in the national press. Realizing that he could not sway proslavery propagandists, and unable to swallow his indignation at ministers who acquiesced to slavery and condemned Elijah, Owen directed his efforts at Protestant newspapers. He attempted to send a copy of his full chronicle to Rev. Joshua Leavitt at the antislavery *Emancipator*, but after the Alton post office failed to mail it, Leavitt continued publishing the views of Elijah's critics. A frustrated Owen wrote Leavitt a second time, and the *Emancipator* published the story in a special December 28, 1837, edition.[22]

Betsey Lovejoy counseled her children from afar, urging Owen, Lizzie, and John not to "harbor any revengeful feeling toward the murderers of your dear Brother."[23] Only God could bring justice. This message seemed to lighten Owen's burden and change his direction. He no longer needed to attend the insincere trials or hold the murderers accountable; the consequences of their disobedience to God's laws would be on their shoulders. He prayed that the murderers would experience "deep repentance before that Power that can pardon the penitent and still maintain the majesty of law."[24] Having put aside revenge, Lovejoy could now seek liberation for himself and for the slaves.

Another momentous letter came to the siblings in Alton, this one from their brother Joseph in Bangor, Maine.[25] Joseph reported that the American Anti-Slavery Society's Executive Committee was offering Joseph and Owen the opportunity to edit a memoir of Elijah.[26] Joseph asked Owen to meet him in New York City as soon as possible. He was certain the memoir would sell if it could be published quickly, and to support publication he had borrowed $6,000.[27] Owen realized that the proposed book would go a long way toward restoring Elijah's good name and might encourage many to join the antislavery movement. In New York City he would also have the rare opportunity to work with experienced black and white abolitionist leaders.

The two brothers met in the American Anti-Slavery Society's New York City offices in early February 1838 to begin their work, three months after Elijah's death. Its headquarters at 145 Nassau Street had been financed by Lewis and Arthur Tappan, wealthy merchants committed to evangelical reform. They had brought together a distinguished team of churchmen that included James Birney and Joshua Leavitt, as well as Utica attorney Alvan Stewart, who developed a legal basis for the antislavery movement, and organizer Henry Stanton, who was usually out in the field working on petition drives.[28] And although evangelist Charles Grandison Finney had left the city and the new Broadway Tabernacle nine months earlier, his presence in the office could still be felt. Finney, now a professor of systematic theology at Ohio's Oberlin College—a radical antislavery institution that enrolled, along with several hundred men, a small number of white women and black men and women—was arguably the most significant religious leader in the first half of the nineteenth century in the United States.[29] In the 1820s he had ignited the Second Great Awakening with his preaching, attracting many young men to the ministry and many young women to benevolence.[30]

But the anchor of the American Anti-Slavery Society office was Rev. Theodore Weld, a believer in radical equality. Some said he was a saint because he worked for little pay, slept in the attic of a black boardinghouse, and wore rough clothes. During an eighteen-day marathon debate against slavery in January 1834, Weld and others had influenced the entire student body at Cincinnati's Lane Seminary to become abolitionists.[31] In December 1836 he and distinguished African American clergyman Theodore S. Wright had trained a corps of more than fifty antislavery agents in racially mixed settings in Oberlin and New York City.[32]

When Owen Lovejoy arrived that winter, Weld was deep in research on several aspects of slavery that Owen would incorporate into his speeches for the rest of his life. Around that time, Weld composed an essay, "Reduction of Persons to Things"; edited an article by James A. Thome titled "Emancipation in the West Indies"; and worked on a book with Sarah and Angelina Grimké that would become one of the most significant of the period, *American Slavery As It Is: Testimony of a Thousand Witnesses.*[33]

Weld's colleague in antislavery training, Reverend Wright, was a local pastor and a national antislavery leader, the forerunner of a new generation of radical black ministers who were outspoken in their demand for equality. Wright asked Joseph Lovejoy, who was ordained, to preach at his church. But Wright also spoke. His description of slavery was an emotional, eye-opening experience for Joseph. Joseph wrote to his wife, Sarah, and urged her to begin immediately to educate their children about the sinfulness of allowing slavery to continue.[34] As a graduate of the African Free Boys' School in New York City, Wright had secured admission to Princeton Theological Seminary in 1825. Upon his ordination, he succeeded his mentor, Rev. Samuel E. Cornish, at Shiloh Presbyterian Church and served on the executive committees of three separate antislavery boards.[35] Although he had many accomplishments, Reverend Wright was often abused by white clergy.[36] Nevertheless, he continued to lead interracial fellowship.[37]

On the weekend of February 28, 1838, Owen was invited to travel to Hartford, Connecticut, to speak at the first convention of the Connecticut State Anti-Slavery Society.[38] White mobs had been destroying houses and businesses of African Americans in Hartford. For example, in 1836 a mob had burned down African American minister Hosea Easton's Talcott Street Congregational Church; while raising money to rebuild the church, Easton had died.[39] The gathering was eager to hear from Owen, a surviving brother of Elijah P. Lovejoy, slain only four months before. Some men at the meeting believed that Elijah's fate had been sealed when he called for the formation of a State Anti-Slavery Society in Illinois. As the meeting in Hartford began, white ruffians forced the delegates to leave the city hall, just as the delegates who formed the Illinois society had been compelled to relocate from the church to Rev. Hurlbut's home. After the Connecticut delegates found space in a local hotel, Owen told them about Elijah. Rev. James Pennington, who was about to succeed Hosea Easton, must have received a full report of the convention.[40]

Joseph and Owen Lovejoy decided to ask John Quincy Adams to write the introduction to Elijah's *Memoir*. Congressman Adams had been reading petitions on the floor of the House of Representatives from the New York Office of the American Anti-Slavery Society. Leavitt and Weld had provided Adams with extensive research on slavery gleaned from the Library of Congress, and the Lovejoys knew that Elijah had written to Adams. Joseph, having volunteered to go to Washington to make this request of the former president, arrived about February 14.[41] On that day Adams presented a mass of 350 antislavery petitions bearing some 35,000 signatures collected across the North and addressed to the House of Representatives.[42] Such petitions had been gathered by antislavery societies, mainly by female societies.[43] Adams spent over an hour with Joseph Lovejoy and agreed to write an introduction to the memoir.

The *Memoir* was an impressive 370-page volume about Elijah. Owen included his own diatribe, titled "To the Citizens of Alton," which admonished the people of Alton to repent of their complicity in Elijah's murder.[44] The book's publication reinvigorated the national antislavery movement and added still more antislavery auxiliaries.[45] The title stated that Elijah had been "Murdered in Defence of the Liberty of the Press," and he became a national symbol for freedom of the press. His death warned northerners that the Slave Power intended to encroach upon the North and demean their constitutional rights.

Finding a Church in Illinois

When he returned to Illinois in April, Owen Lovejoy brought one thousand copies of the *Memoir*, five hundred to Chicago and five hundred to Alton.[46] He sought ordination in the Episcopal Church, but when Bishop Philander Chase informed Owen that he could be ordained an Episcopalian only if he would promise not to preach against slavery, Owen declined. The Alton Presbytery ministers offered to ordain him, but before they did so, Congregational professor Julian Sturtevant and president Edward Beecher of Illinois College at Jacksonville spoke to him about an opportunity in Princeton, Illinois. The two men realized that it would take an unusual parish to absorb the energy Owen intended to expend to keep his vow to Elijah. Princeton's Hampshire Colony Congregational Church, among the first and strongest in the state, needed an interim pastor for one year, as its minister, Yale graduate Lucien Farnham, was ill. Owen traveled to northern Illinois for an interview in late summer and was hired for the interim period, to begin in October 1838.[47]

Hampshire Colony was a choice assignment for Owen Lovejoy. In 1831 thirty Congregational men and women from western Massachusetts had met at Warner's Coffee House in Northampton, where they developed their plan to start a village and church on the Illinois prairie. Motivated by the Second Great Awakening, they were determined to create an antislavery town of spiritual, educational, and agricultural excellence. Other colonies, such as Granville, Galesburg, Geneseo, and Lyndon, would soon be locating in northern Illinois, with plans to dot the West with schools and colleges.[48] The Princeton pioneers were educated middle-class men and women who bought property, wedded in contented companionate-style marriages, and in several cases were experienced operators on the Underground Railroad.

The colony's founders held a bold, progressive vision not shared by all in Massachusetts.[49] A year earlier in Northampton, on July 5, 1830, a local lawyer, speaking at the town's formal celebration of Independence Day, had declared that since the North was complicit in slavery, Northerners should help relieve the South by sending African Americans to Liberia.[50] Many New Englanders were trying to erase the memory that slavery had ever existed in the Northeast. Some were using "warning out" techniques to remove black families from their towns. Others were attacking antislavery lecturers and African American communities.[51] In contrast, the antislavery pioneers, headed toward Illinois colonies, cherished the religious tenet that as all people were created by God, blacks should be welcomed as equals.

Before leaving, the little band entered the Congregational Church in Northampton, once served by Jonathan Edwards, signed their covenant as the future Hampshire Colony Congregational Church in Illinois, and received a silver Communion set.[52] They traveled by way of the Erie Canal and the St. Joseph, Kankakee, and Illinois Rivers, finally arriving on open prairie. The only trails they found were those traveled by Native Americans and horsemen riding from Peoria, stopping at the Smith brothers' Yankee Tavern, a mile north of Princeton, on their way to Galena. Only a few white families had preceded them.[53] One black man named Adams settled in 1829 near their location on a creek that flowed into the Illinois River, and in 1835 an African American man named Henry Love bought a farm a few miles away.[54] When the former New Englanders hired Owen Lovejoy, they had been worshipping in Princeton for only seven years.[55]

After the interview, Lovejoy returned briefly to Alton, where John and Lizzie were staying. In September he traveled to the village of Farmington, twenty miles from Peoria, for the first anniversary meeting of the Illinois State Anti-Slavery Society.[56] Rev. Jeremiah Porter and his wife, Eliza, had moved to peaceful Farmington after a violent antiabolitionist riot in Peoria. Ninety-nine delegates from sixteen counties crowded into Jeremiah's new church. Eliza Porter gathered enough bedding and food for ten delegates to sleep in the Porter house.

The reading at that anniversary meeting of the minutes from the 1837 meeting in Alton was followed by an awkward silence as delegates realized how little they had achieved since Elijah's death.[57] The group had no treasury. There were still 747 slaves (in addition to 1,637 free blacks) in Illinois in 1830 who were harshly discriminated against by the state's Black Laws.[58] Yet the delegates' determination to eradicate slavery and the aggressive spirit of several American Anti-Slavery Society vice presidents, including Owen Lovejoy and Rev. David Nelson, energized the meeting.[59] Owen and Rev. Thomas Lippincott were appointed meeting secretaries. The assembly approved a petition drive to urge the repeal of the Illinois Black Laws and discussed ideas for educating blacks. The best news came when veteran antislavery newspaperman Benjamin Lundy of Philadelphia arrived unexpectedly from his daughters' homes in the new Quaker settlement of Clear Creek, further north on the east side of the Illinois River. The convention eagerly accepted his offer to print his newspaper, *The Genius of Universal Emancipation*, in Putnam County as the state's reborn antislavery newspaper. The delegates would work on a solid agenda, expand their membership, and honor Owen's vow.[60]

After the convention, Owen rode to Princeton with that town's delegate, Butler Denham, an experienced farmer from Massachusetts who bred horses and dairy cows. Butler showed Owen the secret hiding place for runaway slaves he had built under the roof of his cottage.

Owen felt at home in Princeton and intended to bring as many family members as he could persuade to live with him there. Most of the town's two hundred residents at the time were from New England and supported the antislavery movement. However, a contingent of southern Illinoisans, who detested Lovejoy's antislavery position, began to arrive. One man threatened that Owen would be beaten or killed if he dared show himself on Princeton's main street that evening, and a woman offered her pillow to tar and feather the new preacher. But as darkness fell, Lovejoy mounted his horse and, with apparent unconcern, let his animal saunter up and down Main Street.[61] After that show of determination, no one talked about molesting him. Young boys threw clods of dirt at him, but those who sympathized with slaves, and even some who did not, began to admire his courage.[62]

One day Owen crossed the Illinois River to the Quaker settlement at Clear Creek, where he, Benjamin Lundy, and a new Presbyterian minister from Ohio, Rev. James H. Dickey, held a public dialogue on the subject of slavery. The ignited audience of women and men agreed on a robust resolution that praised J. Q. Adams for advocating antislavery petitions, congratulated the British for abolishing slavery, rejected colonization, opposed the annexation of Texas, and declared that Congress had the power to abolish slavery in the District of Columbia. Owen enjoyed these well-informed Quaker and Presbyterian newcomers.[63] He was forming a circle of colleagues and long-lasting friendships.

Owen was further encouraged when Betsey Lovejoy wrote to her children in Princeton—John, Lizzie, and Owen—and announced that she had decided, against Joseph's advice, to move to Princeton. "Don't write me any discouragements!"[64]

In late 1839 the Hampshire Colony congregation called Owen Lovejoy to be its permanent minister. When he was asked, he described his theology as orthodox, but he was not a Calvinist like his father. He preached that the spark of God was in every human being, and therefore there must be a liberality of spirit toward each suffering person. Lovejoy was ordained at Hampshire Colony Church on October 24, 1839, by the Rock River Association of Congregational Churches. During the next five years, the Rock River Association would become one of the most radical associations in Congregationalism on the issue of slavery as Lovejoy and his colleagues embarked on a mission to abolish slavery. They ignored the social code of acquiescence followed by most eastern pastors. These westerners intended to preach against slavery in the pulpit, defy the state's Fugitive Slave Law in their communities, and, if need be, even run for public office.

An event in New Haven, Connecticut, around this time captured Owen Lovejoy's imagination, and others in the Rock River Association also wanted to help. Fifty-one Mendi people from West Africa had been captured by slavers and were imprisoned on the ship *Amistad*, about to be sold in Cuba, when Joseph Cinqué led a revolt. To free themselves, the Africans killed the captain and cook but spared the lives of the Portuguese sailors, whom Cinqué ordered to navigate the ship back to Africa. When the supply of drinking water dwindled to nothing, the desperate Africans swam to land. To their disappointment, the land they reached was not Africa but Long Island, New York. In August 1839, they were arrested and charged with murder. They were jailed in New Haven, Connecticut, and put on trial.[65] Lewis Tappan, Reverend Leavitt, and other colleagues organized the Mendian Committee to seek their release, hoping to demonstrate to the American people the humanity of Africans and the injustice of slavery. Lovejoy's parishioners in Princeton sent frequent contributions for their defense to Tappan. Two and a half years later, on March 9, 1841, following eloquent argumentation before the Supreme Court by John Quincy Adams, the Mendians were freed to go home to West Africa.[66]

Owen Lovejoy and his parishioners were jubilant and African Americans were overjoyed when Cinqué and his fellow captives were freed. James Pennington, the young black Congregational minister who had filled Hosea Easton's pulpit in Hartford, urged blacks to form a new missionary society. On August 18–20, 1841, the Union Missionary Society held its founding meeting at Pennington's church. Forty-three delegates from six states attended.[67] With Pennington as president, the society selected a biracial board of forty-four managers and an executive commit-tee of seventeen. African American Charles Bennett Ray was elected secretary and Theodore S. Wright was elected treasurer.[68] Black churches could not afford to give much money to the Union Missionary Society, and the old established mission societies refused to contribute, but other groups donated. Lovejoy's Hampshire Colony Church voted in 1842 to send all the money it collected at its monthly Concerts of Prayer for the Enslaved. During 1842 Lewis Tappan urged the renamed Amistad Committee and Pennington's Union Missionary Society to combine, keep-ing Pennington as the president but moving its headquarters to New York City, where Tappan, not Wright, would be treasurer.[69] Pennington was well aware of Elijah Lovejoy; he preached about his courage to face racist whites and then asked, "What kind of a spirit was that which shot Lovejoy?"[70]

Owen Lovejoy sent a personal note to Tappan congratulating him for his part in freeing the *Amistad* Africans. "I was particularly struck by Cinque's treatment of the Spaniards—his noble generosity in regard to the use of fresh water on board when it became reduced." Cinqué had given the kidnappers the same portion of water as he gave the kidnapped. "I have read it several times, and yet I believe not without tears. And this is the man on whose neck we are requested to set our foot! This is the race doomed to everlasting inferiority!"[71] The *Amistad* event led to the organization of many new antislavery societies and inspired those who had already been radicalized against slavery, like Lovejoy, to imagine bolder forms of direct action.[72]

Organizing a Political Party to Advocate Equality

In the 1830s, prominent abolitionist William Lloyd Garrison attempted to use newspaper articles, pamphlets, and lectures to persuade slaveholders to free their slaves immediately. By 1840 Owen Lovejoy was beginning to doubt the effectiveness of this approach. Lovejoy also disagreed with Garrison's across-the-board denunciation of established churches and his rejection of political avenues to abolition. By then Lovejoy realized that the Slave Power was not only inching its way into the North but had in fact controlled much of the federal government since the nation's beginning.[73] All presidents, except for John Adams and John Quincy Adams, had been slaveholders representing slave interests, as had the majorities of senators and Supreme Court justices. Through these institutions, the Slave Power had determined the policies of the entire nation.[74]

On April 1, 1840, attorney Alvan Stewart, a friend of Lovejoy's, presided at the Anti-Slavery Convention in Albany, New York. Delegates decided that since both Democratic and Whig parties supported proslavery candidates, they should nominate antislavery James G. Birney for president and pass a resolution to support only independent antislavery candidates for elected office.[75] Lovejoy became convinced that the political route was the best road to slavery's demise.[76]

On July 4, 1840, when the third anniversary meeting of the Illinois Anti-Slavery Society was held in Lovejoy's church in Princeton, he and others tried to persuade the members to join the Liberty Party, an alternative national third party. Six ministers supported the resolution, but the majority voted against it.[77] Some men who voted against joining the movement were Garrisonians who believed that politics was corrupting; some were ministers dependent upon subsidies from eastern mission societies whose boards disapproved of ministers "dabbling" in politics.

The six ministerial supporters of the Liberty Party—Lovejoy, Lucien Farnham, David Nelson, John Cross, Chauncey Cook, and George W. Gale—met the next day and formed the Liberty Party's Illinois branch, the first such action in the West.[78] They had only a few weeks to mount a statewide campaign for the presidential election. The Bureau County Liberty Party received only 13 votes, and there were only 159 votes in the state for James Birney's presidential run. They lacked the support of the Illinois Anti-Slavery Society, owned no statewide newspaper to carry their message, and failed to take advantage of the voters' anger over the Panic of 1837 that struck banking and real estate in Illinois and lingered for several years.[79] Yet they were not discouraged; they were energized by their conviction that slavery was a sin against the laws of God and by their intent to abolish it via political action.[80]

Six months later, on February 25, 1841, Lovejoy and the others had attracted enough additional supporters to hold a Liberty Party convention in the village of

Lowell. An enthusiastic abolitionist printer from Vermont, Zebina Eastman, had recently arrived in Lowell. In New England he had heard of Elijah Lovejoy's murder and had decided to devote his life to the cause of human freedom.[81] After working under editors in Ann Arbor, Chicago, and Peoria, Eastman was well equipped to assist Benjamin Lundy in publishing his newspaper.[82] The convention chose Austin Bryant, one of four Bryant brothers of Princeton, as its president, Zebina Eastman as secretary, and Chicago pharmacist Philo Carpenter as representative of the Chicago activists. Radical minister John Cross was elected as their delegate to the national convention.[83]

A year later, attorney James H. Collins of Chicago, Rev. John Cross, and Owen Lovejoy announced that the group was now strong enough to call the first Illinois State Liberty Party Convention, to be held in Chicago on May 27, 1842. They had obtained delegates from twenty counties, many of them pastors or lay leaders from antislavery churches. Lovejoy delivered a major address, stating, "And first of all we wish distinctly, as a Party, to acknowledge our dependence on God and our amenability to Him. We firmly believe in the natural equality of man."[84] He continued by urging all voters to "cut the bands" that held them to the old Whig and Democratic parties, which had failed to address the abuses of the slaveocracy. He insisted that members of the Liberty Party did not propose to infringe on the moral or constitutional rights of the southern states. Leaving slavery untouched in the South was in accord with the constitutional provision that gave states the right to legislate laws not specifically designated by the federal government, a position that would become the national consensus. Lovejoy ignored the fact that he and other Liberty men continuously broke another provision of the U.S. Constitution by not returning runaways to their masters.

He finished his speech with the even bolder and more audacious phrase: "should the reins of Government fall, as we trust ere-long they will fall into our hands." Lovejoy was expressing the shared confidence that a providential God would bend history toward justice through the acts of faithful believers. "We must ardently hope and confidently believe," he said, "that we are destined to increase till we break up the present party organizations." At some point in time, he believed, the federal government would fall into antislavery hands. With this speech Owen Lovejoy walked onto the political stage.[85] The new third party was firmly established in Illinois.

The activist delegation from Cook County included surgeon Charles V. Dyer, pharmacist Philo Carpenter, and lawyers Calvin DeWolf and James Collins.[86] When publisher Lundy died, they urged the convention to establish a new antislavery paper, the *Western Citizen*, as the official Liberty Party newspaper, with Zebina Eastman as editor.[87] Eastman moved to Chicago and for the next dozen years provided readers in Illinois with the latest local and national antislavery developments and analysis.[88] Dr. Dyer's commitment to abolition started in 1837 when he was so affected by Elijah Lovejoy's assassination that he rented a hall in Chicago and held a protest meeting.[89] Indeed, Elijah's murder had affected many individuals at this convention. By the following summer, these highly motivated churchmen had organized conventions in eleven counties.[90]

Just before Election Day, July 21, 1842, Lovejoy preached a foundational sermon at his church, titled "Religion and Politics." It provided his original idea of both a biblical and a constitutional basis for church members to participate in politics.[91] He combined two concepts. One concept, from political theory, indicated that while in a monarchy like Britain, the king was the ruler, in a republic like the United States, every *voter* was a sovereign or ruler. The second concept, from the Bible, stated that every ruler must be just: "He that ruleth over men must be just, ruling in the fear of God."[92] When these two ideas were brought together in a democratic form of government, it followed that every voter must be a just ruler. Religion and politics had been separated too long, Lovejoy declared.[93] It was a radical pronouncement.

He did not tell his parishioners how to vote, but he clearly hoped they would vote for Liberty Party candidates. He urged women who had arrived at years of discretion, under the guidance of common sense, to exert their influence to repeal unjust laws. Lovejoy cherished the Bible, but he explained that he always consulted several additional authorities before acting: "Whatever the Bible, reason, justice and humanity require of lawmakers, judges, and executives," they also require of every elector.[94] Slavery was neither rational, nor just, nor humane. Every man who voted for a proslavery candidate for public office was voting for the perpetuation of proslavery laws. The voter is as "responsible to God as though he were in the Halls of legislation and said Aye to those laws which passed."[95] Several months later, Lovejoy's sermon covered the front page of Zebina Eastman's *Western Citizen* and was read by hundreds, perhaps thousands, of western church members. Reverend D. Heagle claimed that Owen advocated some aspect of human rights in every sermon he preached.[96]

That year, Owen's mother, Betsey, formed a women's antislavery society in Princeton.

In Illinois, proslavery prosecutors began indicting several individuals for harboring or secreting runaway slaves or indentured servants, breaking the state's Fugitive Slave Law, which stated, "Every such person so offending shall be deemed guilty of a misdemeanor, and fined, not exceeding five hundred dollars, or imprisoned, not exceeding six months."[97] Rev. Samuel G. Wright of Toulon, thirty miles southwest of Princeton, was indicted in an effort to destroy his congregation, which was clandestinely assisting a stream of fugitive slaves. When the governor of Missouri requested that Dr. Richard Eels and Dr. David Nelson of Quincy be extradited to his state, some state officials were eager to cooperate. Four other prominent antislavery men had been served papers. Owen expected to be indicted next.[98]

Antislavery women, not wanting to see their pastors and community leaders intimidated by the courts, attended the proceedings and filled the courtroom. They had already been aiding runaway slaves informally; now they organized formally to let the public know that they were supporting the indicted men.

Proslavery officials felt threatened by this small band of abolitionists. Slavery sympathizers in towns such as Washington, near Peoria, were so angered by the intrusion of lecturers Dickey, Lovejoy, and William T. Allan that they threatened them with violence.[99] The ministers said that they supported the Underground Railroad not to cause disorder, as charged, but to bring about a new order. In Lovejoy's mind, disobeying laws that required fugitives' return to their enslavers was a holy act. In January 1842, when Lovejoy preached his sermon "Supremacy of the Divine Law," based on the text "Obey God rather than man" (Acts 5:29), the editor of the *Peoria Register and North-Western Gazetteer*, labeled him "ultra in the extreme."[100]

Reverend Allan had grown up on a slave plantation in Alabama. He was converted to the abolitionist cause and trained by Reverend Weld at Lane Seminary to be an antislavery agent. He met his future wife, Irene Ball, while instructing antislavery agents at Oberlin College in 1835. Once established in Illinois, Allan was on the alert for religious men with political potential. One day when their paths crossed, Allan told Lovejoy he felt certain he was such a man and he should plan to run for political office. Years later, Allan remembered that young man and described him as "noble, genial, joyous, a beautiful and lovely spirit encased in human form."[101]

Finding a Bride

With the exception of his brother Joseph, Owen's siblings were settled in the West. Lovejoy had been boarding at Butler Denham's homestead for over a year. On August 8, 1841, Butler, Owen's close friend, ally, and generous host, suddenly died. He left two little girls—Lucy, age four, and Mary, age one—and his wife Eunice, who was pregnant with a third child. Early in 1842 the third baby girl was born and named Elizabeth, though Eunice always called her Libbie. Progressive Butler Denham had willed his thousand-acre farm to Eunice and had designated several acres to be sold for his daughters' higher education.

Lovejoy had served Hampshire Colony for nearly three years when a prominent physician requested that he relinquish $150 from his $500 salary. He immediately resigned. But then, drawing on the Lovejoys' family custom of taking important decisions to the family council, he said that he would withdraw his resignation if the whole·congregation, not just a small committee, would decide the future of their minister. The Hampshire Colony congregation stood with Lovejoy. Unlike most congregations in the East, which expected their ministers to accept the norms and standards of prominent ministers as authorities, the Hampshire Colony congregation demonstrated that it intended to be on the forefront of reform in the West and that it was eager to develop the special kind of ministry Lovejoy envisioned.[102] On hearing the crowd of parishioners praise Owen with great enthusiasm, the doctor dropped his recommendation for a salary reduction. From that time on, those who joined the church supported his political sermons and his illegal activity of feeding and sheltering escaping slaves. Members were proud that their minister was a chief operator on the Underground Railroad. Lovejoy was going to stay at Hampshire Colony.[103]

Having made the decision to stay, Lovejoy was able to turn his attention to marriage. Denham's widow, Eunice, had been born to Joshua and Mary Perkins Storrs on September 21, 1809. She was an orphan at ten but well cared for by her maternal grandparents, who brought her up in Trenton, New York, near Utica. She often enjoyed long visits with her grandfather, Reverend John Storrs, in Connecticut, and with her uncle, Reverend Richard Salter Storrs, in Longmeadow, Massachusetts, and with her cousins there, including Reverend Richard Salter Storrs (II), who was later called to serve the Congregational Church in Braintree, Massachusetts.[104] Although the cousins were twenty-one years apart in age, they kept in touch with each other throughout their lives. Cousin Richard gave his name in turn to his own son, Richard Salter Storrs (III), who served a church in Brooklyn before and after the Civil War.[105]

Eunice married Butler Denham in 1835. Sometime after Butler's death, Owen proposed marriage to Eunice, and she accepted. The two were wed on January 18, 1843. The ceremony was performed by Charles Adams, a graduate of the anti-slavery Oberlin Seminary and a Congregational clergyman from the little church at Providence, ten miles southwest of Princeton.[106]

• • •

Five years after Elijah's death, Owen's life was in place—family, church, and political party. He had found mentors in the office of the interracial American Anti-Slavery Society in New York City. He had settled his three siblings and his mother in the West. He was minister to a religious band of people from Hampshire County, Massachusetts, and he had won their allegiance and affection. As he had done in Alton, in Princeton he continued to rescue runaway slaves, whom he found to be strong and intelligent individuals. He was connected with the many members of the Illinois State Anti-Slavery Society.

With the encouragement of highly motivated, theologically active colleagues of the radical Rock River Association of Congregational Churches, and with access to Zebina Eastman's *Western Citizen*, Owen Lovejoy began to widen his sphere of influence. He was no longer thought of as just Elijah Lovejoy's younger brother; he had come into his own. He had witnessed the power of women working behind the scenes in Alton, Farmington, and Princeton. With Betsey, Lizzie, and Eunice backing him up at the church and in the nascent women's antislavery society, he would join his colleagues in organizing new antislavery churches and building a political coalition committed to eradicating slavery wherever it was constitutional to do so.

2. Working against Slavery with Churchmen, Women, and Blacks

1843–1846

At the age of thirty-two Lovejoy was happily married to a gracious partner. He was ready to raise Butler Denham's three daughters and soon his own (Sarah, born in March 1844) in one seamless family. He excelled at managing his own horse breeding business; the farm was among one of the most productive in the area.[1] Thanks to Eunice's inheritance from Butler Denham, Owen had enough money to travel, to initiate new churches, attend regional meetings, and participate in establishing antislavery church practices in an expanding denomination.

But Lovejoy did not settle into a comfortable pastorate. In 1843 he developed his plans to follow Theodore Weld's advice, concentrating on small towns, villages, and farms and staying away from cities where proslavery interests were already solidified.[2] His strategy was to build up an antislavery church, start new ones in the Rock River Association,[3] and over time unify Congregationalists in Illinois in opposition to slavery.[4] He and his colleagues would expand the Liberty Party and eventually win a congressional seat and an antislavery candidate for the White House.

The Lovejoys kept alert for the arrival of freedom seekers from the South. A few weeks after their wedding, Owen and Eunice welcomed a runaway slave named Nancy into their home.[5] She remained several weeks, recuperating from her flight, eating and sleeping under the Lovejoy roof, and working around the house. Nancy spoke so clearly about her experiences in bondage that Owen asked her if she would talk to a group at Rev. John Cross's church in the nearby town of La Moille. On the way, she rode in the buggy sitting beside Lovejoy.

In May 1843, the grand jury of Bureau County served Lovejoy with an indictment for harboring and secreting both Nancy and Agnes, an African American woman who had stayed awhile at the residence eleven months earlier. His case was scheduled to come up for trial in October. The indictment was signed by Norman

H. Purple of Peoria, later appointed to the Illinois Supreme Court, who assisted Benjamin F. Fridley, soon to be state's attorney for Kane County, in the prosecution. Purple, who had recently led a large mob against antislavery men in Peoria,[6] intended to see Lovejoy fined $450 and imprisoned for six months. He expected that this action would break up the Princeton branch of the Underground Railroad, split Owen's congregation, and remove him from the area. But Purple misjudged Hampshire Colony Church. On May 10, 1843, before the indictment was made official, the congregation voted for a resolution that highly approved of Lovejoy's "frequent presentation of the subject of Human Rights from the Sacred Desk as a part of the Gospel of Him who came to preach deliverance to the captives and to set at liberty those that are bound."[7]

Purple's admirers, unaware of Lovejoy's local popularity, approached Fridley, telling him, "we want you to be sure and convict this preacher and send him to prison." Fridley replied, "Prison! Lovejoy to prison! Your prosecution will be a damned sight more likely to send him to congress."[8]

A few days later, after the indictment, on May 24, Lovejoy placed a daring advertisement in the *Western Citizen*:

NOTICE OF THE CANADA LINE OF STAGES. Cheap! Cheap! The subscriber would very respectfully inform the ladies and gentlemen of color of the South, who wish to travel North for the benefit of their condition, or any excursion of pleasure to the Falls of Niagara, that the above line of stages will be in action. . . . For further particulars inquire of the subscriber at his residence in Princeton, Bureau County. OWEN LOVEJOY, Gen. Agent.[9]

At this pivotal time, the effective antislavery editor and lecturer Ichabod Codding came to Princeton to meet Lovejoy for the first time.[10] When lecturing in Maine, Reverend Codding had told Joseph Lovejoy that Elijah's assassination had led him to swear eternal fidelity to the cause of human rights.[11] Betsey and Sarah Lovejoy had written to Owen, praising Codding for his lectures.[12] The men became fast friends. On June 15 Lovejoy took Codding to the district meeting of the Liberty Party and introduced him to the delegates who had formed the Chicago Anti-Slavery Society as a response to Elijah's murder.[13] Dr. Charles Dyer, attorney James Collins, and dry goods merchant L. C. Paine Freer were so impressed with Codding that they persuaded him to stay in Illinois and work with Rev. William T. Allan and Rev. John Cross, who were western Illinois agents of the American Anti-Slavery Society. Codding immediately began lecturing throughout the state.[14] Throughout the coming decade, in antislavery circles in Illinois, Codding's name was closely joined with Eastman's and Lovejoy's. The three men traveled hundreds of miles together as an impressive antislavery triumvirate.

On August 1, 1843, Lovejoy and Codding rode their horses toward La Moille to attend a celebration honoring the day in 1838 on which emancipation of slaves in the British West Indies took place. This festivity was spreading from one black community to another across the North. Free blacks did not celebrate July 4, a time when they were "at risk of attack by drunken whites."[15] Celebrating August First was their way of informing whites that blacks had "proven their success in war and governance in the Caribbean" and therefore deserved to receive their rights as citizens of the United States.[16] White friends were welcomed at these occasions. Lovejoy and Codding expected to join local black and white families eating at tables on the church lawn and hearing rousing speeches in an integrated setting.

However, on the road to La Moille, Lovejoy and Codding passed a well-dressed free black man who told them that he had been cheated out of nine dollars by a Princeton innkeeper named Roth. Lovejoy and Codding returned to the inn to confront Roth. Undeterred, Roth obtained a warrant for the black man's arrest and hired a posse to overtake him. When the posse caught up with the black stranger, one of the gang jumped in front of his horse and drew his knife. But before he could use it, Lovejoy jumped off his horse, brought his foot down on the white man's arm, and held it there until the knife was released. Lovejoy shouted to the black man to leave, which he did. Later, Lovejoy was charged with assault and battery and fined $50 plus $10 for court costs.[17]

When Lovejoy and Codding arrived at La Moille, those gathered praised their heroism, but the event reminded them of the vulnerability of free blacks at anytime, anywhere. Lovejoy introduced newcomer Codding to the crowd, and his electrifying speech quickly revived their spirits.[18]

National Colored Party and Liberty Party Conventions in Buffalo

Lovejoy, not intimidated by his impending trial for harboring and secreting Nancy and Agnes, left Princeton for the National Liberty Party Convention meeting in Buffalo, New York. This was the western entry point to the "burnt-out area" along the Erie Canal where revivalist Charles G. Finney had converted thousands over the previous twenty years.[19] Lovejoy arrived on August 30, 1843. He eagerly joined the early gathering outside the Buffalo courthouse and gave an impromptu address to the crowd.[20]

The National Convention of Colored Men, held in Buffalo, had just adjourned. Lovejoy heard that a black minister, Henry Highland Garnet, had startled delegates with his speech that was from one point of view a sympathetic pastoral letter to the enslaved and from another viewpoint a prescription for slave insurrection.[21] In it

Reverend Garnet had placed the blame for the continuation of slavery upon the shoulders of slaves who acquiesced to that evil system, and he told the delegates that violence was necessary. "Arise, arise, arise! Strike for your lives and liberties! . . . No oppressed people have secured their liberty without resistance."[22] Some said that Elijah Lovejoy's assassination in Alton in 1837 had undercut black loyalty to William Lloyd Garrison's philosophy of nonviolence; Elijah's assassination probably affected Garnet. [23]

But Garnet soon found himself debating with another articulate fugitive over the best tactics to use. That fugitive slave was young Frederick Douglass, who at that time defended Garrison's nonviolent approach. Douglass reasoned that if Garnet's plan were followed, "the impact would be negligible," for their enslavers would soon learn about it and would punish them more.[24] After all the delegates had finished speaking, no strategy had been agreed to. Delegates felt frustrated and hopeless; one stated, "The whole gathering was in tears."[25]

Garnet recovered support later in the deliberations when he introduced a second resolution. It endorsed the white men's Liberty Party, and it carried. As a result, a number of black delegates stayed in Buffalo to attend the Liberty Party Convention.[26] The Liberty Party offered black men a path by which abolition might be accomplished within the law and without violence. Western abolitionists, who believed in political action based on the Constitution as an antislavery document, may have helped slaves believe they could one day feel that America was their home. Blacks might win the battle through a legislative process dominated by whites.[27] Lovejoy was one of those whites, and he wanted to get acquainted with these black men.

At the Liberty Party Convention, Lovejoy told the audience about Elijah's murder and the vow he had made. Massachusetts antislavery newspaperman William Burleigh reported that this speech created a deep impression on Liberty delegates. Lovejoy was asked to close the assembly with prayer.[28]

Both Lovejoy and Garnet had been assigned to the Nominations Committee of the Liberty Party. Though younger than Lovejoy, Garnet had survived the racist squalor of New York City, the physical demands of working on board ships, being targeted by guns along with other black students fleeing from the short-lived interracial Noyes Academy in New Hampshire, and the amputation of a leg in 1840 at age twenty-five. He had met and fallen in love with the gifted antislavery black activist Julia Williams at Noyes, and they had married.[29] Though successful in attracting blacks to the church he served in Troy, New York, he had to scrounge for a salary adequate to feed Julia and their two babies.

While working on the nominating committee, Lovejoy soon realized that Garnet was deeply religious, intensely political, and highly intelligent. Both men viewed the Constitution as an antislavery document despite the fact that major sections of it had been commandeered by the South for the benefit of slaveholders. Both affirmed that the Declaration of Independence, with its claim that all men were created equal, was the better, more patriotic, launching pad for a new political party, and that the ambiguous U.S. Constitution was best interpreted as enabling the process by which the Declaration's vision of equality might eventually be attained.[30]

Lovejoy learned from Garnet that slaves must remind themselves that it was the masters who were dependent on their slaves; once slaves were set free, blacks could take care of themselves. It was a sentiment that Lovejoy would repeat in Congress.[31] Garnet expounded on the interpretations of the scriptures he was developing within the safe space of his black church, where he could freely say what African Americans needed to hear: that God would rescue them from the effects of slavery and deliver them into a promised land where they would be recognized as free and equal American citizens.[32] Both men wrestled with the threat of death: Lovejoy claimed that he was ready to give his life to end slavery, and Garnet insisted that it would be better to die than to bequeath slavery to one's grandchildren.[33] (Later that year, in September, a white mob broke into Garnet's church, carried him out, wrestled him to the ground, and took turns spitting on him. Garnet had to crawl home, for the ruffians had taken away his wooden leg.)[34]

Black minister Samuel Ringgold Ward opened the Liberty Party convention with prayer and then delivered an eloquent formal address. Like Lovejoy, Ward preached Christianity and chose to work within the institution of the church to eradicate slavery. But he agreed with James Birney's thesis that the American church as it existed then was a bulwark of slavery. Both Ward and Lovejoy wanted to save the church from degrading itself. In Illinois, Lovejoy and the other antislavery leaders intended to establish churches to be a bulwark *against* slavery. Ward was one of the few black ministers who served a white church. Called by the radical Congregational church in South Butler, New York, he urged the group to become a "come-outer" church, free from any denominational ties that might try to keep it silent.[35] While Ward believed that most whites were deeply prejudiced, he concluded that God had "enabled *some whites* to do and endure all things for our cause."[36]

The convention appointed five secretaries, Lovejoy among them. African American Charles B. Ray, born free in Massachusetts, was another. Ray was older, educated, and professional, a protégé of Rev. Theodore Wright of New York City's Shiloh Church and a Congregational missionary to African Americans in the city.[37] Ray had lobbied state legislators in New York to regain suffrage for black males. Although he was unsuccessful, he gained political skills in the process.[38]

Lovejoy shared common concerns with Garnet, Ward, and Ray. All four worked on the Underground Railroad, which made existential the biblical metaphor of rescue and deliverance.[39] All four had received frightened fugitives in the middle of the night, shared food with them, and pointed them toward Canada. Ironically, all four served churches in the Congregational and Presbyterian tradition and had faced the necessity of depending on subsidies from the established, conservative eastern mission societies, such as the American Home Mission Society, that wanted them to keep silent on slavery. In one way or another, all four were trying to free themselves from such agencies.

Owen had a transforming experience in Buffalo working with black ministers of his own generation, his equals—determined, creative, educated men. It was a unique situation. Twenty-some blacks participated in the 1843 convention, including an unnamed black delegate selected by the colored citizens of Chicago.[40] Such a positive interracial experience made a lasting impression on the men, and it was invaluable to the Liberty Party.[41] One can imagine that Lovejoy would have stayed up half the night with the young black men in this small circle of equals, exchanging stories of their life journeys.

The black delegates might have told Lovejoy about the steady barrage of torture enslavers used to dehumanize blacks. They might have explained how the concept of racial inferiority was artificially constructed as a weapon for slaveholders to justify their coercive power to oppress a people.[42] Yet Lovejoy would have seen that these men had not been diminished but had somehow expanded their humanity. Buffalo proffered one of those "select situations" in which "activist black clergy won whites over" to a deeper understanding of black perspectives on slavery.[43] It was a moment of the black abolitionist movement radicalizing white abolitionists.[44]

The black delegates—such as Garnet, Ward, and Ray—had been welcomed by the white delegates, but each had faced excruciating rejection elsewhere. Was this experience authentic, with long-term consequences, or just an interracial honeymoon, as Gerrit Smith, the philanthropist and antislavery radical from Peterboro, New York, described it?[45] Even a white benefactor like Lewis Tappan was capable of undermining black agency, keeping James Pennington as the visible and honorific president of the Union Missionary Society but moving its office to New York City and installing himself as treasurer so he could run its affairs.[46] Still, this experience in Buffalo displayed glimpses of equality that were spinning the men off into unfamiliar territory. Lovejoy had one contribution to make to these highly accomplished blacks: he gave them reasons to believe that a victory over slavery might someday be established by law.[47]

In Buffalo, Lovejoy met prominent white leaders as well. Attorney Alvan Stewart was the first person to argue that the federal government had the power under the Constitution to abolish slavery in the slave states, for slavery itself was unconstitutional. He was one of the first to present the idea of forming an antislavery political party, which became the Liberty Party.[48] Stewart's constitutional analysis claimed that Article IV, Section 4, guaranteed that every state in the Union must have a republican form of government, which was denied whenever a state passed laws depriving half its population of the right to participate. He asserted that the Fifth Amendment ("no person shall be . . . deprived of life, liberty, or property, without due process of law") was meant to *include* slaves as persons; otherwise, an exception for them would have been stated. He interpreted the word *person* as "a human being possessed of the natural rights of life, liberty and the pursuit of happiness."[49] He also believed that in light of the Declaration of Independence, tolerating slavery "was a violation of our engagements to mankind and to God." When the southern-dominated U.S. Supreme Court presented proslavery interpretations of the Constitution, Stewart appealed to "the true spirit of the Constitution of the United States."[50] By assembling these arguments, he constructed the legal framework for racial equality. Stewart encouraged Lovejoy to be a political activist.[51] Lovejoy, impressed with Stewart's arguments, adopted his approach that the Constitution was an antislavery document.

Lovejoy was also appointed to work on the platform at Buffalo with Cincinnati attorney Salmon P. Chase. Chase was three years older than Lovejoy, raised in the austere Ohio home of his uncle, Episcopalian bishop Philander Chase. The two young men got along well; it was irrelevant to both that the bishop had blocked Owen from ordination in his denomination. Lovejoy admired Chase's defense of blacks in Cincinnati courts and his expertise in developing legal antislavery strategies within the confines of his view of an antislavery U.S. Constitution. Chase did not call for federal action to end slavery in the southern states where it already existed. Instead, he advocated goals he believed were achievable within the limits of the Constitution, such as ending slavery in the District of Columbia, excluding slavery from the territories, and withholding admission of new slave states, thus containing slavery to the Southeast.[52] For Chase, slavery was only a *local* institution in the South while freedom was the overarching *national* institution of the United States of America.[53] Lovejoy agreed with Chase's strategy and artfully engaged it for the next seventeen years. The resolutions passed by the 1843 convention, differing from Garrisonian positions, focused on goals achievable within the limits of the Constitution, such as ending slavery in the District of Columbia, excluding slavery from the territories, and withholding admission of new slave states, thus containing slavery's growth. Chase, and Lovejoy, saw slavery as a local institution of the South and freedom as the overarching national institution of the United States.[54]

Evangelical Lewis Tappan refused to come to Buffalo. He feared that if abolitionists engaged in politics, they would cease serving God and succumb to their own self-interest. Tappan even criticized editor Joshua Leavitt for remolding the

Emancipator into a political organ for the Liberty Party.[55] Leavitt retorted that a moral third party would be more effective in abolishing slavery than churches had been. The following year, Tappan did vote for James Birney, the Liberty Party candidate for U.S. President in the 1844 election.[56]

Owen Lovejoy refused to separate religion from politics. He intended to join religious and political approaches simultaneously in Illinois.

Lovejoy on Trial in Princeton

Eunice Lovejoy wondered what her family would do if Owen were found guilty. Joseph Lovejoy was concerned also. He had been called as pastor to a large church in Cambridge, Massachusetts, near Harvard College. In September he wrote Owen, concerned about the upcoming trial. "If you should need any funds to pay expenses, just write," he urged.[57] At the last minute, James H. Collins of Chicago took the place of ailing Alvan Stewart as Owen's defense lawyer. Collins, an old friend of radical Gerrit Smith of upstate New York, was a mentor to Owen.[58]

In Princeton the trial lasted a week, and men and women packed the courtroom. Owen's parishioners were called as witnesses, and they worried that their testimony would hurt their pastor. Five women testified that Nancy moved openly about the Lovejoy house and was not secreted.[59] But farmer Isaac Delano told the court that Nancy was indeed an escaped slave, so it seemed that Owen would be found guilty. However, when Collins cross-examined the owner's representative, he revealed that Nancy's enslaver had brought her from Kentucky en route to Missouri, traveling through the free state of Illinois, where she escaped. Collins reminded the court, "She became free when she set her foot on Illinois soil." Lovejoy quoted the English poet William Cowper: "'Slaves cannot breathe in England; if their lungs receive our air, that moment they are free—they touch our country and their shackles fall.' And if this is the glory of England, is it not equally true of Illinois, her soul consecrated to freedom by the ordinance of 1787 and her own Constitution?"[60] On October 7, 1843, the judge, John Dean Caton, gave his charge to the jury: "If the master had traveled with his slave only in slave states, his property would have been secure; but when he voluntarily brought her in transit through a free state, he lost his jurisdiction over her."[61] It would be the last time a court case would be decided on the basis of transit law.

When the jury found Lovejoy not guilty, the Princeton Female Anti-Slavery Society declared it a cause for rejoicing.[62] The society, one of the earliest in Illinois, was organized by Betsey Lovejoy in July 1843.[63] The indictment of ministers had so infuriated these women that they joined together to protect the men they considered courageous.[64]

After the *Western Citizen* published the society's constitution, Betsey sent a press release: "We meet once in two months to work and we hope to pray for the Slave. We have furnished clothing for a number of fugitives that has passed this way. . . . We have sent a box of clothing to Quincy with directions for Mrs. Work to take whatever Articles would be useful to her with five dollars in money." Betsey stated that the group had forty-four members, "and others meet with us but have not put their [signature] to our paper." The society had not publicized its existence, she said, because they had "been in the habit of thinking it was our duty not to let our left hand know what our right hand doeth. But remembering likewise that the Blessed Savior has said let your light shine that others, Seeing your good works, may be led to glorify your Father which is in heaven and as we know it rejoices our hearts when we hear What others are doing we think it may impart the same joy to them to hear from us."[65]

The trial had made Betsey's son Owen a man to be listened to in the Illinois antislavery movement, and with the Anti-Slavery Society Betsey had helped create a space where she could make her own pastoral contribution.

A Mission Society Opposes Radical Clergy

Owen Lovejoy had come to Illinois in the hope of shaping the western churches' responses to slavery, as Weld had in Ohio, before proslavery sentiment became entrenched. In his research, Richard J. Carwardine found that the denominations with the most antislavery members were Free or Reformed Presbyterians, Free Will Baptists, Wesleyan and Free Methodists, "and above all," Congregationalists. Others were Unitarians, Quakers, Disciples of Christ, and German Evangelicals.[66] Lovejoy intended to help organize western religious antislavery people and wanted the churches to lead the way in supporting politicians and political parties opposed to slavery. The clergy in the Rock River Congregational Association, from Princeton, Lee Center, Providence, Polo, Dixon, Lyndon, Byron, La Moille, Rockford, Roscoe, and Geneseo, formed a growing team of radicals who were determined that slavery should be abolished.[67] Their strength expanded as Lovejoy signed twenty applications for new church starts in the area.[68]

In November 1843 Rock River ministers invited distant colleagues to form a statewide Illinois General Congregational Association. When eighty-five Illinois and Iowa Congregational ministers signed the call, they knew there was broad interest.[69] The intent was to establish a religious organization with an antislavery platform and to persuade cautious Illinois associations of Congregational churches to join them. Then together the churches would make demands on the state legislature. As one of the organizers, Lovejoy offered his church for the initial planning meeting on November 15, 1843.[70] He was following the actions of the Congregationalists in Maine who had formed their own state conference.[71]

A formal organizing convention of Congregational churches followed on June 21, 1844, in Farmington. During the meeting Lovejoy and the rest of the ministers took a tough stand against slavery. They agreed to receive no ministers into their fellowship who did not rank slaveholding a heinous sin. They resolved to support the Liberty Party, confront racist actions by the Illinois legislature, and support Underground Railroad operators. They would oppose state laws that subjected operators to "criminal prosecution & incarceration with felons in a common jail for extending to a needy fellow creature that relief which a savage would not deny."[72] They specifically criticized the American Home Missionary Society for subsidizing slaveholding clergy in the South and in Indian Territories. Ministers in the Rock River Association considered the AHMS a major obstacle in the development of the antislavery movement in Congregational churches.[73] Lovejoy knew that criticizing the missionary society was hazardous because most radical ministers relied on the subsidy that came from easterners through the AHMS. Yet to accumulate enough pressure to force changes in the missionary society's policies, the radical clergy needed support from as many Congregational churches in the state as possible.

The AHMS, founded in the 1820s, raised large amounts of money to subsidize pastors as well as funds to build new churches in many states.[74] While Presbyterian churches were organized nationally and had a central authority to which ministers could send grievances, there was as yet no national Congregational denomination to negotiate with, so the Rock River ministers challenged the independent AHMS directly.

After the 1844 Farmington convention, Milton Badger, a national officer of the AHMS, suddenly appeared in Illinois to investigate the leaders of the state's new General Congregational Association; he stayed for weeks. Badger interviewed ministers who were not in the antislavery movement and collected information from them against those who were, filling many notebooks and letters.[75] He reported to the national office that the Reverends Owen Lovejoy and John Cross had been indicted for breaking the Fugitive Slave Law.[76] Badger concluded that western preachers were out of control. These Rock River ministers were rejecting his authority, refusing his supervision, resisting traditional eastern theology and standards of conformity, and substituting their own normative system for those held by the AHMS Executive Committee.[77]

Badger represented well-to-do conservative churches in New York and New England, where slaves had been emancipated for less than a generation. The notion of slavery as a sin was a new view that many long-standing Christians had difficulty accepting.[78] Many churches maintained "Negro galleries," separating blacks from the rest of the congregation. Ministers were in a vocation that had been changing from a state-supported office to a voluntary service-providing profession, resulting in a significant loss of tenure and salary. Facing depletion of class and power, some blamed abolitionists for undercutting their authority and creating chaos in eastern communities, where they felt duty-bound to maintain order.[79] They passed rules to keep abolitionists out of their pulpits and to confine public discussion of slavery to secular literary societies and debating clubs. They considered abolitionism to be a public program, almost a political party, and from their point of view, a misuse of the church.[80] Arriving in Illinois with those presuppositions, Badger considered the unique nature of the Rock River Association and the political activity of its ministers abhorrent. Badger also rejected perfectionist theology associated with Ohio's Oberlin College, whereas the Rock River Association welcomed zealous antislavery ministers from Oberlin.[81]

At the third meeting of the Illinois General Association, the AHMS representatives pressed to remove all traces of Oberlin theology and activism from Illinois Congregational churches. When it appeared that anti-Oberlin ministers had enough votes to eject Oberlin graduates from the group, Lovejoy moved to table the motion, and his motion was sustained. He and his collaborators were relieved for the present, but they saw that the General Association's usefulness as an arm of the antislavery movement was diminished for the foreseeable future.

At the fourth meeting in Farmington, in 1845, a resolution passed that allowed Oberlin pastors to remain members as long as they realized they were on a kind of probation.[82] Lovejoy and his radical ministerial friends had planned to form a much more racially tolerant and progressive association than this one was shaping up to be. They understood that most western pastors were dependent on their subsidy from the AHMS to survive. Because Hampshire Colony rejected any subsidy, Lovejoy was able to maintain his own priorities. The radicals continued to make official protests against the AHMS, to work with individual antislavery churches, and to start new ones. But after the 1845 meeting, they put more of their energy into their political party.

Years later, due to broad consternation opposing the 1854 Kansas-Nebraska Act and the 1857 *Dred Scott* decision, conservative Congregational churches would slowly join with the more radical ones and form a Republican vanguard in Illinois that denounced the *Dred Scott* decision and aided in electing Lincoln. During the Civil War, these northern Illinois churches became fervent supporters of the Emancipation Proclamation,[83] and after the war they aided the building of schools and churches for freedmen in the South. But in 1844–45, the AHMS's Badger punished ministers in the Rock River and Fox River Associations who did not support him. Charles Adams lost his church at Providence, and William L. Parsons of Aurora "heard the crashing storm around his head" and feared he was about to lose his job. Nathaniel Smith of Lyndon was intimidated, and Ebenezer Brown of Roscoe was censored. The Rock River Association quietly dissolved.[84]

Badger had successfully deradicalized the statewide General Association's public statements. But to his great disappointment, this accomplishment did not impede Liberty Party political action. Antislavery Congregationalism in the northern half of Illinois more than doubled from 70 churches in 1844 to 170 over the next two decades.[85] Although they comprised a small minority of the population, they represented a compact group of advocates with a precisely targeted program of political action.[86] Ironically, AHMS censorship strengthened antislavery in Illinois.

The AHMS attacked Lovejoy's black colleagues as well as his white ones. In Troy, New York, Henry Highland Garnet, whom the AHMS considered too engaged in political action, refused his subsidy rather than limit his public speaking against slavery and in favor of the Liberty Party.[87] In South Butler, New York, Samuel Ringgold Ward kept his stipend by modifying his tactics until he was hired by a "come-outer" church in Cortland, New York, that refused AHMS money.[88] Lewis Tappan, furious that the AHMS would punish nascent antislavery churches,[89] gathered evidence that the mission society was supporting slaveholding ministers in the South and appointing slaveholders to its executive board, despite denials. The AHMS had tried to hide from the antislavery people its own report that four out of five missionaries sent to the South became slavery advocates. As Lovejoy and colleagues learned, it was very difficult to get an established organization to change an entrenched self-interested policy.[90]

The AHMS had been so punitive that the existence of the Rock River Association was forgotten for several decades, literally removed from official church memory. In the mid-twentieth century, Frederick I. Kuhns, the society's historian, rediscovered its minutes and corrected the denomination's history.[91] The shortsighted AHMS Executive Board and staff had been asleep to the sweeping social changes taking place in Illinois and in the nation. Not until the Civil War did the AHMS finally amend its practices.

In July 1844, in the midst of the controversy over the AHMS and its use of subsidies to control clergy, Owen Lovejoy focused on what he thought was most crucial in the argument. He preached a sermon on equality titled "Christ Died for All, without Regard to Person, Age, Rank or Color," based on 2 Corinthians 5:14–15. Premise by premise, he developed his egalitarian tenet as a basic belief in Christian theology. "Grateful to the minister of the cross is the task of proclaiming free and full to all that one died for all without regard to person, age, rank, color, country or condition."[92] The Hampshire Colony congregation approved of Lovejoy's sermon;

the Rock River radicals did also, but they feared they were preaching a minority perspective in a state with a proslavery government.[93]

Lovejoy's message was similar to ones given by Henry Highland Garnet and Frederick Douglass. Garnet preached that there were no distinct races of humankind: "There is but one race, as there was but one Adam."[94] When Douglass preached, he quoted Acts 17:26: "God hath made of one blood all nations of men for to dwell upon all the face of the earth." These colleagues were opposing the "pseudoscientific theory" of polygenesis—which proposed that races had different origins—and its claims of "innate and permanent black inferiority," an idea that was spreading west from misguided scientific work at eastern colleges and north from proslavery Gulf states.[95] Frederick Douglass labeled these theories blatant proslavery tools.[96] The slaveholders' scientific racism read the Negro out of the human family.[97]

Antislavery Men and Women Support the Liberty Party

Eastman, Codding, and Lovejoy wanted to draw members of the Illinois State Antislavery Society deeper into the Illinois Liberty Party. To lay the groundwork and provide motivation for this transition, in early 1844 Codding presented an analysis of the national political situation.[98] The nation's Democrats, he pointed out, were intent on making the area called Texas a territory of the United States. If they succeeded, they would try to carve it into several slave states with two senators each, keep control of the United States Senate, and preserve slavery. After Eastman published Codding's prognosis in the *Western Citizen*, Codding toured the state, traveling as far south as Alton. He was a popular lecturer because he knew how to win people of modest education with homely illustrations and how to reach the erudite by using quotes from scholars such as John Stuart Mill, Herbert Spencer, Harriet Martineau, Horace Bushnell, and Ralph Waldo Emerson.[99] By the middle of March he had lectured in eighteen Illinois counties.

At this point, Eastman and Lovejoy joined him on tour.[100] The three men set up district conventions for the Liberty Party in the first, fourth, fifth, sixth, and seventh congressional districts to nominate Liberty candidates.[101] They worked so well together that as a result, the Illinois Liberty Party did not suffer internal strife as some eastern state parties did. They focused on the "one idea": abolition. Many party leaders were clergy and church leaders, but no sect seems to have dominated. By 1848 the Illinois Liberty Party was one of the strongest in the country and may have been the most important Liberty state society in the Old Northwest.[102]

Around the same time, radical women across the nation were forming new political structures and wanted their local women's antislavery societies to parallel and augment the work of the Liberty Party. They were especially motivated by what they had learned about the effects of slavery on women: "Half a million are flogged to prostitution." They saw any system that separated babies from their mothers and husbands from their wives, and that denied individuals marriage and humanity, as antifamily.[103] They were aroused to do more than send charity to slave women; they wanted to fight slavery itself. Although many influential eastern clergymen discouraged women from leaving pietistic activism for political activism,[104] Lovejoy and his collaborators in the West urged antislavery women to participate in political life in every legal way possible. The Illinois Liberty Party included both white and African American women and men.[105]

Local antislavery societies started with diverse leaders. Princeton women, led by Betsey Lovejoy, organized in 1843, the women in Jerseyville in April 1844.[106] Although a proslavery mob in Peoria prevented antislavery men, led by Rev. William T. Allan, from organizing a male antislavery society, Mary Brown Davis and Lucy Pettengill persuaded the men's wives to organize a women's antislavery society there in July 1844.[107] In September 1844 the women of Galesburg, a radical antislavery college town west of Peoria, also formed an antislavery society. Lydia S. Lewis, the daughter of Benjamin Lundy, organized a women's society at Clear Creek, the hamlet centered around the Quaker meetinghouse northeast of Peoria.[108] These societies had members from a variety of denominations—Methodist and Disciples of Christ, Baptist and Unitarian—who came with strong feelings against bondage. Lydia S. Lewis brought the tradition of Quaker activists serving those in need.[109] Galesburg women were Presbyterian and Congregational as their churches shifted denominational affiliations. Irene Ball Allan (wife of William T. Allan), Lucy Pettengill, and Betsey, Eunice, and Lizzie Lovejoy brought the ethos of the Second Great Awakening, which enabled women to step out of what was seen as their sphere to bring comfort and justice to the oppressed.[110]

Mary Brown Davis, wife of newspaperman Samuel Davis, made herself the spokesperson for the women's antislavery movement in Illinois. Having been raised on a Virginia plantation in a predominantly Episcopalian region, she entered the cause after observing in her parents' house the tragedies suffered by slaves she had grown to love.[111] She had rejected the wishes of her slaveholding family when she married Samuel. Years later, when Samuel bought the newspaper in Peoria, Mary worked as his partner while raising five sons. From 1843 to 1853 she wrote over sixty articles about women and antislavery published by Zebina Eastman in the *Western Citizen.*[112]

Although these women could not vote, they became well informed about politics and engaged in political activity outside their homes. While they continued conventional care of their families, they felt called to challenge society's social, economic, and political structures. To maximize their effectiveness, the women announced a statewide meeting in 1844 to organize an Illinois Female Anti-Slavery Society.[113] The call was signed by Peoria residents Mary Brown Davis, Lucy Pettengill, and Irene Ball Allan.

These three women decided to ask Betsey Lovejoy to be the state president. Irene Allan wrote a long, persuasive letter, but Betsey responded with a thoughtful "no." Younger women should take charge, she answered. She was certain that they would succeed and that God would bless their efforts. She warned Irene about the diverse "powers and principalities" conspiring against the downtrodden. She consoled her about the split in the national antislavery organizations and applauded Garrison: "Although the enemy may rejoice for the division that has taken place in the Anti-Slavery movement, don't let it discourage or dishearten you a moment. Garrison has done and is doing good and I can say of Garrison what Cooper said of England 'With all thy faults, I love thee still.' Garrison set in motion a great work." Irene informed Betsey that the second statewide convention, in 1845, would be held in Alton, where her son Elijah was buried. Betsey answered, "It would be a glorification to be with you in person and visit the grave of [my] dearly beloved son, but I must confess, when I think of Alton, I think of Nineveh. . . . I pray that God will bring [his murderers] to repentance and forgive them." As a motherly addendum, Betsey asked Irene to "tell the brethren they must keep a watch" over Owen because he was worn out. "Do not expect him yet too much."[114] Although Betsey refused the presidency, she attended many regional and statewide meetings.

On May 23, 1844, in Peoria, delegates formed the Illinois State Female Anti-Slavery Society. Succeeding annual meetings were held in Alton in 1845 and in Princeton and Chicago in 1846. In 1847 the organization held its annual meeting in two separate locations, in Granville in conjunction with the Christian Anti-Slavery Convention, and in Farmington in 1847.[115] These disparate locations allowed more women to attend. Mary Kellogg, the wife of the first president of Knox College in Galesburg, was elected the society's first president.[116] Newspaper reporter Mary Brown Davis was secretary. Lucy Pettengill, whose husband, Moses, ran local businesses in Peoria, planned activities. Louisa M. Gifford Dyer, the wife of Chicago's leading white male abolitionist, was vice president.[117]

Betsey attended meetings when she could. In March 1844 Eunice had given birth to Owen's first child, Sarah Moody Lovejoy, who would propel him to apply his understanding of women's rights.

From the beginning, the local societies dedicated themselves to assisting runaway slaves. Being ready at a moment's notice to provide assistance to runaway men, women, and children was the business that brought antislavery women together.[118] They also wanted to get black children into schools and hoped to provide scholarships. In 1844 Irene Ball Allan wrote to the managers of the local antislavery societies, urging them to become acquainted with black families and encourage their children to enroll in school. "The colored people are so unused to anything like [the opening of schools], that they will hardly know how to understand us at first. . . . You must get in your wagon, and go out on the prairie to the colored family you may know out there, and see if there is not one that can be spared and induced to go [to school]; then you must go down to [Main] street, where there are several families, and do what you can do there; then, perhaps you know of some living in white families; visit them."[119] At the time, free black families were scattered in villages and along streams over the prairie; some fugitives did not go straight to Canada. In addition to promoting school and providing scholarships, the women offered other kinds of assistance. A Mrs. Wiltslow attended the 1844 state meeting and requested financial aid to purchase her daughter, who remained in slavery in Louisiana.[120]

The Illinois women's antislavery societies of the 1840s did not follow the eastern societies and address women's rights directly. Nevertheless, opponents in the Whig Party accused them of vacating their proper domestic sphere and engaging in improper political behavior. Male criticism against women's political activity outside their homes caused many of the two hundred female antislavery societies in the East to fall apart.[121] But in Illinois, political abolitionist men vigorously defended the women. Eastman spoke for them when he editorialized in the *Western Citizen* by questioning the opponents' manhood. Mary Brown Davis defended her sisters by describing how well they carried out their domestic duties. Mrs. T. C. Hurlbut of Upper Alton accused the male critics of being afraid that their wives would stop cooking for them. Liberty Party wives knew that the opponents were hypocritical because Whig politicians' wives were also busy participating in political activities.[122] The Illinois women continued their work and quickly joined forces with the men in other venues "with interracial activism."[123]

Irene Allan had hoped to take public positions on women's rights, but after her death in 1845 at age thirty, the antislavery women in Illinois returned to focusing on the "one idea." Reforming other evils should, they believed, be postponed until slavery was exterminated. White women in the state did not push for women's rights until at least a decade later.[124]

Female antislavery society members lived far apart; they got together only occasionally, and when they did, they savored the time for fellowship. They also worked zealously to get antislavery men elected to public office. They coordinated their meetings with the men's so that husbands and wives, as well as their young children, needed to make only one trip to enable both men and women to attend their abolitionist meetings. Although they traveled under the guise of belonging to a separate female organization, some women also attended some of the men's meetings. On one occasion in Peoria, forty-five white women adjourned their meeting at noon and walked from Main Street Presbyterian Church to the courthouse to join the Liberty Party gathering.[125] They wanted to learn the latest information, the most persuasive arguments, and the best campaign tactics. They invited Dickey, Codding, and Lovejoy to instruct them. Lovejoy urged the women to hold neighborhood meetings and to chat with friends about Liberty.[126] In Bureau County the Female Anti-Slavery Society raised money to pay a male lecturer to come to Princeton and inform the men.[127] Western women raised money, sewed garments, and collected books for the schoolchildren of freedom seekers in Canada.[128]

At this point, in 1844, antislavery agent William T. Allan urged Lovejoy to run for elective office. Allan later wrote that he had addressed Owen that day out of the commitment he had made at the end of the forty-five-hour, fourteen-day debate against slavery a decade earlier at Lane Seminary. Under Theodore Weld's tutelage, he had decided to become an agent of the American Anti-Slavery Society, and, as one of his challenges, to identify the best candidates for political office. He had looked straight at Owen and said, "Mr. Lovejoy, you ought to be in Congress. You are just the man to lock horns with those bellowing slaveholding animals."[129] Lovejoy responded, "Nothing short of a miracle could compel my congressional district to send an abolitionist to Washington." Then Allan made an unusual promise: "I am going to stump your district. I'll lecture wherever I can get a church, a hall, a schoolhouse, a private home, or a barn. If I can get none of them, I'll call meetings and talk abolition in God's open air, and I'll keep it up 'til the thing is done."[130] As the antislavery agent in Illinois, Allan had studied the potential candidates and concluded Lovejoy was the finest choice.

That summer, Lovejoy campaigned as a Liberty Party nominee to cast the district's electoral vote for president of the United States in the Electoral College. Despite Allan's campaigning, Lovejoy lost on August 5, 1844, but he had put his toe in the stream of politics.

Lovejoy decided to go to the Southern and Western Liberty Party Convention in Cincinnati on June 11–12, 1845. It was the first of three regional conventions planned. The second would be the Great Convention of the Friends of Freedom in the Eastern and Middle States, to be held in Boston on October 1–3, 1845. The third was projected for Chicago in 1846.[131] Charles L. Kelsey, the young attorney who had moved from Connecticut to Princeton, was going with him. The convention's purpose was to bring the enthusiasm of the 1843 Buffalo Liberty Party Convention to people in the West. Two thousand delegates from western Virginia, Kentucky, and nine of the free Northern states attended.[132] Salmon Chase asked his fellow Cincinnatian and talented antislavery newspaperman Gamaliel Bailey to help him

organize this interdenominational convention. Their goal was to form a broader
coalition of all sincere friends of liberty and free labor for the 1848 presidential
campaign. As Chase had argued at Buffalo, the federal government was not authorized to act upon slavery already existing in the states,[133] but delegates could and
did pass resolutions to prohibit slaveholding in the District of Columbia and in
the territories. Chase stressed the law as his basis for action, so the religious tone
of the convention was muted.[134] Following the pattern of interracial programs and
committees featured at Buffalo, African Americans Lewis Woodson and John B.
Vashon came from Pittsburgh to address the delegates.

The black community in Cincinnati presented Chase with a sterling silver pitcher
in gratitude for his defense of blacks facing extradition in Ohio courts.[135]

Margaret Shands Bailey was the unheralded partner of Gamaliel Bailey in their
Cincinnati publication, the *Philanthropist*. Besides writing articles and poetry
for the newspaper, she published the *Youth Monthly Visitor* for antislavery young
people, with instructive stories, poetry, and original music. With a circulation of
three thousand, the monthly paid for itself.[136] In future years the Lovejoys and
Baileys would become close friends.

Back in Illinois, some women were becoming active in the Christian Anti-Slavery
Society, a religious group. Jonathan Blanchard, the new president of Knox College, was the chief organizer. As a young man, Blanchard had been an agent for
the American Anti-Slavery Society in Pennsylvania. There, he had met Mary, a
radical antislavery New Englander who was teaching in Harrisburg and whom
he would later marry. After they were married, Jonathan Blanchard was called to
a Presbyterian Church in Cincinnati, where he and Mary led students from Lane
Seminary in work on projects with African Americans in the city's black neighborhood. In 1844 the family moved to Illinois, and as soon as they were settled, Mary
A. Blanchard joined the Galesburg Female Anti-Slavery Society and became an
officer in the state society, which focused on changing the state's Black Laws.

John and Mary Jones Join the Black Community in Chicago

Earlier that spring, an African American couple, John and Mary Jones, left the black
community in Lower Alton and traveled by stagecoach as far as Ottawa. During
the trip they were nearly kidnapped but were saved by the antislavery driver. They
continued by boat on the canal and arrived in Chicago on March 11, 1845. They
arrived with only $3.50 in currency, but they had professional skills and a strong
entrepreneurial spirit. In Chicago they started a professional tailoring business and
also established careers of fighting for blacks' human rights.[137]

John Jones had been born in 1816 in Greene County, North Carolina, to a free
mulatto mother and a father of German ancestry. Jones's mother, fearing that his

father or other relatives might sell John as a slave, apprenticed him as a very young boy to a white man named Sheppard. When Sheppard moved to Memphis, Tennessee, Jones was moved with him and was later apprenticed to Richard Clere, an expert tailor. Under Clere's teaching, Jones developed excellent skills. In Memphis Jones met and fell in love with Mary Jane Richardson, the daughter of Elijah Richardson, a free blacksmith of African descent.[138] The Richardson family moved to Lower Alton, Illinois. After completing his three-year apprenticeship and saving $100 over that time, in 1843 John Jones followed the Richardsons to Lower Alton. The following year, at age twenty-seven, John married Mary. The couple lived in the strongly proslavery region for several months. Jones deeply resented and never forgot that Illinois State law required him to purchase a Certificate of Freedom from the Madison County Clerk for $50, half of the money he had saved.[139] They decided to leave those restrictions and move to Chicago where the citizenry was more open to African Americans.

In Chicago the Joneses quickly made friends among their black neighbors and white clients. For several months a white antislavery retailer, L. C. Paine Freer, wrote out the legal documents Jones needed for his business, but Freer gradually convinced Jones to learn to read and write. Soon Jones was composing letters to the editor of the early *Chicago Tribune*, organizing meetings, and working closely with African Americans such as Henry O. Wagoner, William Styles, William Johnson, and Rev. Abraham T. Hall, and he and Mary were heading the busy Underground Railroad activities in the city.

The Illinois State Census of 1845 reported that Chicago had 140 black residents out of a total population of 12,088. Most of them lived in the Second Ward between State Street, Clark Street, and the Chicago River. Jones's successful business, "J. Jones, Clothes Dresser & Repairer," was in this area, located at 119 Dearborn. After several years, Jones began investing in Chicago real estate and gradually became well-to-do. John and Mary Jane Jones became leaders of women and men in Chicago's small black community.

Lovejoy sent runaways from Princeton to Liberty Party men in Chicago such as Charles Dyer, Zebina Eastman, Philo Carpenter, James Collins, and Calvin DeWolf, who were members of Presbyterian, Congregational, and other churches in the city. These white men and their families were first clients, then fellow conspirators, and then personal friends of John and Mary Jones and other black families.[140] When the Liberty Party was formed, African Americans participated in its activities "from the party's inception" and were "assuming significant roles within the party itself."[141]

The Liberty Party had been holding interracial and mixed-gender Liberty Association meetings and special lectures "enlivened by the Chicago Liberty Choir and Chicago Brass Band."[142] The party resolution called for members to "carry out the principles of Equal Rights into all their practical consequences and applications."

On Christmas Eve in 1844, an antiabolitionist farmer happened to walk in on their meeting. He saw "every face lighted up with a friendly smile," a white man shaking hands with an African, females of all hues smiling together, and recently arrived slaves—father, mother, and daughter—"raised to the platform of liberty." A speech by Codding so moved him that in a moment he felt his life was changed. He had walked into a Liberty meeting.[143]

John Jones had a specific political agenda. He wanted the Black Laws of Illinois rescinded, the Certificate of Freedom abolished, black suffrage legalized, and public schools opened to black children.[144] The concerns of the Chicago's black abolitionists to safeguard fugitive slaves from federal commissioners and kidnappers and to build an antislavery third political party were almost identical with those of Lovejoy and his colleagues on the Illinois prairie.[145] These whites and blacks, many of whom lived within a few blocks of each other, found themselves meeting informally, building friendships, and quietly creating a coalition for equality.

The Coalition Leads the Liberty Party Campaign

In 1846 Lovejoy decided to seek the Liberty Party nomination for the Fourth Congressional District. The coalition was mobilized, and Dyer, Eastman, Codding, and Lovejoy began to plan a large regional convention in Chicago to report on the Liberty Party's work and provide a platform for congressional candidates, especially Lovejoy.[146] The Illinois Female Anti-Slavery Society decided to meet at the same time as the Liberty Party men and share speakers and resolutions for action.[147] African American Liberty members joined in the preparations, as they had from the party's early days.[148] In March the *Western Citizen* published extensive plans for the convention.[149] In May the state central committee leased a large meeting place in Chicago, the City Saloon, as their base of operations.[150] Then twelve well-known abolitionists signed the formal call and extended it to Liberty Party societies in surrounding states.[151] The coalition intended to hold an exemplary interracial and mixed-gender Liberty Party meeting.

Lovejoy and his friends Charles Kelsey and Ichabod Codding traveled together to the nominating convention held by the Fourth Congressional District at the Unitarian Church in St. Charles on the Fox River. Editor Zebina Eastman took notes on the meeting. On the first ballot Codding was elected to be the nominee, but he quickly declined. Disagreement between moderates and radicals marked a failed second nomination. On the third ballot Lovejoy was chosen, and he accepted.[152] As soon as the meeting ended, Lovejoy rushed to Chicago to the North-Western Liberty Convention. It was a huge affair and required considerable advanced planning. The Cincinnati convention had drawn two thousand attendees and the Boston convention three thousand, but the Chicago convention brought in six thousand.[153]

Hundreds from Indiana, Michigan, Wisconsin, and Iowa were expected to assemble, as well as thousands from Illinois. Charles Dyer called the meeting to order and requested that Owen Lovejoy give the opening prayer, creating a tangible religious context. Dyer appointed Codding, John Cross, and L. C. Paine Freer from Illinois and men from the other states to the business committee.[154] The convention presented the long view when Dyer introduced a resolution to help fund a national antislavery newspaper in Washington. It was approved, and he soon identified Gamaliel Bailey as the man to edit the *National Era*.[155]

Henry Bibb was the guest speaker at the convention. He was the formerly enslaved black son of James Bibb, a Kentucky state senator. Bibb was hired out for ten years to earn money to send the master's daughters to finishing schools, yet he was denied an elementary education. On his sixth attempt, Bibb finally succeeded in escaping.

Lovejoy was the second to speak. He wove Bibb's experience into his own speech, asking the audience, "How did we feel when our friend Bibb told us how his drunken, brutal master [Willard Gatewood] lashed out at Bibb's wife before his eyes, merely because she left a tuft of grass while hoeing in the garden—how, when he knelt at his master's feet and implored him to inflict blows upon him, it only added to the cruelty of her punishment? Couldn't we have torn Gatewood to pieces? I do not suppose we should have done so, for we should have been restrained by Christian principle; but such would have been the first natural impulse. There [is] nothing like talking about the one idea."[156]

Then Lovejoy laced together an image that dramatized the buying and selling of slaves in the District of Columbia, a place he referred to as the Ten Miles Square. He shouted, "Where did this puny white man get the power to insult God, mock humanity, and bid off men like brutes? He got his power from us! Twenty millions of us! We voted for them!"[157] Northerners were as responsible for slavery as southerners because they voted for the congressmen who protected it. Finally, Lovejoy softly described a child sold into slavery. "Perhaps I feel more than I ought; but I remember a little one who makes the light of the household circle, whose eye brightens with joy and welcome when I return home, and I know how my heart would bleed if I should find the house desolate, and the little one sold and gone."[158] His first child, Sarah, was a toddler at the time.

The Liberty Party had put aside all other reform tasks in order to concentrate on abolition, the one idea. Lovejoy argued that the South had its own "one idea" campaign, but it was to perpetuate slavery. If antislavery people could find two hundred thousand men and women in the North who would pledge themselves to do as much for Liberty as the two hundred thousand slaveholders in the South were doing for slavery, Liberty men would be a formidable countervailing power.

Lovejoy had just given his first campaign speech for the U.S. Congress. Someone in the audience yelled, "I'm afraid you'll go to Congress!" He responded, "If I do, I

want to go on the 'one idea.' I want to look those frowning slaveholders in the face.
. . . I shall go there if I get votes enough."[159]

Eastman, Codding, and Dyer worked closely with John and Mary Jones, their
friends, and the black community in Chicago to receive Bibb and include him in all
the meeting's activities. This was an interracial event on a large scale. The numerous
women of the Illinois Female Anti-Slavery Society also made an appearance at the
men's convention. In fact, the invitation to the convention was pointedly addressed
to anyone interested in a "peaceable overthrow of the Slave Power without 'reference to sex, class, or condition.'"[160] The *Western Citizen* had announced that
"Ladies, and gentlemen with their wives, will be provided with places in private
families."[161] As a result, some women attended on their own. At the same time the
Illinois Female Anti-Slavery Society held its own convention. Its women's meetings
were at times interspersed with the men's sessions. The women asked Lovejoy to
address them separately, which he did. Then, at a united assembly, he asked the
males whether they were all "Liberty men." After cries of "Yes, yes!" he next asked,
was every woman a Liberty man? They too answered "Yes, yes!"[162] Liberty Party
men in Illinois clearly wanted women to participate in their meetings and considered their political activity proper and democratic.[163] This convention provided
the opportunity for radical women and men to join forces.

During the 1846 campaign, local women's societies enthusiastically backed Lovejoy's candidacy for Congress on the Liberty Party ticket. The women abolitionists of
Dundee, Illinois, disgusted that neither they nor African Americans were allowed to
vote, demanded that local white men support Lovejoy for Congress because he was
"a living picture of the philanthropist and Christian."[164] Two of the women leaders
in the state's Female Anti-Slavery Society were also the wives of prominent leaders.
Mary Davis's husband, Samuel, presided over the Liberty Party state convention
in both 1846. Louisa Dyer's husband, Charles, ran as the Liberty Party candidate
for governor.[165] Louise became president of the society in 1847.

The North-Western Liberty Convention was the most successful of the three
regional meetings.[166] As a result, the convention provided a solid base for Lovejoy
as he began his campaign. Lovejoy's congressional district stretched from the Wisconsin border in the north, through Chicago, to Champaign in the south, and from
Indiana on the east to Bloomington and Princeton on the west. Lovejoy campaigned
hard to cover such an extensive area.

On Election Day, August 3, Lovejoy and all Liberty candidates in Illinois lost
their bids for elective office, but they interpreted the experience as a step forward.
They had informed thousands of people about slavery; interracial relations were
closer in their coalition for equality; and Lovejoy had obtained one-third of the
vote in his district, receiving more total votes than presidential nominee James
Birney received from the entire state. Reinhold O. Johnson concludes that Lovejoy's

Fourth District was the "heart and soul of the Liberty movement in Illinois," a major center of Liberty strength in the nation. Bureau, Putnam, and DeKalb Counties were "hotbeds." Lovejoy suddenly found himself to be "one of the leading Liberty politicians in the country."[167] The coalition for equality had performed as it had hoped. All its constituencies were deeply involved, working in a spirit of unity, and the antislavery movement had made great gains.[168]

A Windfall to the Antislavery Movement

While Methodists, Baptists, and Presbyterians were divided North versus South over slavery, Congregationalists were divided East versus West. To prevent a national division over the issue, eastern leaders proposed that a conference be held in the West, in Michigan City, Indiana, from July 31 to August 3, 1846. Western pastors hoped the eastern clergy would listen: they did not want to be connected with institutional slavery through the American Home Missionary Society.[169] Lovejoy, campaigning until Election Day, was unable to attend. However, prior to the meeting, Reverend Blanchard spent "a pleasant Sabbath with Br. Lovejoy," during which they undoubtedly developed their united approach to the conference. Blanchard then stopped at Zebina Eastman's home in Chicago to confer with him before continuing on to Michigan City.[170] During the conference, eastern establishment leaders accused the western ministers of unorthodox theology and involvement in politics. Western clergy urged eastern clergy to accept western independence, put aside their unnecessary anxiety over Oberlin theology, send money for the erection of churches, and join the antislavery movement.[171]

A month later, Lovejoy heard news of a momentous decision: on September 2 and 3 in Albany, New York, a group of radical Christian antislavery leaders centered in New York State initiated a new missionary organization, naming it the American Missionary Association (AMA). It was dramatically different from the American Home Missionary Society. The new association was officially antislavery and structurally interracial. White philanthropists Gerrit Smith and Lewis Tappan served on the planning committee.[172] A number of African American ministers Lovejoy knew well, including Theodore S. Wright, Charles B. Ray, and Henry Highland Garnet, were present at the founding. They and Rev. James W. C. Pennington would be on the Executive Committee.[173] The AMA absorbed the former Amistad Committee and the Union Missionary Society.[174] It intended to hire graduates from Oberlin for missionary, pastoral, and staff positions and to subsidize antislavery churches and ministers, black and white.[175]

Lovejoy was immediately aware of the political possibilities the AMA held for the churches of his region. From 1846 to 1865, the AMA subsidized 115 new antislavery Congregational churches in northern and central Illinois.[176] This would alter the

balance between antislavery and silent churches in the Illinois General Association of Congregational Churches and would greatly strengthen the Liberty Party.
The American Missionary Association was the church structure Lovejoy and his
collaborators needed to deliver the West from the Slave Power.

Lovejoy Campaigns as "the Orator of the West"

Lovejoy was surprised and delighted when he received an invitation from the Central Committee of the Massachusetts Liberty Party to come and speak on behalf of
their candidates.[177] They had heard of his outstanding performance as a strategist
and candidate in Illinois. It was a great opportunity. With the election scheduled
for early November, Owen boarded the ship *Niagara* at Chicago and continued his
journey in the "cars" at night along the Erie Canal.[178] He was looking forward to
seeing his brother Joseph and sister-in-law Sarah in Cambridge, across the Charles
River from Boston.

Owen Lovejoy arrived ready to campaign for the Liberty Party. Massachusetts
Liberty leaders were eager to get out the vote for their candidates, and he was a new
voice in the contest.[179] He spoke in different communities around Boston fifty-five
times in forty-one days, often traveling by train. The *Emancipator* called him the
"Lion of the West" and the "Orator of the West."[180] "His off-the-cuff, up-front western style of speaking" attracted eastern audiences. A reporter in Marlboro quoted
in the *Western Citizen* praised the state committee for procuring Owen. "The good
men of the Whig and Democratic parties should call meetings to discuss southern
aggression and northern rights and then call in such a man as Mr. Lovejoy of Illinois
to lecture."[181]

The editor of the *Daily Courier* of Lowell, Massachusetts, agreed with Owen
Lovejoy that slavery must be overthrown but chided him for his choice of remedy.
He argued that the Liberty Party was too weak to accomplish its task, and that Ohio
congressman Joshua Giddings was able to do good things within the Whig Party.
Lovejoy's call for fusion was naive, for if fusion was so easy, "why not fuse all the
churches?"[182] It was clear that Reverend Lovejoy had not been able to bring about
ecumenical unity in Illinois. A third party might sound morally superior, the editor
argued, but it could end up being a spoiler in a three-way race, and "we" could
end up with the Democratic Party, "the worst of the lot"—the standard arguments
against all third parties. Then he suggested that the Liberty Party should join with
the Whigs,[183] who had formed as a reaction to the Jacksonian Democrats in 1834.
They supported banks and economic growth through building infrastructure, and
they generally identified with the interests of the wealthy. Senator Henry Clay, a
slaveholder, was their leading spokesman.

Owen Lovejoy flatly rejected that notion. First, Whigs had adopted racist colonization as a major component of party ideology in order to obtain political clout with its proslavery faction. Second, Whigs had compromised to uphold "universal white manhood suffrage" while systematically suppressing the rights of free African Americans.[184] Whigs had tried—but failed—to keep that deal while pretending to work with supporters of John Quincy Adams and Joshua Giddings who hated slavery and opposed the Slave Power's encroachments on Northern rights. Lovejoy believed that an alternative to the Whig Party was necessary. As he met leading Liberty men and women in Massachusetts, Lovejoy studied their ways of presenting the idea of fusion and got a broader view of the Liberty Party nationally.

In front of the state capitol on Beacon Hill was the Boston Common. Close to it were several avenues with powerful families' opulent homes. Behind the capitol and down the hill were a few narrow streets and alleys where blacks lived in tiny dwellings. The black community had its own modest churches, fraternities, and literary, musical, and mutual aid societies. The red brick Smith Street School was where African Americans had held a memorial service for Elijah P. Lovejoy nine years earlier. A handful of ministers and teachers, one doctor, a printer, and a few store owners, laborers, and sailors made up the town's fragile and rudimentary black middle class.

There was an air of antislavery camaraderie in these side streets behind the capitol. Sympathetic whites provided a buffer between the black community and proslavery whites. Garrison's *Liberator* office was a few blocks away. John Andrew, who often represented the black community in legal matters, had an office nearby. Runaway slaves like Lewis Hayden found employers, patrons, and friends. Near the bottom of the hill were railroad stations whose tracks fanned out to the surrounding towns.[185]

On Election Day, November 4, few candidates in the Massachusetts Liberty Party did well enough to win. Lovejoy explained it in a letter written for the *Western Citizen*: "In the fourth Congressional District [of Massachusetts] the whigs and democrats put up men who were well known for their anti-slavery sentiments in order to sponge up the anti-slavery sentiment. . . . The whigs sail just as close to the liberty Bark as they can, to suck the wind out of our sails."[186]

Before Owen Lovejoy left Illinois for Massachusetts, he had hired David Todd, a young Oberlin seminary graduate, to be his substitute in the Hampshire Colony Church pulpit and to board as a house guest in his absence. Todd was thrilled; he greatly admired Owen Lovejoy and he idolized Eunice Lovejoy. He wrote his fiancée, Charlotte Farnsworth, a student in the Female Department at Oberlin College, about Eunice Lovejoy. "I regard her as a superior woman. . . . Mrs. Lovejoy does admirably in attending to the children. A family better disciplined I seldom have seen. Yet it requires the influence in this case of a master hand. She knows how to see to all the business of the farm & then she is an intelligent & polite lady. . . . Think you not I am fortunate in getting such a place to board? I regard it as home. . . . I am not troubled with any bashfulness, so complete is her politeness. She is at home and makes others so."[187]

Eunice Lovejoy knew her community. She could list all of the weddings and name the newlywed young women. When a husband had to travel and leave his young wife alone in a half-finished cabin on a partially developed farm, Todd wrote, Eunice would invite the newcomer bride to stay with her.[188] If one added to that picture of hospitality the frequent arrival of freedom seekers staying at the Lovejoy homestead on their way to Canada, and politicians stopping by to confer with Owen on their way to Springfield, it would be clear that Eunice Lovejoy included among her other roles those of counselor, innkeeper, and diplomat.

Owen and Eunice Lovejoy had shared four years of companionate married life. There were now five children—three Denhams and two living Lovejoys—and a large farm to care for as well as the church. It was not an easy life for Eunice, who had to cope with Owen's frequent absences. It was also difficult for Owen, who did not want to give up so many days of family life, as his father had. The relationship between Lovejoy and the Hampshire Colony Church had become ardent and trusting. Attempts to radicalize the Illinois Congregational Association had failed, but the new American Missionary Society was about to subsidize clergymen and women's societies that were active in the Liberty Party. Motivated by the experience of blacks, women, and churchmen working together on the Underground Railroad, inspired by professional black delegates at the national Liberty Party conventions in Buffalo, impressed at the achievements of blacks in Chicago in organizing their own businesses, congregations, schoolrooms, and clubs, the trio of Lovejoy, Codding, and Eastman could reflect that a formidable coalition had assembled at the 1846 North-Western Liberty Convention and fought a hard campaign. Although Lovejoy was defeated in his first attempt to win a congressional seat, he had built the most effective Liberty Party state organization in the West, and his persuasiveness was reaffirmed in Massachusetts. Returning home shortly before Christmas, he sensed that the African Americans, the women's groups, and the clergy were ready to try again.

3. Responding to Legislative Maneuverings
1847–1851

John Jones versus the Black Exclusion Referendum

John Jones had been a resident of Chicago less than three years when he and the black community faced a huge challenge. The Illinois legislature voted to hold a constitutional convention to write a new constitution that would reinforce the existing statutory laws by preventing blacks from entering the state in the future. Black abolitionists who wanted family members, fiancées, and friends to move to Illinois were directly affected. It was a provocative, unnecessary, hurtful frontal attack on blacks throughout the state.[1]

Rumors spread before the constitutional convention met that the Democrats intended to include a severe Black Exclusion law. To prevent the convention from presenting such a provision to the public, a coalition led by John Jones wrote a well-crafted presentation against such a law, citing historical and legal precedents. Jones delivered it to the state Senate. On March 1, 1847, the state senate received and approved a report from its judiciary committee recommending that the request of the black community's petition to repeal its immigration and residency Black Laws be rejected. They said that approving the request would invite emigration of emancipated blacks, thus increasing "an evil already felt" in Illinois, and would require state money to remove them, for "nothing [could] raise the African above his current level." If the petitioner was not content, the Senate urged him to return to Africa.[2] In June 1847, when copies of the proposed constitution were distributed, the exclusionary section was listed as Article XIV.

In September 1847, Eastman's *Western Citizen* printed three articles carefully written by Jones, titled "Pleading Their Own Cause." All three opposed Article XIV.[3] Jones stated, "This article is at war with the constitution" of the United

States. He admonished Illinoisans not to insert the word "white" before "citizen" in order to exclude blacks.[4] The evidence showed, he argued, that the Founding Fathers had opposed a similar article in 1776 when a delegate from South Carolina introduced such an amendment to the proposed U.S. Constitution; that motion was voted down. For the same reasons, Jones argued, it should fail in Illinois now.[5]

The black community was totally rebuffed. On March 8, 1848, the new constitution was ratified by a vote of 60,585 to 15,903. In April, the Negro Exclusion provision, Article XIV, carried easily, by 50,261 to 21,297. The referendum for Black Exclusion passed in 87 of the state's 101 counties. However, in the 12 counties where the coalition was strong, it lost. In Boone the vote was 94 percent against; in Lake it was 85 percent against; in Winnebago it was 81 percent; and in McHenry, 75 percent. But in Saline County, in the south, where the statehood constitution protected slavery for the salt mines, the vote in favor of Black Exclusion was 98 percent.[6]

Owen Lovejoy Risks Running on the Free Soil Ticket

Around the same time, the coalition faced a second challenge. In the East a controversial proposal was circulating among political abolitionists: to broaden the Liberty Party's base by fusing with dissatisfied factions of the Whig and Democratic Parties and to change its focus by lending its name to the Free Soil Party. Antislavery men were afraid that this proposal would dilute the strong equal rights platform of the Liberty Party and that it could be a subtle ruse for crass men to use the Liberty Party's goodwill for their own self-interested ends.

Lovejoy wanted to run for Congress again, if nominated, but in 1847 he could not decide which political party to work in. Should he stay with the deeply religious and egalitarian Liberty Party or move into the new, pragmatic Free Soil Party? His colleagues among the Free Soilers were former members of the Liberty Party who still espoused the old Liberty Party platform and remained committed to universal civil rights.[7] They believed that the constitution allowed them to oppose any extension of slavery into the territories. But the other faction of Free Soilers wanted to prevent slaveholders from buying up plantation-sized tracts of land in the new territories[8] and wanted to keep all blacks, whether slave or free, out of the territories so whites would not have to compete with them for land or wages. These latter folks were unconcerned about the rights of blacks or women and shared the latent racism of the North.[9] The one thing that held these two factions together was their determination to prevent slavery from entering the territories.

Lovejoy wanted the federal government to prevent slavery's expansion, which would have the effect of encircling the South with free territories and free labor.[10] He balked against the slaveholders' claim that land expansion was necessary to provide new, rich soil for their growing, slave-dependent cotton industry. He disagreed that slaves were necessary to grow cotton. He wanted to open up the prairies and plains to all free people. Ownership in a piece of land would improve the lives of urban low-wage earners, farmers working on poor New England soil, homeless European immigrants, and free blacks who wanted to escape indenture, apprenticeship, and exploitation as black families in China, Maine, had succeeded in doing.[11] Lovejoy felt much closer to the Liberty Party, but its base was so narrow that it had won very few elections.[12] Ironically, while Free Soil advocates were divided over sharply divergent motives, the party would probably win some electoral victories.

Joshua Leavitt chose to remain in the Liberty Party, and he became its spokesman. He advocated that the national convention be held in 1847. But Salmon Chase and Gamaliel Bailey of Cincinnati urged that a Free Soil Convention meet later on, in 1848, following the Whig and Democratic Party nominating conventions, for they believed it would be easier to attract folks who became dissatisfied with their former affiliations during their conventions and who would then be eager to join a Free Soil Party.[13] The strategy of Chase and Bailey won.

Lovejoy's eastern black friends were suspicious of a national Free Soil Party. Rev. Henry Highland Garnet was well aware that many Free Soilers claimed that public land belonged only to whites. He theorized that economic equality was essential to democratic freedom and was a part of God's plan for the world. Lecturing in Ireland, he had witnessed how land monopolies caused famine.[14] But the most extreme form of monopoly he had experienced was American slavery. Fundamental economic change would be required if blacks were to become citizens. His friend and benefactor, Gerrit Smith, told Garnet that he planned to give plots of land he had inherited in Upstate New York to as many as three thousand poor black city dwellers who were presently denied the right to vote in New York because they owned no property.[15] In 1847 Garnet called the National Colored People's Convention to meet at his church in Troy, New York. Sixty-eight delegates arrived. Garnet softened the speech he had made in Buffalo and no longer called for violence to overthrow the slave system.[16] Instead he insisted that landownership was essential; blacks must have a right to buy land in the territories.

After the African Americans elected their officers, Gerrit Smith made his presentation.[17] This wealthy white man had purchased the freedom of a score of slaves and donated $50,000 to the American Anti-Slavery Society. Now he presented the convention with 120,000 acres of farming and timber land to distribute to several thousand African Americans.[18] He acknowledged that the soil was poor, that it was not located where black people lived, and that many blacks no longer wished to farm. Still, owning a piece of land would make them "men of property," the requirement for a black man to vote in New York State. Smith gave parcels to Frederick Douglass, William Wells Brown, Henry Bibb, and others. Now Garnet felt even more strongly that black people would not be completely free until they were permitted to purchase land of their own.[19]

Coalition Women against Slavery

The Illinois State Female Anti-Slavery Society was in the midst of a campaign of its own. Aware that neither Whigs nor Democrats intended to dismantle slavery, the women continued to build the third party. When the women met during the summer of 1847 in Farmington, they elected two highly motivated women as officers: Mary Brown Davis of Peoria as moderator and Mary A. Blanchard of Galesburg as secretary.[20]

Following the precedent set by eastern antislavery women, who petitioned the U.S. Congress from 1836 to 1840, they planned to circulate petitions statewide asking the state legislature to improve the situation of African Americans. Such petitions performed several functions: spreading information, correcting inaccuracies, awakening sympathy, and influencing public opinion and elected officials. The first bunch of antislavery petitions that reached the floor of the U.S. House of Representatives led the men to institute a gag rule and the rejection of all petitions. As a result, the public became more sympathetic toward the antislavery position, increasing the number of petitions to an avalanche (with hundreds of thousands of signatures) that eventually forced Congress to break its silence and discuss slavery.[21] Historian William Miller seems to assume, despite more recent evidence, that the energy behind the petition movement came from men, as Theodore Weld designed the format of the petitions in Ohio, and that men organized the project and women merely signed the petitions, but congressmen rejected them in part because of their female origin.[22] Historian Susan Zaeske describes women as the visionaries of the scheme, as organizers of the project, and as circulators of the petitions. She goes further, stating that women preceded men in petitioning and taught them how to proceed. In this undertaking, women were making political demands on their congressmen.[23] Women's petitioning helped them develop a language of equality and gave them practice in confronting stiff opposition, advances that significantly redefined American politics.[24]

In lightly populated Illinois in 1847, the women in the Illinois State Female Anti-Slavery Society were disappointed with their statewide petition efforts; although they did not expect to duplicate the flood of petitions and signatures that women in the East had collected in earlier years,[25] the Illinois women collected only hundreds of signatures. They did not succeed in persuading any elected official; they did not have the vote; they were not equal. They decided, then, to engage more fully in political party activism.

The women in Lovejoy's family—Betsey, Eunice, and Lizzie—were solidly behind Owen's campaign. Once, when he traveled to Chicago, the work of his church was still on his pastor-politician's mind. He asked Eunice and Lizzie to "visit the people all you can and keep them easy." He did not want the parishioners to feel neglected. He was depending on all three women to use their pastoral abilities while he was absent.

In February 1847, in Elgin, Illinois, Lovejoy had been overwhelmingly nominated to run again as the candidate from the Fourth Congressional District for the upcoming August 1848 campaign.[26] In October 1847, when Lovejoy traveled to the last National Liberty Party convention in Buffalo, he was still uncertain whether to unite with the Free Soil Party. Idealistic Gerrit Smith gave the opening address in which he described a beatific vision of the Kingdom of Righteousness and universal equality. Lovejoy yearned to retain the religious basis for political action as promulgated by Smith, but he weighed the advantages of applying a more pragmatic strategy in the short run while maintaining equality as the ultimate goal. Smith urged the delegates to "show that they were ready to strike the shackles from the negro, to elevate him and all mankind to a perfect political and social equality." Lovejoy was the next to speak. With Smith's vision of equality still ringing in his ears, he naively denied that there was any difference between the Liberty Party and the Free Soil Party. "There might be [differences] in form—in time—in ideas of expediency, but all were agreed upon the principles advocated by Mr. Smith."[27] Owen convinced himself that both factions had the same goal, the extinction of slavery.[28]

When the vote was taken on accepting Smith's suggested platform, his radical abolitionist remnant of the old Liberty Party was decisively defeated. The majority had voted for Chase and Bailey's plan to develop a broad-based Free Soil Party. It omitted the religious language that radical antislavery leaders like Lovejoy knew attracted many Illinois voters. While Free Soil called for the end of slavery in the District of Columbia, it did not demand the repeal of the Fugitive Slave Act or the enactment of equal rights for blacks. Chase said that he shaped a moderate platform because he feared that an equal rights plank would hinder the possibility of building a wider coalition.[29] In the fray, Lovejoy voted to support the national Free Soil Party.

In Illinois, the *Western Citizen* opened its campaign on behalf of Free Soil candidates, given that the Illinois party "was inclusive in its membership" with significant black and white men and women participating in its events and auxiliaries. The paper attempted to keep its readership aware of the party's activities.[30] It was the first to report that the Illinois State Female Anti-Slavery Society held a special meeting in March 1848 at the home of its vice president, Louisa M. Gifford Dyer, in order to distribute four hundred copies of its new constitution. Dyer's husband, Charles, was running for governor of Illinois on the Free Soil ticket. Assisting her was Mary Jane Eastman, the society's current secretary and wife of Zebina Eastman. Lucy Pettengill's husband, Moses, was running for presidential elector. The women voted to present honorary memberships to several outstanding women leaders in the East, including Lydia Maria Child, an antislavery editor and author of many articles and books, some designed to assist mothers in their children's antislavery education; and Sarah Grimké and Angelina Grimké Weld, who were organizers and circulators of petitions, researchers, and lecturers on slavery and women's rights.[31]

The *Western Citizen* kept clergymen of local communities informed about Lovejoy's campaign schedule. In one article Eastman boasted that his "county by county listing of speakers supporting Lovejoy" showed that "an innumerable number of preachers, too many to call out in this way, will do their best to send one of their order to Congress."[32] The April 18 edition listed Lovejoy's itinerary; he would be visiting a different town each day in April and May. Eastman also published editorials and reported Lovejoy's positions on issues. In March he wrote the headline "What our neighbors think of the Illinois Vote on the Black Clause." He warned that the recent vote in favor of Black Exclusion, cast against white residents' black neighbors, unfortunately disclosed the real feelings of the people of Illinois.[33] In April he complained that religious journals, with the exception of the *Presbyterian Reporter*, had remained silent on the new Illinois Constitution's adoption of the Black Clause. The May 2 issue invited all voters to "Come and hear the history of wrongs you have committed at the ballot box." Eastman was clearly disturbed by the referendum proposing a Black Exclusion Act.

The recent passage of the Black Exclusion referendum made the coming congressional election even more critical to the coalition of blacks, women, and churchmen. A committee of five managed Lovejoy's campaign for Congress; they raised $388 by subscription. By April, Lovejoy was on the stump, traveling over his enormous district. James Perry, a popular Liberty Party singer, provided music. On a balmy spring evening in Chicago, Owen found a crowd of eager supporters. But in Ottawa, where the Fox River flowed south into the Illinois River, the leading churchmen boycotted his speech; they said he was too radical.[34] In DeKalb County he left his buggy and horses in the barn of the Pritchard family near Waterman, and while he was speaking, opponents incinerated the barn and the buggy and burned the horses alive.[35]

When Chicago attorney James Collins advised Lovejoy to move closer to the political center and answer practical questions on the voters' minds, Lovejoy listened and made a major shift from the "one idea," addressing multiple issues confronting Illinoisans. Collins arranged for the *Aurora Guardian* to publish an open letter he had written to Lovejoy.[36] On July 18, 1848, the *Guardian* printed Lovejoy's answers. On the issue of slavery, Owen stated that Congress had the right to abolish slavery in all U.S. territories and in the District of Columbia and to make slave trading a crime. Furthermore, Congress should open up public lands in limited quantities at no charge to settlers. This policy would foster the growth of the middling class, which he believed was the backbone of a democratic country. In a clear appeal to women, Lovejoy recommended that couples should not be evicted from a homestead they were developing, for "the homestead should be inalienable without the free and unconstrained signature of the wife."[37] In sum, Lovejoy had taken a moderately progressive stand. The *Western Citizen* reported that at the state convention, on July 4, Owen Lovejoy was officially nominated for the Fourth District on a ticket with Charles V. Dyer for governor, L. C. Paine Freer for Cook County auditor, and Moses Pettengill of Peoria for presidential elector.

Lovejoy had advocated the nonextension of slavery into the territories since the 1842 Liberty Party convention in Chicago. Now that same policy was part of the 1848 Free Soil platform, leading some voters to think that the purpose was to facilitate white people's migration to the West, where they could buy land, while at the same time protecting slavery in the states where it already existed. But the reverse perspective of this policy, what James Oakes calls the containment theory of slavery, had an additional, aggressive purpose: If the South were surrounded by free territories, the theory went, it would become isolated, its economy would shrink, and slavery would gradually disappear. As scorpions were known to kill themselves when surrounded, slavery, cordoned off, would eventually annihilate itself.[38] Frederick Douglass had called for the South to be "surrounded by a wall of antislavery fire."

Election Day in Illinois, August 7, 1848, brought Lovejoy his second congressional defeat. In the Fourth District, Democratic and Whig candidates had shrewdly claimed that they too were Free Soil men. Democrat "Long John" Wentworth of Chicago won reelection to the U.S. House of Representatives with 11,857 votes, while Lovejoy came in third place, having polled only 3,159.[39] It was little consolation, but still noteworthy that Lovejoy received more votes as a Free Soil candidate than he had as a Liberty Party man. Furthermore, Reinhard Johnson points out that the Illinois Free Soil Party, despite its across-the-board defeat, had made the strongest showing of any state west of the Allegheny Mountains, and that it had been energized by devout Christians from a number of denominations with deep antislavery commitment. In Illinois the political momentum for ending slavery had been slow to develop, but by mid-1848 it was the strongest and most united in the

Old Northwest.[40] Eastern observers noted that Owen Lovejoy deserved much of the credit for this minimal success, but they seemed unaware of the African American defeat over the Black Exclusion referendum. The northern Illinois coalition for equality was set back on its heels.

Lovejoy Joins National Free Soil Party; Blacks Hold Back

Before the Illinois tally was final, Lovejoy left for Buffalo. On August 9, 1848, he joined a throng of twenty thousand Free Soilers there. Among the Illinois delegates to the National Free Soil Convention were John Cross, James H. Collins, and Charles Dyer, who was now Chicago's surgeon and city health officer as well as partner with African American John Jones in the operations of the Chicago Underground Railroad.[41]

Again Lovejoy served on the resolutions committee chaired by Salmon Chase. Historian Frederick J. Blue describes the limits of the party's platform. It pledged that the party would maintain the rights of Free Labor against the aggressions of the Slave Power and would secure "Free Soil for a Free People." It denounced any extension of slavery but made no mention of black rights, black suffrage, or racial equality.[42] Samuel Ringgold Ward, Henry Bibb, Henry Highland Garnet, and Frederick Douglass found the tone so different from the 1843 Liberty Convention that they wondered why they had bothered to come or how they could endorse the new party.[43]

It may have been at this conference that Lovejoy and Douglass met for the first time. If so, they would have had a lot to discuss. Douglass had been lobbying the New York State legislature the previous winter to return the ballot to blacks. In July he had given a decisive speech advocating women's suffrage at Seneca Falls.[44] But the party platform was silent on women's rights and black suffrage. Historian Philip S. Foner wrote, "Next to Abolition and the battle for equal rights for the Negro people, the cause closest to Douglass's heart was woman's rights."[45] Douglass declared that blacks were deeply indebted to the "tireless efforts of the women's anti-slavery societies" and that women too should have the right to vote. At the Free Soil Convention in Buffalo in August, Douglass was invited to speak, but as he had just had an operation on his throat, he said only a few words. The official reporter recorded, "The audience appeared to feel a great disappointment when they learned that Mr. Douglass could not address them."[46] However, unofficially, several white delegates yelled that "they didn't want a 'nigger' to talk to them." Yet more deeply affecting than those slurs was Douglass's disgust with the party's tone-deaf platform with regard to race.

Samuel R. Ward agreed. In his view, the radical Barnburners in the Free Soil movement made it clear that they were "as ready to rob black men of their rights now as ever they were" when they blocked the extension of the vote to blacks during New York State's constitutional convention.[47] Henry Bibb told the Free Soil Convention's audience, "Given the racist views of most of the delegates, it is not surprising that the party never considered an attack on northern discrimination."

After the convention, Garnet took the train home to Troy. A conductor attacked him, choked him, injured his eyes, struck his temple, and severely hit his chest. Dependent on his wooden leg, Garnet fell down, helpless against the attack. But it was not only the attack that led him to despair; it was the loss of the egalitarian ethos of the Liberty Party, the coarse grain of the Free Soil Party, and the hypocrisy of its presidential nominee, Martin Van Buren.[48]

Lovejoy went home with the credulous hope that former president Van Buren had reformed. The Van Buren White House, 1837–1841, had been staffed with slaves and suffused with efforts to please the Slave Power. Lovejoy must have hoped the despair of his black friends would diminish if some candidates actually won seats in Congress. In his letter to his potential constituents, published in the *Western Citizen*, he wrote, with an extravagant pen, that the convention had been "a political Pentecost where more than three times three thousand received the baptism of Liberty."[49] Later, he must have regretted using those words with their powerful religious symbolism, for unlike Pentecost, the convention had not united a wide variety of peoples. Fusion had not taken place.

A Dozen Free Soilers Enter the U.S. Congress

The national antislavery movement gained some clout from the election of 1848. Fourteen Free Soil men were elected to Congress. Two, John P. Hale (an incumbent) of New Hampshire and Salmon P. Chase (newly elected) of Ohio, would serve in the Senate. One of the twelve who won a seat in the House of Representatives was George W. Julian, a Quaker from Indiana. Julian described eight of the newly elected men who would sit with him, beginning their tenure in the Thirty-First Congress in early December 1849.[50] The antislavery leader in the House was veteran representative Joshua Giddings of Ohio, John Q. Adams's successor on the issue of slavery. He was as familiar with the slavery question as he was with the alphabet.[51]

Despite these additions, it was a bittersweet time. Active Free Soiler congressmen had the comfort of living in the same boardinghouse run by Mrs. Anna G. Spriggs, who had boarded Theodore Weld, Joshua Leavitt, and Abraham Lincoln in previous years. Giddings was able to make plans with a close-knit antislavery congressional cluster. But his euphoria with the Free Soil caucus did not last long. Senators John Calhoun, Daniel Webster, and Henry Clay were preparing to announce their recommended compromises on settling the slave question once and for all.

The end of 1848 was a dismal time for Lovejoy. He saw the abject suffering in the black community resulting from the Illinois Black Exclusionary referendum and the state legislature's castigation of the community's petitions. He felt deep disappointment over losing his congressional campaign. The Free Soil experiment, a detour from the intended route, had failed to create a third party tenacious enough to achieve emancipation. The antislavery movement in Illinois was in disarray.

Cleveland Convention and Appeal to Illinois Legislature

Illinois blacks had been bruised. To renew their energy, they elected John Jones and Rev. Abraham T. Hall to be the black community's representatives to the National Colored People's Convention in Cleveland that began on September 5, 1848. Hall had little formal education, but he "exuded the characteristics of an AME clergyman." He ran a successful barber shop at Canal and Lake, which served as the meeting place of the prayer group that had laid plans to organize Quinn Chapel, Chicago's first African American church.[52] In Cleveland, Frederick Douglass was elected president and John Jones was elected a vice president of the convention, and they began to work together closely. Eager to use the talents of western blacks, Douglass appointed Jones to the Committee on Agriculture, which would deal with Gerrit Smith's gift of 120,000 acres in New York. Douglass also appointed Jones to a committee of five to select the convention's next set of officers. Thirty-one-year-old Douglass seemed keen to take Jones under his tutelage, but he soon discovered that the thirty-two-year-old Jones was already a seasoned and articulate politician.

Jones proved his skill by negotiating what could have been a thorny compromise: black delegates did not endorse the Free Soil Party because they knew it contained many prejudiced whites who wanted homesteads and jobs for whites only. However, Jones needed to support his close white friends in Chicago, including Dr. Charles Dyer, who had just run for governor of Illinois and was one of the vice presidents of the national Free Soil Convention.[53] Therefore, Jones deftly recommended that the convention accept the Free Soil Party's preamble with its slogan "Free Soil, Free Speech, Free Labor, and Free Men" because, he argued, the preamble showed "an interest in the downtrodden." The convention agreed to do that. Douglass and Jones forged a long-lasting relationship that would affect Illinois directly.

When Jones and Hall returned to Chicago, they immediately plunged into state and local political work with urgency. The black community felt vulnerable to the newly adopted, regressive 1848 Constitution, approved by referendum, that had instructed the state legislature to "pass laws as will effectually prohibit free persons of color from immigrating to and settling in this state."[54] Jones and his black colleagues in Chicago formed a correspondence committee, which passed a number of resolutions condemning laws that deprived free men of their rights as delineated in the U.S. Constitution.[55] First, the committee assessed that it had the manpower to circulate petitions throughout the northern counties that asked for the repeal of all Illinois Black Laws. Then it took a survey of blacks throughout the Fourth Congressional District, listing their names and addresses.[56] With fierce determination, Jones and the committee called for a meeting to be held in Springfield in December 1848 to demand that the General Assembly repeal the Black Laws when it opened in January.[57]

By then it was clear that Lovejoy and Jones held almost identical agendas on policies affecting African Americans: abolish slavery in the District of Columbia; free those slaves who were transported into the free state of Illinois by their masters; and repeal the state's Black Laws, especially the laws prohibiting free blacks from immigrating into Illinois and requiring expensive Certificates of Freedom.[58]

When the General Assembly convened at the state capitol on January 2, 1849, a bill implementing the Black Exclusion measure as mandated by the new constitution was introduced, but it did not pass.[59] Voters in the recent referendum desired it and the new constitution required it, but the representatives in the General Assembly held back, for unknown reasons.

At the same time, the number of blacks escaping slavery and entering Illinois was increasing. Underground Railroad passengers could appear at the Lovejoy homestead at any time of the day or night. In October 1848, Lovejoy received a letter from a colleague in a neighboring town informing him that a freedom seeker had left his watch with his host on purpose so it would not be stolen, but now that the fugitive was safely on his way, the host would send it to Mr. Lovejoy, for Lovejoy would know where the fugitive had gone. If runaways arrived at the Lovejoy homestead at suppertime, the Lovejoy children knew that their portions would be smaller than usual.[60] If fugitives turned up on a Saturday night, they might go to worship at Hampshire Colony Church the next morning and tell their stories.[61]

Lewis Tappan's Response to Antislavery Lethargy in Washington, D.C.

Several years before the confluence of the 1850 senatorial orations by Calhoun, Clay, and Webster rocked the congress, Lewis Tappan had foreseen the limitations of the Free Soil Party's contradictory compromise and the party's probable downfall. As a careful strategist, he knew the movement would need an inspiring national voice. His response was to finance a national antislavery newspaper in Washington close to the apex of the Slave Power and to where congressmen deliberated. In 1846 he had hired editor Gamaliel Bailey to leave Cincinnati and establish the *National*

Era.[62] In the past, John Quincy Adams and Joshua Giddings had relied on the research of Weld and Leavitt in the Library of Congress for data about slavery.[63] They could not offset the effects of widely read national proslavery newspapers that deliberately praised the activities of slaveholders and distorted the work of antislavery congressmen. Lewis Tappan wanted to see an antislavery editor and his monogamous, companionate, antislavery family set an example before the male-dominated planter's family structure of Washington, D.C. Gamaliel and Margaret Bailey would set an example.[64] While the *National Era* readership grew steadily to some 50,000, the southern society of Washington City scorned Margaret, taunted the Bailey children, and invaded their home.[65]

When the new cluster of Free Soil men arrived in Washington, D.C., the Baileys provided them a hospitality center and salon where they could gather and greet antislavery visitors such as Oberlin College president Asa Mahan, Rev. Henry Ward Beecher of Brooklyn's Plymouth Congregational Church, and artists, missionaries, and moderate congressmen from other parties. The Baileys were relaxed hosts. Their children added to the informality. The food was good and served by free black men. Margaret Bailey's evening occasions deliberately blended women and men. She invited bright and vivacious women visiting in town from New England who added a literary as well as political tone to the Baileys' soirees. In seven years Lovejoy would join the forum and feel at home at the Baileys'.[66]

Lewis Tappan wanted to bring more progressive Congregational ministers to New York City churches to counteract the ethos spread by prominent city clergy who tolerated bondage.[67] As wealthy southern planters regularly received loans from New York banks, vacationed in New York hotels, and contributed generously to its major churches, their prejudices were transferred to local clergy.[68] At the same time, thousands of young New Englanders moving to New York City were looking for congregations with antislavery sentiments. Tappan wanted them to be able to find antislavery ministers. Within a rather short time, four highly educated evangelical New England ministers received calls to strong churches. Tappan's friends anticipated that they would expand an antislavery evangelical Congregationalism with experiential, New Divinity theology, historic biblical criticism, and political comment in the city, much as Lovejoy and his colleagues were doing through the small churches of rural northern Illinois.[69]

Lovejoy had personal connections with three of the four ministers. He had not met Joseph P. Thompson, a scholarly man who was called to Broadway Tabernacle in 1845 and who immersed himself in a new exegesis of the Bible—finding the original meaning of passages by studying the history, rhetoric, and grammar of each biblical author and audience.[70] But Lovejoy had connections with the other three men. Richard Salter Storrs (III) was the son of Eunice Lovejoy's first cousin of the same name. The younger man was called to the Church of the

Pilgrims in Brooklyn in 1846. He was intellectual, moderately antislavery, refined, and aloof.[71] George B. Cheever, whose grandmother was the sister of Lovejoy's grandmother, arrived at the Church of the Puritans on Union Square in Manhattan the same year. He had graduated from Bowdoin College as Lovejoy had entered. He traveled abroad, authored twenty-one books, and became radically antislavery.[72] Lovejoy also knew of the gregarious Henry Ward Beecher, whose brother Edward had boarded with them in Alton the week before Elijah Lovejoy's murder.[73] Beecher, the best known of the four New York City clergymen, became the pastor of Brooklyn's new Plymouth Church in 1847. His popular preaching ignored Calvinist theological anxieties and focused instead on God's love, delivered in contemporary parlance.[74] He and his congregation championed the Underground Railroad and the antislavery movement in the 1850s. These four pastors changed the religious conversation in the city. Three of them would later participate in Lovejoy's funeral.

Lovejoy Goes on the Offense against the Fugitive Slave Law

On January 1, 1850, Lovejoy sat mulling over the outline of his sermon at his desk, surrounded by shelves of books, his satchel on the floor, a pile of letters and a pot of ink and quill before him. Three weeks before, he and Reverend Codding had succeeded in organizing antislavery people in the towns along the Fox River, holding meetings night after night in Aurora, Batavia, Geneva, St. Charles, Elgin, and Dundee in Kane County.[75]

They were informing antislavery people about another major compromise that was being floated in Congress. Now, as he looked out of the window over fields to the open prairie, Lovejoy knew he had to discuss this bitter reality with his own congregation. But in what context should he challenge them? He had grown up in Maine detesting the Compromise of 1820. Now members of the U.S. Congress were threatening to offer the Compromise of 1850. The very word *compromise* was distasteful to Lovejoy.

Senators and representatives were making inflammatory statements: "the 31st Congress might decide whether the Union should continue to exist."[76] Pressure was felt all around. With a crisis brewing, Illinois senator Stephen A. Douglas, a Democrat, was convinced that citizens cared less about *how* slavery was settled than that it should be settled. Lovejoy disagreed. He cared very deeply how slavery matters were decided. One prong of the proposed Fugitive Slave Bill would target the Underground Railroad, including parts of the network that were operated by members of Hampshire Colony Church and colleagues in the coalition from Chicago to the Rock River. Compromises constructed by slaveholders, as the 1850 bills would be, always directly assaulted African Americans and racial equality.

Although at first glance it seemed irrelevant, Lovejoy decided to give a foundational New Year's Day sermon. He was not privileged to present a State of the Union message as congressmen did in the U.S. capital, but as a minister he had a pulpit. On January 1, 1800, clergymen in New England had preached sermons summarizing the state of the country at the turn of the century; in like manner, on January 1, 1850, Lovejoy prepared to preach a half-century sermon. His title was biblical—"Signs of the Coming Reign of the Messiah"—but his message was contemporary: despite dire signs, progress is possible if we keep our vision before us.

Lovejoy began a circuitous discourse by showing how Calvinism was being altered. In the early 1800s, he said, "a limited Salvation was doled out to the favored few; and although it was 'not pretended' to point out the individuals to whom alone the offers of Salvation were made, yet it was confidently affirmed that there were those for whom there was no hope, no life—Whose name had been written in the book of damnation from the depths of eternity."[77] Lovejoy considered theories of predestination to be both irrational and unscriptural. "They have been exploded," he told his congregation. By 1850, he noted, pulpits were proclaiming Arminianism, "a full and free Salvation to all who will accept it." Each person could decide, and every person was included. "Religion has not as much of gloom or terror and more of love," he said.[78] Lovejoy lifted up Calvin's compassion for the oppressed and expanded it to include all humanity. If human beings could change their understanding of theology within a few years' time, he reasoned, then within a few more years they ought to be able to change their view of African Americans from inferior beings to persons of equality.[79]

Historian Eric Foner points out that while "the abolitionist movement played a major role in developing the concept of human rights" as universal, "unbounded by race and nationality," and "belonging to a common humanity," these ideas were linked more often to liberty than to racial equality.[80] But this sermon makes it clear that Lovejoy was one of those who linked antislavery with equality.[81]

Lovejoy told his Hampshire Colony congregation that equality among whites in the United States had been ascending until 1789, but by 1850, equality for blacks and Native Americans was on a downward slide. A contagion was spreading across the nation, a "propaganda war" intended to degrade how white Americans thought about blacks.[82] By 1850 pseudo-ethnologists were propagating polygenetic theories claiming that there were separately created and unequal races of human beings defined by their color (black, white, yellow, and red), that these races were ranked, and that blacks were the lowest of the four. Such racist theories of black deficiencies were presented as justifications for buying and selling human beings.[83] In his half-century sermon Lovejoy rejected these falsehoods. He hoped that as religion had become more humane in a short period of time, this trend toward inequality could be reversed.

"That which characterizes the present age above all others—that which is shaking our own land and all the nations of Europe to their very center, is the overshadowing question of human rights—of human equality," he preached.[84] John Milton's principles of "sweet equality," which came over to America with the Pilgrims, had found their way back across the ocean and were shaking the nations of Europe.[85] In America, he continued, the first obstacle to equality was slavery. After the Revolutionary War many thought that slavery would gradually disappear, but instead it "overleaped the Alleghenies" and was struggling to "overspread the Pacific Coast with its mildewing curse." Yet in the face of this curse, "the pulpit is dumb, the press muzzled or subsidized, the governmental offices monopolized."[86] Therefore, the Slave Power must be destroyed; no other reform would take place until this happened. But he consoled his congregation not to be discouraged; the antislavery movement was making progress. "Why, we have ten reliable men in the House [of Representatives] . . . together with two senators."[87]

Lovejoy reminded his congregation that the primacy of human rights came not only from the Bible but just as strongly from three other authorities: reason, justice, and humanity.[88] These four authorities formed the quadrilateral he followed. Lovejoy ended by focusing on the concept of the soul expounded by William Ellery Channing, the Unitarian minister who had organized a meeting at Faneuil Hall in Boston in 1837 to protest Elijah Lovejoy's murder.[89] Channing wrote, "Into every human being God has breathed an immortal spirit, more precious than the whole outward creation. No earthly or celestial language can exaggerate the worth of a human being. . . . To live in the truth or divine spirit of Christ is to be freed from the always-evil desire to dominate any other human being."[90]

Lovejoy's sermon, provoked by the rumor of a federal Fugitive Slave Law to be passed as part of a proposed 1850 Compromise, traveled around the region.

The legislative attack began in Congress on February 5, 1850, when Senator Henry Clay of Kentucky, a slaveholder, insisted that a new armistice was necessary to keep the country from falling apart. Clay had brokered the Missouri Compromise in 1820 and 1821 by pitting Missouri against Maine.[91] Now Clay issued an omnibus proposal: admit California to the Union and let its people vote on whether to become a slave or free state; divide the remainder of the land purchased from Mexico into two territories, New Mexico and Utah, and organize them without reference to slavery; pay off Texas's debt to Mexico; end the slave trade in the District of Columbia but not slavery itself; and enforce the constitutional provision for returning fugitives, increase the federal government's powers to do so, and provide stringent penalties for anyone assisting a fugitive.[92]

The second attack came on March 4, when Senator James Mason of Virginia read the speech written by the dying South Carolina senator John Calhoun. Unless the North allowed Southerners to bring slaves into new territories and consented to a constitutional amendment that would maintain a balance of power, the South would secede.[93]

The third legislative attack came on March 7 from Massachusetts senator Daniel Webster in the form of an oration. In addressing the Senate, Webster supported Clay's resolutions and blamed abolitionists for tearing the country apart.

If the new federal Fugitive Slave Law passed, it would be a federal crime not to report someone who aided a freedom-seeking slave. Lovejoy knew that he and his collaborators on the Underground Railroad, as well as all the black runaways, would be in great jeopardy because this stricter law was to be enforced by federal officials. Ironically, the Southern advocates of states' rights uncharacteristically wanted to require the federal government to take on the task of capturing their runaway slaves.[94]

Lovejoy enlisted the help of three semi-dormant organizations to combat this new threat from the federal government. The first one was a regional interdenominational organization. He joined with Jonathan Blanchard and Zebina Eastman to revitalize the Illinois branches of the Christian Anti-Slavery Society to work politically against the Fugitive Slave proposal. Second, he spoke to the remnant of the Free Soil Party in northern Illinois and urged them to act against Clay's plan. Third, he worked to resuscitate the Illinois Antislavery Society. The idea was to empower religious people of all denominations to work politically against the proposed Fugitive Slave law.[95]

Blanchard helped organize a large Christian Anti-Slavery convention in Cincinnati, Ohio, with eight cooperating Protestant denominations on April 17–20, 1850; African Americans Lewis Woodson and John B. Vashon came from Pittsburgh to reawaken the crowd.[96] In July, a Northern Christian Convention was held in Chicago, and Blanchard and Lovejoy encouraged people to prepare for a new antislavery third party; it had no name as yet, but one idea floating around was the Free Democratic Party. The convention's central purpose was to organize the antislavery grassroots to demand the end of slavery by political means, and doing so required a political party.[97] At another Illinois Christian Anti-Slavery Society meeting, in Ottawa, Illinois, on May 7, Lovejoy railed against the proposed Fugitive Slave Bill. On the same day, Frederick Douglass attacked it in Rochester, New York. Douglass, who was a devout Christian and licensed preacher, also published reports on the Illinois Christian Anti-Slavery Society in the *North Star*.[98]

A closer relationship between Lovejoy and Douglass was developing. Douglass, who gave lectures in Illinois, was effective in combining themes from the Bible, politics, and western populism.[99] Lovejoy was one of the men Douglass kept tabs on in his newspaper and "kept company with" when he was in the West.[100] At one of the Christian Anti-Slavery Society conventions, Lovejoy told his black ministerial colleagues that white ministers bore much of the responsibility for perpetuating racism. The *Western Citizen* editorialized that Protestantism itself was endangered by its alliance with slavery.[101] In 1851, when another convention took place in Cincinnati, women were in charge of a special preliminary gathering.[102]

A second organization from which Lovejoy sought support was the remnant of the Illinois Free Soil Party. In an announcement he said, "It is high time we were up and organized and doing."[103] The delegates decided to hold a nominating convention in Elgin in August 1851, for the upcoming election.[104] Lovejoy assumed that he would be nominated again. But when he arrived in Elgin, he found out that the editors of the *Chicago Tribune*, which wrote nativist editorials in the early 1850s, had already endorsed Chicago businessman William B. Ogden, a Democrat with moderate antislavery views, for the seat. Owen's hope of sending the House of Representatives an Illinois voice calling for rejection of a Fugitive Slave Bill was smashed.[105]

A third organization to which Owen had access in his campaign against the Fugitive Slave Bill was the old Illinois Anti-Slavery Society, begun by Elijah in 1837. Eastman and Lovejoy, hoping to revitalize the organization across the state, arranged a convention for men and women to be held on July 29 in Aurora, with two impressive speakers, Samuel Ringgold Ward, advertised as "the eloquent and educated colored man," and Henry Bibb, "an eloquent, self-emancipated slave." Owen was quoted as saying, "We wish to make this the impetus of new activity in the Anti-Slavery reform in this State. We have been inactive too long."[106]

Ward told the convention that white Americans judged blacks to be inferior so they could oppress them guiltlessly. They denied the intellectual equality so well demonstrated by the achievements of a long list of men including Henry Highland Garnet, Alexander Crummell, Frederick Douglass, James Pennington, and James McCune Smith.[107] Racism, Ward said, was not incidental to the religion of America, it was essential to it. He considered "American" and "Negro-hater" to be synonymous terms. "What the Negro needs is what belongs to him—what has been ruthlessly torn from him—and what is, by the consent of a despotic democracy and a Christless religion, withholden from him, guiltily, perseveringly." Africans had a great history, he repeated, but the dramatic story of the African diaspora had been reduced to the slave trade.[108]

Ward and Bibb led the audience to repentance and action to halt the set of laws that made up the Compromise of 1850. But it was too late; Congress enacted the laws. Two months after Ward's speech in Aurora, he and his wife went on a lecture tour in Ohio and quietly slipped across the border to safety in Canada.[109]

While Lovejoy's three attempts aroused antislavery people in northern Illinois, they failed to stop the new federal Fugitive Slave Act. In September 1850, President Millard Fillmore signed the complex Compromise of 1850 into law.[110] From that moment the Fugitive Slave Act was a calamity for African Americans.

Despite the failure of Lovejoy's campaign against the proposed laws, it was clear that Lovejoy was back in the fight again. He grew increasingly adamant as he saw the panic and anxiety on the faces of his black friends and colleagues.

In Chicago, L. C. Paine Freer, Charles Dyer, John Jones, Calvin DeWolf, Louis Isbell, and H. O. Wagoner contracted with the quiet assistance of Col. Charles G. Hammond, past superintendent of the Michigan Central Railroad, for ten train cars to take the fugitives then living in Chicago to Canada.[111] Left behind were their homes and their belongings. In Pittsburgh, John Vashon said farewell as most of his African Methodist Episcopal congregation departed.[112] In Rochester, Frederick Douglass saw almost all the members of Rev. Horace H. Hawkins's Abyssinian Baptist Church, also known as Third Baptist Church (African), enter Canada near Niagara Falls, leaving jobs and homes behind.[113] Fear of capture by federal commissioners was draining the nation of its most educated blacks.[114] It is estimated that across the North, as many as fifty thousand slaves escaped to Canada from 1830 to 1860, with as many as 40 percent of those leaving in the 1850s.[115]

In Chicago, a furious John Jones concluded that the Fugitive Slave Law not only was unconstitutional and un-Christian but was a deep assault on the free and self-emancipated black community. He was convinced that blacks must have a vigilance committee to alert escapees when federal agents were in the area.[116] On September 30, 1850, three hundred free Chicago blacks rallied at the AME Church on Wells Street to decide how they would resist the new law.[117] They chose a committee of seven—Henry O. Wagoner, Richard S. Cooper, Barney Lewis Ford, William Johnson, Thomas Styles, Henry Bradford, and leader John Jones—to draft resolutions.[118] The vigilance committee they established consisted of an unofficial black police force of seven divisions, with six persons in each division, to patrol the city each night, keeping their eyes open for official interlopers. In addition, the black community formally denounced the law because it did not guard against false claims.[119] Mary and John Jones's home became the city's center for black vigilance as well as escape to Canada.[120]

On October 21, 1850, the white Common Council of the City of Chicago, following the recommendations of its Resolutions Committee, declared the Fugitive Slave Law unconstitutional and suspended its operations in the city.[121] Collins, Codding, Lovejoy, and Eastman gave stirring addresses on the topic before every audience that appeared. Enormous public meetings supported the council's decision. But on October 23, Senator Stephen A. Douglas arrived on the train from Washington and addressed a meeting of four thousand.[122] He accused the council of treason, and the following day an intimidated Common Council repealed its resolution.[123]

Watching Chicago's officials lose their courage so quickly, and realizing that the city that had once been a sanctuary for refugees would become a battlefield against federal commissioners, Dyer, Freer, Philo Carpenter, and other Underground Railroad operators formed a Committee for the Relief of Fugitives in Canada. Eastman kept the group's financial records.[124] Lovejoy responded to Douglas's heavy-handed accusation by preparing a resolution to call for a new party and a national nominating convention. Such a resolution would shake up the Washington establishment.[125]

Meanwhile, the New York *Independent* had taken a big gamble by editorializing against the Fugitive Slave Act. New York was a city interlocked with southern commerce. Antislavery readers who depended on the *Independent* feared its avant-garde position might force the newspaper out of business. A loss of subscriptions would indicate a loss of widespread antislavery sentiment. In the center of the commercial district of New York City, five thousand merchants had rushed to Castle Garden to endorse the Fugitive Slave bill. Filled with consternation, Henry Bowen, the *Independent*'s publisher, and Lewis Tappan, Bowen's wealthy father-in-law, quickly organized a meeting of countervailing abolitionist businessmen who vigorously rejected the bill.[126] Then Bowen declared on his newspaper's front page that the Fugitive Slave Law was evil.

Bowen's editorial writers, the four prominent Congregational pastors in New York City, supported his decision. Twenty-nine-year-old Richard Salter Storrs preached a sermon against the law in the form of an attorney's brief that was published in the *New York Observer*, the Old School Presbyterian paper that had vilified the deceased Elijah P. Lovejoy twelve years earlier. Rev. George Cheever suffered directly from repudiating the law; a leading layman denounced him publicly and urged members to leave the church, and many did so.

The *Independent* lost half of its six thousand subscriptions, but over the following days, five thousand new subscriptions came pouring in. Bowen had won his gamble and widened his reputation. This dramatic shift in readers led Bowen to advocate an even more aggressive antislavery stance in his newspaper.[127]

Protecting the Antislavery Church in Washington and Princeton

In the midst of this tumult, Tappan announced another radical plan: to start an antislavery church as a bulwark to the *National Era* newspaper enterprise in Washington, D.C.[128] He quietly identified a suitable property in the old Trinity Church on Judiciary Square and found a young graduate of Oneida Institute and Auburn Theological School, Josiah Bushnell Grinnell, to fill the pulpit. But as soon as Grinnell delivered one of the first sermons ever directed against slavery in the national capital, to parishioners such as Senators John P. Hale and Salmon Chase, Representative Joshua Giddings, and Gamaliel Bailey and family, he became a marked man to the proslavery population of the nation's capital.[129] The sheriff charged Grinnell with giving a young mulatto couple a lesson in locating the North Star, and banished him from the city by putting him on a train headed north. In the 1850s, the little D.C. congregation limped along with guest preachers. Tappan's radical plan to establish another antislavery foothold in the white, privileged Washington had faltered.

In contrast, Owen Lovejoy's church in Illinois was flourishing. The year 1851 was a low period of political activity but a high time in the life of his local church and family. During that year he presented powerful sermons to a growing congregation in an impressive new church building. He ignored doctrinal distinctions and emphasized taking action. He preached that God's kingdom would one day come on earth. After raising money for a church bell, he traveled to the ironworks in Troy, New York, to select the one whose tone he liked. It was placed in the belfry at the center of Princeton village, and townspeople called it the "Lovejoy bell." Whenever an African American was "caught in the meshes of the law," the bell rang out to urge everyone in the town to come to his or her defense.[130]

The increased peril caused by federal commissioners enforcing the new Fugitive Slave Law led Hampshire Colony Church to rededicate itself to civil disobedience. In Princeton, one way to enact that was to hold a revival. Lovejoy asked one of the busiest Underground Railroad operators in the area, Rev. Samuel Wright of Toulon, Illinois, to lead it. Wright was a local hero, unapologetic before the judge and immovable from his Underground Railroad work. Wright reported that he spent "two weeks and one day" in Princeton and preached eighteen times. As a result, forty local men and women were converted to Christ. Many of them then felt emboldened to defy the Fugitive Slave Law and to support others who defied it.[131]

• • •

Lovejoy applied the western political antislavery approach to abolition. The Free Soil Party's 1848 campaign was intended to widen the base of supporters by addressing political issues beyond the nonextension of slavery, but in August, Lovejoy and the Free Soilers lost by a wide margin. The Illinois antislavery coalition felt betrayed by national Free Soil ideology that wanted to protect territorial land for whites only. Another defeat took place the same year when a large majority of white Illinoisans voted in favor of a new, exclusionary state constitution that rejected black suffrage and prohibited black immigration, revealing the extent of racism in the state. African Americans led by John Jones had put enormous effort into their campaign to block the constitution, but they had persuaded only voters in the state's northern counties.

When congressmen proposed the collection of bills known as the Compromise or Armistice of 1850, coalition women circulated petitions against it and Lovejoy preached for human equality and revitalized three dormant antislavery organizations to help oppose the bills, to no avail. After the president signed the bills, entire neighborhoods and congregations of talented African Americans fled to Canada. Lovejoy and the coalition realized that it was time to shape a new antislavery political party, one that was united in the religious belief that God created one race of all humankind.

4. Organizing a Christian Political Response to Win Elections

1852–1854

Codding came up with the idea for the announcement, Lovejoy was willing to go along with it, and Eastman wrote it up in style. The three men had met in the office of the *Western Citizen* at the corner of Lake Street and Clark in Chicago as the year 1851 waned. It was daring to plan an important meeting in Illinois for the cold of January, but they couldn't wait for spring.

Eastman wanted to get the call for the meeting into the mail before Christmas—in two days—so all would have time to make the necessary plans. Although he and his African American compositor, Henry O. Wagoner, were tired from getting the newspaper out, both men felt light-hearted. As soon as this issue of the *Western Citizen* was in the mail, he and Wagoner and their families could spend an evening with old Liberty Party friends and Underground Railroad co-conspirators, black and white, who lived just a few blocks from each other. Wagoner spread the news among black Chicagoans.

The invitation was to all "Friends of Liberty" to join a new political party and make a fresh start on January 21, 1852, at Hampshire Colony Church in Princeton. The call read: "Friends, will you not turn out by the thousands to the Princeton Convention to meet there Lovejoy, the martyr's brother, to meet there the men who stood by the martyr at his death—to meet there those who have stood together so many years. It will be a glorious time we believe—Oh! Let your old enthusiasm be aroused."[1]

The three familiar strategists, Eastman, Codding, and Lovejoy, had decided to follow the plan of action developed by Joshua Giddings of Ohio the previous September, when Giddings invited a small, select group of national antislavery leaders to Cleveland. They included editor and party organizer Sherman Booth of Wisconsin, philanthropist and Underground Railroad operator Francis LeMoyne of Pennsylvania, congressman George W. Julian of Indiana, evangelical entrepreneur Lewis Tappan, and several others. The Free Soil concept had not elected many congressmen, but the approach of the platform just written at Cleveland felt right. All in this newly energized group agreed to enlist only those recruits who would put the plight of the slave first.[2] They would call it the Free Democratic Party.

On January 21, 1852, Owen Lovejoy welcomed the initial meeting at Princeton in a buoyant, optimistic mood. His religious antislavery followers, white women and men from the towns and farms of the region, filled the sanctuary of the enlarged Hampshire Colony Church. It was warmed by two new stoves and the embraces of old friends. Former state legislator John Howard Bryant was elected president of the state convention. He was the youngest brother of William Cullen Bryant, editor of the *New York Evening Post*, and of three other brothers and a sister who lived in Princeton. He was quick to remind the crowd that any hope of the slaves getting their freedom would depend on ministers and churches. Then he endorsed the new name for the party.

Princeton attorney Charles L. Kelsey, a friend of Lovejoy's, headed the Resolutions Committee. Foremost was the resolution that the Fugitive Slave Law must be repealed. Lovejoy recommended that a national convention be organized to name presidential and vice-presidential candidates. Then the group solemnly agreed to meet on the second Wednesday of every month to organize northern Illinois and campaign door to door to identify untapped men and women who held antislavery beliefs.[3]

Mr. Thomas, a reporter for the *Frederick Douglass Paper*, quickly sent that paper a summary of the Princeton convention. Thomas could not forego chiding the Illinois men for yielding to the presidential nominee's "Van Buren tornado" back in 1848, but he congratulated them for being "among the first to speak out and gather again in fifty-two" to form a party that would be better than Free Soil. Frederick Douglass applauded the action of the Illinois radicals and urged other states to follow their example. He was so encouraged by these developments that he urged philanthropist Gerrit Smith to accompany him to the upcoming national meeting.

Blacks and Whites Build a Political Force in Tandem

Lovejoy was elected to head the Illinois delegation to the national Free Democratic Convention in Pittsburgh that Congressman Giddings and others were organizing. The unofficial central committee in Illinois also chose businessman Moses Pettengill of Peoria, agricultural scientist and minister Jonathan Turner of Jacksonville, Knox College president Jonathan Blanchard, and ten others to go. It was a strong delegation. The convention was not the throng of twenty thousand who had congregated

at the Free Soil Convention in Buffalo in 1848, but the two thousand who went to
Pittsburgh in 1852 were solidly against the extension of slavery and solidly for the
repeal of the Fugitive Slave Act, and their views were based on religious beliefs.
Lewis Tappan reassured all the "Old Liberty Party men" in the assembly that they
were welcome and needed.[4]

In downtown Pittsburgh, where the Monongahela and Allegheny Rivers join
and flow into the Ohio River, former Democrat Henry Wilson of Massachusetts
was elected chairman of the convention. He asked Lovejoy, his fellow egalitarian,
to open the convention with prayer. When Frederick Douglass and Gerrit Smith
arrived, a chorus of greetings filled the auditorium. Lewis Tappan immediately
nominated Douglass to be a secretary of the convention, and Douglass was quickly
installed by acclamation and asked to speak. Lovejoy had been out of the hall, but as
he reentered, he identified the voice at once as Douglass's and was moved to tears.
Douglass's self-transformation from slave to national orator and editor enthralled
everyone at the convention.[5]

Giddings chaired the Platform Committee, and Lovejoy joined it. The two men
quickly gravitated to each other and developed a strong, personal friendship. John
Quincy Adams had mentored Giddings, and after Adams's death, Giddings had
become the leading antislavery voice in the U.S. House of Representatives. Lovejoy
was eager to learn from him about Congress. In Pittsburgh the committee reaffirmed
the principal planks of the 1843 Buffalo platform, condemned the Fugitive Slave
Act, and opposed extension of slavery into the territories. It also acknowledged
that the U.S. Constitution prevented Congress from interfering with slavery in the
South. That disappointed Gerrit Smith and Frederick Douglass, who wanted the
platform to state that slavery was illegal everywhere and to support equal rights
for all persons regardless of color or gender. Unlike many at the 1848 Free Soil
Convention, most delegates at Pittsburgh favored expanding human rights, but not
as a first step. Lovejoy was impatient with those who forgot the party's strategy.[6]
Some delegates incorrectly interpreted the platform committee's unwillingness to
list suffrage for blacks and women as items in the platform as proof that they did
not believe in human equality for blacks or women.[7] For this reason, many African
Americans refused to align with the Free Democratic Party. Other blacks saw it
as the only party in 1852 that confronted the issue of slavery.[8] Despite their different strategies, Lovejoy and Douglass shared a deep passion for equality. In a year,
Douglass would be lecturing in Lovejoy's church.

Lovejoy was appointed to the National Executive Committee of the Free Democratic Party. The convention chose Senator John P. Hale of New Hampshire as its
candidate for president and Quaker U.S. representative George Julian of Indiana
for vice-president.[9] In most states the Free Democratic Party failed to become an

effective instrument to organize antislavery forces, but in northern Illinois it was quite successful. It built up a formidable foundation for the Republican movement that would emerge in 1854.[10]

Two weeks after returning home, on August 25–26, 1852, Lovejoy brought the latest news from Pittsburgh to the delegates at the Illinois State Convention of the Free Democratic Party in Granville. John Howard Bryant presided over an immense crowd. Fifteen hundred farmers and townspeople came by horse and carriage. Some said the turnout was so high because the Fugitive Slave Act had rubbed the sensibilities of antislavery folks raw.[11] Others said so many had attended because everyone was reading *Uncle Tom's Cabin*, Harriet Beecher Stowe's vivid dramatization of slavery's cruelties.[12] Jacksonville merchant Elihu Wolcott and agronomist Jonathan Turner had formed a committee to buy five hundred copies so everyone in their town could read it. Illinois College president Julian Sturtevant stated that he had never witnessed such a revolution in public sentiment, for the book was filled with a holy purpose by painting a great national crime in all its enormity, with the aim of eliminating it.[13]

Within a few days the Free Democratic Party held conventions in each of four congressional districts in northern and central Illinois as well as a number of county conventions. When the convention for the Third Congressional District met, it nominated John Howard Bryant, one of Lovejoy's closest Princeton friends, for its seat in Congress.[14] Although Bryant was a former state legislator and a proven local civic leader, his chances of winning were not good. Farmers, in the midst of a painful recession, were afraid to leave their fields before the harvest to go to distant voting polls.

However, there was increased excitement when H. Ford Douglas, a young black activist, plunged into the Free Democratic Party campaign. The talented Ford was a former slave and a barber who had lobbied legislators in Ohio and was a popular lecturer in northern Illinois.[15] Plans were laid to invite other outstanding African American speakers to upcoming conventions.

Lovejoy campaigned hard for his good friend, but Bryant lost. It was a consolation for the Free Democratic Party that it succeeded in sending four Illinois antislavery men to the U.S. Congress: Elihu B. Washburne, Jesse O. Norton, Richard Yates, and James Knox.[16] While the four still labeled themselves Whigs, they publicly campaigned for the Free Democrats' central policy of nonextension of slavery in the territories. The Whig surge in Illinois was ironic, since nationwide, the party was dying.

Feeling fresh energy, Illinois African Americans hoped some positive actions would result from the next state legislative session. Their Literary and Debating Society of Chicago planned a mass meeting for December 27, 1852, to approve circulating a huge petition that would ask the legislature for one item only: to allow blacks to testify in court. The most educated and politically astute black men planned this project. The society deputized Joseph H. Barquet, author of the petition, to carry it to the citizens of the northern counties of Illinois in order to obtain as many additional signatures as possible. Barquet had been educated in the Charleston, South Carolina, area before coming to the North and was well equipped for the task.[17]

Henry O. Wagoner was optimistic. He too had been educated as a youth. Although his father was a slave, one of his grandfathers, a white man who had once been High Sheriff of Washington County, Maryland, had sent his grandson to school.[18] Wagoner had wide experience as both a teacher and a newspaperman in Canada, Galena, Illinois, and Chicago.[19] He was an experienced operator on the Underground Railroad.[20] Wagoner kept his colleague Frederick Douglass in Rochester, New York, informed, expressing his hope that the petition would convince the Illinois General Assembly to repeal the part of the Black Code that prevented blacks from testifying.

But when Chicago's white state senator Norman Judd presented their petition to the General Assembly in Springfield in January 1853, the black community was greatly disappointed. The bill accompanying the petition was rejected, 41 to 16.[21] To further demolish the plans of Barquet, Wagoner, and Jones, a newly elected state representative was determined to fulfill the requirement of the 1848 Constitution by passing Black Exclusion legislation. First-term twenty-six-year-old John A. Logan, from Murphysboro in southern Illinois, introduced a bill that would make it a crime for anyone to bring a free African American or mulatto into Illinois.[22] Such a person would be fined not less than $100 or more than $500 and would be imprisoned for not more than one year.[23] Blacks entering the state under their own volition and remaining more than ten days would be subject to a fine of $50 and, if the fine was not paid, they would be sold to any person who would pay the fine.[24] On February 5, 1853, in a separate bill, legislators voted 45 to 23 to retain the Illinois Black Code as it was.[25] It was hardly surprising, then, that on February 11 they voted overwhelmingly to pass Logan's bill with its additional, onerous restrictions on African Americans.[26] These actions pleased most southern Illinois voters, but it distressed the coalition and the elected representatives from the fourteen northern counties who favored black suffrage.[27]

The editor of the *Congregational Herald*, published in Chicago, was furious, for Barquet's petition, which had been signed by ten thousand people, was totally ignored by the Illinois legislature.[28] Blacks had been disrespected, and northern whites, who had emigrated from regions where they had held power, had been disregarded. Barquet had made an eloquent presentation "to the people in the northern portion of the state" in order "to obtain signatures to a petition to repeal Illinois's black laws" that denied blacks' right to citizenship—a presentation that was treated with contempt.[29] Barquet then remonstrated in a letter to the *Western Citizen* that there was a humane concern involved. Since most African Americans in Chicago were men, there was therefore a severe shortage of African American women. Logan's resolution would discourage additional women from entering Illinois, for a man would risk losing his wife if she stayed more than ten days. Barquet asked the white legislators if they had thought about that.[30]

Ironically, almost every newspaper of both parties in the state opposed Logan's Black Exclusion law. But the cocky majority dominating the Eighteenth General Assembly ordered the authorities to enforce the Black Laws even more stringently.[31] Blacks and whites in the coalition had shouldered the task of petitioning together with tremendous energy and astute finesse, but they had failed miserably.

Churches Handle Racism in Contradictory Ways

After the defeat of the Free Soil Party and passage of the Black Exclusion Act, political abolitionists in Illinois were wondering what do next. In the early 1850s, Lovejoy's preaching at Hampshire Colony Church was said to be powerful in the extreme. He would often sit in his pulpit and read his newspaper while the congregation sang the first hymn; then he would read from the newspaper some account of the return of a fugitive slave or similar incident and break out into a passionate appeal for justice and humanity.[32] His religious vision and political goals were irretrievably intermeshed.

On October 5, 1852, delegates from Congregational churches from around the country gathered in Albany, New York. Western and eastern church leaders still differed. Eastern churchmen still believed that Congregationalism could not thrive in unformed communities on the frontier,[33] and they still pressed their positions on the same four areas of disagreement. First, polity: keeping decision making in the hands of the clergy and deacons rather than encouraging congregational democracy; second, theology: preserving conventional orthodox beliefs and not permitting perfectionist or other alternative progressive theologies to develop; third, missions: allowing proslavery or slavery-sympathizing missionaries to have standing as clergy rather than forbidding slaveholders to preach, hold membership, or take communion; and fourth, politics: forbidding clergy to participate in politics.

Lovejoy did not go to Albany because he was campaigning at that time for John Howard Bryant; but Rev. David Todd, his young clergy friend at the Providence Church, did go. Todd and other Illinois delegates were in agreement with Lovejoy's views, which contradicted those of eastern churchmen in all four areas. When

Lovejoy heard reports of the meeting, he knew that the balance of power was shifting in the assembly of Congregationalists. Because of the coalition's work, the American Missionary Association decided that northern Illinois was a ripe field for antislavery growth. It invested its funds into vital subsidies for the churches and small salaries for politically involved Illinois antislavery pastors who publicly supported the third-party movement.[34] The Albany convention created a new policy that placed all privately managed mission societies under the authority of a national denomination that, when formalized in 1866, would be called the Congregational Church. Meanwhile, easterners pledged $50,000 to aid in the erection of sanctuaries in the West.[35] The young Rev. Richard Salter Storrs of Church of the Pilgrims in Brooklyn, the son of Eunice Lovejoy's first cousin, gave a major address favoring basic cooperation between East and West.

Leading African Americans and Women Spell Out Their Rights in Public

In 1853 the people of Illinois began reading about radical proposals to expand human rights, proposals that national speakers were delivering on lecture circuits. Five years after the Seneca Falls Woman's Rights Convention, a young white antislavery lecturer, Lucy Stone, came to Chicago in the cold of January to present six lectures. She found a respectable audience but not enough support to hold a convention. However, Mary Brown Davis publicized and partially endorsed Stone's views. Davis's husband had suffered severe injuries from the antiabolitionist riots in Peoria and later had succumbed to disease. After his death, Mary Davis moved to Galesburg while her five sons attended Knox College. Later she moved to Chicago to make her living as a woman journalist and social worker. She attended Stone's lectures and wrote that Stone was "a very extraordinary woman, quite handsome, very eloquent, graceful, and prepossessing in appearance. . . . Her mission seems to be a good one—to elevate her own sex and place them on an equal footing with men in education and capacities for earning a livelihood. So far I can go with her, but to go in person to the ballot box, to ascend the sacred desk or even the public platform, I think is a little out of the sphere of the daughters of our land."[36] Davis, an ardent abolitionist who had stood courageously against proslavery mobs, was rejecting women's suffrage and women's ordination. Upon reading this, Lovejoy realized that a major woman supporter of his was not ready to advocate for a full range of women's rights.

In September 1853, another call for human rights took place in New York City, and it made a big splash in the *Chicago Tribune*. It focused on an intriguing interracial trio composed of Frederick Douglass, William Lloyd Garrison, and Theodore

Parker, a Unitarian minister from Boston. The three men advocated legal expansion of human rights. They also shared the platform with two women, Lucy Stone and her former roommate at Oberlin College, Antoinette Brown.[37] Stone had been lecturing at antislavery conventions and women's rights meetings in the East for several years, often "wearing a black velvet coat and knee-length skirt worn over black silk breeches, her hair cut short and combed straight back," making a political statement with her clothing.[38] Antoinette Brown had been installed as the first ordained pastor of a Congregational Church in the small town of South Butler, New York, where African American Samuel Ringgold Ward had ministered before her.[39] On the tour, the two women were chaperoned by the older, highly respected Philadelphia Quaker Lucretia Mott. When the five speakers advocated equal legal property and inheritance rights for women, they were heckled by rabble-rousers. When Reverend Brown said, "The day is dawning when women shall be recognized as the equal of men in everything," a storm of hisses assailed her. The *Chicago Tribune* printed a vivid, detailed report of the New York event, labeling the male audience shameful and describing the women speakers as enlightened and unrelenting.[40]

The speakers' demands would soon be followed by another set of radical requests that would fill Chicago newspapers in October when African Americans held their First Illinois Convention of Colored People, with Frederick Douglass as the featured speaker.

African Americans' rising concern over their lack of human rights led to the announcement of another national black convention. Historian Philip S. Foner notes that from 1848 to 1853, "the national convention movement lay dormant." After Congress passed the Fugitive Slave Act in 1850, blacks became too terrified to attend public gatherings.[41] But in July 1853, the National Negro Convention gained new momentum and met in Rochester. John Jones and James D. Bonner attended as representatives from Chicago. Frederick Douglass and John Jones were reunited and both were named vice-presidents of the convention. Rev. James W. C. Pennington, who had just received an honorary doctorate from Heidelberg University, Germany, was elected president.[42] Nine states sent a total of 140 delegates to Rochester. Douglass opened the proceedings by presenting a speech titled "Address of the Colored Convention to the People of the United States," which set forth "the basic demands of the Negro people for justice and equality."[43] He urged that "the doors of the school-house, the work-shop, the church, the college, shall be thrown open as freely to our children as to the children of other members of the community." He called for four standing committees to establish a manual labor school, start protective unions, advocate black businesses, and support publications that improved the lives of African Americans. This was his answer to colonizationists who urged emigration to Africa as the solution to whites' unwillingness to accept blacks as American citizens. Delegates once again formally rejected the Fugitive Slave Act, the exclusion of black children from public schools, and the prohibition of black adults from serving on juries.[44] In eighteen months Lovejoy would bring these issues before the Illinois state legislature.

But the idea that shook the convention hall with greatest enthusiasm was Frederick Douglass's plan for the convention to build a manual labor college for black students. Young African Americans were in great need of advanced education. Such a college would be the first in the nation. In the following weeks, many black state and local meetings concurred with the convention's ambitious plan. But as the months went by, they were not able to find the money.

When John Jones returned to Illinois from Rochester in 1853, he and his friends completed arrangements for the First Convention of Colored People of the State of Illinois, to be held in Warner's Hall in Chicago, October 6–8, 1853.[45] He worked closely with Barquet and with Wagoner, president of the Chicago Literary and Debating Society. The black community had lobbied against the state's Black Laws the previous year and failed, but now they were preparing to lobby again.[46] Jones invited Frederick Douglass to be the convention's keynote speaker. The *Chicago Tribune* felt obliged to make it clear to its readers that it was "Douglass the slave, not Douglas the slaveholder," who was the star of the conference.

Forty black delegates came from eleven counties. James D. Bonner called the meeting to order; Jones was elected president and Wagoner and Barquet were elected secretaries.[47] Jones and Bonner were selected as Illinois representatives to the new National Council of Colored Men. The convention arranged for five Chicago men to be elected to the Illinois subsidiary of the National Council.[48] Then the delegates discussed the same problems raised at Rochester. A major difference was that intimidated blacks living in the Alton area asked only for segregated schools.[49] But those in the Chicago area, led by John and Mary Jones, insisted that black children be educated in integrated schools. The resolutions on colonization, Black Laws, and education were the proposals Jones and the convention wanted to see presented to the state legislature.

During this time, Eastman, Codding and Lovejoy were campaigning around the state to elect white antislavery state legislators who would vote for those very bills in the Illinois General Assembly. As soon as the convention ended, another trio of men went on a lecture tour together. Frederick Douglass, John Jones, and young H. Ford Douglas spent the next three weeks traveling to dozens of Illinois towns by train, speaking to local African American groups and to white audiences in places such as Geneva, St. Charles, Elgin, Rockford, Aurora, Joliet, Ottawa, Cortland, and Freeport. They were building a constituency to repeal the Black Laws and to secure black rights.[50]

Frederick Douglass Demands Action
at Hampshire Colony Church

The central committee of the Free Democratic Party, led by Lovejoy, invited Frederick Douglass to bring his radical message to Illinois's state convention on October 26, 1853, at Hampshire Colony Church in Princeton.[51] When white antislavery men across northern Illinois got the news that the renowned Frederick Douglass was coming to speak to them on their own turf, they eagerly made plans to attend. Douglass would go on to become a regular visitor to Illinois.

During this period of his life, Douglass spoke out against Christian churches that shielded American slavery. He preached that white churches possessed a splendid revelation from Christ, but failed to apply it.[52] "The slave fears everything. He had rather meet a wolf than a Christian—had rather encounter a rattlesnake than a man with a prayer-book under his arm."[53] These were the pinpricks that Eastman, Codding, and Lovejoy hoped Douglass would bring to the serious, religious members of the Free Democratic Party. Douglass spoke with both apocalyptic and millennialist imagery. Although America was doomed by sin, he said, it was a nation that could be propelled by an unbounded mission: "Christ will have a Second Coming in the 'new Israel' of America." America could be offered a second chance to become a redeemer nation and perform a special role in history, but this could happen only through repentance, testing, and suffering.[54] Lovejoy was not an apocalyptic or millennialist preacher, but he used some of the same words metaphorically. As for Douglass himself, he said he did not intend to wait for God to abolish slavery; God's will and purpose could be realized only through human action.[55] Years later, at a critical time, Lovejoy would echo those words.

Douglass's cutting speech sliced through the brisk autumn air as he repudiated Henry Clay's Compromise of 1850, denounced the Whig and the Democratic Parties, which had submitted to the gag rule and destroyed *habeas corpus*, and attacked John A. Logan's newest Illinois Black Exclusion Act. He berated the audience for its lack of religious insight. Did they not see that there was a significant and terrible difference between the Christianity of Christ and the Christianity of this land?[56] "No wonder you are not disturbed by the Fugitive Slave Law. Your religion is not a religion of justice and mercy. I wish you could open your eyes and see that this law has forbidden the preaching of the gospel. My friends, this ought to arouse you. . . . Need I tell you what is your Christian duty here?"[57] Douglass's speech was a jeremiad, a lamentation for the sins of the world that had injured four million people. Puritan ministers had used jeremiads in seventeenth-century New England to strengthen parishioners against the natural and self-inflicted disasters they faced. African American ministers utilized jeremiads to unite black worshippers in the face of unending oppression, to offer solace, and to bring the inspiration of a shared history endowed with divine meaning. They preached jeremiads to give black parishioners courage to demand justice and to give white Christians the conscience to grant the rights and liberties denied African Americans.[58] Inside the church Lovejoy served, Douglass spoke jeremiads to the white Free Democratic Party—a deep lamentation over a monstrous injustice perpetrated by whites. This was the message Eastman, Codding, and Lovejoy wanted everyone to hear.

Douglass's peroration was a razor-sharp prologue to the productive business meeting that followed. The report from the unofficial central committee announced that Codding and Eastman had been in the field organizing full-time, preparing to spread the party statewide.[59] So far, they had organized twenty-four northern and central counties in Illinois. "A State board of directors numbering twelve was to sit at Chicago and undertake the effective reorganization of the party."[60] They had formed working groups of five persons in each county and three persons in each town. Nineteen Free Democratic county associations had been established over the previous year. They had never worked so hard at organizing. Impassioned by Douglass's lecture, the delegates were now exhilarated by the impressive report.

In addition, a newly reorganized newspaper, *Free West*, was approved, with Eastman and journalist Hooper Warren as its editors. They placed Frederick Douglass's speech on the front page of the first issue, December 1, 1853.

As soon as the meeting adjourned, Douglass, John Jones, and H. Ford Douglas continued their extensive three-week tour of northern Illinois towns, riding by train as well as buggy, giving speeches every day, staying overnight, and taking the pulse of the citizenry on the Black Laws of Illinois. The reinvigorated team of Eastman, Codding, and Lovejoy followed their example and took to the field again to enlist still more new members. Frederick Douglass's presence in Hampshire Colony Church and his message before the people of northern Illinois had been the high point and culmination of their year's labors. The convention had been a huge success, surpassing Lovejoy's expectations.[61] Like the old Liberty Party, the new Free Democratic Party was going to be radical, egalitarian, and interracial. Human Rights were in the air again.

The Nebraska Bill Accelerates Early Republican Growth

Ten weeks after Frederick Douglass preached in Princeton, Senator Stephen A. Douglas from Illinois unintentionally dropped a gift in the lap of the Free Democratic Party of Illinois. On January 4, 1854, Douglas introduced the Nebraska bill in the U.S. Senate. He proposed to admit a part of the territory of Nebraska called Kansas into the Union and to allow emigrants there to vote on whether it would be slave or free. The Nebraska bill infuriated and mobilized antislavery people because it would demolish the Missouri Compromise of 1820 and shatter the sacred bipartisan promise made in trust to the people of the nation to keep all land north of the 36°30' parallel free. Douglas's bill would set a precedent by making slavery national and perpetual and legalizing white supremacy and black inferiority. In what was about to become the Kansas Territory, southerners were already building homesteads to ensure the area would become a slave state, even as northerners were arriving daily by wagon to ensure it would remain free. Violence would be inevitable. Lovejoy and his colleagues predicted a major political battle. They intended to make every effort to prevent the bill's passage.

In Washington, Senator Chase and Congressman Giddings were outraged and drafted "Appeal of the Independent Democrats in Congress to the People of the United States." The response was loud and the audience was vast, reaching as far as Illinois.[62] Gamaliel Bailey's *National Era* warned its fifty thousand subscribers that Douglas's bill was a new plot to expand slavery. Previous plots had sought to divide Texas into five states, annex Cuba, invade Haiti, and carve a slave state out of southern California.[63] Clergy across the North united in their condemnation of the bill. In March, three thousand New England clergymen signed a very long petition against it.[64] New York City clergy wrote a letter in opposition circulated by Lovejoy's cousin Rev. George Cheever. Chicago clergy sent their denunciation of it. In defiance, Douglas directed his wrath at the ministers, accusing them of desecrating the pulpit and prostituting the sacred desk. In Washington in April, Israel Washburn, a Universalist and an antislavery Republican from Maine, rose in the House of Representatives and charged that the Nebraska bill threatened free institutions everywhere. He declared that the South was trying to swindle the North out of territory that has been reserved for the free farmer ever since Maine became a state. He called for the overthrow of the Slave Power.[65]

On May 30, 1854, President Franklin Pierce, ignoring all opposition, signed the Kansas-Nebraska Act into law. All antislavery people despaired when they heard the news. Black abolitionists watched as one more domino fell. The Fugitive Slave Act had made recapture of slaves or kidnapping of freemen possible at any moment; no place was safe. Now, four years later, the Kansas-Nebraska Act allowed any territory to vote to become a slave state—another protection demolished. What would the Slave Power get next? In the face of increasing uncertainty, blacks faced a difficult choice.[66] Should they leave the United States or stay? Some advocated building a new nation elsewhere. Others were determined despite great barriers to gain citizenship in America. Many met at the National Emigration Convention in Cleveland on August 24, 1854, to discuss the question. Frederick Douglass was appalled by the disunity evident there, for he could see that the convention would split the black consensus he had built in Rochester and further undermine his plan for a manual labor college.[67] The issue stirred emotional conflict and fear among the delegates, and debate heated up. One view considered colonization an open door to true black democracy; the other imagined it to be a great white threat ready to swallow blacks into oblivion.

Many blacks still hoped white Americans would rid themselves of their prejudice against blacks and offer them full citizenship. Other delegates had given up in despair and, while trying to avoid Liberia, were searching for alternative locations in Central America, Haiti, or the Niger Valley of West Africa. Delegates debated, argued, prayed, wept, and finally parted over the issue.

Throughout this long controversy, both Douglass and John Jones steadfastly advised African Americans to remain in the United States and demand their rights as citizens. They continued to push ahead in their political efforts to gain human rights.

Lovejoy's mother, Betsey, had urged her children to reject colonization from the time she began reading Garrison's *Liberator* in Maine. Lovejoy shared the vision that Douglass and Jones held of a racially integrated democratic society of equals in America. The Illinois African Americans in the coalition opposed colonization and sent no delgates to the Cleveland convention.[68]

In contrast, white colonizationists were not distressed by the Kansas-Nebraska Act. The American Colonization Society had revived itself, having paid off its debts and gained contributions from the state legislatures of Virginia, New Jersey, Pennsylvania, Maryland, Missouri, and Ohio. Its agent, Rev. James Mitchell, was currently touring Indiana, Illinois, Michigan, Wisconsin, and Iowa, asking these legislatures to appropriate money for the resettlement of blacks in Liberia.[69]

Northern congressmen who had voted against the Kansas-Nebraska Act were unsure what to do after President Pierce signed the law. However, "even as the midnight defeat was taking place in the House of Representatives," the farsighted congressman Israel Washburn of Maine invited those who voted against the act to meet the next morning for breakfast at his Washington home. Thirty furious anti-Nebraskans came. Washburn told them it was time to shift the federal balance of power to the North but that the present parties were inadequate to deal with the "southern steamroller." They must form a new political party. Kelsey claims that Washburn gave it its name: "Call it the Republican Party," Washburn suggested. The congressmen who were despondent the night before burst into applause.[70]

Senator Douglas had given the coalition for equality an enormous campaign opening. Many ordinary Illinois citizens were so angry at the Kansas-Nebraska Act that they were willing to break old party ties and join a new alliance. Lovejoy said that he had never seen politicians struggle so hard to keep up with the rapid shift in popular sentiment.[71] The Free Democratic caucus in Illinois hired Codding to organize an alliance of all those opposed to Douglas's act and call them Anti-Nebraskans.[72] By July 20, 1854, Codding was traveling Illinois roads, rivers, canals, and trains, working furiously for fusion. Sensing fresh possibilities, Chase and Giddings came to Illinois and brought Frederick Douglass with them.[73] John F. Farnsworth, a U.S. congressman from Illinois, joined Lovejoy in touring. They relished their interracial team. They urged citizens to come together to rescue the federal government from the Slave Power.

In the Maine legislature, Democrats and Whigs dissatisfied with their own parties' position on slavery took the political risk to fuse with antislavery stalwarts. News came from Ripon, Wisconsin, and Jackson, Michigan, that similar peoples' parties were forming, calling themselves Republicans. This was the moment the coalition of clergy, women, and blacks in Illinois had been working for.

John Howard Bryant also jumped in. He decided that if fusion could take place in other states, he would help it happen in Illinois by inviting all the anti-Nebraska Democrats and Whigs in Bureau County to an organizing meeting on July 4, 1854, at Bryant's Woods, a picnicking ground adjacent to his red brick house at the southern edge of Princeton. He nominated Lovejoy to run for a seat in the state legislature on what he called the Republican ticket. Lovejoy received the nomination by acclamation.[74]

Then, using extensive contacts with blacks and whites, men and women, who had been welcomed by the Free Democratic Party, the earliest Illinois Republican organizing committees proceeded to set up three congressional district nominating conventions in Ottawa, Rockford, and Aurora.[75] After these successes, the *Free West* published a summons to a statewide convention at the State Fair in Springfield, where politicians annually vied for supporters. They set the date for October 4 and 5, 1854.[76] The invitation was to all citizens who were opposed to the repeal of the Missouri Compromise and who were in favor of overthrowing the existing national administration.[77] Codding and Lovejoy would lead the meeting.[78] Codding had returned from a long lecture tour of the state and was enthusiastic about the possibilities.[79]

The Illinois leaders of the Free Democratic Party were encouraged by the formation of Republican parties in Connecticut, Vermont, Iowa, Ohio, Indiana, New York, and Maine, as well as Wisconsin and Michigan. They wanted to pass on this good spirit to the freemen of their state and others.[80]

On October 3, 1854, Lovejoy arrived ahead of time. For the first time he heard Abraham Lincoln speak. Lincoln called for the restoration of the Missouri Compromise that Douglas's act had just repealed. Lovejoy was deeply moved when he heard Lincoln say that he hated slavery and was outraged that human beings were treated like animals. Lincoln said, "No man is good enough to govern another without that other's consent."[81] Lovejoy saw great political potential in Lincoln.

Codding and Lovejoy welcomed delegates like young Paul Selby of Jacksonville to help write the platform. Republican editor H. M. Sheetz of the *Freeport Journal*, an important delegate, reported that a good-sized crowd had gathered and a number of mild resolutions were agreed to, although there was no mention made of repealing the Fugitive Slave Law. He wrote that the speakers were dignified and moderate.[82] However, the next day, Democrat Charles H. Lamphier, editor of the Springfield *Illinois State Register* and Douglas's right-hand man, attacked the early Republicans with a scalding piece, claiming erroneously that only a scattering of people attended and that the resolutions they passed were radical and included the repeal of the Fugitive Slave Law. Lamphier claimed, "Ichabod raved, and Lovejoy swelled."[83] Clearly, Lovejoy and Codding were challenging Douglas's formidable political machine. The misrepresentation of the first Illinois Republican Party convention by the Democrats has had long-lasting consequences, for historians including Arthur Charles Cole wrote confidently that the convention was a failure and that the early Republican Party would soon die. Yet the party was on the eve of a big success.[84]

In the midst of this intensive campaign, Lovejoy was surprised to learn that Senator Douglas planned to debate him in Princeton. Certainly Lovejoy, twice defeated for Congress, must have looked like a small fish to the famous senator. Teenager Peter Bryant, son of Cyrus and Julia Bryant, heard that Douglas planned to speak for forty-five minutes and then let Lovejoy talk for fifteen minutes, after which Douglas would answer him. However, halfway into Lovejoy's response, the chairman pounded that he must stop, and then Douglas spoke for two and a half more hours.[85] The local Republican group was not prepared to handle the shenanigans of a national celebrity.

However, Senator Douglas did not win every contest. On October 17 Frederick Douglass made plans to campaign in Aurora, where Stephen Douglas was also scheduled to appear. It appears that a group in Aurora had cleverly arranged for the two famous men with the same last name to appear on nearby platforms. Frederick Douglass's presence caused the Illinois senator to cancel his scheduled address.[86] The symbolism of a short white man followed by a tall black man, both self-made, both strong orators, was too much for Douglas. But Frederick Douglass continued to campaign. In Chicago on October 30 at Metropolitan Hall, fifteen hundred people came to hear him speak on the politics of the day.[87]

The early Republicans conducted an aggressive congressional and state campaign. Just before Election Day, Lovejoy, who was campaign manager as well as a candidate, wrote his oldest step-daughter, Lucy Denham, "Everything looks favorable unless the Democrats play some devilish trick. I do not see what can prevent the republican ticket from success. Your loving Daddy, Owen Lovejoy."[88]

For the first time, Lovejoy won. In fact, the early Republicans had unexpectedly won a huge upset victory across northern Illinois. Twenty-five candidates would accompany Lovejoy to Springfield in January under the Republican label.[89] The broader, more moderate, anti-Nebraska portion of the assembly, which included some anti-Douglas Democrats and anti-Nebraska Whigs, working together with the early Republicans, would control both houses of the Illinois General Assembly. For the first time the Democratic juggernaut in the state legislature was broken.

Winning felt wonderful to Lovejoy. He wrote Giddings that he desired to share this moment with a good friend. "It is gratifying to me inasmuch as I have been cursed and abused and vilified for a long series of years. I was drawn into politics on the antislavery principle apparently from the necessity of the case, and in consequence brought down upon me a great deal of wrath."[90] He asked Giddings to excuse his egotism: "My head has been filled with elation." He also thanked Giddings for his help during the campaign: "We all liked you hugely, as Uncle Toby would say. Your visit did me good." He reached back to his religious moorings: "I never have felt more of the religious sentiment than in this campaign." Then, as he was already hoping to run for the U.S. Congress, Lovejoy asked Giddings to be his mentor.

The Illinois anti-Nebraska campaign organization won five of nine congressional seats, including Elihu Washburne for the First District (Galena) and Lyman Trumbull for the Eighth (Alton). Republicans made even greater gains in other states. As a result of this, after years of domination, the Democrats in the U.S. House of Representatives lost their majority.

In Chicago, out of the exuberance of victory and gratitude to the women who had worked hard during the campaign, Eastman hired Hannah Cutler to be the correspondent on woman's affairs for the *Free West*. Cutler was a graduate of Mary Lyon's Ipswich Seminary, where Lovejoy's sister Lizzie had studied. Cutler became the president of the Ohio Woman's Rights Association and lobbied in Springfield, Illinois. Eastman placed the profiles she wrote about leading woman's rights activists on the front page, starting with a profile of Lucretia Mott, a great organizer and circulator of petitions.[91] Most women who were involving themselves in the women's rights cause had been active in the abolitionist movement.

Illinois Republicans planned to use winning twenty-six seats out of one hundred as leverage to obtain a Speaker who would give them appointments to important committees and allow slavery issues onto the agenda. This would give them the experience they needed to go to the U.S. Congress. Democrats, in turn, intended to hold on to as much power as they could. Senator Douglas returned to Washington but directed Governor Joel A. Matteson to introduce some new issue in his annual message to the General Assembly that would divert attention away from the controversial Kansas-Nebraska Act and split the alliance of early Republicans and other anti-Nebraskans.[92]

While Democrats were facing up to the reality that they were in the minority in the General Assembly, Douglas gave them instructions to reelect U.S. senator James Shields. Abraham Lincoln was strategizing for the same seat. Lincoln's best hope lay in gaining the support of the political abolitionist coalition for equality represented by Lovejoy. Giddings wrote to Lovejoy that he should support Lincoln. Anti-abolitionist judge David Davis of Bloomington, Lincoln's close associate, believed it was necessary to make some kind of deal with Lovejoy's group. Lovejoy biographer Edward Magdol said in the 1960s that he had insufficient evidence to prove that a deal was made,[93] but since then, information has accumulated that substantiates it.[94] At some point Lincoln and Lovejoy, either personally or through surrogates, negotiated an agreement helpful to both. Lovejoy or his core group promised to support Lincoln's nomination to the U.S. Senate on the first three ballots. In return, Lincoln's longtime Whig friend in the Illinois statehouse, Representative Stephen T. Logan, would cast the deciding vote in the General Assembly on a resolution instructing Illinois congressmen to vote against any extension of slavery into the territories. As a part of this unusual deal, Lovejoy would be permitted to speak on this resolution publicly and then present it on the floor prior to the election for the U.S. Senator.[95]

In December the early Republicans met in the village of Somonauk, Illinois, to plan their strategy for the upcoming session of the General Assembly, which would begin on January 2 in Springfield. Their modest Republican State Central Committee could not claim to be a truly statewide committee because it had failed to draw membership from the southern section of the state. However, the early Republican Party did not collapse as its foes had hoped. Historian Victor Howard's research has found that the party was already a powerful influence in northern Illinois. There was no doubt that the party would survive.[96] Three concerns at the 1853 Colored People's Convention in Chicago—repealing the Illinois Black Laws, granting blacks the right to *habeas corpus*, and opening public schools to black children—required state action.[97] Lovejoy considered these concerns of the coalition for equality to be Republican priorities.

• • •

In 1852 Lovejoy and the coalition for equality had announced a bold plan to organize the Illinois Free Democratic Party based on religious and constitutional principles. Frederick Douglass called for the party to take radical action, John Jones announced the first Illinois State Convention of Colored People, and a national women's rights lecturer came to speak in Chicago. In 1854 the leaders of the Free Democratic Party organized three congressional district conventions, and Codding and Lovejoy led the first early Republican Party Convention. Some antislavery Whigs and Democrats joined the early Republicans, and together they elected Lovejoy and twenty-five other Republican Party members to the state legislature. As a result of the election, in January 1855 the Democratic Party majority in the Illinois General Assembly would be displaced for the first time since 1818. Through the Republican Party, the coalition for equality strategized on how to open Illinois courts and schools to blacks and how to instruct Illinois congressmen to vote to prohibit slavery's extension into the territories.

5. Achieving Political Fusion and Winning a Seat in Congress

1855–November 1857

The city of Springfield, Illinois, was modernizing. It was installing gas lights along major streets and in the statehouse. Arriving four days before the opening session of the state legislative, Reverend Lovejoy avoided the new hotels. Instead he stayed at the home of Ebenezer Phelps, a jewelry maker who had led the colonists to Princeton in 1831 and served as president of Hampshire Colony Church until he moved his business to Springfield. On New Year's Eve, a Sunday, Lovejoy worshipped at Phelps's antislavery Second Presbyterian Church.[1] Lovejoy planned to bring up African American priorities before the Illinois General Assembly.[2]

There was a feeling of success in the air as the coalition had come together and elected twenty-six friends to the legislature. The black community in Chicago sent James D. Bonner to observe the actions of the 1855 Illinois legislature; he planned to keep Frederick Douglass informed.[3]

On New Year's Day one hundred members of the Nineteenth General Assembly of the Illinois legislature were converging on Springfield. Prominent well-to-do women of the city opened their houses, and the governor held a reception at the capitol. The unpaid-for statehouse dominated the square. The pillared Hall of Representatives on the second floor displayed impressive fenestration looking toward the western prairie.

The makeup of the Nineteenth Illinois General Assembly was entirely different from the Eighteenth. The House now had thirty-four Nebraska Democrats who would support Senator Douglas's wishes versus forty-one members of the House who were opposed. They were composed of anti-Nebraska Democrats, anti-Nebraska Whigs, Fusionists, and Republicans. The Senate had eleven Nebraska Democrats and fourteen anti-Nebraska members.[4]

Lincoln's first law partner, Whig Stephen T. Logan, proceeded to start the election of officers. Dr. William Lyman, an antislavery military physician who resided in Rockford, nominated Hon. Thomas J. Turner for Speaker on behalf of the anti-Nebraska faction. Turner, at thirty-nine, was a moderate antislavery lawyer from Freeport. The Democrats nominated Dr. John P. Richmond, a conservative physician from central Illinois. Turner won with forty votes to Richmond's twenty-four. Physician Charles Henry Ray, editor of a Galena newspaper and neighbor of Congressman Elihu Washburne, was hired as Clerk of the Senate. Ray wanted to start an antislavery newspaper in Chicago.[5] Turner appointed Lovejoy to be the chair of the House Committee for the State Library and a member of the Education and Licenses standing committees.[6]

As Senator Douglas had instructed, Governor Joel A. Matteson's annual message contained a surprise to draw attention away from the controversy over the Kansas-Nebraska Act and put the Assembly's focus on a fresh distraction. Matteson asked the Assembly to consider supporting a colony in Liberia.[7] Democrat Richmond favored investigating the possibilities. Lovejoy said that he opposed turning the state into a colonization society. Blacks in the coalition were also against it. Barquet had written to the legislature explaining, "we will not go—we will linger here in our birthplace."[8] Richmond retorted by claiming that the legislature had the power to determine the destiny of the entire black population of Illinois, which sounded like a threat to expel blacks from the state. At that point it was announced that the agent of the American Colonization Society, Rev. James Mitchell, was in town to answer any questions the members might have about the society and about Liberia.[9] Governor Matteson speculated that this issue would split the anti-Nebraska coalition. Lovejoy calculated that several anti-Nebraska legislators would support the American Colonization Society as their Christian duty, but that most core Republican legislators believed blacks should become citizens of the United States.

Richmond compiled a list of questions to ask Reverend Mitchell, including the cost of sending blacks to Liberia, its living conditions, and how willing blacks were to go there.[10] At this point, outspoken Rockford Republican William Lyman snidely labeled Richmond's resolution "a magnificent piece of humbuggery."[11] Then, with the intent of defeating the governor's colonization bill, Lyman offered an amendment and a parallel set of questions for Mitchell to answer. First, what were the claims of Canada as a place for colonizing people of color compared with those of Africa? Second, what was the comparative expense of colonization in those two countries? Third, what were the comparative numbers of persons annually colonized in these two countries? These questions blatantly trumpeted the illegal activity in which many core Republicans, including Lyman himself, were engaged—the unlawful Underground Railroad. Lyman's brazen amendment siphoned the breath away from the men sitting in the Hall of Representatives.[12] Up in the balcony, James Bonner must have chuckled.

The official House *Journal* did not report Dr. Lyman's proposal. Only Zebina Eastman's *Free West* printed the story for the public.

On January 12, 1855, astute antislavery Republican Rev. Daniel J. Pinckney, principal of the academy at Mount Morris, Illinois, introduced "An act to incorporate the Illinois State Board of Colonization." Speaker Turner appointed a select committee of nine to consider making a contribution to Liberia.[13] Its actual purpose was to kill the idea. Turner appointed a majority of anticolonization men, including Lovejoy, to the committee, and apparently it never met.[14] In Chicago, John Jones and his colleagues must have been relieved that colonization was buried in committee.

Lovejoy was determined to place the coalition's priorities before the General Assembly. He searched for a way to bring up the inflammatory issue of the Illinois Black Laws, so important to the delegates at the First Convention of the Colored Citizens of Illinois, which Jones had held in Chicago on October 6–8, 1853. Just two years before, in 1853, the legislature had passed ever more onerous laws. Lovejoy speculated that discussion of any Black Laws would not be allowed on the official agenda, but, since Turner had appointed him chairman of the State Library Committee, he could obtain the privilege of speaking. He stood and audaciously introduced a bill titled "An act to expurgate the public library" and spoke under that ruse. As soon as the Democrats realized that his intent was to permit African Americans to testify in court, they broke into pandemonium. After long, chaotic minutes, Turner adjourned the meeting.[15]

The next day, January 12, an unintimidated Lovejoy made a memorable speech, which Eastman later published in the *Free West*.[16] "If the gentlemen had allowed that bill of yesterday to have taken its regular course through the House—had extended to its friends the usual parliamentary courtesies, and then consigned it to the tomb of the Capulets, they might have done with it, and I should have been content. But if this bill and kindred subjects [about African Americans] . . . are to be thrust out of the House unceremoniously, nay, almost contemptuously, then I will tell the gentlemen, it will occupy a deal of the time of the House."[17] After that speech, it was clear that Lovejoy was the preeminent antislavery speaker in the legislature.[18] Reverend Pinckney of Mount Morris later explained to the legislature, "Lovejoy is so far ahead in this [discussion on] race as to be nearly out of sight of the most of us."[19]

Lovejoy regularly presented petitions from blacks. Several came from those living in the Alton area.[20] It is probable that some of the petitioners sat in the gallery and watched Lovejoy discussing them. On January 12, the day on which Lovejoy admonished the House, the editor of the *Alton Telegraph* reported that Alton blacks had submitted a petition in which they opposed going to Liberia because "blacks and mulattoes cannot live harmoniously together." They refused to go "unless separate colonies were assigned to those of different shades of color" and "unless they were educated before they were sent to West Africa."[21]

If the *Telegraph* article was frivolous and untrue, its purpose may have been to retaliate against Lovejoy for his admonition or to target him with rancid humor.[22] Slavery-sympathizing whites could guffaw at the notion that Alton blacks were as racist as they were.[23] If the accusations were accurately printed, it is suspected that the black petitioners were being sarcastic.[24] If the black petitioners were serious and did not want to leave America, they had hit upon an effective way of discouraging the Assembly from expelling them to West Africa, as the state was deeply in debt. The cost of education, dual facilities, and transportation was prohibitive. Historian Clarence E. Walker perceptively notes that whites were known to fabricate accusations of color discrimination among blacks as a political weapon against oppressed peoples or as a rationalization for white prejudice.[25] When the *Alton Telegraph* criticized Lovejoy for introducing petitions from blacks, he responded that he would always present petitions, whether he agreed with them or not, because all people had the constitutional right to petition.[26]

Illinois blacks watched every day to see how Representative Lovejoy was doing in the General Assembly. On January 18, 1855, African American James D. Bonner wrote to Frederick Douglass and told him that Owen Lovejoy "has proved himself as true as steel, and we love and honor him." Douglass reprinted Bonner's letter in *Frederick Douglass' Paper* on February 8, 1856.[27]

The Coalition Attains Mixed Results in the General Assembly

On January 20, 1855, a giant snowstorm swept over most of Illinois. For almost two weeks the legislature lacked a quorum. When members finally reassembled, an unusual announcement was made that Lovejoy would give an address in the Hall of Representatives on the evening of February 6, 1855, and the public was warmly invited. This remarkable concession was permitted by a slim majority of votes. Lovejoy began his speech with Thomas Jefferson's words that all men are created free and equal, and the assertion that the U.S. Constitution was basically an antislavery document. "Never was this government organized in any wise to extend and propagate slavery! Never, Never, Sir."[28] He was picking up steam in his full-throated voice as his forehead and neck were wet with passion. "No power on earth has the right to make a man a slave. . . . God made that man as he made you and me in his own image. . . . You had better take your foot from his neck, you might as well trample the Son of God. There is the divine miniature, and you squatter sovereigns had better take your feet from off him."[29]

Lovejoy won over many doubters in the audience. The *Western Citizen* announced that this was the first exposition of antislavery doctrine ever heard in the Illinois statehouse.[30] This speech reverberated within the Republican Party. Lovejoy and his western allies were carving out a position that viewed the U.S. Constitution as antislavery and that accepted its provision of not interfering with slavery where it already existed, but insisted that Congress held the exclusive jurisdiction to keep slavery out of the territories.[31] Historian David Brion Davis sees the application of the concept of containment as one component of "a larger project to abolish slavery in the nation,"[32] and James Oakes sees Lovejoy as a prototype implementer of the containment policy.[33] In coming years this policy formed the Republican platform and mandate.

The next afternoon, February 7, 1855, Speaker Thomas J. Turner announced that the order of the day would begin with Mr. Lovejoy offering three resolutions. Fulfilling the part of the bargain agreed to earlier by either Lincoln or his surrogates, Lincoln's former partner, Whig Stephen T. Logan, moved to make the resolutions offered by Lovejoy the special order of the day, and his motion passed by one vote.[34] The first resolution, which urged Illinois congressmen to prohibit any extension of slavery into the territories, was the decisive one. Amazing everyone, it passed forty-one to thirty-two.[35] In 1860 this plank of nonextension would fuse various factions and carry the national Republican Party to victory. The second resolution, to prohibit the admission of any new slave state, was not part of the bargain, and it failed, thirty-three to forty; Lovejoy had lost the votes of eight former Whigs led by Logan.[36] The third resolution would repeal the Fugitive Slave Law. Sensing that he did not have support for that resolution, Lovejoy asked to modify the motion to secure the right of *habeas corpus* and trial by jury before the regularly constituted authorities of the state on behalf of all persons "claimed as owing service or labor."[37] Such a provision would protect free blacks who were being kidnapped by slave catchers and sold into slavery. While the third resolution lost twenty-five to forty-seven, it was astonishing that twenty-one early Republicans plus four anti-Nebraska Fusion men supported this radical resolution.[38] Lovejoy's success in obtaining the support of a majority of the House of Representatives for the nonextension of slavery into the territories—the first resolution—was a personal victory for Lovejoy and a bellwether for the nation. Seven years later Lovejoy and Chicago congressman Isaac Arnold would shepherd such legislation through the U.S. House of Representatives, and President Lincoln would sign it. This would deliver the Republican Party's premier plank to the citizenry.

The following day, on February 8, the whole legislature was scheduled to vote on the occupant of the contested U.S. Senate seat.[39] As the early Republicans had agreed, and apparently Lovejoy had promised, they voted for Lincoln on the first three ballots.[40] Initially Lincoln was ahead, but he could not get the necessary majority. After James Shields lost, Governor Matteson garnered some votes but then slipped behind anti-Nebraska Lyman Trumbull. After nine tallies, Lincoln released his supporters to vote for Trumbull rather than allow Democrat Matteson to win. Lovejoy voted for Trumbull on the final three ballots.[41] On the tenth ballot, Trumbull was declared the victor. Seating Trumbull in the U.S. Senate was great news for the antislavery coalition. He detested slavery and had a fine judicial acumen.[42] The *Rockford Republican* wrote on February 21 that Trumbull's election rendered complete the anti-Nebraska triumph.[43]

Lovejoy wanted the legislature to approve public education for all children in Illinois. He was the one who called for the third reading of the act to make valid a school tax. But Ninian Edwards, interim Superintendent of Education, prepared a public education bill with the discriminatory word "white" in it in order to exclude black children.[44] The coalition of churchmen, women, and African Americans wanted schooling for all children; the early Republican core legislators came to Springfield fully prepared to integrate the public schools. Speaker Turner had appointed Lovejoy and four other progressives to the nine-member education committee. Core Republicans wanted Edwards's bill to be amended to include black children.

On January 18, Lovejoy read a petition from two black men, Aaron B. Church and William Bacon, who were probably listening. They would settle for segregated schools, but they protested against forcing blacks to pay a school tax while denying their children the right to attend school.[45] On their behalf, Lovejoy introduced "an act to remove certain legal disabilities of colored persons; and moved its reference to a select committee."[46] His bill would instruct school boards to allot blacks' portion of the school taxes to a fund established specifically for black children's education. Loud resistance erupted against this idea, and it lost, albeit not by much: thirty-three to thirty-six. Lovejoy reproved the legislators who had voted against it, saying, "Now, I conceive it is not altogether a question of what we owe to the colored population, but also a question of what we owe to ourselves; not only a question of what the five thousand colored people of this State can endure, but also a question of what we, clothed with authority, can afford to impose upon them."[47]

On February 8, 1855, the legislature addressed the subject of establishing a state public school system. Such a bill had failed to pass in the previous session. The chairman, Dr. Lyman, reported the main bill from the education committee.[48] Several core Republicans introduced amendments to include black children.[49] On February 9, the amendment of Republican Samuel J. Brown of Galesburg would allow each county to decide for itself whether to integrate its schools.[50] But Democrat Chauncey Higbee from downstate Pittsfield interjected with a substitute amendment to keep public schools for whites only in *all* counties.[51] Then Higbee forced a lengthy postponement of the main vote. Only after he was assured that little or no money would go to black children did he allow the body to vote on Lyman's motion to establish a state public school system.[52] It was finally decided in the affirmative: forty-seven yeas, with Lovejoy and his core voting for it, and fourteen nays.[53] The next day the Senate concurred with the House. For the first time Illinois had a public school system, but it was for white children only. Curiously, Lovejoy's amendment survived in a minor section of the law, but blacks received very little money from it.[54] African Americans felt defeated once again as the state denied their children a public education.[55]

When the General Assembly closed on February 15, 1855, the early Republicans had scored on the national issue over territories but had been outmaneuvered on state issues. Northern Illinois whites had participated as the conscience minority in the Assembly, but despite Lovejoy's strong efforts, blacks had made little progress. When John Jones returned to Chicago from national committee work in New York City, he quickly called for a Second Illinois State Colored People's Convention, to be held in Alton in 1856.[56] In the Twentieth General Assembly, opening in January 1857, Democrats would likely be back in control, and public education for blacks would be derailed again.[57] Some southern Illinois African Americans were dismayed when they heard that Lovejoy might not be returning to the legislature to fight for their causes.

Despite little progress on state issues, Lovejoy had established himself as the white political antislavery leader of Illinois, and with that record, he would run for the U.S. Congress. He had won the crucial vote on nonextension. Joshua Giddings wrote from Ohio congratulating Lovejoy on managing the passage of that important resolution and predicted that Illinois voters would support Republicans in the next national election.[58] Horace Greeley boosted Lovejoy by placing an account of his February 6 speech on the front page of the *New York Tribune*.[59]

The Ad Hoc Republican Central Committee

In the spring of 1855, the challenge before the coalition was to elect a radical man to Congress. To do this, Lovejoy's colleagues in the ad hoc Republican Central Committee believed that they must have a statewide daily newspaper, support from Lincoln, and a broader-based party attained through fusion. It looked impossible. First, Eastman could not finance a daily paper. Lovejoy asked editor Austin Willey, Joseph Lovejoy's friend in Maine, if he would move to Illinois and start such a newspaper. Willey came for a visit, but he too could not arrange solid financial backing. Second, Eastman and others doubted Lincoln's sincerity, and they traveled to Springfield to investigate whether Lincoln was really antislavery. Though Lincoln's friends tried to reassure him, the radical Eastman lost enthusiasm, despaired of Lincoln, and tried for several years to make his living in real estate. Some African Americans considered Lovejoy's strategy, of limiting the party platform to nonextension in order to get Lincoln's support, to be only a tiny gain for blacks, who needed far more leverage in such an important negotiation. Third, it was necessary to build a broader-based party, but blacks remembered that when Liberty Party men had tried to win elections through compromise with Free Soilers, they made no progress at all. They feared the same would happen again if fusion became the linchpin of the Republican Party. Furthermore, Lovejoy's vision of ending slavery through Congress seemed illusionary to them.

Despite uncertainties, Lovejoy made his decision. He was going to run for the U.S. Congress on the Republican ticket. He told the people at Hampshire Colony Church that he planned to resign as their minister at the end of 1855. It was not easy to end the close relationship he had with these unusual parishioners. They did not want him to resign; he had been their minister for seventeen years.[60] But should he win, he would need all his energy for his new duties. And he needed to win to keep his vow. If he was elected, the family would continue to live at the homestead in Princeton that Eunice owned. During the congressional sessions, traditionally the months of December through March, he would stay in Washington, and Eunice would come to be with him for a few weeks during the winter social season.

In April and May 1855, the ad hoc unofficial Central Committee of the Illinois Republican Party negotiated the purchase of a newspaper. Codding, Eastman, Lovejoy, Charles H. Ray, and Chicagoan Henry W. Blodgett met with Joseph Medill and John C. Vaughn, former editors of the *Cleveland Leader*. They decided to purchase the *Chicago Tribune*, which in the past had leaned toward Know-Nothing Party editorial positions, and to remodel it into a solidly antislavery Republican Party newspaper.[61] From this group, Ray and Medill were able to make payments of one-third each. This statewide daily would give the Republican movement its own megaphone to compete with the popular, partisan Springfield presses—the Democrats' *Illinois State Register* and the Whigs' *Illinois State Journal*. This was a huge step for the unofficial Central Committee to take.[62] On April 14 Codding and Lovejoy reveled at the *Tribune*'s possibilities.[63] On April 21 Ray wrote his friend Elihu Washburne that the purchase was about to be made.[64] In September Ray and Vaughn became editors, and together with Medill they incorporated the firm.

To broaden the Republican Party's base, the unofficial Central Committee hired Codding to organize a second tour for statewide political fusion. While he was on the road lecturing, his fiancée, Maria Preston, kept track of the locations where he spoke.[65] At each place, he hunted for common ground that would unite

Republicans with the various political factions that were opposing the Nebraska Act. At the end of July 1855, Codding lectured for five days in Quincy, where, after his fifth address, Archibald Williams, a Whig candidate for Congress, announced that he could agree on two resolutions. The first opposed the extension of slavery to the territories, and the second pledged to refrain from interfering with slavery in the states where it existed.[66] In that way, Williams offered the simple formula that combined these two policies and the two wings of the proposed party. It was this formula that allowed the first fusion to take place in central Illinois.[67] When the ad hoc central committee members heard this good news from Codding, they quickly centered on this wording as the basis for a statewide Republican Party. This formula had been Lovejoy's position for a decade.

That summer the ad hoc committee began by inviting leaders to an Anti-Nebraska convention. Lovejoy was asked to write Williams, Trumbull, and Lincoln to ascertain their interest in a state convention be held in the fall.[68] But Williams believed that the Whig newspaper editors in the central part of the state remained cautious, still stereotyping the early Republicans as anticonstitutional Garrisonian abolitionists.[69] Lincoln replied that he was willing to unite along the lines of Williams but was not ready to attend a fall convention.[70] On August 23, Trumbull answered, saying that there was so great an aversion against fusion in southern Illinois that very few Democrats would be likely to unite in a convention composed of all parties.[71]

Historian Victor Howard declares, "Thus it appeared—to Twentieth Century historians at least—that the Republican Party was dead."[72] Arthur Cole came to that same conclusion in 1919. In 1986 Louis Fuller wrote, "The effort of the Illinois abolitionists to organize was a failure," and William Gienapp agreed.[73] Historians of the Republican Party have generally concluded that the rejections by Williams, Lincoln, and Trumbull ended the radicals' leadership in the party's formation.[74] But further research by Victor Howard, Matthew Pinsker, and William F. Moore indicates instead that these radicals understood the need to postpone the autumn statewide convention idea while public opinion caught up, and to focus for the time being on other organizing strategies.[75] They scheduled two large regional conventions, in Chicago and Galena, and sponsored a lengthy downstate tour by Codding and Ohio's Giddings, who urged all to forget their animosities and unite as Republicans. In other words, they proceeded with their strategy for political fusion.

During this time the ad hoc Central Committee developed a two-part plan for February 1856. They were hunting for a way to bring southern Illinois conservatives and northern Illinois progressives together. Lovejoy developed the metaphor, calling it a "two-bobsled" tactic, referring to a method used to pull large logs over uneven terrain.[76] One "bobsled," composed of the more radical northern Republican leaders, would attend the national planning meeting in Pittsburgh on February 22, with Lovejoy as the head of their delegation. The meeting's purpose was to prepare for the first National Republican Nominating Convention, to be held in Philadelphia in June. The other "bobsled"—a meeting convened by Paul Selby, a moderate anti-Nebraska editor of Jacksonville in central Illinois—would bring together radical *Chicago Tribune* editor Charles Ray with Abraham Lincoln and his more conservative central-southern Illinois network at a meeting of newspaper editors in Decatur on February 22.[77] There, they would plan an anti-Nebraska convention to be held in Bloomington in May to bring both parts of the state together and nominate candidates for statewide offices. It was an impressive plan, for both bases would hold their meetings on the same day—the birthday of the greatly revered president George Washington. Regardless of which faction initiated the approach, the leaders of both northern and southern factions were cooperating in arranging for two simultaneous meetings on February 22. Biographer Edward Magdol was aware of the letter that discussed this two-bobsled plan but did not see that it directly connected Codding and Lovejoy with the Bloomington Convention outcome. According to Selby, who convened the Decatur meeting, the symmetry of the two meetings was not a coincidence.[78]

Charles Ray left Chicago by train early on February 22 with George Schneider, editor of the *Illinois Staats-Zeitung*, who represented antislavery German Americans in the Chicago area. Snowdrifts on the tracks, caused by a heavy snowstorm, did not stop the train, and the two editors spent the trip drafting the platform for the Decatur meeting.[79] At the Decatur hotel they met Selby.[80] Despite the storm, eleven editors came. Some were from central Illinois—Decatur, Jacksonville, Quincy, and Peoria, for example. Many others, contrary to the usual narrative that only central and southern men attended, traveled from northern towns such as Chicago, Princeton, Lacon, Dixon, Rock Island, and Rockford.[81] Lincoln was the only lawyer at the meeting.[82]

Selby was chosen chairman and Ray was put in charge of resolutions. The group wanted to see the 1820 Missouri Compromise restored, with the guarantee that states in the Nebraska territory, such as Kansas, would be kept free from slavery.[83] They called for a "State Delegates' Convention to Nominate Candidates for State Offices" to be held in Bloomington on May 29.[84] The editors purposely sidestepped the divisive name Republican and selected moderate positions. It had been agreed beforehand in Chicago that candidates for state offices would not come from the northern, radical antislavery early Republicans for fear that they would frighten off the moderate southern Illinois conservative office seekers they hoped to attract.[85]

At the same time, Lovejoy led the Illinois radical delegation to the Republican convention in Pittsburgh. Delegates included Codding, Kelsey, and Bryant, Medill and Vaughan from the *Chicago Tribune,* and others, like state senator Wait Talcott of Rockford, who attended out of religious conviction. Joshua Giddings and James Mitchell Ashley of Ohio and George W. Julian of Indiana greeted them. All were determined to solidify their state societies into a national Republican Party; the Pittsburgh event was an intermediary step.[86]

As soon as Lovejoy arrived in Pittsburgh on February 21, he was hustled into a small emergency meeting to approve Francis P. Blair as chairman. Lewis Tappan said it was unconscionable to select a slaveholder as the chairman of a political party pledged to restrict slavery from the territories, but Gamaliel Bailey had carefully picked Blair as a way of attracting Democrats.[87] Since so many delegates were clergymen and evangelical laymen, it seemed natural for the program to begin with "The Rev. Owen Lovejoy addressing the Throne of Grace." Lovejoy delivered a pointed prayer. He asked God to enlighten the president's mind, and "if this was not possible, to take him away, so that an honest and God-fearing man might fill his place."[88] The delegates, who considered President Franklin Pierce immoral, unresponsive, and a betrayer of Northern values, reacted with an audible murmur of pleasure at the thought of him being voted out of office through God's influence. Later, Lovejoy gave an address in which he declared the existence of "a Divine Power ruling over all things" and "a higher law than that created by demagogues." God had not designed this nation for slavery, he professed, but designed it instead to demonstrate the divine truth that all men were equal and that the miniature God within all persons must not be crushed.[89]

Frederick Douglass decided not to attend the Pittsburgh or Philadelphia Republican conventions, as the platforms focused only on preventing the extension of slavery into the territories. It did not condemn the Fugitive Slave Act, call for slavery to be eradicated in the District of Columbia, or demand equal rights for blacks in the North. In his view, this new party was not an advance but a retreat. Instead, Douglass participated in Gerrit Smith's Radical Abolition Party convention, with its "unprecedented moment of interracial unity and collapsing of racial barriers."[90] Yet Douglass and Lovejoy continued their friendship, as both were deeply religious and incisively political, and both had committed their lives to the eradication of slavery.[91] However, they played separate political roles at that time: Douglass kept his followers' gaze on the unadulterated goal while Lovejoy worked to broaden the base for intermediary objectives, moving step by step toward what he hoped would be the political takeover of Congress and the White House.

On April 16 the Decatur editors' group agreed to announce the fusion convention to be held in Bloomington on May 29. As the day of the conference came closer, the ad hoc Central Committee sensed that anti-Nebraska conservatives in the southern part of the state were still afraid that radical northern Republicans would take over the convention and capture the nominations for state offices. To quell southern fears, Charles Ray put an important notice in his *Chicago Tribune* on May 17, promising once again that Republicans would not seek statewide offices: "The Republicans of the North wish to testify their sincerity by taking the places of privates in the ranks."[92] The early Republicans promised to be foot soldiers and to help moderates and conservatives win the state offices. In return, it was hoped that early Republicans would be supported in their 1856 campaigns for seats in the U.S. Congress.

Early Republicans in Bloomington and Philadelphia

Despite violent events in Kansas and Washington that were shocking the nation, the atmosphere inside the Bloomington Convention was enthusiastic that May, and delegates had high expectations. Lovejoy was in his element, buttonholing delegates in the huge crowd outside the hotel and exuding charm. His young antislavery friend Joseph O. Cunningham, the editor of the Urbana newspaper, described him thus: "The athletic personality of Owen Lovejoy" was seen "making love to the abolitionist haters of the center and south."[93] The gregarious pastor greeted every delegate in sight. Those who met him for the first time saw a solidly built man with a healthy complexion and thick black hair. He had a thin, wide mouth that could purse up into a silent admonishment or bloom into the happiest of smiles. A key conservative man from southern Illinois, Jesse Dubois, had been skeptical about coming to the convention, for he had heard reports that Lovejoy was a fanatical abolitionist. When he spied him in Bloomington for the first time, he left the scene. Later on, however, he was persuaded to return to the square.

There were 270 white delegates. At the last minute, word passed that Paul Selby had been assaulted by a proslavery gang and would not be able to come. When Orville Browning, the leading Whig in Illinois, arrived in Bloomington on May 28 on the 4:00 p.m. train, he found himself taking over Selby's responsibilities. Browning was a Henry Clay devotee—he was not against slavery, only against its extension. He quickly made out the next day's speaking schedule. Fifteen to twenty of the leading men of all shades of opinion would be allowed to speak.[94]

Outside the hotel on that warm spring evening, a number of men gave spontaneous speeches, including Owen Lovejoy, Democrat John M. Palmer, and "Long John" Wentworth, the popular six-foot, six-inch former Democratic congressman from Chicago.[95] Finally, six-foot, four-inch Abraham Lincoln had his turn.

The convention opened on May 27, and Palmer was elected its president.[96] The body supported the slate of candidates that had been put together at Decatur. It included Whigs, anti-Nebraska Democrats, German Americans, and Know-Nothing men but, as promised, no early Republicans. Palmer kept most committee positions in conservative anti-Nebraska hands, and an official statewide Central Committee was appointed. The convention also unanimously passed a resolution against the extension of slavery.[97]

Lovejoy was the next-to-last speaker. Although no reporters wrote down exactly what he said, they remembered one part well: he vigorously stated that he would never propose any political action by Congress that would interfere with slavery in the states where it now existed; his focus was on prohibiting the extension of slavery into the territories. Conservatives, who had expected him to speak like a Garrisonian abolitionist, were surprised. They praised his moderation and assumed that he had changed, when in fact he was restating a position he had held for over a decade. When he finished, the mixed crowd of Fusionists rose to their feet and shouted a passionate approval for Lovejoy. Journalist and historian Charles A. Church later wrote that this was "the occasion when Lovejoy gained stature statewide."[98]

Abraham Lincoln had not been scheduled to speak. On the main floor very few official delegates were antislavery, but up in the gallery there were many antislavery nondelegates who now called loudly for Lincoln to address the convention. When Lincoln's speech was over, many in the audience said, "It surpassed all others—even himself. His points were unanswerable, and the force and power of his appeals, irresistible—and were received with a storm of applause." Although the reporters were apparently too "spell bound by the power of his arguent, the intense irony of his invective and the deep earnestness and fervid brilliancy of his eloquence" to write a verbatim account of Lincoln's oration, they remembered the "glory" of it for years afterward.[99] From then on, they considered Lincoln the leader of the anti-Nebraska movement in Illinois.

During the business meeting that followed, John Wentworth of Chicago introduced a resolution to appoint delegates to the National Republican Nominating Convention in Philadelphia, convening in June. Both Lincoln and Lovejoy were among the delegates elected, although Lincoln did not attend because he was still afraid that he might be identified with more radical positions than he was prepared to take on at that time.[100] Again, Lincoln's refusal has been interpreted by Democrats and historians as an indication that the early Republican organization was dead or dying. William E. Gienapp wrote, "Lincoln's decline [to join the Republicans in 1854] symbolized the failure of the fusion movement . . . that doomed it to ineffectiveness."[101] Actually, the radical abolitionists' strategy succeeded: fusion took place, Lincoln's and Lovejoy's reputations were enhanced, and all the radicals in the balcony were primed to campaign hard in the 1856 election.

In June, when Lovejoy got to Chicago, he wrote an apologetic letter to his mother, Betsey, who was eighty-three and ailing. She had always followed presidential politics closely and coveted knowing every detail. He reassured her, "I think the cause of Freedom shall triumph next Fall."[102]

The Republican Nominating Convention in Philadelphia opened on June 16. The leading candidate for president was John Frémont, a popular explorer of the western frontier and a military hero whose positions on slavery were unknown and who would not offend moderates. The Illinois delegation at Philadelphia was more conservative than the group that went to Pittsburgh. Accompanying Lovejoy were antislavery newspaperman George Schneider, moderate congressmen Jesse O. Norton, and Cyrus Aldrich of Dixon in Lovejoy's district. But they were counterbalanced by conservatives General W. H. L. Wallace, John Palmer, and Norman Judd, who all limited their commitment to keeping slavery out of the territories.[103] On the floor of the convention Lovejoy carefully moved the assembly to include a reference to the Declaration of Independence, with its unequivocal pledge of equality, as the foundational document of the party.[104]

Abolitionist Albert Barnes, a minister who had sponsored Elijah Lovejoy's licensing ceremony in 1833 and had been tried for heresy by Old School Presbyterians in 1836, gave the opening prayer. He was now a national Republican leader. Seventy antislavery clergy delegates attended the convention. One spectator likened it to a sober Methodist conference, "oozing order and decorum" with earnestness and determination, in stark contrast to "raucous boozy" Democratic conventions.[105] However, historian Richard J. Carwardine cautions that the political force in the Republican Party was "the product of impressive political calculation and not a spontaneous creation of evangelical fervor." It was the product of "managers, discipline, and professional politicians as much as ideological enthusiasts."[106] Radical ministers like Owen Lovejoy and churchmen like Joshua Giddings worked to ensure that the party's platform remained true to "God's revealed Word" and to Jeffersonian imperatives on equal rights.[107] Some sectarian ministers could be divisive, Carwardine acknowledges, but Lovejoy seemed able to bring factions together into a coherent force with the "rag-tag and bob-tail gang" of anti-Nebraskans in Illinois.[108] Ten years earlier, Lovejoy had fretted over recalcitrant eastern churches, hoping they would join the political antislavery struggle. Finding so many ministers in Philadelphia indicated to him that a lot of eastern clergy had broken their silence and now joined the political abolitionist route to slavery's eradication.[109]

Lovejoy Campaigns and Prepares for Congress

Lovejoy returned home from Philadelphia ready to campaign for himself and for the Republican Party and its presidential candidate, John Frémont. But on July 2, when he went to Ottawa to the convention of the state's Third Congressional

District—which had at the time the largest constituency of any district in the United States[110]—to win the nomination for his own seat in Congress, he faced formidable and unexpected opposition from bolters, or party members who did not support the party's nominee.[111] The bolting clique was dominated by devotees of Henry Clay who advocated a position of nonextension while still owning slaves themselves. As Whigs, Clay's admirers in central Illinois favored policies of internal improvement but ignored African Americans' predicament. Their leaders traveled the Eighth Judicial Circuit with Abraham Lincoln of Springfield, Judge David Davis of Bloomington, and attorney and former judge T. Lyle Dickey. Among them was lawyer Leonard Swett. Many Whigs considered Lovejoy a fanatical abolitionist and wanted to see Swett in Congress, and Swett expected to obtain the nomination. Yet after two tallies at the separate bolters' meeting, Swett lost and Lovejoy won.[112]

Republicans in Princeton planned a big rally for July 4. Lovejoy, their district candidate for Congress, was the major speaker. Little-known Lincoln and others were also invited to address the Independence Day rally in Princeton. The huge turnout of eight to ten thousand demonstrated Lovejoy's popularity with the voters and won over Lincoln's tepid support of Lovejoy. Lincoln informed two of his Whig colleagues, young Henry Whitney and Judge Davis, that he grudgingly accepted Lovejoy's nomination. But Judge Dickey was still not willing to accept Lovejoy's nomination and arranged to hold a bolters' convention in Bloomington on July 16 at the Court House Square. The bolters labeled Lovejoy a Garrisonian abolitionist who disregarded the sacred property rights of slaveholders and an "immediatist" who would interfere with slavery in the South and disregard the U.S. Constitution.[113] They expected that once they spread such negative disinformation about Lovejoy, his influence would diminish.[114]

But Quaker Jesse Fell, publisher of the Bloomington *Pantagraph* and a founder of Illinois State College, learned of the planned meeting. The antislavery Fell and his wife, Hester Vernon Fell, had assisted runaway slaves along the Mackinaw River for years. Fell let Lovejoy know that the bolters intended to take the nomination away from him. Lovejoy, realizing that he had to confront the dissidents face-to-face, came to the gathering and stood unnoticed at the back of the crowd. Many of the things speakers said about him were provocative and fabricated. One man called him a "nigger thief" and another suggested hanging him. The group proceeded to nominate Dickey, who enthusiastically accepted.

Initially Lovejoy's presence was "wholly unsuspected" by the crowd, but after Dickey accepted the nomination, someone recognized Lovejoy in the crowd and asked him to speak. This was the first moment that the crowd realized Lovejoy was present. Most did not know him personally but knew him only by his reputation as a "prominent abolitionist." Lovejoy tried to control his feelings. A *Pantagraph* reporter frantically scribbled, "It took considerable effort to overcome evident embarrassment. His voice shaking with emotion, he confessed that he had no heart for 'this personal contest.'" However, his daring appearance "secured him breathless attention."[115]

In response to the accusation that he was a "nigger thief," Lovejoy told the audience what an abolitionist really was. "I am accused of aiding fugitive slaves. I do not know that I ever gave aid to a slave. My Bible tells me to feed the hungry and clothe the naked, and I have done so to the best of my ability without reference to whether the applicants were bond or free, white or black, or some other shade of color." In other words, he did not stop to investigate whether a person was a slave or free before relieving his or her needs; "It is enough for me to know that he or she is a fellow creature in need of food, clothing, or shelter."[116]

Lovejoy's speech ended the bolting rally.[117] The *Pantagraph* reporter wrote that Lovejoy had "so entranced the audience with his logic, wit and eloquence, and the pathos of his pleas, [and] moved the men of Bloomington, that they were then quite as ready to mob his enemies as they had been anxious to defeat him a few minutes before."[118]

Owen Lovejoy spent the summer campaigning for presidential candidate John Frémont and for himself. His rallies drew great crowds of five thousand to thirty thousand. White and black women and men prepared huge amounts of food, and brass bands led processions of youthful white men and women. Democratic newspapers described Lovejoy's campaign rhetoric as "freedom shrieking," but the *Pantagraph* endorsed him.[119] Fell declared that the charges made against Lovejoy were untrue: "Almost all the crimes of the Decalogue, and a legion of others which the Decalogue makes no mention, have been laid to [Lovejoy's] charge." Echoing William T. Allan, Fell depicted Lovejoy as a man "whose teeth won't chatter, whose knees won't smite together every time some lordly slave breeder threatens to dissolve the Union."[120] Fell had assessed correctly that Lovejoy could not be intimidated. At the humiliating bolting rally, he had proven his character.

African American William Wells Brown, whom Elijah Lovejoy had once hired as a slave boy to run errands for the *St. Louis Observer* and who was now an antislavery lecturer and author in New England, accurately described the challenge Lovejoy would face in the U.S. House of Representatives.[121] An antislavery man in Congress would have to face the Southern congressman: "the bully, the duelist, the woman-scourger, the gambler, the murderer." It would be like "taking your little son from the country and sending him to the city, where he finds a thousand rude boys who insult and abuse him. Men in the South who are accustomed to flog old men and young women, and to sell children from their mother's breast, are more than a match for your Northern men."[122]

Lovejoy won his seat in Congress by 6,069 votes, which was 59.42 percent of the total.[123] In addition to Lovejoy, two other northern Illinois Republicans he knew well were elected: Elihu Washburne of Galena and John Farnsworth of St. Charles. Conservative Republican William P. Kellogg of Canton in west-central Illinois was also elected. On December 10, 1856, these Republicans celebrated their victory in Chicago at the Tremont House,[124] but when the Thirty-Fifth Congress opened in December 1857, Republicans would still lack a majority.[125]

Nationally, Frémont received 114 electoral votes and 1,341,264 popular votes, but James Buchanan received 174 electoral votes and 1,838,169 popular votes.[126] John Jones saw nothing good coming from a Buchanan White House or from the Illinois General Assembly, where Democrats would once again be in power. But with his connections in Alton, he put together the Second Illinois State Convention of Colored Citizens. It was held at the Colored Baptist Church in conservative Alton on November 13–15, 1856. Their purpose remained the same as the previous convention's: repeal the Black Laws. Blacks were restricted: lacking the right to vote, denied the right to testify against a white man, and forced to pay school taxes while unable to send their children to public schools.

In 1856 blacks in and around Alton still saw their situation differently from blacks from Chicago. Living among the remnants of slavery in Alton, they doubted that the state's General Assembly would ever vote for public integrated schools and concluded that they had to accept segregated public schools, while blacks from Chicago demanded integrated public schools. Some Alton blacks were so discouraged by white intransigency that they did not discount colonization, while those in Chicago continued to demand full citizenship. Despite these differences in opinions and circumstances, delegates made a long-term commitment to create a Repeal Association and raise one thousand dollars to make it operational: to collect statistics on blacks in Illinois, hire agents to traverse the state, hold township and county conventions, and gather petitions to repeal the Black Laws.[127] The November black convention also elected a state Central Committee.[128]

In Washington, D.C., southern congressmen were furious that the presidential race had been so close. Democrats blamed Protestant clergy for Frémont's relatively strong showing. President Franklin Pierce called it a perverted and desecrated pulpit and said that the preachers were fiercely and fanatically against him.[129] Democrats complained that clergymen stood at the polls all day trying to influence voters. It was true that Rev. Henry Ward Beecher stumped in Brooklyn for the Republican ticket and Charles G. Finney led daily prayer meetings in Oberlin the week before the election.[130] However, looking back at the historical evidence, clergy power may have been overstated, for evangelical voters did not constitute a voting bloc.

Carwardine reminds the reader that Republicans and Democrats both won votes from all Protestant groups.[131]

Lovejoy, elected in November 1856, would not go to Washington until December 1857, giving him a year to prepare himself for Congress. In December 1856, the economy in the West suffered from inflation caused by land and commodity speculation, and then in 1857 it fell into a deep depression. Lovejoy worried about the financial situation of his large family, now totaling nine children. He wrote Gerrit Smith and asked him for a loan of up to five thousand dollars. On Christmas Eve, Smith put a draft in the mail, which Owen received in Princeton on January 20, 1857.[132] Smith urged Lovejoy to obtain a law license, which he gained in the spring from John D. Caton, now the chief judge of the Illinois Supreme Court.

That year, Lovejoy performed two sad family funerals. His mother, Betsey, died on April 23 and his older sister, Sibyl, on November 11.

Although Lovejoy remained at home, he began to follow the news from Washington very carefully as the Second Session of the Thirty-Fourth Congress opened on December 1, 1856. Both major parties seemed to be uncomfortable. President Pierce, ill at ease and ineffective, would remain in the White House until March 1857. In that atmosphere several shocking events took place. First, a leading Ohio Republican, John Sherman, snubbed a man of his own party. To demonstrate leadership, first-term representative Sherman felt he needed to reposition the Republican Party. On December 8, 1856, Sherman repudiated the positions taken by Joshua Giddings, the House's venerable religious abolitionist spokesman.[133] He denied that Republicans in the House were working to repeal the Fugitive Slave Law or to abolish slavery in the District of Columbia and urged the House not to take Giddings seriously. Reading Sherman's speech in Illinois, Owen Lovejoy realized that Giddings, an outstanding antislavery congressman and Lovejoy's mentor and personal friend, had been humiliated by someone from his own party. By implication, Lovejoy perceived that his own potential steps toward equality were being rebuffed.

The second tremor to reach Princeton came from Southern Democrats demanding to reopen the Atlantic slave trade. Such a resolution was introduced on the floor of the U.S. House of Representatives. Old-time Northern congressmen grumbled that they had voted to make slave trading illegal in 1807 and asked why it was being discussed in 1857. Then, to their amazement, when the vote was taken, fifty-seven slaveholder congressmen—a minority, but an alarming number nevertheless—voted to reopen the slave trade. This brazen reversal appeared to be gaining popularity.[134] Its most vigorous advocates were secessionists who wanted to split the nation in two and form a confederacy of the South.

Lovejoy's third shock was perpetrated by the U.S. Supreme Court. A few days before James Buchanan was inaugurated as the fifteenth president on March 4, 1857, the Court announced the *Dred Scott* decision. Chief Justice Roger B. Taney himself wrote the decision that slaves remained property whether or not they were taken into free states. Seven of the nine justices agreed,[135] bringing the slavocracy to the pinnacle of its power prior to the Civil War. The decision dragged to a new low the morale of African American Illinois residents.

The state's coalition for equality disagreed with every part of the *Dred Scott* decision, believing that it had the effect of overturning the Bible, the Declaration of Independence, and the Constitution all at once. It essentially declared that blacks were less than human, had no souls, and could never be equal.[136] It also declared that the Republican platform's central plank, prohibiting slavery in the territories, was unconstitutional.[137] Radical black and white northerners erupted in anger, disbelief, and sorrow. Still reeling from Illinois's 1848 Constitution and Black Exclusion Act, the Compromise of 1850, and the 1854 Kansas-Nebraska Act, they had received another assault on their principles. The *Dred Scott* decision permitted slaveholders to bring their slaves and reside in free Northern states or the territories at their own pleasure, thus affecting every American and every institution.

As soon as the decision was made public, President Buchanan made the momentous announcement that slavery now existed in all the territories, by virtue of the Constitution.[138] Henry Highland Garnet was outraged and chagrined by the decision.[139] Frederick Douglass wrote that Judge Taney could not reverse the decision of the Most High. Nor could he make evil good and good evil. Then, with tongue firmly in cheek, he advised, "Look at it in a cheerful spirit."[140]

As Lovejoy's November 1857 departure for Washington, D.C., came closer, Hampshire Colony Church prepared a festive farewell. The congregation passed a resolution praising Reverend Lovejoy's accomplishments in the pulpit as well as in "the philanthropic and reformatory movements of the day."[141] "Owen Lovejoy loved people," the church committee said, and they insisted that they were not saying so just to be polite. The congregation genuinely believed that Lovejoy was a great preacher, a great pastor, and a great friend. The church's historian wrote that for seventeen years Lovejoy had swayed the hearts and minds of the church and the community. Then he listened to the larger call of the nation, and Congress heard the voice that always rang true to freedom and righteousness.[142]

• • •

The coalition for equality helped elect Lovejoy and twenty-five other Republican representatives to the Illinois General Assembly in 1854. African Americans became an aggressive presence there as spectators and petitioners. The passage of

Lovejoy's resolution before the Nineteenth General Assembly in 1855, instructing Illinois congressmen to vote against any extension of slavery into the territories, was a major victory for the early Republicans and became the organizing principle of the Republican Party. While Lovejoy and other early Republicans prevented the state from funding colonization, they failed to modify any Black Laws or obtain public education for black children. They identified a two-pronged basis for anti-Nebraska fusion—nonextension of slavery into the territories and noninterference with slavery where it already existed. However, African Americans felt left out of the national Republican platform. They held their own state convention in Alton and established a politically oriented Repeal Association focused on the state's Black Laws. Changes took place within the coalition as Codding and Eastman left and the *Chicago Tribune* became the statewide Republican newspaper. In 1856, four Illinois Republicans, including Lovejoy, won national congressional seats. Abraham Lincoln continued as the state leader of the anti-Nebraska movement. In late November 1857, Lovejoy left for Washington, but the intransigence of the General Assembly, volatility in Kansas, and the Dred Scott decision cast a cloud over the coalition in Illinois. Of the many antislavery clergy in Illinois, the one that the clergy wanted to represent them in Congress was Owen Lovejoy.

6. Confronting the Slave Power
and Unifying Illinois Republicans

November 1857–November 1859

In late 1857 African American colleagues of Lovejoy heard frequent stories of racial murder in Illinois. One Negro had been beheaded; two had been buried alive.[1] They reminded Lovejoy of the deep seriousness of his purpose as he packed to go to Washington. Activists who had worked with him in the coalition for almost two decades sent him off to Congress with their hopes for some lessening of the daily tragedies blacks faced.

The major issue before Congress was whether to admit Kansas into the nation as a slave state. Rumors spread that on October 22, in Chicago, Democratic senator Stephen A. Douglas had met with staunch New York Republican William Henry Seward, hoping to garner Republican support for his upcoming political ambitions. In a surprise move, Douglas proposed to reject the Lecompton Constitution, written by Kansan slaveholders in support of Kansas statehood, and in this way fit in with the Republican position of a free Kansas.[2] He hoped that doing so would soften his position on popular sovereignty as not being explicitly proslavery and in this way gain some Republican friends.[3] Soon after the meeting, Douglas left Chicago to prepare for the opening session of Congress. First-termer Lovejoy would have to maneuver carefully between these two Senate giants.

At the end of November, Lovejoy and another Illinois freshman member of Congress, conservative Republican William P. Kellogg from Canton, traveled together by train to eastern Ohio. At the Relay House, where two railroads joined, they met Representative Joshua Giddings and Senator Ben Wade, who had come south from Ohio's Western Reserve. Both men had grown up and practiced law in Jefferson, the county seat of Ashtabula County. Giddings had suffered a stroke in January but felt strong enough to return to Washington. Lovejoy was relieved that Giddings was able to travel. At Wheeling, West Virginia, they met U.S. Supreme Court justice

John McLean from Cincinnati, who had, a few months earlier, written a moderate dissenting opinion to Taney's *Dred Scott* decision.[4] Conversation kept the men awake on much of the long trip.

Either on the way to Washington or a few days later, Lovejoy made a special trip to New York City to keep a special unrecorded appointment with New York's governor, William Seward. With unexpected hospitality, Seward showed him around the city.[5]

In Washington, Giddings must have taken Lovejoy to the Republican caucus. The three Washburn brothers were there. Lovejoy knew Elihu Washburne well and soon engaged in banter with his brothers Israel, from Maine, and Cadwallader, from Wisconsin.[6] The brothers, all antislavery Republican congressmen, were living together. They hired a black cook, chambermaid, and butler, and their wives would join them during the social season.[7]

Lovejoy entered the chamber of the U.S. House of Representatives for the opening session of the Thirty-Fifth Congress on December 7, 1857. As a result of the 1856 election, Democrats had regained a total of 131 seats. Republicans had 92 seats (having lost 16 of the seats they had won in the 1854 election), and there were 14 "others."[8] The first order of business was the election of the Speaker of the House. Lovejoy was assigned to the lackluster Revolutionary Claims Committee.[9] However, Israel Washburn was asked to continue as chairman of the Committee on Elections, an assignment that would soon prove to be of great value to the antislavery bloc.[10] Lovejoy had no secretary. On one day he wrote twenty letters to his "dear constituents."[11]

Taking Leadership in the House of Representatives

Lovejoy quickly realized, as he and the other incoming representatives socialized in the House chambers, that Giddings was no longer the outstanding antislavery spokesman he had been for years. Second-term congressman John Sherman of Ohio was leading the Republicans.[12] Lovejoy knew that the custom was for freshmen members of Congress to be seen and not heard, but he intended to challenge slavery soon.[13]

He renewed his acquaintances with colleagues he had met at the Pittsburgh and Philadelphia conventions. He greeted Edward Wade, with whom he had stayed overnight in Cleveland. He was welcomed by John Armor Bingham, a man with a sharp legal mind, from Cadiz and New Philadelphia, Ohio, and by Amherst College alumnus Galusha Grow of Pennsylvania, who was a veteran of the House, having been first elected in 1850.[14] Justin Smith Morrill, a merchant and horticulturalist from Vermont, was starting his second term.[15] John Fox Potter, born in Augusta,

Maine, had been elected as a representative from Wisconsin.[16] All of these acquaintances were vigorous and ambitious antislavery men.

Harper's Weekly reported that Lovejoy "at once took a commanding position" in the House of Representatives.[17] Friends claimed that he stood out among the class of entering freshmen because of his powerful frame, strong feelings, and great personal magnetism.[18] Although opponents called Lovejoy an agitator, neutral observers said that he did not look like one but had "a kind and intellectual face."[19]

As January began, President Buchanan ignored Stephen A. Douglas's recommendation and endorsed the proslavery Kansas state constitution that had been adopted at a convention in Lecompton, Kansas. On January 7, Committee on Elections chairman Israel Washburn of Maine reported that fifteen of Kansas's thirty-four counties were not represented at the Lecompton convention and that "fraud after fraud" had taken place. Lovejoy confided, "I do not believe that the Administration ever intended that Kansas should be a free state."[20] The Senate approved the constitution, but the House rejected it and laboriously developed a compromise, called the English Bill, which eventually required Kansans to start the process toward statehood over again.[21]

Southern congressmen soon attacked Lovejoy as a formidable enemy of slavery, and Lovejoy was ready to spar with them. Editor J. G. Hewitt of the new *Bureau County Republican*, hired by John Howard Bryant to keep Lovejoy's district informed, described some congressional skirmishes in the newspaper's first issue on January 14, 1858. Hewitt relayed to the folks back home "a hot exchange of words over fugitive slaves" that took place between Lovejoy, the Washburn brothers, and earnest radical Galusha Grow of Pennsylvania versus volatile Lawrence M. Keitt and John McQueen of South Carolina and William Barksdale, Reuben Davis, and Lucius Q. C. Lamar of Mississippi.[22] On January 25, after a disagreement, Georgia congressman Lucius Gartrell parried, "I will ask the gentleman a question and I hope he will answer it categorically. Does the gentleman consider the African equal to the white man?" Lovejoy answered blithely, "That depends altogether upon his character, sir," a response that provoked laughter from other House members.[23]

Lovejoy intended to expand his Illinois coalition for equality by making friends with black and white churchwomen and men in the Washington, D.C., area. Sundays offered him good opportunities. Most of the white churches in Washington projected a Southern mentality and preached proslavery sermons. However, there were a dozen African American congregations in the District of Columbia, and Lovejoy felt at home in the worship services of these churches. Carl Sandburg's researcher, Katherine Turner, reported that Lovejoy had "the habit of attendance" at a black church.[24] Other antislavery men such as Joshua Leavitt and Theodore Weld had worshipped in black churches previously.[25]

Lovejoy also attended Lewis Tappan's struggling interracial antislavery Congregational church in Washington. The small congregation included several young black students and black and white teachers whose illegal schools were sponsored by Northern churches and regularly accosted by local police for breaking the law by instructing African Americans.[26] Among the worshippers were Giddings and Senator Charles Durkee of Wisconsin. Lovejoy made contributions to these schools. Defying local racial and class mores, several blacks invited whites for visits to their homes, and a few whites invited blacks to theirs.[27]

The Reverend George W. Bassett had been called in 1858 to be this antislavery church's minister. In a sermon Bassett declared that "God Almighty is for the negro"[28]—an astounding statement in the slaveholding city. Gamaliel Bailey, editor of the *National Era* and leading member of the laity, came to the unwelcome conclusion that Bassett was too close to radical political abolitionists to attract new church members in such a racially polarized city.[29] Josiah Grinnell had been banished in 1854, and Bassett would depart in 1860.

Congregationalists were not alone in their inability to stabilize a Washington interracial church. The Unitarian Church in the city hired twenty-four-year-old antislavery Moncure Conway in 1854, but after he stated in a July 6, 1856, sermon that he "refused to submit any longer to the grasping demands of slavery," he was dismissed as pastor of the Washington Unitarian church.[30]

Lovejoy eagerly awaited his wife's arrival in Washington. He sent Eunice a lighthearted letter addressed to her cousin's home in Braintree, Massachusetts: "I guess you had better come round this way and make me a visit on your way home and then you can take your plants and roots home with you . . . sweet potato bulbs."[31] He maintained a good relationship with her host, Richard Salter Storrs, despite their differences on slavery: "You will, I judge, be at Braintree when this reaches you. I have had a letter from Dr. Storrs saying he had received speeches and such and had a very charming visit from my lovely daughter and now he enjoys one from my lovely wife, his 'dear cousin,' as he calls her." Eunice stayed in Washington for several weeks, met her husband's colleagues at social gatherings, and saw the unfinished capitol dome, art galleries, museums, and specialty houses in their wintery garb of snow, slush, and mud.

On February 17, 1858, Lovejoy had been in Congress little more than two months when he delivered a major address titled "Human Beings not Property."[32] He let everyone know his intentions by directly confronting the conflict in the nation—the conflict between freedom and slavery.[33] He challenged the men of the South to become "true heroic men" and foreswear allegiance to slavery now.[34] Then he attacked the dogma of slaveocracy. "The chief deceit of slavers," he told them, was "the notion that a human being can be reduced to a thing." Building on that falsehood, slavers had formulated a deviant religious creed and constructed an inhumane legal and political structure based on violence to enforce it. This greed should stop, he demanded. In contrast, he described the "God man" who lay down his life to "expiate the sins of man." "Did Christ shed his blood for cattle?" he asked the House. "No; Christ shed his blood for all people, black and white." Then he declared, "Every human being stands on the broad level of equality."[35] Slavery was, he said, contrary to the Christian message, the Golden Rule, and all Ten Commandments.

Next, Lovejoy analyzed the U.S. Constitution: "In no article, in no section, in no line, no word or syllable, or letter, is the idea of property in man expressed or implied."[36] Lovejoy offered an alternative way of governing—"not by slavery and not by the rule of kings but by a new theory of government."[37] It is called democracy, he explained, and "America is the theater where this great experiment is taking place." "It does not say all English men are born equal, or all French men, or all Scotch men, or all Dutch men, or all white men, or all tawny men, or all black men, but ALL MEN."[38]

Lovejoy had gone straight to the core of the slaveholder's interpretation of the U.S. Constitution when he said, "And all this upon the false, atrocious and impious argument that human beings are property. . . . The Supreme Being never intended that human beings should be property." He told the men from the South that though the U.S. Constitution gave them the right to pass local laws that reduced humans to property, it did not give them the authority to mandate them nationally. Lovejoy's speech was widely distributed at the time and remains his most frequently reprinted speech today.[39]

Lewis Tappan of the American Missionary Association had hoped Lovejoy's first major speech would attack Buchanan's policy on Kansas. But Lovejoy suspected that slaveholding congressmen had never heard a basic antislavery speech. They had been fed so much disinformation that one must begin at the beginning.[40] In the North, liberty was defined by laws formulated by the broader community and rooted in egalitarian principles of faith, but in the South a small hegemony of elitists, reinforced by hierarchical views injected into their religion, dominated everything.[41]

As Lovejoy plunged into work for his constituents, he discovered how federal government departments routinely denied basic civil rights to free blacks. When Lovejoy requested a passport from the secretary of state, Lewis Cass, Cass refused because the applicant, a free black man, was not an American citizen.[42] When Lovejoy queried the secretary of the Treasury, Howell Cobb, about the procedures by which an African American could preempt a quarter section of the public land, Cobb replied that they were not allowed to buy public land. He added that a black man was not allowed to command an American merchant vessel, even one he owned.[43]

Lovejoy heard how Southern extremists had taken control of the Southern Commercial Convention and blindly asserted that the South had enough industrial and commercial resources to exist as a separate, viable confederacy, more than equal to the North in strength.[44] These Fire-Eaters wanted to secede.[45] On March 11, 1858, the legislature of the State of Louisiana voted to reopen the Atlantic slave trade, despite the fact that it was illegal for a state to take such action.[46]

Lovejoy Seeks Reelection and Lincoln Fights for a U.S. Senate Seat

Although Lovejoy had been in Congress for only six months, it was necessary for him to campaign for his second term during the summer of 1858. Judge T. Lyle Dickey was trying for the second time to unseat Lovejoy, but a group of Quakers informed Lincoln about the plot and Lincoln immediately informed Lovejoy.[47] Lovejoy quickly wrote to Jesse Fell in Bloomington and asked for his endorsement in the *Pantagraph* again. When it was settled that Lovejoy had been renominated, Judge David Davis acknowledged that the abolition element was entirely in the ascendancy. The intended takeover had failed before Lovejoy even returned to Illinois.[48]

It had been Lovejoy's hope that Abraham Lincoln would someday head the Republican ticket in Illinois. It was about to happen on June 16, 1858, when Lincoln presented his "House Divided" speech and the state Republican convention officially nominated him as its candidate for the U.S. Senate. Included in that speech was the observation that the cause of solving the conflict over slavery must be entrusted to and conducted by those "whose hearts were in the matter and care about the results."[49] With those words, Lincoln showed his growing appreciation of Lovejoy's antislavery coalition, but he disappointed a few powerful conservative friends.[50]

Lincoln's unwieldy Illinois fusion consisted of white conservatives, Nativists, German immigrants, educated Whigs, upwardly mobile Democrats, and antislavery Republicans, including a few Garrisonian abolitionists. This was the ragtag alliance Lovejoy foresaw in 1854 when he said that Lincoln was the only man who could keep them all together.[51] These disparate subgroups of the party all agreed on one thing: slavery must not be allowed to go into the territories. The purpose of Lincoln's fall campaign was to get enough Republican state legislators elected who would vote for him to go to the U.S. Senate. In support of this purpose, Lovejoy campaigned for unity: "The sooner we forget what we have been and only remember that we are Republicans now, the better."[52] The election would take place in the General Assembly in Springfield in January 1859.

Lovejoy arrived in Princeton in mid-June after being absent for six months. The pile of accumulated mail on his desk remained unopened until he reunited with his growing family. His nine sons and daughters thrived when he was home, and so did he. Sophie, his sixth daughter, remembered that on warm evenings he would hitch the horses to the wagon, load it up with the children, and pick up their friends, singing and telling stories along the way.[53]

Before long, Lovejoy was in the midst of Illinois congressional district politics again. On June 30, 1858, he was in Joliet to accept his nomination. He opened his campaign in Princeton at Bryant's Woods again. Opposition rose in the community immediately, and a voice scoffed that Lovejoy was afraid of slave drivers. J. G. Hewitt quipped that Lovejoy could whip a dozen in a fair fight, "either with words and facts, or by physical strength."[54] But the radical wing of the Republican Party, and Lovejoy in particular, faced a bigger problem: how could a candidate affirm black equality when campaigning for white voters who were afraid of or prejudiced against blacks? In 1858 Democrats accused Lovejoy of supporting "Negro Equality," a term they used to frighten voters who feared black competition. As a result, Lovejoy sometimes withheld mention of racial equality while adding his own standard—the Declaration of Independence. This tactic alienated Illinois Garrisonians who wanted candidates to speak distinctly for black suffrage. Some Garrisonians refused to join the Republican Party.[55]

Lovejoy was pleased that the first debate between Stephen A. Douglas and Abraham Lincoln was going to take place in Ottawa, in Lovejoy's own district. Lovejoy was LaSalle County's popular congressman and had campaigned in that area for twelve years. In contrast, Lincoln was almost a stranger. Twelve thousand were present on August 21.[56] Trees shaded the dignitaries sitting on the platform in the prominent New England–style square of the busy river town. Chief Shabbona, the most prominent Native American leader in the region, sat on the platform wearing a feathered headdress. In the ensuing debates, slavery was the dominant subject. Douglas deliberately baited Lincoln by calling him a "Black Republican" and likening him to Lovejoy—a drawback in his view. Lovejoy's name is mentioned forty times by Douglas in the seven debates.[57]

During the debate, Lovejoy sat close to Lincoln, sometimes whispering advice into his ear. Douglas verbally attacked Lincoln, accusing him of planning to bring Old Line Whigs into the abolition camp and then transfer them over to rabid abolitionists such as Joshua Giddings, Salmon Chase, Frederick Douglass, and "Parson Lovejoy," who were "ready to receive them and christen them in their new faith."[58] Douglas delivered the statement as a chastisement of Lovejoy, but the crowd didn't take it that way. They cheered enthusiastically for their congressman.[59]

Douglas asserted that Lincoln followed the example set by "interfering minor preachers" such as Lovejoy—"all the little Abolition orators, who went around and lectured in the basements of schools and churches, read from the Declaration of Independence that all men were created equal, and then asked how can *you* deprive a Negro of that equality which God and the Declaration of Independence awards to him."[60] After making fun of Lovejoy in that manner, Douglas bragged, "For my own part, I do not regard the Negro as my equal, and positively deny that he is my brother or any kin to me whatever." Conveying a sense of contempt, he concluded, "Lincoln has evidently learned by heart Parson Lovejoy's catechism."[61]

That evening Douglas left town on the earliest train to Chicago. Lincoln and Lovejoy were invited to dinner at the home of Mr. Joseph O. Glover, the mayor of Ottawa.[62] After supper a large crowd gathered outside the mayor's house and shouted for Lovejoy to give a speech. A band escorted him to the courthouse, where Lovejoy "rolled up his sleeves and went to it."[63]

On August 27, Lovejoy took the train to the second Lincoln-Douglas debate, in Freeport in northwest Illinois. On the train he met Benjamin Shaw, editor of the *Dixon Telegraph*. Lovejoy told him that Douglas had impishly called Lovejoy a Garrisonian in the Ottawa debate.[64] He also said that Douglas had falsely accused Lincoln of seeking to repeal the Fugitive Slave Law.

In the second debate, Douglas intensified his attack on Lovejoy by reading to the audience the three resolutions Lovejoy had presented to the 1855 General Assembly: keep slavery out of the territories; refuse to admit new slave states; and repeal the Fugitive Slave Law. Douglas decidedly disagreed with all three, but when he read them out loud, the men and women in the audience cheered for them. Irritated, Douglas then erroneously asserted that Lincoln's "friends" in the state legislature had supported all three resolutions when in fact they had supported only the first one. This mistake gave Lincoln opportunity to expose the false assertions Douglas made and to set the record straight, indicating that the Republican Party had only one goal—to prevent slavery from going into the territories.[65]

Since there was no meeting that evening in Freeport, citizens urged Lovejoy to speak. A dry goods box was improvised as a platform in front of the Brewster House. Lovejoy stepped up onto it, and an eager crowd gathered to hear his rebuttal to Douglas. Lovejoy attacked Douglas for downgrading black human beings to property and relegating white citizens to bloodhounds who must chase and capture runaways. He sketched two figures. One was a man "innocent of crime with only a polar star to guide him to a freedom justly his." The other was "a man-greyhound in hot pursuit, lapping the mire by the wayside to quench his hellish thirst for blood."[66]

As Douglas proceeded around the state, he relied increasingly on race baiting and racist deceit by claiming that Frederick Douglass had been seen in Illinois campaigning for Lincoln, "'reclin[ing]' in a carriage next to the white driver's wife." Using that fabricated story, the Democratic Party was having a negative effect on Lincoln's chances.[67]

Lovejoy directed his campaign to the east-central town of Paris, Illinois, known as an antiabolitionist stronghold. He asked the hostile audience to pick twelve men to be his jury. They jockeyed until a dozen sat before him. Then he described in biblical terms a fugitive who had come through Princeton, a girl the age of his daughter, in need of clothing, food, and money, which he provided.[68] "She was unable to reach the next station and I sent her to it. So from station to station she crossed the Northland far from baying dogs on her trail and out from under the shadow of the flag we love and venerate, into Canada. Today she lives there a free and happy woman."[69] Then he thundered, "As you shall answer to God, what would YOU have done? Rise, men, and give me your verdict." The twelve on the jury rose up and shouted back, "You did right! We would have done the same!" A reporter asked a listener what he thought of it. He replied, "One of the best speeches that ever came out of a man's mouth. No more abolition than I've believed in all my life."[70]

Despite his persuasiveness in Paris, many citizens disdained Lovejoy. Samuel Pike, editor of the Democratic McLean County weekly *National Flag*, "loved to bellow against Lovejoy, that 'notorious Abolitionist and nigger stealer.'" Pike derisively defined the Republican Party, writing, "It's the marriage of conservative niggerism to radical niggerism with the notorious nigger stealing Lovejoy officiating."[71]

In 1858 Lovejoy won reelection to the U.S. Congress by 7,325 votes, a larger margin than in 1856,[72] and with more than 55 percent of the vote in nine of his thirteen counties.[73] Republicans won statewide offices, but the General Assembly remained under the control of the Democrats, who reelected Stephen A. Douglas to a third term in the U.S. Senate. However, conservative politicians woke up to the jarring fact that a larger number of people had voted for pro-Lincoln state legislators than had voted for pro-Douglas legislators. If senators had been elected by popular vote, Lincoln would have won.[74] The population in northern Illinois was exploding as new immigrants arrived by train and wagon every day, and their young men, voting for the first time, tended to vote for Republican candidates. Lovejoy foresaw that in the presidential race of 1860, the growing number of newcomers might produce a majority for Lincoln, shifting substantial power to northern Illinois.

Blacks in the state were stymied. During the 1858 senatorial campaign, Lincoln seemed to shift inconsistently from racist remarks in his speech in Charlestown to egalitarian ideas in his speech in Alton and back again. White Republicans appeared satisfied with the weak platform, but it did not arouse African American enthusiasm. They were glad Lovejoy would return to Washington for a second term, but what good could he do for them there? In January 1859, Democratic representatives in the Illinois General Assembly had voted once again to withhold public education from their children. In Chicago blacks held a mass meeting at Quinn Chapel and rejected colonization once again.[75] John Jones, refusing to accept the status quo, redoubled his efforts to raise money for the Repeal Association and make it operational.

Finding Colleagues at the Baileys

Lovejoy returned to Washington for the Second Session of the Thirty-Fifth Congress, which began December 6, 1858. Upon arriving, he visited Gamaliel and Margaret Bailey. Antislavery congressmen in Washington "gravitated to the Baileys' parlor."[76] Gamaliel Bailey had been a Washington resident for a decade, editing the *National Era*, and was a repository of information about Congress and the city. Republican congressmen also met at Bailey's office, away from the hostile eyes of the Democrats. In December 1858, Joshua Giddings, Preston King of New York, Schuyler Colfax of Indiana, and Lovejoy returned almost every day as the session got underway in order to strategize. Bailey was not well; he was too weak to walk to the capitol.[77]

The social season in the Southern city of Washington took place in January and February. Republicans were seldom invited to the parties in the mansions hosted by Southern ladies and gentlemen. In such a polarized environment, the Baileys provided a weekly Saturday evening social affair for antislavery congressmen. As Lewis Tappan had envisioned, the Baileys exhibited that rarity in the District: an egalitarian abolitionist family, a companionate marriage, and a democratic lifestyle in the midst of a Southern city characterized by hierarchy, patriarchy, and hegemony.[78]

The Baileys gave women an important place in their establishment. Margaret Bailey, who worked with Gamaliel as an equal, was considered a "superior woman and very companionable." Gamaliel was a benevolent father and partner. "The Doctor snaps out occasionally, but never to me," Mrs. Bailey told young Mary Abigail Dodge, who tutored the Bailey children and wrote for the *National Era* under the pseudonym of Gail Hamilton. "And when he does to his wife," Dodge noted, "she only laughs at him." Describing the weekly social events, she wrote, "In the evenings guests played backgammon or whist, listened to the Bailey's [*sic*] son practice at the piano, or engaged in literary and political conversation until midnight."[79] Intelligent, witty conversation remained the mainstay.

The regulars from Congress were the antislavery guard: Lovejoy, Seward, Giddings, Thaddeus Stevens, David Wilmot, Henry Wilson, Preston King, Galusha Grow, James R. Doolittle, Salmon Chase, and Israel Washburn. In addition to the women on the newspaper's staff, Margaret Bailey invited wives, widows, and single women, providing a gathering place for them in an otherwise hostile city. Lovejoy enjoyed meeting prominent guests like Philadelphia antislavery feminist Lucretia Mott, who hosted the wedding of Angelina Grimké and Theodore Weld, performed by Rev. Theodore Wright, and their interracial wedding reception.[80] These women were united in purpose with those in his Illinois coalition.[81]

Mary Abigail Dodge crafted an artful portrait of the informal Lovejoy. Lovejoy was usually in the center of the most invigorating conversation in the room. "He was such a good-natured, sleepy-eyed lion, roaring at you so gently, for all his shaggy strength, so meek and submissive, and long-suffering. When his antagonisms were lulled asleep, and he could, with good conscience, take his ease among his friends . . . he was an irresistible target for teasing."[82] The banter apparently brought him back to his youth, to the time when he and his sisters and brothers teased each other: "The heavier and harder the storm of banter and brow-beating that pelted him, the more he enjoyed it. No sharper weapon than a Latin epigram, or a verse from Virgil, or some quiet little home-bent blade did he ever draw upon his assailants, but so apt and ready was he with this sort of small arms that he generally came off victorious."[83] Dodge marveled that Lovejoy was quick to let go of resentments: "But conquered or conqueror, his good-nature was invincible." She described him as having a low, deliberate voice. He mixed the rural richness of plain talk with unexpected biblical allusions. He had a smile "mingled of amusement, assumed toleration, real enjoyment, and all manner of good wit and good will." He could get excited, "roused sometimes, even in the pleasure of social talk, to indignation and loud-voiced eloquence over the wickedness which it was his life-trust to combat," but he was willing to be interrupted or criticized. "He was always tolerant of the hand that pulled the valve-string of his balloon, and he ever came earthward again with a half-ashamed smile, with a deprecatory look, or a mock ferocious threat."[84] This was a genial, affable man whose deep hostility was directed toward slavery, whose gregarious spirit and keen wit endeared him to many, and whose practical wisdom earned him respect.

Women Go to Springfield and the "Black Trio" Tours Northern Illinois

In Illinois, radical women focused on electing Republican candidates to contain slavery. A smaller group of women's rights advocates was pressing state legislators to change laws concerning women.[85] Antislavery leaders Hannah Cutler and Frances D. Gage, visiting from out of state, lobbied extensively in Chicago and Springfield for a married woman's property bill that would allow women to own and dispose of their own property, but in 1859 it failed to pass in the state legislature. That year the only new legislation women obtained was the right to reclaim their original surname after divorce.[86] The Married Women's Property Act would not pass until February 1861.

Eunice owned Butler Denham's farm in her own name because Butler had designated it to her in his will. Lovejoy respected his friend's decision and did not request a transfer of the property to his name, even though, when he married Eunice in 1843, he had a legal right to do so.

In February 1859, Frederick Douglass traveled to Chicago by train from his home in Rochester, New York, to be the guest of honor at a gala reception at Quinn Chapel, the AME Church on Jackson Street. The next day Douglass, John Jones, and H. Ford Douglas began another interracial campaign tour by train. This trip lasted for an arduous seven weeks.[87] The men went with the coalition's blessing to test public opinion prior to the 1860 presidential election. Douglass believed it was changing: "The public sentiment has been gradually rising. . . . We think a Negro lecturer an excellent thermometer of the state of public opinion on the subject of slavery, much better than a white man. . . . Put him in a rail car, in a hotel, in a church, and you can easily tell how far those around him have got from barbarism towards a true Christian civilization."[88]

The trio gave nearly fifty speeches in Illinois towns and villages, starting with Waukegan, Bloomington, Elgin, Belvidere, and Rockford. H. Ford Douglas had lived in Rockford previously and was known there. In Rockford, despite severe cold, they addressed audiences of four to five hundred on February 9 and 10, 1859.[89] Ford's lecture was titled "The Essential Wickedness of Slavery." Next, the trio spoke in Janesville and Beloit, Wisconsin, before returning to Illinois to visit Freeport, Dixon, Mendota, Princeton, Galesburg, Peoria, Ottawa, Morris, and places in between. The people of many of these towns were Lovejoy's constituents. These three black men were witnessing to their own humanity and that of all African Americans. Frederick Douglass recounted, "Times have changed very much of late. The Abolition lecturer speaks to a different audience, moves in a different atmosphere, and treads a less rugged pathway. . . . Those who came to hear us, were confessedly the most valuable and intelligent of the people in each community visited. . . . Slavery was really the thought uppermost in the minds of our hearers."[90]

When Douglass, Douglas, and Jones returned to Chicago, they spent several days together debriefing as guests in the homes of their closest white antislavery colleagues. First, they stayed with Charles and Louisa Dyer and their children, on Lake Street at State; next they visited at the home of Philo Carpenter and his wife and family; and finally they relaxed at the residence of L. C. Paine Freer, on Monroe between Clark and Dearborn Streets. With all three families, core members of the coalition for equality socialized and strategized in a stimulating interracial setting.[91]

Owen Lovejoy Defines Democrats as the Fanatics

In Washington on February 21, 1859, the news passed quickly from desk to desk in the House chambers. Congressmen hushed their conversations, put aside their letter writing, and folded up their newspapers as the fireworks were about to begin: Owen Lovejoy was going to speak.[92] His subject was the fanaticism of the Democratic Party. He began by addressing arguments presented in President Buchanan's annual message to Congress. For years Democrats had applied the word *fanatic* to abolitionists, and Lovejoy intended to turn the tables: President Buchanan and the Democrats, he claimed, were the real fanatics. Buchanan, Lovejoy continued, called slavery a blessing that should be extended to the territories, to Cuba, and to another slice of Mexico,[93] and he recommended an appropriation of $30 million to carry out his imperialist plan.[94] Democrats claimed that the Bible approved slavery, but actually, Lovejoy said, they were breaking all the Ten Commandments and defying the Son of God by denouncing racial equality. The fanatical voice of the slaveocracy was not God's voice, he assured the congressmen; it was only the siren of a tiny clique of slaveholders.

Lovejoy turned another favorite word of the Democrats upside down: *nigger*. He attacked them first by using the word hypocritically and then by redefining it paradoxically:[95] "The Democracy party pretends to have a great horror of 'niggers,' but their acts belie their words." In fact, he said, "slaveholders have a very close relationship with 'niggers.'" They are nursed by "niggers." They are clothed by "niggers." They are put to bed and led to school by "niggers." In return, they regularly rape them. And then they run for Congress to represent a constituency of whom three-fifths are "niggers."[96] These self-contradictory Democrats degraded the very people who had nurtured and cared for them. Historian David Fischer traces certain folkways that produced and permitted such contradictory behavior.[97]

Concluding his speech, Lovejoy said that he refused to be reincarnated into a bloodhound tracking down fugitives: "Sir, I never will do it. Owen Lovejoy lives in Princeton, Illinois, three-quarters of a mile east of the village, and he aids every fugitive that comes to his door."[98]

Democrats were extremely angry. At the very time when they had plans to expand slavery in a swath across the continent and around the Caribbean, Lovejoy was attacking the slave system's fundamental premises. He was getting too big a following; he was dangerous. Democrats tried to think of something they could do to undermine his popularity or destroy his ebullient spirit.

As the session of the Thirty-Fifth Congress prepared to close on March 3, Lovejoy watched Giddings warn Washington for the last time with a massive academic and historical attack against reopening the Atlantic slave trade. Upon his retirement, 104 House members celebrated his career with the gift of a solid silver tea set, and African American Henry Highland Garnet, who would soon become pastor of Washington's prominent black Fifteenth Street Presbyterian Church and deliver a sermon in the Hall of Representatives, presented him with a gold watch "from the colored people of New York and Brooklyn."[99] Along with radicals James Ashley and John Bingham, Lovejoy would become a successor of Giddings—each following him in his own way.[100]

The specter of a reopened Atlantic slave trade stalked the capitol. Bailey wrote in the *National Era*, "There can be no doubt that the idea of reviving the African Slave trade is gaining round in the South. But of late there has been an ominous silence upon the subject."[101] In May, the Southern Commercial Convention voted to reopen the slave trade.[102] In his own newspaper, Douglass quoted Alexander Stephens as crowing that slavery was in its infancy, not its ultimate demise.[103] The *New York Times* editorialized that the forces for moderation in the South had been gagged: "The hotspurs would have their day."[104]

Summer in Princeton Ends in a Quandary

Lovejoy left Washington and scheduled a stop in Chicago to attend a meeting with Colonel Charles Hammond, Rev. Jonathan Blanchard, pharmacist Philo Carpenter, and others at Chicago Theological Seminary, the first major Congregational seminary in the West.[105] Lovejoy believed that a western seminary would be better than the eastern seminaries at training the next generation of western ministers in the battle for human rights. As a member of the Licensing Committee of the Illinois State House of Representatives, Lovejoy had called for the seminary's incorporation on February 13, 1855.[106] The affluent Hammond, the railroad superintendent who arranged the transport of fugitives to Canada, was an active member of the Board of Trustees and the new seminary's major contributor.[107]

After unpacking his belongings in Princeton, Lovejoy traveled to Bloomington. There he asked Jesse Fell, who was about to be chosen secretary of the Illinois Republican Party, to also be the manager of his personal 1860 reelection campaign. Warmhearted hostess Hester Vernon Fell invited many guests at various times to eat dinner in her dining room. These included Lincoln, Lovejoy, John Howard Bryant, and editor William Cullen Bryant, who came from New York to visit his mother, sister, and brothers, as well as her prominent neighbor Judge David Davis. Guests often stayed after dinner for lengthy political conversation.[108] Considering how important each of these men would soon be in Lincoln's election, one can imagine that several, or perhaps all of them, sat around Hester Fell's dining room table in July 1859 and discussed the 1860 presidential campaign.

That summer in Washington, Gamaliel Bailey, like many terminally ill patients at that time, sought health from ocean waters. He boarded a ship headed toward Europe and died at sea.[109] It was a triple loss for Lovejoy: the probable end of the *National Era*, the loss of the life of a valued political abolitionist, and the end of revitalizing Saturday evenings at the Bailey home.

Lovejoy continued to lay the groundwork for his 1860 congressional campaign by writing Illinois secretary of state Ozias Hatch and telling him that in 1860 he wanted to campaign in "Egypt," as southern Illinois was often called. He thought it was important to confront one's opponents: "You can never catch the Devil napping. . . . You have got to meet him face to face. We cannot beat the Democrats by strategy, cheating, or lying but we can beat them by the open manly and earnest discussion of our principles."[110]

That autumn, while riding from one speech to the next, Lovejoy wrote "An Agricultural Poem" praising the farmer, the land, and the God who created it. In October he read it to the Bureau County Agricultural Society; the farmers did not mind its poetic imperfections.[111] What Lovejoy's farmer constituents did care about was Congress's failure to establish a U.S. Department of Agriculture. Lovejoy was determined to start one.

Information reached Lovejoy that in early February white abolitionist John Brown had traveled with a dozen freedom-seeking runaways from Kansas to Chicago. John Jones had gone downstairs to answer his doorbell and found John Brown standing there with a number of men. Mary Jones fed them all. Having received word of the arrival, abolitionist and future detective Allan Pinkerton stopped by to meet Brown. Then Dyer and Freer arrived; seeing Brown's disreputable outfit, they suggested that a new suit of clothes would be a better disguise for the rustic itinerant, and they bought one for him. Mary Jones was later known to have said, "I guess John Brown was hung in those clothes." The day after Brown arrived in Chicago, a network of black and white operatives moved Brown's fugitives from Chicago to Detroit, possibly by steamship, possibly by rail under the auspices of Colonel Charles Hammond.[112]

In October, Princeton received news by telegraph of a raid on a U.S. arsenal at Harpers Ferry, Virginia, led by Brown. Lovejoy realized that this attempt to start a slave revolt was immensely important to the nation. Southern strategists would label it an invasion, raise hysteria, and call for secession. Radical Republican analysts would wonder how it would affect the chances of electing a Republican to the White House in 1860 and the likelihood of it leading to the abolition of slavery. Lovejoy craved every bit of information he could gather about the raid. He learned by telegraph that Brown's incursion had been financed by Northern abolitionists and that Governor Henry A. Wise of Virginia had put out a warrant for the arrest of six white men, Gerrit Smith, Theodore Parker, T. W. Higginson, Samuel Gridley Howe, Frank Sanborn, and George Luther Stearns, and three blacks—Frederick Douglass, Lewis Hayden, and Harriet Tubman.[113]

When the young man at the Philadelphia telegraph office received word of a warrant for Douglass's arrest, he realized that Douglass was giving a speech nearby. He quickly had Douglass notified and delayed delivery of the telegram to the sheriff. Douglass had just enough time to leave the city on the train.[114] If he was arrested in Virginia, where the proslavery Wise was governor, execution was certain. Douglass headed for his family in Rochester and then continued on to Montreal, where he already had a ticket to sail to Great Britain.

Lovejoy struggled to sort out his own feelings as he thought about the warrants for his friends. The idea of these treasured individuals—Smith, Hayden, Douglass, and the rest—being hunted down must have made him miserable. That night he could not sleep, walking back and forth from one end of the small farmhouse to the other. His anguished pacing shook the frame building all that long night.[115]

As Douglas was leaving Rochester for Montreal, he prepared an article on John Brown for *Douglass' Monthly*. If John Brown were hanged, he wrote, the North would unite against slavery.[116] Lovejoy must have pondered Douglass's words carefully.

At first Lovejoy refrained from public comment. He remembered that in 1837, Brown had announced that Elijah Lovejoy's murder had caused him to dedicate his life to abolition. Lovejoy did not talk about Brown to Congress until April 1860. At that time, he chose to portray him in the ironic pose of a wounded lion: "You want me to curse him. I will not curse John Brown. . . . I believe that his purpose was a good one . . . no one can deny that he stands head and shoulders above any other character. . . . He was not guilty of murder or treason. He did unquestionably violate the statute against aiding slaves to escape, but no blood was shed, except by the panic stricken multitude."[117]

African Americans across the North cast John Brown, executed in December 1859, as a martyr. When no one else seemed able to break the national stalemate on slavery, Brown had taken a bold action and forfeited his life. After Brown's hanging, blacks eulogized him, saying that he went to the gallows in complete possession of himself for the sake of the slave.[118]

• • •

Although freshman congressman Lovejoy was elected by the minority party, in his first weeks in Congress he exposed the slaveocracy's core fallacy in his oration "Human Beings not Property," while slaveholding congressmen plotted to reopen the African slave trade. Lovejoy expanded the Illinois coalition with black clergy, white clergy, and leading women at the national level. In Illinois, Democrats tried to denigrate Lovejoy's catechism and conservative Republicans attempted to take Lovejoy's seat again, but he was reelected by a larger margin than before. In 1859 Lovejoy demolished Southern justifications for slavery in "The Fanaticism of the Democratic Party." In Illinois, visiting women lobbied for women's rights, and three black leaders toured Illinois and Wisconsin to repeal Black Laws. Many in the coalition for equality called John Brown a martyr, and Frederick Douglass predicted that Brown's sacrifice would solidify the North.

7. Electing Lincoln and Holding the Party Together

December 1859–June 1861

In late autumn of 1859, the Illinois coalition was on edge over numerous rescues and kidnappings. In October in Ottawa, Jim Gray, a fugitive slave from Missouri, was whisked out of the courthouse door by eight white men and into a waiting carriage, escaping to Canada.[1] But in November, in Centralia, "as the noon train was about starting for Chicago, several white men sprang upon a Negro and claimed he was a fugitive slave," kidnapping him in broad daylight.[2] "Almost every week some poor black man is literally put upon the block to pay jail fees" because of the Fugitive Slave Act, declared Rev. W. W. Patton at the Northwestern Christian Anti-Slavery Convention in Chicago.[3] There seemed to be no way to stop the suffering the law caused. Militant abolitionist John Brown had called on all slaves to flee through the Appalachian Mountains, but that had not worked.

Lovejoy was hoping a political solution would come out of the 1860 presidential election. As he stepped off the train in Washington, D.C., ready to begin his second term in Congress, his immediate focus was specifically political. He had made careful plans to move into a room at a Mr. Joy's at the corner of Eighth Street and Pennsylvania Avenue, where he would share accommodations with two politically powerful men: his good friend Henry Wilson of Massachusetts, the pragmatic antislavery leader in the Senate, and John Sherman of Ohio, the popular moderate in the House of Representatives who was the leading Republican candidate for Speaker. This location put Lovejoy at a center of information for both chambers. He was eager to be appointed chair of a committee this term; if elected Speaker, Sherman would assign the chairmen. Wilson was chairman of the Senate Committee on the District of Columbia, and Wilson and Lovejoy both wanted to reduce the regulations controlling free and enslaved blacks in the city and expand their rights.[4]

Both the Illinois coalition and the coalition he was identifying in Washington were deeply concerned.

As Lovejoy entered the capitol on December 5, 1859, he tried to prepare himself for the scene inside. Only three days had passed since John Brown's execution, and several Southern congressmen were storming into the House of Representatives armed with pistols and knives, ready to challenge any admirer of Brown to a duel.[5] It was obvious to all that trouble lay ahead, but enough order was established for the first session of the Thirty-Sixth Congress to begin.

Lovejoy analyzed the composition of the new House. The Democratic Party held 101 seats, the Republicans more at 113, but that was still 13 short of the majority required to select a Speaker of the House or to pass a bill. The remaining 23 House members came from Southern states and were listed either as Americans (Know Nothings) or Whigs.[6] Thus, the balance of power rested on these minuscule parties. The Democratic caucus had lost control of the House and feared it might lose the White House in the coming election in November 1860.

The antislavery leadership in the House of Representatives was composed of Lovejoy's colleagues from the previous Congress, including Galusha Grow of Pennsylvania, John Bingham and Edward Wade of Ohio, and the brothers Elihu Washburne of Illinois and Israel Washburn of Maine. Stern-looking, high-powered parliamentarian and indomitable abolitionist "steamroller" Thaddeus Stevens, sixty-seven, from Lancaster, Pennsylvania, joined the leadership that December. He had served in Congress as a Whig from 1849 to 1853. Now, after an absence of seven years, Stevens was returning to Congress as a Republican.[7]

In addition, several promising new antislavery congressmen had joined the House in March 1859. One was radical James Ashley, age thirty-three.[8] He had grown up near Portsmouth, Ohio, working first as a riverboat operator and later as editor of the *Portsmouth Dispatch*. Although he was the son of an itinerant proslavery Campbellite minister, James deplored his father's views. After passing the bar exam, Ashley moved to Toledo and was elected to Congress.[9] Another new congressman was progressive John A. Gurley, a Universalist minister and newspaper editor in Cincinnati. Both were eager to broaden equality under the law.

An Opening for Lovejoy and a Hint of Lincoln's Candidacy

The inevitable conflict over the election of the Speaker of the House erupted in an unforeseen way. Lovejoy's fellow boarder John Sherman, who was the lead candidate for Speaker, was suddenly eliminated because he had endorsed a new book, *The Impending Crises*, which Southerners hated for its antislavery arguments. However, the Democrats lacked the votes to select the next Speaker. For seven weeks the parties wrangled. The long stalemate finally ended when moderate William Pennington, a former Whig and former governor of New Jersey, was elected on February 1, 1860. He was seen as a compromise candidate because he refused to support the repeal of the Fugitive Slave Law. However, Pennington showed his Republican commitment by selecting strong antislavery committee chairmen: Grow to the Committee on Territories; Sherman to Ways and Means, with Vermont's Justin Morrill writing tariff laws; Elihu Washburne to Commerce; Indiana's Schuyler Colfax to the Committee on Post Offices; and Lovejoy to the Committee on Public Lands, an assignment Lovejoy savored.[10] With these appointments, real power had shifted into Republican hands, and more than that, into several radical antislavery hands.

On his way to Washington, Lovejoy had stopped in New York to meet with Colfax and *New York Tribune* editor Horace Greeley. At this time politicians were busy identifying and evaluating electable Republican nominees for the presidency of the United States. Lovejoy may have heard before he left Illinois, or learned while he was with Colfax and Greeley, that Lincoln had received an invitation dated November 1 to address the Young Men's Lecture Series at Henry Ward Beecher's Plymouth Church in Brooklyn in early 1860.[11] Plymouth Church had the reputation for being a mighty engine for the Republican cause.[12] It was one of the few eastern churches that appeared popular, prosperous, and unapologetically antislavery.[13] Organizers of the lecture series included Lewis Tappan's son-in-law Henry C. Bowen, publisher of the *Independent*, and William Cullen Bryant, editor of the *New York Evening Post*, whose brothers in Princeton were Lovejoy's close friends. Lovejoy had ties with all the men. He also held expectations for Lincoln but had not shared this in public. The committee intended to introduce Lincoln to easterners as a possible candidate for the presidency. Other prominent competitors were also included in the series, and Beecher's sponsorship made the offer attractive. Lincoln enthusiastically accepted.

The lecture was scheduled for February 27, 1860. Lincoln assembled "an arsenal of answers" to the key constitutional question: did the thirty-nine Founding Fathers include in the Constitution anything that forbade the federal government from controlling slavery in the territories? Starting with this carefully worded question, he concluded that Congress had the authority to keep slavery out of the territories. Furthermore, the South could choose to end slavery in the states where it already existed. Lincoln had carved out for himself a solid middle position between the more radical-sounding William Henry Seward and the more conservative Edward Bates. As interest rose, the lecture was moved from Brooklyn to the larger Cooper Union in Manhattan, and final plans were made in William Cullen Bryant's office at the *Evening Post*.[14] When Lincoln arrived in New York on Saturday, February 25, he visited Henry Bowen's office, and on Sunday he attended Beecher's church.[15] On

Monday evening at the Cooper Institute, Lincoln sat on stage with Bryant, whom he had first met in Illinois during the Blackhawk War—and later, probably in the parlor of Jesse and Hester Fell.[16]

Several weeks later, on March 26, 1860, an energetic Lovejoy stood before the House of Representatives as chairman of the Committee on Public Lands and presented the latest form of the Homestead bill, a concept he had supported since 1848. This legislation was a favorite with women.[17] As new territories became part of the United States, millions of acres of public lands became available for sale to ordinary families. Democrats had scuttled previous homestead bills, preferring a narrow policy that gave land corporations the first opportunity to pick the choice tracts and make private profits that would consolidate the nation's wealth and power in select families. The remaining land would then be sold at higher prices to ordinary families.[18]

Slaveholders opposed the Homestead bill, fearing that a tide of Free Soil farmers would make land unavailable for plantation owners. Southern congressmen could see that Lovejoy's bill, if signed by Buchanan, would result in new free states adding new senators whose numbers would tilt the Senate's balance of power to the north, endangering the perpetuity of slavery.

Lovejoy advocated selling land in small tracts to bachelors and young families at a low price per acre, putting a free labor model in place, setting some land aside for public schools and land-grant colleges. He said this land use policy fit the American theory of government, for in a democracy, the government is "simply an agency through which the people act for their own benefit."[19] Such a federal Homestead Act would relocate and raise the standard of living for the urban poor, European immigrants, and eastern farmers plagued with poor soil. It would raise the standard of living for women and enlarge the middle class.[20] A strong middle class would reduce the gap between rich and poor and hold the society together.[21] The middle class, he assured House members, was the heart of democracy. It was in this class that the government would find support, permanence, and prosperity: "the farmer who cultivates the soil which he owns, and returns at evening to meet the 'wee ones' running out to greet their father, and to enter the white painted cottage to partake of the frugal evening meal with the mother and children."[22] It was this middle class that would fight battles against a foreign enemy, control politicians, and protect human freedom.[23]

The House passed the popular bill. The Senate passed a weakened version, but eventually the two chambers reached an agreement. But then, just three days before the end of the session in June, President Buchanan vetoed it. Republicans realized that until they occupied the White House, their policies would remain subject to veto. Lovejoy knew the homestead issue would be central in the fall campaign of

1860.[24] His constant references to the vetoed Homestead bill would, he believed, help Republicans win the presidency.

As a time of collision between Democrats and Republicans drew near, victims and perpetrators increased their activity. Lewis Tappan, Gerrit Smith, and African American minister Charles B. Ray found themselves arranging increasing numbers of flights for runaway slaves.[25] Douglass, who had returned from Britain, reported from Rochester to his overseas friends that he had never seen so many fugitives running away.[26] More runaways were arriving in Illinois from the South. At the same time, the illegal slave trade was accelerating fast. From January 1859 to August 1860, almost one hundred illegal slave ships left New York City harbor; the city had become the greatest slave-trading mart in the world.[27]

National Newspapers Discuss Lovejoy's April Speech

Speaker Pennington scheduled Lovejoy to speak for an hour on April 5, 1860, ten days after Congress passed the homestead legislation. Israel Washburn was presiding. Tension filtered through the hall. Rhetorician George V. Bohman opines that no congressman was recognized as better qualified than Lovejoy to attack slavery with the varied intellectual, temperamental, and physical talents expected of a first-rate orator.[28] Even Lovejoy's antagonistic colleague Samuel S. Cox, Democrat of Ohio, agreed that Owen was the most remarkable man in the Thirty-Sixth Congress.[29] Nevertheless, Democrats did not want to hear his lecture.

Lovejoy's title for his speech was "The Barbarism of Slavery."[30] His choice of the word *barbarism* was deliberate. It was usually applied to African Americans, but Lovejoy applied it to slaveholders who had created a barbaric system.[31] Lovejoy's intent was to demolish Taney's *Dred Scott* decision and challenge slaveholders to free their own slaves. He began adroitly: "Slaveholding has been justly designated as the sum of all villainy."[32] "You are joking!" a member interjected. "No, sir, I am speaking in dead earnest, before God, God's own truth. It has the violence of robbery, the blood and cruelty of piracy, it has the offensive and brutal lusts of polygamy, all combined and concentrated in itself, with aggravations that neither one of these crimes ever knew or dreamed of."

Lovejoy listed three arguments regularly used to justify slavery. First, slavery was justified because the African race was inferior. If we were to concede that were true, he argued, then logically it would also be right to "trip a cripple, strike a weak old man, take advantage of an idiot, and deceive a child."[33] Lovejoy was not able to finish this sentence, for a fracas broke out on the floor of the House. Young first-term congressman Roger Pryor of Virginia got out of his seat, advanced from the Democratic side of the House into the area where Mr. Lovejoy stood, and accused him of entering Democratic floor space. In seconds, thirty or forty congressmen lunged toward the front of the hall, shoving and shouting.[34] Fists, shrieks, and even a toupee flew through the air. When a couple of congressmen cocked their pistols, Elihu Washburne, John Fox Potter, and other Republicans rushed to defend Lovejoy. Lovejoy simply observed, repeating "Nobody can intimidate me."[35] After twenty tense minutes, with Pennington pounding the gavel throughout, everyone gradually stepped back, and Israel Washburn was able to call the House back to order.

When the melee quieted down, Lovejoy resumed by stating a second popular justification for slavery: that it imparts Christianity and civilization. Scowling as he lifted his eyebrow, Lovejoy disagreed, saying that slavery could not be a mode of imparting Christianity because it relied on torture and coercion. Slavery could never be a means of imparting civilization, for it forbade civilization's essentials— marriage, family, and home. Then he presented the third justification for slavery: the U.S. Constitution protects it. That was not true, he shouted. "In no article, in no section, in no line, in no word, in no syllable, can there be any recognition or sanction of human slavery found in the Constitution of the United States."[36] Then Lovejoy attested that the Constitution was in essence an antislavery document.[37] It was meant to reflect the Declaration of Independence and was a beloved and precious work destined to be perfected in the future. "I love the Constitution, not in consequence of these [proslavery] things which are alleged to be in it, but in spite of them."[38]

With a burst of explosive statements, Lovejoy thrust questions and answers up toward the chandeliers. Is slavery crushing the black family? Yes; you steal babies from their mothers' arms.[39] Is the South despotic? Yes; you slaveholders are despots because you silence dissenters and threaten them with tar and feathers and prison.[40] If we do not right this wrong, he assured them, "the whole civilized world will snuff it in the air; and it will return with awful retribution on the heads of those violators of natural law and universal justice."[41] Then he brought his speech to its highest pitch: "Here and now I break the spell and disenchant the republic from the incantation of this accursed sorceress."[42] "This is the question: Whether these twenty-eight million people shall be accommodated or two million people be accommodated."[43] Is the United States a democracy or not? Are we ruled by a pervasive special interest or by the people? Slaveholders in Congress must overturn the assumptions of their worldview and repent. They "ought to put on sackcloth and ashes."[44] Concluding, Lovejoy called upon the slaveholders to emancipate their slaves themselves: "I offer you a quarter of a century; if you want half a century, you can have it. But I insist that this system must ultimately be extinguished."[45] Slavery, he warned them, was going to melt like an iceberg in tropical waters.

At the end of Lovejoy's speech, stunned silence filled the hall. After a moment Congressman Elbert Sevier Martin of Virginia hurled his own invective at Lovejoy: "If you come among us we will do with you as we did with John Brown—hang you up as high as Haman. I say that as a Virginian." Lovejoy responded, "I have no doubt of it." Alexander Stephens said that he felt dishonored by Republicans like Lovejoy and Lincoln, who, by calling slavery wrong, put the Southern states "under the bar of public opinion and national condemnation." Such rhetoric was cause for revolt.[46] Historian William W. Freehling writes that with this speech, Lovejoy furthered the rift that would shortly lead to secession and war.[47] Bohman points out that Lovejoy's proposal, to take fifty years for the Southern states to emancipate their own slaves gradually, was never seriously considered, for by then, Southerners identified emancipation in any form as treason and heresy.[48]

Fifty-five newspapers carried all or parts of Lovejoy's speech, often omitting the conciliatory parts. Until that speech, Lovejoy had been seen as a regional radical organizer, a coalition spokesman, a committee chairman, a floor manager—a collaborator. After that speech, he had his own power, his own voice, and it seemed that everyone was listening. Southern congressmen threatened to expel him from the House of Representatives as they had expelled Joshua Giddings and attempted to expel John Quincy Adams, yet they did not try.[49]

A few days after the speech, Lovejoy received word that he had won the support of leading women in the East. Lydia Maria Child, an accomplished editor, scholar, and radical abolitionist, wrote to a close friend, possibly Harriet Beecher Stowe, that Lovejoy had "poured the hot coals upon slavery, to my heart's content."[50] She wrote another colleague, "How I want you to read Lovejoy's speech in Congress! He came down upon the slave holders like 'a thousand of brick'! He is the brother of the martyred Lovejoy, and the mantle of Elijah has fallen on a prophet worthy to follow him."[51] In a separate letter she expressed exasperation when a third associate advised her to wait for a better time. "Is the truth then never to be spoken, till there is no election to be endangered by it, and no measure that may possibly be postponed by its utterance? This miserable doctrine of present expediency operates like a magician's spell in the hands of the slave-holders." She was tired of pussyfooting. "Thankful was I when Lovejoy broke the spell, and disenchanted the House."[52] In a reply to Child's gratitude, Lovejoy downplayed his preparation: "It was in me and would come out."[53]

His boardinghouse mate, Senator Henry Wilson of Massachusetts, recorded later that, "maddened" by Owen's "accurate" portrayal of slavery, the slaveholders revealed their reasons for "stigmatizing him with rude and vulgar words," calling him thief, villain, wretch, and devil for criticizing their "monstrous iniquity."[54]

The 1860 Campaign in Nation and State

Weeks later, in late April 1860, an implosion took place at the Democratic Nominating Convention in Charleston, South Carolina. The convention disintegrated, preventing any nomination from being made. Later, three nominations were announced. On May 10, the Southern Democrats who did not advocate secession formed the Constitutional Union Party and selected John Bell of Tennessee as its nominee for president.[55] On June 20 in Baltimore, the residue of the Democratic Convention nominated Stephen A. Douglas.[56] On June 22 the secessionist Democrats held a convention of their own in the Maryland Institute Hall and nominated John C. Breckinridge of Kentucky. At that point there were three viable presidential candidates to run against the Republican nominee.

The Republican Party began its nominating convention in Chicago on May 16 while congressmen stayed in Washington. In Chicago's Wigwam meeting hall, the party platform set the parameters for the campaign: there is no property in persons; the recent attempt to reopen the African slave trade is shameful; and freedom is the normal condition of all territories. These policies that Lovejoy valued were strongly affirmed. In addition, all schemes for disunion were abhorred; each state controlled its own domestic institutions; any lawless invasion by armed forces into any state would be a grave crime; workers should be paid generous wages; the homestead measure should be passed; naturalization laws should remain unchanged; rivers and harbors should be improved; mail should be daily; and a railroad to the Pacific Ocean should be built.[57] Lincoln received the nomination for president on May 18. When Lovejoy heard the news, he was jubilant.[58]

Stuck in Washington till the end of the session, Lovejoy felt a personal loss when Israel Washburn told him that he was leaving Congress to campaign for the governorship of Maine. Lovejoy's mentor Giddings had retired in March 1859, and his colleague Gamaliel Bailey had died that summer. Now, in May 1860, his Maine friend was returning home. Lovejoy wondered with whom he would spend afternoon tea and any free time during the next session of Congress.

Lovejoy Campaigns throughout Illinois

In late May, Lovejoy was increasingly frustrated that he was still required to be in Washington. He wanted to start campaigning, for everything he had been working for over the past twenty years depended on the November election's outcome. He began organizing for his own renomination while he was still in the District of Columbia. Lovejoy wrote a congratulatory letter to Lincoln in Springfield, Illinois, and also sent a book, title unknown, to Mary Lincoln, "which I hope she will be kind enough to accept." Mrs. Lincoln loved literature as Lovejoy did. On June 15 Lovejoy continued the connections Giddings had made while in Washington with Underground Railroad operatives by penning an unnamed associate his assurance that he had received his "shipment" and sent him north: "Yours of the 6th came safely."[59]

As soon as the first session of the Thirty-Sixth Congress ended, he took the train to New York City to confer again with Seward's political associate Thurlow Weed and then continued to Albany. While there, he received a telegraph from Jesse Fell informing him that he had been renominated for his third term in Congress.[60]

Codding came from his pastorate in Wisconsin and helped coordinate the campaign for Lincoln. When Lovejoy finally got home, he launched his crusade in southern Illinois. Fell had convinced the central committee to let Lovejoy go to "Egypt" and campaign for Lincoln there.[61] It was timely, for on July 20 John M. Palmer, who had chaired the Bloomington Convention in 1856, announced that he would refuse to take the stump for the Republican ticket unless the Central Committee would send some prominent antislavery orator into southern Illinois. His section of Illinois, with its history deeply rooted in slavery, indenture, and white migration from the South, would be persuaded only by an exceptional speaker. The committee sent Lovejoy. Isaac Arnold of Chicago commented, "As a stump speaker, it would be difficult to name his superior."[62]

Lovejoy met Palmer at Tegard's Mill, near Alton. It was notoriously called the most unhealthy spot on earth for abolitionists.[63] Lovejoy and John Howard Bryant arrived the night before the meeting, and they had trouble finding a place to sleep. The next day an immense crowd of thousands came to have "some fun with the black abolitionist," despite the heat and harvest time. Palmer dramatically introduced Lovejoy by breaking off the front railing of the speakers' platform and then tantalizing the audience to look at the cloven hoofs, horns, and tail of the devil Lovejoy for themselves.[64] After this humorous beginning, Lovejoy "held them entranced for two hours by the most brilliant political oration."[65] He reminded them that Elijah had been murdered at nearby Alton: "The blood of my brother, slain in these streets, ran down and mingled with the waters of the mighty river which sweeps past your city to the sea." He recited a line from a poem, "Avon to the Severn runs, the Severn to the sea. And Wickliffe's dust shall spread abroad Wide as the waters be." He closed by showing how his brother Elijah's death had changed many attitudes toward slavery, just as John Wycliffe's death had spread far and wide the news of Christendom.[66] The correspondent for the *New York Times* reported, "A general impression prevails (and rightly) that [Lovejoy] is furiously ultra . . . 'the man who takes a couple of darkies to breakfast.'" But then "a bland, portly gentleman appears, three parts benevolence and the rest fun and jollity, and the audience, after laughing with him for a couple of hours are ready to scout the notion of his being a fanatic."[67]

Frederick Douglass had been hesitant about Lincoln, fearing that he was too conservative on matters of slavery and race, but Douglass admitted that if Lincoln should win, it would be a great improvement to have an administration that refrained from supporting slavery. Douglass spent the fall urging the New York State legislature to rescind its requirement that blacks must own property in order to vote. When he discovered that white undercover conservatives of the Republican Party were trying to "create a new character" for the party that would be less threatening to Southerners, he called their intent despicable, and he aggressively defended the original core of antislavery Republicans, proclaiming that antislavery sentiment was the vital element of the Republican Party: "The Republican Party has its source in the old Liberty Party. . . . Antislavery positive opposition to slavery is the main and all-sustaining element of the Republican Party."[68] However, Douglass did not quell the criticisms of Lincoln expressed by many African Americans; doubts about Lincoln continued to simmer on the back burner.

After a successful tour in southern Illinois, Lovejoy returned to northern Illinois and was soon in Freeport, speaking to a huge crowd of young men and women. He looked for new voters: those turning twenty-one, foreign-born men newly eligible to vote, and emigrants moving from the East. He appealed "to a constituency that could not vote and had previously been largely ignored but that nevertheless wielded tremendous influence: women."[69]

Lovejoy unapologetically crafted many of his speeches to appeal to women. On this occasion, he explained that he chaired the committee that had proposed the homestead bill. Democrats, he clarified, opposed allowing bachelors to develop a homestead and insisted that a man must be married before he could start his farm. Lovejoy claimed that it was cruel to take a bride to a plot of ground that lacked even a shanty. He advised young women to ask young men, when they came calling, which party they planned to vote for—a party "that will morally compel William to wed Mary and then expose her to all the hardships of the first beginning of a settler's life" or one "that allows William to go first to his land and build a log house, not very magnificent of course, but a comfortable shelter, turn over a few acres and thus get ready to go after Mary, and then raise some garden-stuff, some cabbages, and, and—other domestic products . . ."[70] Great laughter and applause followed Lovejoy's unfinished reference to the raising of homesteading offspring, but Democrats later criticized him for making the women blush: "He turned himself into a circus clown, mimic, a buffoon, an ape, to make a few score of whittlings laugh, as many more young women blushed."[71]

The Homestead bill prepared by Republicans would give any white person over age twenty-one a quarter section at 12.5 cents per acre, half of what Democrats wanted to charge. In contrast, Democrats recommended letting speculators take the lion's share of the land first, and then ordinary citizens could buy the refuse, the swamp lands and sand hills. Lovejoy said that was like being offered the blue skimmed milk after the cream was taken.[72] God did not make the world for speculation, he roared. The land was made to be cultivated, not to be exploited. The air and the water and the land were the three basic elements everyone needed for life. "You might just as well bottle up the air and let rich men turn the key on it, and then dole it out for us to breathe; as to place the land in the hands of capitalists, to be given out in little tracts at exorbitant rates to the poor settlers. That is *ultra*, is it?" He lowered his voice. "It is not *ultra* if it falls within the idea and design of Infinite Wisdom when he made the world, and I believe it does."[73]

Lovejoy warned the crowd to consider the consequences of their vote: "A vote for Douglas is a vote for the slave system. Under the Democratic Party you may lose your right to print your own newspaper, your minister may be tarred and feathered for quoting Helper, your local free school may go unfunded, and if you travel into the South you will have to hold your tongue."[74]

In 1860 white and black women played a significant role in Republican Party activities. Women wrote letters and articles, developed talking points, distributed tracts about candidates, persuaded neighbors to attend rallies, influenced men of their acquaintance, provided food at major events, and offered overnight hospitality to speakers and organizers.

Women were involved in preparing every aspect of a big rally in Princeton. Thousands of members of Wide Awake clubs formed by Republican youths from surrounding towns marched with brass bands, glee clubs, and flags and banners in grand and imposing style.[75] They formed the symbolic army of Republican political foot soldiers.[76] Princeton Wide Awakes displayed "their superior drill and general Zouavity of demeanor."[77] Thirty-three young women dressed in white robes, one for each state, rode on wagons, surrounded by young men wearing oilcloth capes to protect them from the burning flares they carried, symbols of intelligence and truth. This dazzling demonstration enveloped Princeton on September 28, 1860.[78] Lovejoy spoke for three hours: "The world is watching to see if we will live up to our declaration of equality. Our image in the world depends on ending slavery."

From July 20 to November 6, Owen was away from home almost every day. It was said he gave one hundred speeches in support of Lincoln. The Illinois State Republican Committee wanted to thank Lovejoy and other campaigners for their stellar performances. They invited the Lovejoy family to be their guests at the Briggs House in Chicago on October 15. Wide Awakes accompanied Lovejoy by torchlight from the Briggs House to a huge celebration at the Wigwam.[79] Lovejoy launched into a speech. He was with his audience and they were with him.[80]

Garrisonians Accuse Lovejoy of Racism

During the 1860 campaign a false accusation surfaced against Owen Lovejoy from an unexpected source. It said that "Lovejoy had sunk to proclaiming Negro inequality."[81] The accusation hit the newspapers when an anonymous letter writer, who claimed to be from Princeton, Illinois, wrote to William Lloyd Garrison, editor of the *Liberator*. The letter claimed Lovejoy had said that people of African descent were inferior to the white man and that "the government of the United States belonged only to the white man."[82] This was the position Douglas repeated often and emphatically while running for the presidency in 1860, and it was also the position of many conservative Republicans. Judge David Davis, Lincoln's conservative Republican colleague on the circuit court in Illinois, spoke in such terms.[83] But it was not the position of Lovejoy or radical Republicans. It was the antithesis of Lovejoy's stump speeches.

When Garrison received the letter in Boston, a thousand miles to the east, he assumed that the accusation was true, and he mentioned it in his November 11 issue of the *Liberator*. His response has been summarized as, "William Lloyd Garrison was saddened to find that Lovejoy had sunk to proclaiming Negro inequality and to declaring that the government of the United States belonged only to the white man."[84] During that period, Garrison's strategy was to discourage his followers from fusing with the Republican Party because it pledged only to withhold slavery from the territories, while Garrison was urging his supporters to maintain their highest ideals during the 1860 campaign by insisting on full equality and suffrage for blacks.[85] The anonymous letter writer's message seems to fit Garrison's directive.

It is unfortunate that this anonymous letter has been at times taken at face value. In 1967, the same year that Edward Magdol's biography depicted an effective and egalitarian Lovejoy, Eugene H. Berwanger published his widely read study of the 1860 election. In an otherwise thoughtful work, Berwanger accepted the veracity of the letter and wrote, "Representing the 'most abolitionized district' in the state, Lovejoy's acid comments on the 'peculiar institution' were well known. However, even as early as 1856 he assumed a more conservative position, and by 1860 he repudiated the abolitionists in his hometown, Princeton, Illinois."[86] This is the view of Owen Lovejoy that many historians hold today. Both Lawrence J. Friedman and William Lee Miller have perpetuated this misunderstanding.[87]

Evidence indicates otherwise. At the height of the 1860 campaign, in his standard speech given at Freeport, Lovejoy spoke clearly: "I am an Abolitionist, you are an Abolitionist, every man is an Abolitionist if he brings the question home to himself. Personally, I may, in my opinions go further than the Republicans, but I go so far with them, my way, as they go. If I want to go to Chicago and you offer me a ride half way, I go with you as far as you go."[88] The radical western political abolitionist leaders and Garrisonian abolitionists shared the same goal of ending slavery, though they differed on when and how.

Other than the anonymous letter, there is no known source for asserting that the radical Republican Lovejoy had proclaimed racial inequality. Some historians have tried to modify this curious characterization that Lovejoy was a racist. Eric Foner wrote in 1970, "Especially in the West, Republican spokesmen insisted that they, not the Democrats, were the real 'white man's party,' and they vehemently denied any intention of giving legal or social equality to free Negroes."[89] But Foner qualified his statement by applying it only to the conservative and moderate factions of southern Illinois Republicanism. Then he devoted his next chapter to describing the work of the radical Republicans who lived predominantly in fourteen northern Illinois counties. Foner pointed out that the anonymous letter writer's description did not describe northern radical Republicans accurately: "The fact that so many Republican leaders had defended the rights of free Negroes and fugitive slaves in the 1840's and early 1850's should be strong evidence that there was more to Republican attitudes than mere racism."[90] Indeed, there was much more. In 2011, John Ashworth goes further in correcting this historical narrative: while some Republican Party spokesmen were guilty of virulent utterances, "recent historians had probably exaggerated this point."[91] Thousands of radical Republicans in Illinois fought for equality. Back in 1970, Foner did not identify Owen Lovejoy as their religious-political abolitionist leader, first in Illinois and then in the U.S. House of Representatives. However, in 2010, in *The Fiery Trial*, he recognizes Lovejoy as the leader of the northern Illinois abolitionists and places him among the leading five radicals in the U.S. Congress—along with James Ashley, George W. Julian, Thaddeus Stevens, and Charles Sumner.[92]

Lovejoy was accused of vacillating over racial equality, but this was not so. For more than a decade he had advocated prohibiting slavery in the territories as the best strategy for gaining political power for the antislavery cause. Lovejoy and Lincoln had formed a political party based on this policy of nonextension. That was the central promise Republicans made in the 1860 campaign, and they had designed it to give the party its broadest possible electoral appeal. While Lovejoy had repeatedly spoken in favor of full rights for blacks, the party had agreed not to emphasize them in the campaign. Both Lovejoy and Lincoln hoped and expected that the South would eventually take the initiative to free their slaves themselves after the fading institution had been decisively cordoned off and contained.[93] Lovejoy's commonsense view was that the eradication of slavery must be achieved first before full rights could be obtained.

Lovejoy occasionally used the word *inferiority*, but not to comment that any race was inferior—rather, he used it to arouse compassion and "humanity," to call for justice and to bring about abolition. In two published speeches Lovejoy used the word *inferior* to describe the contemporary oppressed situation of blacks in American. When he used the term, he was not referring to any natural or inherent condition of African Americans. Rather, he was referring to whites withholding from blacks their basic needs—food, clothing, housing, education, and empathy—as well as denying them their constitutional rights—natural, civil, political, and social.

Indeed, Lovejoy used the word *inferiority* as some of his African American colleagues used it. In 1863, for example, William Wells Brown described induced inferiority when he said, "I admit that the condition of my race . . . at the present time cannot compare favorably with the Anglo-Saxon."[94] Two decades before that, Garnet had said, "It is one of the most malignant features of slavery that it leads the oppressor to stigmatize his victim with inferiority of nature, after he himself has . . . brutalized him."[95] Lovejoy must have remembered the thesis of Hosea Easton, who wrote in Hartford in 1836 that slavery was responsible for the "deformity of two and a half millions of beings, who have been under its soul-and-body-destroying influence."[96]

Lovejoy's campaign speeches in Freeport in September and in Chicago in October 1860 were resounding calls for ending bondage and initiating avenues of equality. In Freeport he said, "Mr. Douglas declares that the words in the Declaration of Independence applied only to British subjects. . . . What do you think of that, Germans, Irish, and all you citizens of foreign birth?"[97] Lovejoy continued, "Now what does this language—that all men are equal—mean? Equal in size? No! . . . in intelligence, in natural gentility, in manners? No! How then? All men are equal in their right to life, to liberty and to the products of their honest labor."[98] Then Lovejoy raised the standard for equality by evoking his own highest authority: "Call Lovejoy a radical if you wish. To be a radical means to go to the bottom of things. Such a radical was Christ. He was a negro equality man, for his divine precepts apply to ALL men."

On October 15, before the huge audience in Chicago, he admonished, "It is a mistake to say that the Republican Party is only the white man's party. It is not the white man's party, nor the black man's party, nor the tawny man's party. . . . It is the party of equality, justice and humanity to all men." Then Lovejoy asked himself a rhetorical question: "Mr. Lovejoy, Do you believe that all men are created equal?" He answered his own question with a resounding affirmation, "Yes I do." Then his tone changed and he talked plain facts: "I know very well that the African race as a race is not equal to ours. I know very well as a matter of fact, that in regard to the great overwhelming majority, this government may be considered in a certain sense a government for white men, but I say that the theory of our government, contrary to the old theory of despotism that kings rule by divine right, is that all men are equally entitled to those natural rights which the common God and Father gave them by an inalienable title." The Democrats were not going to shake him from this position: "I will not give up the glorious Declaration of Independence, which comes to us baptized in the blood of the purest patriots that ever lived, because there is a miserable prejudice against the colored man. I will not do it. . . . I defend universal liberty and the equality of man."[99]

The attention given to an inaccurate anonymous letter continues to have unfortunate reverberations in recent scholarship. It has altered the standard narrative about Owen Lovejoy in many renditions and should be reexamined. In 1860 Owen Lovejoy was not a localized, expedient, prejudice-tinged fallen Garrisonian. He was a rising political abolitionist leader and a national, egalitarian emancipationist who announced his plan in the 1840s and proceeded, almost always on the same course, through eight years in Congress, until his death in 1864.

Remaining Steady through the Southern Secession Storm

On November 6, 1860, Owen Lovejoy was reelected to the House of Representatives for a third term,[100] and Abraham Lincoln was elected president. Lovejoy marveled that after twenty years of effort, a man with unusual political acumen and deep moral convictions would move into the White House. In the midst of brutal politics, a man with a moral compass had emerged. In the North, Chicago congressman Isaac Arnold felt a dramatic change in the air: "This presidential campaign has had no parallel. The enthusiasm of the people was like a great conflagration, like a prairie fire before a wild tornado."[101]

But difficulties were multiplying. Due to the four-way race for the presidency, Lincoln had received less than 40 percent of the national popular vote. Many Republicans naively assumed that Democrats would let Lincoln govern. They had not foreseen that Lincoln's election would trigger secession, and they were not prepared when it did.[102] Northerners had assumed that the extremists in the Deep South were bluffing and that slaveholders realized secession would be against their own self-interest. On November 29, even *New York Evening Post* editor William Cullen Bryant wrote to his brothers in Princeton, Illinois, that "Nobody but silly people expect [war] will happen."[103] But the Bryants in Princeton continued to worry.

African Americans in Illinois, also fearing war, clung to any signs that sensible whites in the South wanted to stop secession.[104] But having suffered under slavers for so long, Illinois blacks were afraid that Southern planters would reject all compromises affecting slavery. Slavery was crucial to plantation life's aristocratic subculture, with its mockery of equality, predatory relations with women, practices of torture, and habits of overextended indebtedness. Blacks saw planters as fatalistic gamblers who would go to war without evaluating their future.[105] Closer to home, African Americans imagined slaveholders from Missouri and Kentucky invading Illinois and destroying local black communities. Meanwhile, recently arrived Irish laborers had already taken away some of their jobs.[106]

African American H. Ford Douglas was pessimistic about Republican Party resolve: "It is yet to be seen whither they will drive in the political storm they are creating, and which is now raging."[107] Lovejoy wrestled over how to hold together the befuddled Republicans in the House and how to assist president-elect Lincoln in concrete ways that would reassure Douglas and others that the president would not cave in to proslavery demands.

On December 3, 1860, Lovejoy returned to an anxious Washington for the Second Session of the Thirty-Sixth Congress. He held in check his own feelings of elation about Lincoln's victory, for the nation was in peril and many Northerners feared that the government would cease to function and the nation would break apart.[108] Republicans had won the White House, but James Buchanan would live in it for three more months, during which time the pledges the Republican Party had made to the American people could be forgotten if the party split. Some, fearing disunion or war, considered offering compromises with the South; others, doubting secession or unafraid of war, hung on to the platform agreed to at the Chicago Wigwam and envisioned the end of slavery.

William Pennington of New Jersey was still the Speaker of the House. At the beginning of each session of Congress, members could give State of the Union messages. During the winter of 1860–1861, more than sixty such speeches were printed in the appendix of the *Congressional Globe*. When Lovejoy realized that President Buchanan was paralyzed and would not act against the rebels, he decided that he must be ready to deliver a State of the Union message himself.

Lovejoy had several concerns. He gave his immediate attention to the secession taking place. Fire-Eater extremists were propelling South Carolina toward secession. Its legislature had waited only four days after Lincoln's November 6 victory before it scheduled a date for selecting delegates to a secession convention.[109] It became increasingly apparent that President Buchanan did not plan to resist the Confederacy; his government allowed the South to capture forts, shoot down the national flag, and fire at the unarmed government vessel *Star of the West*. Southern members of Buchanan's cabinet resigned.[110] An indecisive Buchanan did not arrest secessionists. He believed that neither he nor the Congress had the authority to compel a state to remain in the Union by force of arms.[111]

In contrast, Republican governors Richard Yates of Illinois and John Andrew of Massachusetts urged the government to use the whole power of the nation to defend itself.[112] On December 17, early in the congressional session, Lovejoy focused on this fundamental constitutional matter by introducing a simple resolution: "We deprecate the spirit of disobedience to the Constitution, wherever manifested. . . . It is the duty of the President of the United States to protect and defend the property of the United States." In response, critics targeted Lovejoy with unmerciful insults and charges because he had gone to the core issue again. His resolution was approved 136 to 0, but Southern representatives had refused to participate in the vote.[113] The resolution provided a basis for the next president to protect federal property if needed. But what was at stake was more than federal property; it was the question of whether a national experiment embodying freedom and equality could endure.

A second concern of Lovejoy's was that Southern congressmen were tempting Republicans with calls for compromise. Lovejoy and other leaders of the Republican caucus directed its members to reject all of the many proposals for compromise and to keep as silent as possible on the floor of the chamber. However, everyone wanted desperately to state their position on slavery one last time before the end came. Some Northerners were willing to give in to the South's demands. Among the members who refused to do so, despite intensifying pressure, were Elihu Washburne, Thaddeus Stevens, and Owen Lovejoy.[114]

On December 18, Lovejoy listened intently as John Crittenden of Kentucky, gaunt and sober, pressed upon the Congress a package of constitutional amendments that he called a compromise.[115] Like Henry Clay's Missouri Compromise of 1820, it would allow the extension of slavery into territories south and west of the latitude of Missouri's southern border—of 36°30'—and in this case it would cover not only the Louisiana Territory but all territories "hereafter acquired," even to the Pacific Ocean.[116] In the minds of the slaveholders, this extension of slavery also included Cuba, Central America, or parts of Mexico that might be obtained for a larger slave empire.[117] It allowed new slave states to be admitted and designated that slavery would be permanent. It prohibited abolishing slavery in the District of Columbia and allowed domestic slave trade. If passed, it would decimate the core of the Republicans' Chicago Platform.[118] President-elect Lincoln secretly communicated to his men that under no circumstances would he compromise on the nonextension of slavery in the territories.[119]

Then Lovejoy faced a further anxiety. He received warning of an assassination plot. Most congressmen had gone home for Christmas, but he was alone in his apartment when Joseph Medill, publisher of the *Chicago Daily Tribune*, knocked on his door. Medill brought Lovejoy the news that conspirators were plotting to assassinate Lincoln on the way from Springfield to his inauguration in Washington. Allan Pinkerton of Chicago, who had used stealth to protect John Brown and fugitive slaves on the Underground Railroad, would now serve as a detective to protect Lincoln. A secret organization, later identified as the Disunion Vigilance Committee, intended to prevent Lincoln's inauguration by ambushing him in Baltimore on February 23, 1861, aiming to have Breckinridge, who had the next highest number of electoral votes, installed as president.[120] Medill and Lovejoy knew the information's secrecy could not be guaranteed if they sent Lincoln word of the plot by regular mail; it would be more secure if sent with a congressman's "frank." The men sent the troubling information to Lincoln in an envelope stamped on December 26 with the frank "O. Lovejoy."[121]

After the holidays, members gave their State of the Union speeches. On January 12, Senator Seward of New York presented his conciliatory message orally; he was willing to forgive the disunionists. His priority was to preserve the Union rather than to restrict slavery.[122] Afterward, his Quaker wife, Frances, sent him a "blistering" letter saying, "Compromise based on the idea that the preservation of the Union is more important than the liberty of nearly 4,000,000 human beings cannot be right."[123] In his own State of the Union speech, Congressman Charles Francis Adams suggested that New Mexico might possibly be allowed to become a slave state; his Massachusetts constituents quickly chastised him.[124] When conservative Republican William Kellogg of Canton, Illinois, offered a compromise, he was repudiated by his home district and read out of the party, according to the *Chicago Tribune*.[125]

On his last day in the capitol, January 21, 1861, Senator Jefferson Davis of Mississippi denied any personal responsibility for the crisis facing the nation as he presented his State of the Union speech. "Your voters refuse to recognize our domestic institutions [slavery]." "You refuse us that equality without which we should be degraded if we remained in the Union." "You elected a candidate who made a distinct declaration of war upon our institutions."[126] Lost in the midst of his farewell, but picked up by Lovejoy, was Davis's unyielding biblical assertion that "slavery existed in the tents of the patriarchs, and in the households of His own chosen people." "It was established by decree of Almighty God . . . and sanctioned in the Bible—both Testaments—from Genesis to Revelations." In this speech Davis declared that slavery was the cause of disunion and slavery would be the reason for going to war.[127] Davis would soon go to Montgomery, Alabama, to form the Confederacy before Lincoln's inauguration.

At this crucial juncture, on January 23, a determined Lovejoy gave his own State of the Union speech orally before the remaining members of the House of Representatives—Northerners and border state men.[128] Lovejoy did not address the

Democrats in the chamber but directed his words to his wobbly fellow Republicans. Then he gave a long series of admonishments: Remain united. Do not amend the Constitution; this was no time to tamper with that holy instrument.[129] Put aside fear; no state could dissolve the USA.[130] The Chicago Platform had declared secession to be treason: "It is a crime to make shipwreck of this Government."[131] Remember that the Republican Party won the election fair and square; now the party must stand united on its principle that slavery must not be extended into the territories. The platform was oriented toward the future, filled with magnificent programs that would help the nation grow into its potential for greatness.

Lovejoy called on the disunionists to repent, using the religious term deliberately. He would arrest individual traitors, but he opposed a lawless invasion by any state. He refused to compromise with the South because it had no genuine grievances, and he chastised Republicans who were willing to concede to the slaveholders. "We appointed a committee of compromise—a grave mistake for us, a carnival for the Democracy."[132] They were poor negotiators: "We reach out our wrists for handcuffs, and console ourselves by saying, 'It is not as bad as it might be; we can move our fingers a little.' Sir, the whole history of these compromises should teach us that this slave power [has] insatiable demands." The United States was not a federation of states as Jefferson Davis claimed; it was a union of the states. "Who made this Government?" Lovejoy shouted.[133] "We, the people of the United States!" he answered. "We are the rulers, not the states." "Let the American people who made this government preserve it consecrated to freedom."[134]

Democracy, Lovejoy proclaimed, was supposed to operate by majority rule, not by a minority of self-interested slaveholders. He opposed allowing a minority of self-interested slaveholders to rule the majority. The Chicago Platform commended liberal wages for working men, mechanics, and manufacturers, but the Slave Power had been withholding wages from blacks and obstructing national development by the federal government for thirty years. Slaveholders constituted less than 25 percent of the population of the South and less than 7 percent of the nation's population.[135] "At a liberal estimate there are not more than two millions of people in the United states interested in slave labor," he stated. "There are only four hundred thousand slaveholders. There are thirty millions of people in this county. There are twenty-eight millions interested in the system of free labor, . . . And this is the question: Whether these twenty-eight million people shall be accommodated, or two million people be accommodated."[136] Yet this small clique held the majority of seats in the powerful Senate and was now fomenting disunion. Slaveholders were operating as an oligarchy, contrary to the spirit of the Constitution.[137] A few in the South were rich, but the vast numbers of white yeomen were poor, and the black slaves had next to nothing. The slaveholders were accumulating conspicuous wealth off the backs of a subjugated people who lived under utter oppression.

Lovejoy, having identified a potential split in the Republican Party, warned that the party must remain united. A group of conservative Republicans were willing to bargain with the South but feared that the radicals like Lovejoy would refuse to negotiate and bring the nation into war. These conservatives were trying to isolate Lovejoy and the antislavery faction, but Lovejoy exposed their plot. In his witty, sardonic way, Lovejoy pointed out that without the true antislavery men and women in the ranks of the party, there would have been no Republican organization. Speaking to those who wanted to reorganize the party with the radicals excluded, he said, "I wish you a merry time of it, my masters. A very interesting play, *Hamlet* with Hamlet left out!"[138] Lovejoy was reminding frightened Republicans that "originally" the party "had absorbed into its complex body" the "political wing of a great crusade, namely the antislavery radicals."[139] Without them, there was no Republican Party. Lovejoy was the heart of the radicals.

Historian James Oakes points out that the secession by the Southern states allowed the Republicans to move from their policy of gradual abolition by way of containment to a policy of immediate emancipation to be granted as a military necessity.[140]

The Divide between Opposing Religious Interpretations Sharpens

Lovejoy had worshipped in black churches since he arrived in Washington. As hostilities and fears between South and North rose, he developed even closer ties. An authentic friendship was developing between him and one of the leading local black pastors. On the Sunday before he gave his State of the Union speech, Owen worshipped at that church. He confided to the pastor that he had planned to make an antislavery speech that week directed against the Fugitive Slave Law, aware that its enforcement caused agony daily to African Americans in the city of Washington and elsewhere. But when the day came, and he felt the mounting chaos in the House chamber, he changed his focus and made an "anticompromise speech" instead. "Owing to the peculiar state of affairs in the House," he implored Republican congressmen not to compromise with slavery and called for desperately needed party unity instead.[141]

However, after he gave his January 23 address, the politically astute African American pastor wrote a column in the *Evening Post*, in which he criticized Lovejoy's speech as too soft. Lovejoy read his review, and on February 4, 1861, when they met again, Owen responded enthusiastically to the man's article, but in his own defense, he teasingly reminded the pastor, "You exhorted me at the door of the church 'to speak the truth in love.'" Then he continued the thought, "As I meant to be unyielding in my votes, I thought perhaps I had better be not severe in words." But after explaining himself, Lovejoy apologized: "I did not mean to lower the standard any." He then confided that he too was impatient with gutless speeches. "Seward behaves badly," he noted, referring to his recent speech. "Timidity is as calamitous in times of battle as treachery. He is where Webster was in '50 and his utterances are . . . just as though Slavery was not a crime."[142] With their direct give-and-take, these two clergymen demonstrated their collegial friendship. But there was the mark of admonition as well as friendship taking place in the interaction. African American churches, more than any other institution in Washington, mediated between the black community that had developed under slavery and the white-dominated world of federal politics.[143] The black minister was conveying to his friend Lovejoy that the black community as a whole thought his speech did not go far enough.

When the South Carolina convention met on December 24, 1860, they had adopted a resolution warning their people to reject antislavery religion. "All hope of remedy is rendered vain, by the fact that public opinion at the North has invested a great political error with the sanction of more erroneous belief."[144] They were accusing northern religious leaders of teaching Christianity in a way that forced Southerners to secede from the Union. This did not seem to make sense, as most Northern clergy and professors of theology had concurred with the opinion that the Bible supported slavery. The resolution seemed to target Lovejoy's religious views and those of western political abolitionists specifically in order to defend their own dehumanization of African Americans.

Six weeks after Jefferson Davis took the oath as president of the provisional government of the Confederate States of America, Alexander Stephens, its vice president, asserted that "the old Constitution set out with a wrong idea: that African slavery was wrong and would be extinguished. But time has proved the error and we have corrected it in the new Constitution. We have based ours upon the principle of the inequality of the races—and the principle is spreading."[145] Slavery was clearly the central institution of the Confederacy.[146]

It remained a secret that the Confederate cabinet sent propagandists to London to take over a docile Anthropological Society of London in order to have them say that blacks were a separate and inferior race, thus undercutting the antislavery assertion that all human beings came from common descent. The Confederate secret service, bankrolled by the Richmond administration, succeeded in planting its proslavery lobby within that society.[147] They also sent proslavery clergymen to inculcate British churchmen with the myths of the "kind master" and the "happy slave."[148] Frederick Douglass had been farseeing when he warned in 1854 that the pseudoscientific theory of polygenesis—that blacks and whites had separate origins—posed a great threat to the future integration of blacks into American society.[149]

On March 4, President Lincoln gave a moderate inaugural address. The winter of secession was over. The Lincolns moved into the White House, and the Lovejoys went home.[150]

The Fugitive Slave Act—Obey or Repeal

Lovejoy was caught by surprise when President Lincoln enforced the Fugitive Slave Act within a month of taking office. On April 3, 1861, in Chicago, a federal commissioner arrested Mr. and Mrs. Harris and their three children and remanded them to slavery in Missouri. The coalition in Illinois was distressed, and African Americans living along Lake Michigan were panic-stricken. Three hundred blacks left quickly for Canada West, which would soon be called Ontario.[151] The black community was decimated; empty houses were left behind, and those who remained were bereft. The *Bureau County Republican* on April 11 wrote scathingly, "It is humiliating that the first federal Marshall under the Republican Administration should have violently arrested a family of color in Chicago."[152]

Illinois newspapers were full of rumors that the South was getting ready to capture Fort Sumter. On the evening of April 11, organizers corralled a great crowd in the streets of Charleston, Illinois. As night fell, former congressman Roger Pryor, who had started the brawl during Lovejoy's April 1860 address, gave an electrifying summons that galvanized the throng.[153] After midnight, on April 12, shots were fired on Fort Sumter. War had begun.

Lovejoy immediately began to raise volunteers for the army. It was a cumbersome process, with private citizens recruiting volunteers who elected their own officers and gathered their own supplies, including horses. By April 25 Lovejoy had organized a company,[154] and the local paper listed a total of five companies from Bureau County. Lovejoy said, "It seems to me that the booming of cannons against the forts of the United States, the seizure of federal property, and the dishonoring of our flag for the first time since we became a nation, ought to arouse our patriotism without much speech-making. . . . I am not going to urge the young men to enlist under a fit of enthusiasm or whiskey. If you enlist I shall expect to hear that you have done your share; and if you die or get killed, we will embalm your memories in our hearts." At a mass meeting on the twenty-fifth, Lovejoy urged the distracted county to organize for any emergency[155] because rebels in Kentucky and Missouri could easily invade. Lovejoy had applied to Secretary of War Simon Cameron for a position in the Union Army. His colleagues urged him to serve in the army only until Congress opened in early December.[156]

Frederick Douglass had been ready to sail to the Caribbean and consider the ramifications of supporting colonization by visiting an actual colony there, but when he heard that Fort Sumter had been fired upon, he was greatly relieved. He unpacked his bag and breathed, "God be praised!"[157] Seeing the implications immediately, he announced that war was necessary to complete the unfinished American Revolution. He predicted that two things must be done to win war. First, the slaves must be freed as a war measure; and second, blacks must be recruited into the Union Army. "The Negro is the key to the situation—the pivot upon which the whole rebellion turns." Then he added a third action necessary for a true peace: African Americans must be integrated more fully into the mainstream of American life.[158] His second recommendation was quickly thwarted when Chicago rejected black recruits for the army.[159] Boston blacks who requested permission to form black drill societies and join the Massachusetts militia were refused by the state legislature. African American volunteers in Washington, D.C., were sent home.[160]

Then, without asking anyone, some black slaves in Virginia emancipated themselves. In May 1861, a number of enslaved blacks broke through military lines at Fort Monroe, Virginia.[161] Slaves flocked to the Union Army and were ready to act as guides, to dig, to build, and to fight for liberty. White officers did not know how to respond. Some officers enforced the Fugitive Slave Act by permitting masters to enter their lines and carry away their slaves by force.[162] Others, like General Benjamin F. Butler, declared that the law did not apply to Confederates. The Confederacy was now a foreign country, and the Fugitive Slave Act applied only to states within the USA. Butler protected the African Americans and allowed them to stay. By the end of July, over 850 blacks had escaped to the fort.[163] The word *contraband*, usually applied to animals and materiel confiscated by victors in a war, was now the label used for this growing influx of freedom seekers.[164] Blacks were liberating themselves.

• • •

In January 1860, Speaker William Pennington appointed Lovejoy to chair the Land Use Committee, who shepherded the Homestead bill through the House of Representatives. President Buchanan vetoed it, but it became a major point in the following Republican campaign. On April 5, 1860, Lovejoy admonished slaveholders for distorting Christianity and urged them to free their own slaves; Southern congressmen said that his speech insulted their honor. That summer, Wide Awakes, churchmen, women, and blacks campaigned actively for Lovejoy, who solidly won reelection. Lovejoy also campaigned vigorously for Lincoln. Southerners feared that an inaugurated Lincoln would invade the South, while African Americans in Illinois feared that angry Southern armies would invade Illinois. Fire-Eaters urged secession while radical Republicans in the House called the frightened Republican caucus to remain united and keep their platform promise for nonextension of slavery. Lincoln became president, war began, and "contraband" crossed lines. Radicals changed their strategy from containment to emancipation by military necessity. The Fugitive Slave Act was broken beyond repair.

8. Promoting Emancipation in the Thirty-Seventh Congress

July 1861–August 1862

Special Session of the Thirty-Seventh Congress, July 1861

The movement to obtain rights for blacks in Illinois was at a dead end. The coalition had tried every democratic technique available to persuade the white people of Illinois to repeal the Black Laws. And now the federal government in Washington was in peril and the ill-protected Union was at war. The great question facing the Special Session of Congress and the new president remained unanswered: what was the purpose of the war? Conservatives wanted to preserve the Union. Radical Republicans wanted to end slavery.

Members of Congress called by President Lincoln assembled with urgency for the Special Session of the Thirty-Seventh Congress on the symbolic day of July 4, 1861. There was a quick consensus to elect antislavery Republican Galusha Grow of Pennsylvania, a cheerful, jovial attorney, as Speaker of the House of Representatives.[1] Grow appointed radical antislavery men as chairmen of all the major committees, forming for the first time a vital circle of radical leadership in the House. Lovejoy was in the center of House action. While his official base was his appointment as chairman of the Committee on Agriculture, he swiftly involved himself in other committees' progressive efforts as well.

Lovejoy had another line of influence that was just as important, but he waited for a propitious occasion to furnish a bridge of trust between the House of Representatives and the White House. When he had first come to Washington in December 1857, he had had the advantage of spending Saturday evenings with colleagues at Gamaliel Bailey's home. After Bailey died, he received an open invitation to afternoon teas at Israel Washburn's home. Now Lincoln was living in the White House, and he had extended a standing invitation to all the "Illinois friends" or "home folks" to come over at any time and enter by way of the side door. Lincoln intended to be accessible, and Lovejoy was available.[2]

The opening session on July 4 was the first opportunity for Congress to set goals. Everyone placed importance on preserving the Union, even as individuals differed widely on how to accomplish it, but there was very little discussion about slavery—whether to keep it or end it. However, Lovejoy and the other radical Republicans were intent from the start on finding ways to abolish slavery. In the meantime they would try to limit it by outlawing it in Washington, D.C., and by excluding it from federal territories.[3]

The secession had significantly reduced the size of the chamber. Only 178 representatives remained in the House, as 55 members had resigned. Republicans were clearly in the majority with 108. Most of the 44 Democrats came from Northern states but were still protective of slavery in the South. Most of the 28 "others" called themselves Unionists and represented the border states.[4] They wanted to stay in the Union and keep their slaves. A gaping division among Republicans was also becoming noticeable. Conservative Republicans restrained the radical Republicans' legislative initiatives whenever they could. When they found common cause with the Democrats and/or Unionists, they created a recalcitrant majority. When they were persuaded by Thaddeus Stevens and Lovejoy and the radical clique, there was movement toward emancipation. Despite this vacillation, the Thirty-Seventh Congress would be among the most productive congresses in American history.

Speaker Grow appointed Lovejoy to chair the Agricultural Committee. He chose Stevens to chair the powerful Ways and Means Committee; Stevens arranged the order of business for the House and, as parliamentarian, moved bills speedily through the House.[5] He was as dedicated as Lovejoy to expanding blacks' rights. Others in the circle of chairmen were Elihu Washburne of Galena, Illinois, who led the Committee on Commerce; James Ashley of Toledo, Ohio, who headed the Committee on Territories; John Hickman of Pennsylvania, the supportive chair of the Committee on the Judiciary (though the radicals counted more fully on aggressive John Armor Bingham of Cadiz, Ohio, to look out for their legislation on that committee); John Potter of East Troy, Wisconsin, who led the Committee on Public Lands; and Justin Morrill of Strafford, Vermont, who prepared the land grant bill. All seven were determinedly antislavery. Four of these chairmen were from states west of the Allegheny Mountains. The West had played a significant role in the Republican Party's growth, and western leaders of the Republican caucus were creative proponents of progress in the House throughout the Thirty-Seventh Congress, pushing the programs agreed to in the Republican platform—homesteading, public higher education, agricultural research, a transcontinental railroad, expansion of the middle class, and the prohibition of slavery in the territories.

Harper's Weekly reported that since Lovejoy arrived in Congress in 1857, he had been a voice of authority in the House, but now that his party was in the majority, he could get bills passed.[6] Biographer Edward Magdol concluded that beyond the confines of the House, Lovejoy had become "the voice of the antislavery sentiment in the land."[7] Historian Allan G. Bogue calls him "the most effective Republican abolitionist on the floor of the House."[8] Another historian, Hans Trefousse, writes that on matters affecting blacks, Stevens and Lovejoy worked together as a team closely managing the floor; "Lovejoy's opinions were Steven's own, and they had to be furthered by every possible means."[9] Historian Heather Cox Richardson identifies Lovejoy as the mover and shaker on the issues of public land and agriculture.[10] As chairman of the Agriculture Committee he brought together an informed group of agriculturalists, and they urged that a new federal department be formed to increase the farm families' productivity through scientific research and marketing. Technically, she noted, Lovejoy's leadership was confined to the chairmanship of the House Committee on Agriculture, but on the floor of the House, "his most effective and dramatic actions were on the slavery question."[11] Lovejoy would make every possible issue a platform for ending slavery and introducing some measure of racial equality. On these issues Lovejoy had become a necessary bridge to the White House.[12]

Lovejoy was drawn to a major issue in July when he introduced a resolution that would protect slaves who were escaping across Union Army lines. Women and children in need of aid were arriving on the northern side of military lines. Lincoln was forced to confront the political question: who was now responsible for enforcing the Constitution's Fugitive Slave Clause?[13] On July 7, Lincoln told Illinois senator Orville Browning that he did not want the federal government to send any escaped slaves back to bondage. The next day, five days into the session, Lovejoy introduced a resolution to deal with these escaped slaves.[14] His words were similar to Lincoln's: "It is no part of the duty of the soldiers of the United States to capture and return fugitive slaves."[15] Lovejoy's resolution passed in the House ninety-three to fifty-five along party lines. Although the bill did not come before the Senate, it left its mark on both chambers, for it expressed the abhorrence Republicans felt for the practice of returning runaway slaves to their masters.[16] And Lovejoy would soon bring up the issue again.

On July 16, eastern activist Lydia Maria Child, who followed Lovejoy's legislative actions, knew that Lovejoy's crucial resolution had passed the House but feared the Senate would not act on it. Child wrote her Massachusetts senator Charles Sumner on behalf of her friend Harriet Beecher Stowe as well as herself, urging him to convince the Senate to approve it. "I watch the game with trembling anxiety. Under the Fugitive Slave Law I *will* not live. So help me God! I have always disobeyed it, of course. But I will not submit to the ignominy of being subject to it. . . . How I thanked Owen Lovejoy for his manly resolution! How I rejoiced over the vote in the House! The spirit of our fathers is not quite dead, as I have feared."[17]

Illinois senator Lyman Trumbull had the same situation in mind when he brought a similar resolution to the U.S. Senate, that "any person claiming to be entitled to the labor of another person, and who allowed such person's labor to be used for the rebellion, shall forfeit all right to such service or labor." While drafting the resolution, Trumbull had changed the word *property* to *persons*. With the passage of Lovejoy's resolution in the House and Trumbull's in both chambers, it was clear that Republicans were in support of freeing slaves that were used to support the rebellion. Congress was not only legislating about confiscation of material property but was now emancipating human beings.[18]

Lovejoy was certain that the measure was constitutional, but Lincoln feared it would alienate the congressmen from the four slaveholding border states, Delaware, Maryland, Kentucky, and Missouri, that had remained in the Union. On August 6, 1861, President Lincoln reluctantly signed the bill, but he ordered his attorney general, Edward Bates, not to enforce it. For that reason, the legal status of such blacks remained unclear; "They no longer owed labor to their owners, yet the act did not explicitly emancipate them."[19] Within a year of the initiation of General Butler's contraband policy at Fort Monroe, tens of thousands of slaves had become liberated.[20]

In 1926 revisionist James Garfield Randall looked at this sequence of events from the viewpoint of a Democrat of that day. He "dismissed evidence that Republican policymakers were interested in attacking slavery as early as July, 1861," thus denying that the momentous action of freeing slaves began so soon and so decisively. In contrast, James Oakes sees the passage of Lovejoy's bill and Trumbull's similar resolution as the moment when the Republican policy of military emancipation became operational. These combined acts of legislation formed "the first federal law in American history designed to emancipate slaves in states where slavery was legal,"[21] and Lovejoy had initiated it.

When Lovejoy's resolution passed, Frederick Douglass applauded in his newspaper, but later he expressed his frustration at the administration's refusal to enforce it. "When Congress voted upon the resolution of Mr. Lovejoy, declaring the recapture of runaway slaves no part of the present business of our army, we seemed on the verge of the right path; but when the Government decided that no more slaves should be allowed within the lines of our army, and that none should follow our soldiers, the loss was greater than the gain."[22] Douglass and Lovejoy consistently held similar views. At this point they agreed on policies concerning contraband. Whether it was by coincidence, independent invention, or private conversations, it seemed that Douglass would publicize an idea for action in his newspaper and then Lovejoy would introduce it as a resolution in the House, or vice versa. The two men were working in tandem.

On July 22, 1861, Lovejoy and other congressmen and civilians went to observe the Battle at Bull Run/Manassas, a few miles from Washington, D.C., in Virginia. Charles H. Ray, editor of the *Chicago Tribune*, went with Lovejoy. They were shocked to see how slaves had been ordered to build a honeycomb of batteries that effectively repulsed the Union soldiers. After that, Lovejoy and Ray began to speak publicly about recruiting black men to work for the Union.[23]

As soon as Congress adjourned, Lovejoy returned to Princeton. On August 17 a telegram from Secretary of War Simon Cameron informed him that his request to enlist had been accepted. On September 27, 1861, Lovejoy left for St. Louis wearing a colonel's uniform.

During that autumn, both black and white women in Illinois faced tough situations at home. Husbands left home for war work and women suddenly became the breadwinners for their families, often taking work outside the home.[24] Farmers' wives were harvesting the crops planted by their husbands.[25] In Chicago, black parents suddenly faced new restrictions placed against their schoolchildren by local white officials.[26] Black families accepted refugees into their homes.[27] Black and white women sewed garments, canned food, packed supplies, and sent packages to their men through their churches and through the United States Sanitary Commission.[28] A few white women entered professional roles for the first time as nurses and managers under stressful conditions.[29] In Princeton the small black community organized an African Methodist Episcopal Church and found a minister for the harried flock.[30]

Colonel Lovejoy Sees Slavery Disintegrate in Missouri and Devises a War Plan

Lovejoy arrived in St. Louis on September 27 and reported to General John C. Frémont. He spent several days of his two months in the Union Army working as a member of a three-judge Claims Commission with the German American Illinois lieutenant governor, Dr. Gustave Koerner, and abolitionist editor and congressman Rev. John A. Gurley of Cincinnati. Their charge was to adjudicate which Missourians should be reimbursed for material property taken by the Union Army. Koerner remembered that Lovejoy "was more prepared to allow claims than I."[31] Koerner was referring to food, horses, or ammunition taken by the army. However, when slaves escaped across Union lines and their owners pursued them, Lovejoy's fellow officers, in jocular fashion, would refer the slaveholders to Lovejoy. He invariably rejected their applications to recapture their slaves. He saw hundreds of black refugees, and he sent some to Illinois, where they became a part of his ever expanding coalition for equality.

In Missouri Lovejoy saw firsthand that the Union Army lacked a firm policy on how to deal with ex-slaves. In the middle of the battle, many blacks did not know what to do, where to go, or whether they were free.[32] "Nine contrabands came into camp today, father mother and indeed I think eight children," he wrote.[33] He advised General Frémont to send such families to Illinois, a policy for which he would suffer as a candidate in the 1862 campaign. He told Eunice: "A man came in this [group] and I have taken him for a servant. I do not know how he will turn out."

Lovejoy described to his family how he had slept one night in a secessionist's farmhouse, and early the next morning the owner, an old gentleman, came to his room, "forlorn and nearest broken," and said that his negroes had all left him during the night and that he "would not be able to get me any breakfast." The two women and their children had promised never to leave him, he cried. He managed to prepare breakfast, but "the loss formed the theme of conversation during breakfast. . . . He asked me how to proceed but I told him I had no idea what course he had better pursue. I sympathized and consol[ed] with him as I could under the circumstances. You may suspect I had something to do with the slaves' decision to run away but really I did not know a thing about it directly or indirectly."[34]

Lovejoy left Missouri in November with a more realistic understanding of what the Union Army was facing. As he traveled home, he formulated a pragmatic program to test on his constituents in Princeton and to introduce through a series of bills in the House of Representatives in December.

Lovejoy spoke to the citizens of his district gathered together in Princeton in front of the courthouse. First, he advocated expanding the Confiscation Act to give actual freedom to all slaves who crossed Union Army lines. Second, although he would never accept the slaveholders' view that people could be property, he was now willing to give compensation to loyal border state slaveholders if they freed their slaves. Third, in the past Lovejoy had supported the constitutional requirement of allowing slavery to remain in the states where it already existed. But that was during times of peace, and this was a time of war. Therefore, that promise no longer applied.[35] Now, Lovejoy declared, the Lincoln administration should end slavery in the Southern states. Presidents John Quincy Adams and James Monroe, Harvard law professor Theophilus Parsons, and others had concluded that in time of war, if necessity demanded it, the president had the right to abolish slavery.[36] These experts agreed that the U.S. Constitution conferred these powers to the president as Commander-in-Chief in order to protect the nation.[37]

With this third point, Lovejoy was calling for universal military emancipation. "What right do we have to destroy slavery? I answer briefly, that if we do not destroy it, it will destroy us."[38] In Oakes's view, the idea to deploy military emancipation as a means of destroying slavery was revolutionary.

Fourth, Lovejoy said that in order to win the war, the nation had the obligation to enlist black troops from among the four million loyal African Americans. He testified to the extensive relationships he had with African Americans over many years. "If we proclaim freedom to these men, they will do nobly for us. I have seen a great many, and know how they feel. They are our natural allies, our natural friends."[39]

The *Bureau County Republican* published Lovejoy's speech. Members of the coalition for equality heard news of Lovejoy's intent to introduce key legislation in Congress.

Republicans Take Charge in the House of Representatives

On December 2, 1861, Lovejoy moved into an apartment in the Washington home of surgeon Dr. Allen G. Breed and his wife, Gulielma, who engaged in social work as a full-time volunteer. They were Quaker activists who had been supporting the Underground Railroad, the education of black children in the District of Columbia, and medical care of slave and free black residents and fugitive newcomers for years. That February, Gulielma Breed published *An Appeal of the National Association for the Relief of Colored Women and Children*. In the following eight months the core group of radicals would initiate debates, bills, and resolutions for the purpose of ending bondage, and while pushing President Lincoln, wait for public opinion and congressional approval to move closer to their goals.

On December 3, Lovejoy mingled with the other 182 members of the House. Lovejoy and his antislavery colleagues who headed committees—Stevens, Julian, Ashley, Gurley, Bingham, Elihu Washburne, and Morrill—planned to offer major bills to increase prosperity, weaken slavery, and advance equality. J. G. Hewitt, Princeton newspaper editor, described Lovejoy as "the acknowledged leader in all the great reforms in our national legislation."[40] Although the core group had developed mutual trust over the years and none of them sought stardom, they occasionally stumbled and got in each other's way. Potter was briefly furious at Lovejoy for introducing his committee's legislation at Grow's request; Stevens and Lovejoy threw epithets at each other on the floor of the House; and Ashley and Bingham did not always agree on Lovejoy's recommendations.

Almost every day in December, Lovejoy was on the floor of the House. Almost daily he brought a specific concern related to his experience in Missouri. The first

Confiscation Act had intended to protect escaping slaves who crossed the Union lines, but Lovejoy saw in Missouri that a stronger law was required. A consensus was developing in the House of Representatives that if army work was available, blacks should be employed and the principle of universal freedom applied.

On December 9, Lovejoy introduced a bill making it a crime for anyone in the army or navy "to capture or return, or aid in the capture or return, of fugitive slaves."[41] His former boardinghouse mate Henry Wilson introduced a similar bill in the Senate. Negative reaction came quickly. Congressman Philip B. Fouke, a downstate Illinois Democrat, scolded Lovejoy: "If my colleague would pay less attention to the Negro and more to the interest of the country we would get along much better with this war."[42] In March 1862 the House approved, by a vote of eighty-three to forty-two, the bill prohibiting the U.S. military from enforcing the fugitive slave clause. Lincoln signed it on March 13, 1862. While it settled an immediate problem, Lovejoy realized that radicals must deal with the much bigger task of drafting a more comprehensive confiscation bill. Lincoln had indicated that he would consider it.

On December 20, Lovejoy kept pushing his plan by trying to bring out of the Judiciary Committee a bill that would "confiscate the property of rebels, unconditionally liberate their slaves, and protect slaves from recapture by rebel masters."[43] Although in a climax of complicated maneuvers he tabled his own motion, the committee retained the proposal. Passage of a second Confiscation Act would take the greatest effort of any bill in the Thirty-Seventh Congress. On this day, his motion fell eight votes short. Confiscation was complicated because it contained a dozen points of controversy, and the House had to find a compromise for each one. In such skirmishes, Lovejoy could count on about 50 radical members to back him up, but 39 additional men were required to reach a majority in the 183-member House.[44] To find them was the task of the core, antislavery group that included Lovejoy.

Frederick Douglass was following what happened to Lovejoy's confiscation bill. When it was defeated, he wrote in frustration to Gerrit Smith, "I am bewildered by the spectacle of moral blindness . . . which the government of Lincoln presents. Is there hope? I shall think there is not if all the antislavery measures now before Congress are laid aside as was Lovejoy's resolution of Friday."[45] He could not understand how it could fail, for such a large majority of the House members were Republicans.

Lovejoy was able to pass resolutions to establish diplomatic relations with Haiti and Liberia.[46] Recognition of Haiti had special significance for the black community because it provided an "irrefutable argument" that "the descendants of Africa were never designed by their Creator to sustain inferiority, or even a mediocrity in the chain of beings."[47] Lovejoy also introduced a bill, much desired by John Jones, to repeal the law requiring blacks to carry passes while traveling in the North. The bill passed.[48]

Lovejoy was deeply irritated by a nettlesome but ubiquitous question raised by members of the House: "What shall we do with the Freedmen?" the questioner would ask in a condescending tone. To avoid the obvious answer, conservative whites repeated the question. Frederick Douglass gave his answer: "Do nothing with them; mind your business, and let them mind theirs. Your *doing* with them is their greatest misfortune."[49]

Lovejoy recognized that any plan for slave emancipation to require appropriations or reparations to the ex-slaves would lead conservatives to reject it.[50] He wanted to introduce legislation to assure that freedmen would at least receive all the rights enjoyed by whites—the right to join the army, travel without a pass, serve on a jury, have children educated in a public school, purchase land, and vote. He assumed that once freed, blacks should be equal citizens.

African Americans were daring to think ahead, beyond the end of the war to an era without slavery. Two associations of African Methodist Episcopal churches invited Lovejoy to come and speak with them about their future. One event was held at Israel Church near Capitol Hill on January 25, 1862. A packed audience surrounded Lovejoy as he gave a discourse described by the church's secretary as "logically, prophetically, clearly, and forcibly, carrying his audience clear through the vast wilderness of prejudice and slavery, into the fruitful 'promised land' of equality."[51] He lifted the assembled clergy beyond their present situation to one they longed to imagine, a vision of life for people of color in the years after emancipation. When the black trustees showed Lovejoy that they had procured a permit to hold the assembly legally, Lovejoy tore it into fragments as a remonstrance against slavery and the bureaucracy that dismissed freedoms of speech and assembly. Black freedom would not be enough; equality demanded that African Americans receive the entire Bill of Rights as well.

A few weeks later Lovejoy spoke at an AME Church Conference in Baltimore. Its trustees also procured a permit from the mayor to hold the assembly. When they showed it to Lovejoy, he took a match and burned it in protest "against this species of despotism."[52] In mid-March Lovejoy was scheduled to lecture to another large audience of black people, in Washington again.[53]

One day in the House of Representatives, after Lovejoy eviscerated slavery in a debate with Kentuckian John Crittenden, slaveholder Charles A. Wickliffe, also from Kentucky, put Lovejoy on the spot, saying, "I hear that, at a meeting of an association of blacks in the city, some members of Congress attended and edified them with about such a speech as we have heard here to-day." Lovejoy answered, "I have, during this session, twice addressed an assembly of colored people." He said he told them nothing he would not say in the halls of Congress. "I told them they had just as much right to hang their masters as their masters had to hang them; just as much right to sell their masters' children as their masters had to sell theirs."[54]

Each time the question "What shall we do?" came up, in January, February, and March, Lovejoy tried to reassure Congress about the future self-sufficiency of colored people.[55] However, historian V. Jacques Voegeli writes that Lovejoy's proposal ignored reality and public opinion, and that Lovejoy naively believed that liberation from slavery alone would erase white people's racial prejudices, which were virulent in the North, especially in Illinois.[56] Another historian, James M. McPherson, disagreed that the abolitionists were irresponsible and insisted that they understood much more than their critics alleged.[57] Voegeli may have been unaware of the practical bills on landownership, homesteading, and agriculture that Lovejoy would introduce in the House during the Thirty-Seventh Congress, all of which were intended to provide a legal and economic foundation for the freedmen's self-sufficiency. Lovejoy was painfully aware of what needed to be done.

From a different perspective, author Herman Belz supports Lovejoy's and Douglass's views and recommendations, warning that paternalism built on prejudice, as expressed in Congress, was inevitably destructive, whether in the form of a gradual release from slavery, colonization, apprenticeship, or sharecropping. Supervising the freedmen would deny their free status.[58] Douglass noted the irony that from the slaveholders' perspective, British West Indian emancipation had failed, but from the perspective of former slaves, their condition was vastly improved; they had created their own farms, set up residences as families, and achieved some civil rights.[59]

Lovejoy had grown up with free and self-sufficient blacks in Maine. He had observed there that when states and municipalities refrained from passing prejudicial laws against them, and when communities ceased discriminating against them in education, housing, and employment, blacks managed well.[60]

When the question arose in Congress once again, an exasperated Lovejoy aimed directly at the slaveholders' unspoken dread: "They can not only take care of themselves, but they can get along without their masters much better than their masters can without them."[61] He had seen that in Missouri.

Bills on Sequestration, Agriculture, and Homesteading

The pragmatic Lovejoy believed that landownership was the major path to stabilizing a middle class and achieving social equality. It was generally illegal for blacks to buy land. If Lovejoy's three bills became law, they would help freedmen achieve economic freedom.[62]

On January 8, 1862, he presented a sequestration bill that would confiscate land from traitors and make it available for purchase by freedmen and whites. It outlined a legal process by which blacks could purchase land abandoned by rebels. Union Army generals posted in the rebel states would appoint commissioners of sequestration, who would be authorized to sell abandoned property and to send the profits to the United States Treasury. Sequestered homesteads of not more than 150 acres could be auctioned to families who would develop them over three years. If they succeeded as farmers, the land would become their own, as in the West. Although the House approved, fifty-two to zero, to send Lovejoy's resolution to the Committee on Public Lands, the committee was unable to resolve deep differences of opinion among its members and could not bring a recommendation to the House floor.[63]

Lovejoy's sequestration legislation was needed right away on the Sea Islands off South Carolina's coast. Confederate owners of prime cotton-growing plantations there had quickly abandoned them under fire. The U.S. Treasury Department was charged with selling the land. Without a sequestration policy, the usual Northern real estate developers would arrive from New York and Boston and snatch up large acreages at big profits. Only the worst land would be available for African American farmers. On June 7, 1862, an act was passed whereby property could be seized from traitors but kept only during the new owner's lifetime.[64] Lovejoy's bill would have established purchasers as permanent landowners. What actually happened aided white buyers instead. Most congressmen's reluctance to take the radical step of confiscating land and redistributing acres to freedmen would be a major factor in the postwar failure of interracial integration and reconciliation.

Lovejoy's second initiative was a major success. It offered practical assistance to farmers through scientific agricultural research. On February 11, 1862, Lovejoy, known by many as "the Farmer's Congressman," as chairman of the House Committee on Agriculture brought to the House floor a bill to establish a Department of Agriculture.[65] The effect of this new department would be immense, as farming was the chief occupation of the vast majority of Americans. When conservatives tried to reduce the bill's scope from a department to a bureau, Lovejoy accepted it with equanimity, knowing full well that it would soon expand from citizen demand. Editor J. G. Hewitt had described his congressman's breadth of concerns accurately when he wrote that Lovejoy had proven himself not only the champion of freedom but also the real working friend of the laboring classes.[66]

Lovejoy had worked hard on a third path toward building a society of equals, through the wide distribution of public lands. Although President Buchanan had vetoed the 1860 Homestead bill, President Lincoln made it clear that he was eager to sign it. On February 28, Speaker Grow, a veteran of several failures to pass such legislation, requested that Lovejoy ask the late-arriving Public Lands Committee chairman, John Fox Potter, to present the Homestead bill to the House for a vote. Once it had passed both chambers, Lincoln signed this plank of the Republican Party Platform on May 20, 1862.[67] Essentially the same bill that Grow had initiated and Lovejoy had managed the previous year,[68] it gave hundreds of thousands of families the opportunity to buy a farm and start an independent life as landowners. The bill was a priority of women. Revolutionary as it became for the growth of a sturdy white American middle class and for the prosperity of the nation, it did not provide African Americans opportunity to buy land. This omission had to be a great disappointment to Lovejoy and an even greater disillusionment to blacks who were watching in Washington and Illinois.[69]

Freeing and Educating Slaves in the District of Columbia and Territories

The radicals decided the time had come to introduce the emancipation bill for the District of Columbia. Lovejoy's close friends, Senators Henry Wilson and Charles Sumner of Massachusetts, began the process in the Senate on March 30, 1862. Wilson said it was the first installment of the great debt all white people owed to an enslaved race and would be recognized as one of the victories of humanity. Yet half of the senators held a very different vision and voted to make it a requirement that all freed D.C. African Americans must move to Liberia. At the last moment, ardent antislavery Republican vice-president Hannibal Hamlin of Maine broke the tie, removing mandatory colonization from the bill.

On the day of the vote, April 9, the galleries of the House of Representatives were filled and the corridors were jammed. African American men stood close to the back wall of the gentlemen's gallery. Prior to Grow's election as Speaker, any black person who dared come to the door of one of the galleries would have been denied entrance. Grow changed the rule, and on this occasion many blacks were present.[70] Lovejoy let his House colleagues take the lead on the bill. Thaddeus Stevens had expedited the bill's scheduling, and Lovejoy's neighboring congressman, Chicagoan Isaac Arnold, presented it to the House. Next, Stevens, Bingham, and others lined up to speak.[71] Opponents were city councilmen, border state congressmen, and D.C. slaveholders. Lincoln had said that he would sign the bill only if it was amended to provide compensation to D.C. slaveholders. Roscoe Conkling of Utica, New York, quickly specified a compensation of approximately $300 per slave. With three thousand slaves in the District, the total cost would be nearly $1 million.

Lovejoy was content to rely on his colleagues, but when a member of Congress— speaking on behalf of the slaveholders who had ruled the District of Columbia for six decades—complained that $300 per slave was below the fair market price, Lovejoy jumped to his feet and waved a piece of paper in his hand. He was holding a pledge that a conniving slaveholding woman had given to the free husband of one of her slaves, promising not to sell the man's wife and child. Then she sold them anyway. "Talk about robbery! *Every* slave here has been robbed and stolen, and *every* man who holds a slave is a man thief."[72] Then he displayed the paper on which Louis Mackall, the slaveholder, had promised freedom after receiving payment from the man for his wife and child but had taken them instead to the slave pen in Baltimore and sold them. "In this house brazen men stand up and talk about robbing, because we give only $300 apiece on average to deliver these poor oppressed beings from a condition of brutism. It is the sublimity of impudence."[73]

The debate had reached its decisive moment. In the men's gallery, affected slaveholders gripped their fingers tight. A cluster of African Americans from the Washington Island United Literary Association leaned away from the wall, trying to hear every word. One of them, John W. Lee, observed that Lovejoy had spoken until his locks were wet with perspiration.[74]

Then it was time to vote. The count in the House was ninety-two to thirty-eight.[75] Every antislavery congressman relished his moment of glory as he cast his vote for freedom.[76] J. G. Hewitt wrote in the Princeton newspaper, "Every Negro in the District of Columbia looks upon Lovejoy as the deliverer of the race." He was a moving spirit behind the legislation and had pushed the House to approve D.C. emancipation—the published goal of his brother Elijah. Lovejoy admitted he was most proud to have his name attached to this act.

The slaves would be freed at exactly midnight on April 15. On that day, the seventeen black churches began to fill up with men, women, and children ready to express their jubilation. At the Union Bethel Church, African American parishioners gathered, sang, and prayed as they watched the clock strike twelve. As the new day began, "the crowd was crying, 'Glory to God! Glory to God!' Suddenly someone shouted out, 'Glory to Lovejoy! Glory to Lovejoy!' But the minister reminded his flock, 'No, I tell you, Glory to God!'"[77]

In Chicago, after many newspapers repudiated the act of emancipating D.C.'s slaves, a mass meeting of African Americans was held at the AME Church, now on the corner of Jackson Street and Fourth Avenue. Led by their president, John Jones, they remonstrated against those proslavery editorials with a series of carefully crafted resolutions prepared by their committee, which included stalwarts W. R. Bonner, M. L. Lewis, E. R. Williams, L. Isbell, H. Bradford, J. Patrick, J. F. Platt, J. L. Thomas, and G. Lee. "The meeting in all its details was harmonious and enthusiastic," yet its attendees were unaware that this was just the first step toward emancipation.[78]

On Monday morning, May 8, 1862, there was probably a liveliness in Lovejoy's step. On behalf of the House Committee on Territories, of which he was an active member, he was going to present his friend Isaac Arnold's bill to abolish slavery in U.S. territories.[79] Preventing the extension of slavery into the territories had been Lovejoy's desire since Congress had voted for the Missouri territory to become a slave state when he was a boy in Maine. It had been his written goal since 1842, the purpose of his maiden speech at Springfield in 1855, and the centerpiece of the Republican Party platform. Because Lovejoy had been associated with this proposal for so many years, the *Chicago Tribune* called the new statute the "Arnold-Lovejoy Act."

Democrat Samuel S. Cox from Columbus, Ohio, demanded an amendment. He lamented that the House was doing nothing for the white race, nothing, "except for the negro."[80] Lovejoy responded, "Men jeer about the 'everlasting nigger.' You cannot get rid of him, sir. You might just as well try to wipe out Jehovah's government, and crumble the pillars of God's throne. In the Negro just now are embodied and represented here before us the RIGHTS OF MAN." Then he added with a twinkle, "They are here to punish us." At that, laughter from many congressmen broke the tension.[81]

A few days later, on May 12, Lovejoy presented a simplified bill. Horace Greeley, editor of the *New York Tribune*, was watching and later wrote that Lovejoy "pressed" it "to a vote."[82] It passed the House, eighty-five to fifty. Then Illinois senator Orville Browning reported Lovejoy's bill to the Senate, and it agreed, twenty-eight to ten, to insert "That, from and after the passage of this act, there shall be neither slavery nor involuntary servitude in any of the Territories of the United States." Predictably, all Democrats voted against the bill, but on June 19, 1862, Lincoln signed it.[83] Democrats were well aware that this decision shifted power from slaveholders to Northern interests.[84] The *Chicago Tribune* chose to honor the two Illinois representatives behind the new law and named it the Arnold-Lovejoy Act.[85]

For many years Lovejoy had urged officials to offer public education to black children only to have Democrats vote against it. As an active member of the Committee on the District of Columbia, he supported Senator Henry Wilson, who introduced a bill titled "Providing for the Education of Colored Children."[86] In 1862, local D.C. law required that 10 percent of property and real estate taxes be allocated to a public school fund. Lovejoy knew that, just as in Illinois in 1855, African American taxpayers derived no benefit from the taxes they paid since the public schools supported by the fund were for white children only.[87] On May 9, 1862, the senate passed Wilson's bill, a week later the House agreed, and on May 21, President Lincoln signed it into law. For the first time, the District of Columbia public school system would provide education for black children, and the taxes from local property owned by African Americans would be set aside to finance schools for black children. That year it amounted to $265.[88]

Lovejoy identified a problem that arose. The law instructed Secretary of the Interior Caleb Smith to appoint a board of trustees for black schools, but Smith was preoccupied and had not done so.[89] On June 23, Lovejoy introduced a bill to transfer power from the nonfunctioning board to a new group that included his host, Dr. Allen G. Breed, founder of Freedman's Hospital in Washington, D.C.[90] Lovejoy's bill became law on July 11, and the new board finally began to function.[91]

Two Lovejoy Speeches Push the Stalled House

Resolutions to expand the first Confiscation Act were submitted to the House Judiciary Committee as early as December 1861, but Chairman Hickman of the Judiciary Committee did not put them on the House agenda until March 20, 1862. The long interval indicated what Lovejoy had suspected all along, that this would be the most difficult legislation to negotiate.[92] The author of one of the bills submitted, young Thomas Dawes Eliot of Massachusetts, was designated the point man. Democrats and Unionists opposed any confiscation bill, knowing that "once it passed, the old ways could not be restored."[93] Conservative and moderate Republicans tried to water down each section.[94] But radical Republicans considered this legislation a necessary stepping-stone to emancipation.[95]

Lovejoy and his radical colleagues had submitted several bills with varying approaches to this complicated and controversial subject, hoping that one would win enough votes to pass. They hoped that once enacted, it would provide the preliminary legal foundation for the revolutionary military emancipation of all slaves. Bingham had saved Lovejoy's comprehensive bill, which would confiscate the property of rebels, unconditionally liberate their slaves, and protect slaves from recapture by rebel masters. Although Lovejoy had unintentionally tabled it, Bingham preserved it along with the others.[96] It was not surprising that Bingham and Lovejoy looked out for each other in this way, for the radical friends shared a similar outlook. Bingham grew up in the extreme antislavery Associate Presbyterian Church and graduated from the denomination's Franklin College, sometimes referred to as the fountainhead of the abolition sentiment in eastern Ohio.[97] Bingham wanted to be sure he had all three of Lovejoy's elements available for consideration when constructing the final bill.

What came to be called the Second Confiscation Act dealt with the constitutional basis for confiscation of property; the categories of slaves to be freed; the legal proceedings necessary to remove slaveholders' property and to protect former slaves from recapture; and the applicability of the war powers theory.[98] It had to state who should decide when the moment of military necessity to free the slaves had been reached—the Congress or the president. Finally, it dealt with whether blacks should be recruited for the Union Army.

Lovejoy, determined to change votes, made two significant public appearances during the fractious conflict over confiscation, both at crucial times. The first crisis came when Democrats and conservative Republicans defeated the radicals' emancipation bill on April 22, 1862, and a shocked Thaddeus Stevens cried out, "The rebels have a majority of the house!"[99] With the radicals' bill in peril and the radicals in disarray, the politically savvy Crittenden from Kentucky shrewdly calculated that this might be a time when he could pick up some moderates and make it impossible for the radicals to legislate any second confiscation bill. On April 23, in a major speech to the House, Crittenden offered a proposition to President Lincoln: if he would halt all attempts to free the slaves and begin to compromise with the South, there would be a niche for him in history and a statue next to George Washington in the capitol rotunda.

Republicans were outraged. When the Republican caucus met that evening, they chose Owen Lovejoy to make the formal, eviscerating response to Crittenden. The next day, April 24, Lovejoy began with a sweeping, full-length denunciation of slavery; then in a dramatic rhetorical gesture, he recast Lincoln—perhaps for the first time—as the true liberator and emancipator: "Let Abraham Lincoln make himself, as I trust he will, the emancipator, the liberator, as he has the opportunity of doing, it."[100]

Lovejoy's speech had a powerful impact on the temporarily set back radicals, helping them regain their determination to find enough votes to pass the Second Confiscation Act. That evening, Isaac Arnold took Lovejoy's speech to the White House and read it aloud to Lincoln, who heard those majestic words—*liberator*, *emancipator*—perhaps for the first time applied to him.

The second crucial occasion on which Lovejoy spoke was after the House had voted to accept a watered-down *substitute* for the confiscation bill that remained unclear on key points. The New York City Emancipation League invited Lovejoy to speak at the Cooper Union on June 12, 1862. They hoped his speech would inspire citizens to press House members to vote for a stronger bill. Lovejoy hoped it would persuade league members to be patient with Lincoln and persuade the president that the time had come to act. He hoped his message to abolish slavery would bolster the hopes of African Americans, women, and clergy in Illinois, and everywhere, who had been supporting him for so many years. William Cullen Bryant, lion of New York City's cultured society, introduced Lovejoy to the crowd.[101]

Lovejoy announced to the Cooper Union audience that "emancipation of the slave is essential to the safety and perpetuity of the Republic" and "emancipation is a national necessity."[102] The time had come for Congress to pass the Second Confiscation Act and for President Lincoln to prepare an emancipation proclamation. Having stated his position, Lovejoy presented a simple, foundational idea that had undergirded his thinking: the equality of human beings. "What is the central thought, the nucleus idea around which our organic political elements crystallize? You know that this nuclear thought is the equality of mankind. This is the sun around which our political system revolves. . . . Every piece of mechanism must have a unity of design and of execution. It must have some one central portion to which all its parts are adapted. . . . If this is not the case, then part will clash with part, cog grate against cog, collision and repulsion occur, and destruction to the machinery ensues" He likened government to machinery: "Any foreign or discordant element or theory introduced will, if not removed, cause friction. Slaving is that foreign and discordant element. It throws it out of gear and if not extracted will break and destroy it. . . . It does not accord with our theory of government." What makes government operate smoothly is equality: "This equality of the human race is the pivot upon which our government rests and resolves and its practical denial is the virtual overthrow of our theory of government."[103]

Lovejoy ended his lecture with "Long live the republic! Let it be perpetual! . . . But American Slavery . . . let it perish! PERISH! PERISH!"[104] This address was the apex of Lovejoy's rhetorical career. His friends had previously invited Lincoln to speak at Cooper Union; now they had invited Lovejoy.

Soon after Lovejoy returned from New York City, on June 18, the emancipation bill passed the House by a vote of eighty-two to fifty-four, but it did not pass the Senate.[105] Congress spent another week in open debate and commissioned a conference committee between the two chambers from which came the final form of the Second Confiscation Act, combining both confiscation (material property) and emancipation (persons), signed by the president on July 17.[106] Edward Magdol claims that this act contained the heart of Lovejoy's original bill.[107] The carefully crafted Second Confiscation Act obliterated the slaveholders' claim that there was "property in man." This new understanding, planted years ago by the antislavery movement, was finally bearing fruit.[108] The president could now employ persons of African descent to suppress the rebellion; he could, without warning, authorize seizure of the property of officers of the Confederate government and, after sixty days' warning, the property of all others supporting the rebellion.[109]

In 1926, historian James Garfield Randall went out of his way to deplore both the Confiscation Act and the Second Confiscation Act, judging them so legally incoherent that the attorney general never bothered to issue the instructions for implementing the law.[110] In sharp disagreement, nearly a century later James Oakes found the two statutes legalizing *military* emancipation to have been well crafted and appropriately implemented by the secretary of war.[111] Unfortunately, Oakes believes that as a result of Randall's appraisal, scholars over the years have paid little attention to the original Confiscation Act, which was one of Lovejoy's major initiatives.

While the Second Confiscation Act represented great progress toward the ultimate goal and made it clear that Republicans intended to destroy slavery in the seceded states, it was still not the universal emancipation that Lovejoy and other radicals sought.[112] Nor did it protect former slaves from reenslavement.

The session of Congress was ending when Isaac Arnold and Owen Lovejoy visited Lincoln at the Soldiers' Home, three miles north of the White House, on the sultry Sunday afternoon of July 13. His "Illinois friends" visited Lincoln often. This time Lincoln repeated his hope that the border states would accept the grand proposition he had offered them for the gradual, compensated emancipation of their slaves.[113] "Then you, Lovejoy, and you, Arnold, and all of us, would not have lived in vain! The labor of your life, Lovejoy, would be crowned with success. You would live to see the end of slavery."[114]

But the next day, the border congressmen rejected the president's proposal. Lincoln fell into a deep depression. He found himself imagining the painful changes the ending of slavery would bring to white Southerners and to destitute freedmen, and the enormous ramifications and unanticipated consequences for the whole nation. The weight of the responsibility paralyzed him. Robert Browne writes that a seriously depressed Lincoln asked Lovejoy to come to the White House and listen to him. As Lovejoy entered the mansion, he passed Thaddeus Stevens, who was leaving. Stevens whispered to Lovejoy, "The president needs your support and strongest encouragement. He is in deep melancholy. No one could better come. You know how to . . . help this burdened man."[115] Lovejoy listened to Lincoln for a long time. Then, as Lincoln sat in silence, Lovejoy observed, "I do not believe that God will [save the Union.] but I do believe the contrary, and that he will let this Nation go to destruction, as he has let hundreds before us for lesser oppressions of mankind if we do not" end slavery. After lengthy conversation, Lincoln responded, "I know you do not desire me to say more now than this. But I do want to assure you that it will be settled, so far as I can determine and take it."[116] Lincoln kept his decision to himself.[117]

Lovejoy headed back to Illinois. He did not know what Lincoln had decided to do, but he had the satisfaction of knowing that he and his colleagues in the House of Representatives and Senate had, through the Second Confiscation Act, provided the president with the legal foundation to proclaim emancipation.

He stopped in Chicago for a huge "war meeting" on August 2. There, he was reunited with black and white coalition friends. Those who participated in the

coalition were stunned at the changes taking place in Washington and at the bills
Lovejoy had initiated and President Lincoln had signed. In Chicago, he told the
audience that the government must enlist African Americans in the army: "These
Negroes know all the roads, all the swamps, all the country, and they are above all
the loyal people in the South that have helped us, and I would proclaim freedom
to them all, not for the sake of the Negro, but for the sake of the government."[118]
His black colleagues must have mused at his backhanded compliment.

• • •

From July 4, 1861, to July 1862, the Thirty-Seventh Congress revolutionized American society. As a leader of the inner circle in the House and a bridge to the White
House, Lovejoy introduced a resolution in July to begin dismantling slavery, a
central part of the first Confiscation Act. As a colonel in Missouri, he recommended
applying presidential war powers to free the slaves as a necessity to win the war,
and to recruit black soldiers. In 1862, Lovejoy and colleagues pushed legislation
reflecting the priorities of blacks, women, and churchmen in the coalition for
equality: D.C. emancipation, territorial emancipation, the Second Confiscation
Act, recognition of Haiti and Liberia, public schooling for black children in the
District of Columbia, homesteading made easier for women, agricultural research
for prospering farm families, and making sequestered land available to freedmen.
Women leaders corresponded with Lovejoy, and African Americans invited him
to speak. However, the more Lovejoy accomplished in Washington, the more the
Slave Power distorted, subverted, and castigated his achievements in his newly
drawn congressional district in Illinois.

9. Struggling to Enact Legal and Enduring Equality

Autumn 1862–March 25, 1864

Late in the summer of 1862, Lovejoy learned that he would face opponents in the coming campaign for his seat in Congress. In early August, a local Stephen A. Douglas supporter in Princeton was heard to say that he "didn't want to get down on his knees to Sambo and pray Oh! Niggers for God's sake save us."[1] The label "Sambo" had long been the caricature of one who was lazy, childlike, dependent, irresponsible, and black.[2] Princeton had diversified as southern white Illinoisans had moved into the antislavery town. Young Peter Bryant wrote his brother Marcus, who was studying at West Point, that the campaign was headed toward a low level of discourse.[3]

Many white Illinoisans' negative attitudes toward African Americans had not softened after the Civil War. As the slave system began to collapse and slaves ran away from besieged plantations, fear increased that blacks would encroach on Northern white communities and threaten white prerogatives and privileges.[4] Indeed, some escapees were finding their way to Chicago. Racial antipathy pervaded Illinois and was affecting the 1862 campaign.[5] The cardinal tactic the Democracy Party employed was to generate hostility toward African Americans in order to defeat Lovejoy.[6]

The Democratic majority in the state's General Assembly redrew the boundaries of Lovejoy's congressional district. Lovejoy had never campaigned in five of the seven counties in his new Fifth Congressional District. Many of the young men he had recruited for the Union Army were stationed far from polling places. His military service in Missouri in the fall of 1861 had kept him away from his constituents. Even his own Bureau County was conflicted. Lovejoy had not previously faced vicious campaigning, but now powerful political forces were deliberately working to defeat him.[7] The antislavery arm of the Republican Party supported

Lovejoy more than ever, but conservative Republicans like Senator Orville Browning kept silent, dedicated only to preserving the Union and stopping the spread of slavery into the territories. They did not favor emancipation and did not endorse Lovejoy.

In September, President Lincoln announced a preliminary Emancipation Proclamation. Blacks hesitated to rejoice. The proclamation would not free slaves in the border states or protect freed slaves in the South, and it had no enforcement powers. Frederick Douglass wrote to his readers, "We shout for joy!," but privately he was viscerally afraid that the Confederacy just might accept Lincoln's offer—take their last chance to return to the Union and save slavery. They had until December 31, 1862, to make up their minds. As the fourteen long weeks passed slowly, Douglass's anxiety increased: a week before the deadline, he wrote, "The suspense was painful."[8]

Southern-leaning whites in Lovejoy's district reacted differently. At first, all seemed cooperative. But then the preliminary proclamation heated the political atmosphere throughout Illinois. On September 25, the bipartisan statewide Union Nominating Convention, agreed to by both Republicans and Democrats when war broke out, met in Springfield. Lovejoy intended to obtain a rousing resolution from the delegates in favor of the proclamation. Young Illinois Republican Joseph G. Cannon, who would become Speaker of the U.S. House of Representatives decades later, watched what happened. When the prepared resolutions were passed out to the delegates, not one contained an endorsement of the proclamation. Lovejoy immediately stood up and addressed the chair. Suddenly, cries of "Sit down!" erupted all over the hall. Sensing hostile intruders, Lovejoy exclaimed, "God helping me, I will not sit down. I will be heard!"[9] Then Lovejoy spoke "as never a man spoke before," fighting for the delegates to affirm Lincoln's proposed proclamation.[10] When he could feel that he had a majority with him, he quickly offered a resolution endorsing it. Just as quickly, it was carried, as it "passed over all other justifications." He had barely prevailed; something was amiss.

At the same convention, Ebon C. Ingersoll, a War Democrat from Peoria, was nominated for the at-large seat in Congress. Perceiving that realignment was taking place within the two parties, Lovejoy and Ingersoll got together and planned their own united campaign. Lovejoy was willing to enter this cross-party collaboration because Ingersoll was willing to let slavery come to an end. The collaboration was essential for Lovejoy, who needed to obtain votes from Ingersoll's wing of the Democratic Party, especially in the Peoria area, to make up for the conservative Republican votes he was losing.[11]

Late in the campaign, just a month before the election, Lovejoy discovered a second group of men, also craftily calling themselves Unionists, suddenly appearing in his district. They held a clandestine and rigged nominating convention and enticed a respected but slavery-sympathizing Republican legislator, Colonel Thomas J. Henderson, then serving in the Union Army, to run for Congress against Lovejoy.[12] Secretly, Copperhead Democrats, not genuine Unionists, ran Henderson's campaign.[13]

The campaign, marked by bitterness and duplicity, became a heavy burden for Lovejoy. It required all the physical stamina he could muster. By November 1 he was exhausted.[14] The election took place on November 4, 1862. Lovejoy barely won, by a mere 641 votes.[15] Two years before, he had won by over 9,857.[16]

This backlash was not just happening in Illinois but was sweeping the North. Nationwide, thirty-four of Lovejoy's Republican collaborators in the House of Representatives lost their seats, including John A. Bingham of Ohio. However, five antislavery northern Illinois Republicans—Elihu Washburne, John Farnsworth, Isaac Arnold, Jesse Norton, and Lovejoy—would serve in the Thirty-Eighth Congress. Republicans retained control of the House, but Democrats increased from forty-two to eighty.[17] When the Thirty-Eighth Congress opened in December 1863, radical Republicans would have a narrower base to carry out their program. Fortunately, a regular Second Session of the Thirty-Seventh Congress would occur first, starting in December 1862.

The season had also been acrimonious for nonvoting African Americans in Illinois. As the day of emancipation came closer, pro-Confederate Democrats became angrier. In Chicago, hysteria triggered the "Omnibus Riot" in July and the "Riverbank Riot" in August, and blacks often became targets of violence. Some were able to protect themselves by aligning with prominent whites.[18] Hundreds of black refugees newly released from slavery were finding their way into Illinois towns; they did not know whether they would be treated as fugitives or as free persons. These newcomers also waited for news from family members dislocated during the war. One historian, Christopher Reed, describes some of the self-freed blacks arriving with social, psychological, and physiological scars so severe that many would never heal.[19] Another, Jennifer Harbour, describes daily hardships as well as attempts African Americans made to help one another.[20] Most white people, however, ignored the refugees' plight.

During this time additional black churches organized in Chicago, and they helped assimilate the hundreds of refugees. On September 7, 1862, Chicago coalition leaders held a public meeting to press President Lincoln to end the Fugitive Slave Act. They sent a delegation to talk with Lincoln the following week.[21] In these critical times, John Jones single-mindedly continued writing, cajoling, and meeting to build up the Repeal Association and to persuade white voters to give blacks the right to give testimony in court against whites.[22]

The racist backlash unleashed by Northern Democrats in the 1862 campaign disturbed everyone in the coalition for equality. Their hope lay in January 1, 1863—a date they referred to as Jubilee.

Lovejoy Calls for Universal Emancipation and Recruitment of Black Soldiers

Owen Lovejoy was home only thirteen days after the election; on November 17 he was on a train headed for Boston. On Saturday, November 22, Lovejoy was the special guest at a testimonial dinner held in his honor at the revered Parker House, flanked by his friends John Andrew, now the governor of Massachusetts, and Senators Charles Sumner and Henry Wilson. Lovejoy and Andrew gave speeches on the immediate necessity of recruiting black men for the Union Army.

The venerable abolitionist Theodore Weld, who had mentored Owen as he compiled Elijah's *Memoir* in 1838, was also present. Weld and his wife, Angelina Grimké, had moved to a home near Boston.[23] Lovejoy reminded Weld that William T. Allan, one of the seventy antislavery agents Weld had trained, was the first man on the prairie to urge Lovejoy to run for political office: "I owed my seat in Congress to Allan. He abolitionized my congressional district and sent me to Washington."[24] Allan never stopped working for Lovejoy from 1846 through 1862. In the recent deplorable campaign, Allan's work in Henry County had probably saved Lovejoy's seat.

The following Tuesday, November 25, Lovejoy was the heralded speaker in a lecture series sponsored by the Fraternity of the Twenty-Eighth Congregational Society, the reform-minded Unitarian Church in Boston started by the Reverend Theodore Parker.[25] It was held at the Tremont Temple, where events of Boston's black community often took place.

In early December the Second Session of the Thirty-Seventh Congress began. Days later, a group of Unionist congressmen tried to pass legislation that would stop Lincoln from making the revolutionary Emancipation Proclamation announced for January 1, 1863, but "Lovejoy, the bellwether of the House radicals, quickly moved to table the resolution."[26]

Just two days before Christmas, Confederate president Jefferson Davis had provocatively announced that he too planned to sign a proclamation—an ordinance that all black Union fighting troops should, if captured in the South, be dealt with according to the laws of the state in which they were seized. Historian Benjamin Quarles explains that this punishment was the equivalent of a death sentence.[27] Frederick Douglass predicted that after emancipation, freedmen would find themselves entrenched in racial prejudice: "The slave having ceased to be the abject slave of a single master, his enemies will endeavor to make him the slave of society at large."[28]

On New Year's Day, 1863, in Washington, D.C., after the president signed the Emancipation Proclamation and the telegraph wires carried the news, Lovejoy probably joined the huge black crowd gathered around Israel AME Church to hear the minister read the proclamation from a newspaper.[29] In Chicago, Quinn Chapel held morning and evening services of solemnity and celebration. The next day, however, anti-black hysteria in Chicago grew in intensity.[30] Aware of the proclamation's limitations, John Jones and his colleagues continued to urge white friends to act "in their behalf politically with the President and the Congress."[31]

The Second Confiscation Act of July 1862 had authorized the president to enlist black troops, but the Lincoln administration was holding back.[32] Finally, in early January 1863, the War Department gave Governor John Andrew of Massachusetts permission to form the Fifty-Fourth Massachusetts Regiment, the first black regiment to be recruited in the North.[33] In Boston, Lewis Hayden had prepared 125 black men in a drill company, and he announced that they were ready to enlist. Frederick Douglass became a recruiter; among his enlistees were his sons Charles and Lewis. Governor Andrew visited the Twelfth Baptist Church, a short walk from the state capitol, and told disappointed black recruits that the Secretary of War, Edwin M. Stanton, intended to appoint only white men as their officers, and that he "was powerless to correct this discriminatory situation."[34]

Disappointed, Thaddeus Stevens and Lovejoy decided to exert pressure on the War Secretary. On January 12, with leading black ministers watching from the gallery of the House, Stevens introduced the Negro Regiment bill, authorizing Lincoln to raise 150,000 black soldiers; slaves who enlisted, and their families, would become free, and the government would pay monetary compensation to slaveholders who were loyal to the Union.[35]

Lovejoy stood beside Stevens as he spoke and was the second to address the House. He reminded the House that additional troops were greatly needed; that white men were refusing to volunteer in sufficient numbers; that congressional Democrats were purposefully delaying a draft while black men were eager to volunteer. Therefore, Lincoln should order the large-scale enlistment of black troops.[36] Feeling resistance from Charles Wickliffe of Kentucky and other conservatives in the hall, Lovejoy shifted to another line of argument: black troops, he noted, could save the lives of as many as one hundred thousand white troops.[37] In the month of February 1863, more than sixty thousand "boys in blue" were sick every day, and the death rate from disease amounted to the equivalent of twenty-seven regiments in the past year. Army hospitals were overcrowded with victims of ague and malaria. Therefore, the North should recruit Negro soldiers.

Then Lovejoy made a greater demand: black men should serve as officers in black regiments. His young friend H. Ford Douglas of Illinois was ready to prove that he could be an accomplished officer of black troops. Democrats sitting in the House responded with jokes and jeers at the notion of "general Sambo," "colonel Sambo," and "captain Sambo."[38] But Lovejoy ignored their hoots; he had assisted so many strong, intelligent, courageous freedom seekers escaping to Canada that he knew the stereotype of blacks as lazy and irresponsible to be outrageous. Instead, he latched on to the slaveholders' insulting label and gave it a sarcastic twist. "Why, sir, I do not advocate putting white men under black officers. Nobody else does or ever did," he said with the pretense of haughtiness. Then, having coated their racism with ridicule, Lovejoy roundly repudiated it:[39] "But, as God is my judge, I would rather follow the black man than a slaveholder as an officer, for I would expect that the one would betray me, whatever his ability, while I am sure the other would be loyal and true, and fight it out." Laughter followed this remark. Lovejoy said that he would like to see some of "these gentlemen" sinking in the river, having sunk twice and about to go down the third time, with a black man on shore throwing out a coil of rope, and the Democrat refusing to grasp it to save his own life. "Colonel Sambo" would draw the white soldier ashore anyway.

As weeks went on, evidence mounted—as Lovejoy had predicted—that black troops were excelling. The first news came that the black Massachusetts regiments, led by Robert Gould Shaw into Charleston Bay, had proven their courage. Then the report that black soldiers had fought superbly at Milliken's Bend near Vicksburg brought further vindication. Lovejoy heard from Princeton that under the command of his young white neighbor Julian Bryant, a newly formed black regiment that was attacked by Confederate soldiers beat back their attackers with hand-to-hand combat of the deadliest kind. When the fighting was over, Bryant discovered that hundreds of his freedmen had been killed, and he was one of the few officers to survive.

Assistant Secretary of War Charles Dana concluded that "the bravery of the blacks in the battle of Milliken's Bend completely revolutionized the sentiment of the army with regard to the employment of Negro troops."[40] Adjutant General Lorenzo Thomas hailed Julian Bryant for leading his men despite having seen the skeletons of white officers who, commanding African American troops, had been captured, crucified, and burned.[41]

Despite blacks' excellence as soldiers, Secretary of War Stanton decided that the Union Army would not give equal pay to whites and blacks. Julian Bryant was so infuriated that his brave black soldiers received less pay that he protested to his uncle "Cullen" Bryant, who soon published an editorial in the *New York Evening Post* demanding equal pay for black soldiers.[42] Meanwhile, Julian Bryant was promoted to lieutenant colonel of the Ninety-Sixth U.S. Colored Infantry, which he commanded.[43]

In Chicago, black leaders including John Jones, Henry O. Wagoner, and Lewis Isbell were recruiting soldiers. In north-central Illinois, H. Ford Douglas was seeking both recruits and a command position. Joseph Barquet, who had moved to Galesburg, recruited a dozen men, who all served together.[44] In Lovejoy's Bureau County alone, eighteen black soldiers served in the Twenty-Ninth U.S. Colored Infantry from the small towns of Princeton, Ohio, Dover, Concord, Manlius, and Brawley; twenty-one men enlisted in the Eighth U.S. Colored Artillery; and five from the Illinois villages of Clarion, Ohio, Grover, and Berlin enlisted in the Thirteenth U.S. Colored Artillery.[45] By the end of the war, 70 percent of black males of military age had joined the Union Army.[46] And Owen Lovejoy never stopped telling Secretary Stanton that black soldiers deserved equal pay.

Lovejoy Falls Seriously Ill and Convalesces at Home

In late February 1863, Owen Lovejoy became desperately ill with smallpox. He was residing at the boardinghouse run by Margaret Bailey.[47] When Eunice learned from Margaret that Owen was severely afflicted, she sped there to care for him. Lovejoy remained in bed for weeks. Several times passersby saw President Lincoln enter Margaret Bailey's house, where he visited an emaciated Lovejoy in his apartment. After one such visit, a reporter wrote that "Lovejoy was thought to be better by the hopeful, cheerful [manner] of his visitor." But his recovery was still in question.[48] Concerned African Americans stopped by the apartment every day and asked what they could do to help.

Although he was very ill, Lovejoy tried to serve his constituents. He responded to a request from H. Ford Douglas to help him get transferred to build an all-black South Carolina regiment in which he would become a black officer.[49] Lovejoy requested that Rev. Henry McNeal Turner, the black minister of AME Israel Church, be appointed chaplain for the First Regiment of the U.S. Colored Troops; Turner became the first black army chaplain in the United States.[50] When her son was killed in action, Elizabeth Keckly, Mary Lincoln's dressmaker and confidante in the White House, asked Lovejoy to help in obtaining the pension that was her due. Owen asked his brother Joseph, who was working in the Patent Office, to see that her claim was processed.[51]

Eunice read aloud each letter that was delivered during his affliction. In 1863 Lizzie's oldest son, Austin Wiswall, became a white lieutenant of a black regiment in Virginia. He wrote from the battlefront, "For miles in every direction the Slaves have left their Masters bringing with them all the horses mules cattle and whatever else they could get hold of. Their places must be filled by soldiers from the Army or the people must starve. And the more intelligent of the citizens admit it."[52] Many Southern white soldiers were deceived into enlisting, more were forced in, and the majority were "heartily sick" of army life. "Neither are the Slaves as ignorant as they have been represented," wrote Wiswall. "The majority of them are more intelligent than the poor Whites." At the time of his letter, he believed that "there would be scarcely a word said, against the enlistment of colored soldiers, where six months ago there would have been open Mutiny. Owen and Eunice Lovejoy returned to Illinois in mid-April, and Owen began months of convalescence at home.

Over the preceding year Frederick Douglass had thought out a framework of what an interracial American future might look like and what must be done to build it. First, the Union Army should give white and black soldiers equal pay, equal work, and permission to appoint black officers. Second, the government and philanthropic societies should train a new class of men by establishing a legal basis for family relations, organizing schools for ex-slaves, and holding forums to explain democratic institutions to the freedmen. Third, it should provide opportunities for blacks to farm abandoned lands in the South. These actions would initiate a full civil and political equality for all blacks.[53] Either by coincidence or by collabora- tion, Lovejoy had presented bills for equal pay for blacks, public education in the District of Columbia for black children, and availability of sequestered land for freedmen. Lovejoy and Douglass were of like minds.

Lovejoy read the latest articles about the Sea Islands off South Carolina's coast, where the Union Army now controlled the land and supervised the freed slaves. Announcements from headquarters at Port Royal carried distressingly contradic- tory accounts of that land experiment. The Treasury Department had allowed wealthy Northern real estate speculators to buy land;[54] it inaccurately assumed that freedmen would want to be wage laborers, when in fact some had saved enough money to purchase lots. Finally, on September 16, 1863, Lincoln gave instructions that certain plantations should be reserved for heads of families of the African race, subdivided into twenty-acre lots, and sold at $1.25 per acre. By then, however, very little land on the islands was left for the freedmen.[55] But at the last minute, some African Americans combined their savings and made a small number of purchases.[56] The preference given to speculators foretold how paternalistic whites would set new boundaries around ex-slaves and obfuscate African American answers to the prime question: What should freedmen be allowed to do within the nation's economic structure after the war?[57]

That autumn, Mary Livermore of the Chicago-based North West branch of the United States Sanitary Commission (USSC), a relief agency that supported sick and wounded Union soldiers, asked Lovejoy to give an inspirational talk to the white women from Illinois and adjacent western states who were in charge of organizing the Chicago Sanitary Fair for the entire region. She requested that he ask Lincoln to send a copy of the Emancipation Proclamation, which would be put on sale at the fair, and he did. She also asked him to give a major address at the fair.[58] He did not tell her that his doctor had urged him to make no speeches at all; instead, he accepted all three requests.

Without fanfare, African American women who were able to do so participated in the United States Sanitary Commission.[59] H. Ford Douglas had married Sattira Steele, a gifted young teacher, in 1857, and they had a daughter, Helen. Sattira Douglas supported the fair by raising money, collecting donations, and urging other black women to assist the enterprise. However, neither she nor other black wives and mothers relied exclusively on the USSC to meet the needs of their husbands and sons in the army. Within the black community they organized the Chicago Colored Ladies' Freedman's Aid Society and the Ladies Loyal League and sent supplies to the men of their families directly.[60] Black Christian women multiplied their efforts by corresponding with each other through the *Christian Recorder*, the African American newspaper of the African Methodist Episcopal Church.[61] But Sattira Douglas's work was suddenly interrupted; she was urgently called to St. Louis to take care of her husband, who had contracted malaria in Mississippi while performing his duties with the Tenth Louisiana *Corps d'Afrique* and was in a frightfully emaciated condition. Somehow she managed to bring him to her parents' home in Chicago. Near the end of the war he received his commission as an officer, one of very few given to blacks, but he died soon after.[62]

The North West Sanitary Fair opened in six large buildings in Chicago on October 27, 1863. It continued for two weeks and raised almost eighty thousand dollars for soldiers' homes and hospitals.[63] Lovejoy's speech drew a big crowd. He offered honorary commissions of captain and major general to Livermore and the other women organizers of this enormous event. He also announced that his major legislative initiative in the upcoming Thirty-Eighth Congress would be a bill for universal emancipation that would make slavery a crime.

On Thanksgiving Day, Reverend Lovejoy was invited to speak at Hampshire Colony Church in Princeton. As the congregation gathered around him in his weakened condition, he led the pastoral prayer. He took his time. He thanked God for freedom of thought, worship, speech, and press, and most especially for the principle of equality that white people generally enjoyed but that God had intended for all. "We have been guilty in that we have oppressed our fellow man, in that we have robbed the slave of his wages, and his most valuable and sacred rights. Our Father, thou has had a controversy with us on this subject . . . thy judgments are upon us."[64] Later, he repeated his intention to introduce a bill in the House to make freedom universal and slavery a crime punishable by fine and imprisonment. He believed it was essential to exact punishment for reenslavement in order to break the Slave Power once and for all.[65]

Lovejoy Returns to Washington to Prevent Reenslavement

Eunice packed to go to Washington with Owen, who was very frail. They had wavered over a historic invitation from William Lloyd Garrison. The thirtieth anniversary of the American Anti-Slavery Society was being celebrated in Philadelphia almost on the day that the Lovejoys would be passing through on the train to Washington. Finally, Lovejoy sent an answer of regret, explaining that he had to save his strength for vital legislative initiatives.[66] Old friends read Lovejoy's letter at the banquet: "I am in favor of an act of Congress abolishing slavery throughout the entire limits of the United States and making it a penal offence to hold or claim to hold a slave."[67]

Lovejoy's resolutions fluttered in his fist as he slowly climbed the White House steps to the office of Lincoln's secretary, John Hay. It was a bustling Sunday morning, December 6, 1863, and Lovejoy was eager to introduce his bills onto the floor of the House of Representatives. Hay missed the gravity of Lovejoy's personal situation. Others who saw him that morning recognized his unnatural pallor and guarded gait.[68] But Hay did catch a definitive aspect of Lovejoy's relationship with Lincoln. He wrote in his diary that night that Lovejoy had "avowed his faith in Lincoln, though there is nothing subservient about it.'"[69] Whether Hay realized it or not, this was the key to Lovejoy's success in building relationships with other people: for no matter how powerful or how weak they were, he seemed to see everyone as an equal.

That evening Lovejoy attended the caucus. He wanted to submit his name for Speaker; he thought he could win, but he refrained. His close colleague Schuyler Colfax won. When the First Session of the Thirty-Eighth Congress was about to open on Monday, December 7, 1863, a diplomatic Colfax honored Lovejoy by asking him to call the session to order. Colfax appointed the same core men to be committee chairmen, asking Lovejoy to chair the House Committee on the District of Columbia. Thaddeus Stevens continued as chair of Ways and Means. George W. Julian of Indiana would chair the Public Lands Committee, and James Ashley of Ohio would take the Committee on Territories.[70] John A. Bingham of Ohio, who had lost his seat in the 1862 election, would be replaced on the Judiciary Committee.

Lovejoy formally introduced his resolutions on December 14, 1863.[71] These bills, if passed, would move African Americans well beyond the Emancipation Proclamation. It would declare the slaves free, protect them from unlawful search and seizure, and extend to them the right to testify in court, to sue and be sued in the same manner as other free white citizens.[72] Republicans realized that they must repeal old laws protecting slavery.[73] Lovejoy had been impressed by the legal research of William Whiting, a New England lawyer appointed solicitor in the War Department in December 1862, who argued that freeing four million slaves by federal proclamation did not, in itself, abrogate the local laws that established and protected slavery; he noted that further action beyond presidential emancipation would be necessary to "render slavery unlawful."[74] Therefore, slavery must be declared a punishable crime; any person convicted of an attempt to reenslave another person could be punished by imprisonment for one to five years or fined between one thousand and five thousand dollars.[75]

Unless slavery was made a crime, Lovejoy was certain that many whites would reenslave blacks after the war. Attorney General Edward Bates of Missouri had already ruled that free and freed blacks were citizens of the United States, thereby making reenslavement "a palpably unconstitutional deprivation of the 'privileges and immunities' of citizenship."[76] Even so, in 1863 reenslavement was no abstract threat. It took place routinely during the war as Southern congressmen threatened publicly to reenslave any individual they could get hold of.[77] In fact, reenslavement was the official Confederate policy for dealing with captured former slaves.[78]

Lovejoy was blocked. Without an aggressive radical member like John A. Bingham on the Judicial Committee, his bill would get no traction. Lovejoy knew that his bill for universal emancipation was ahead of public opinion and that the House was not ready to act on it, even though taking action to criminalize slavery was indispensable. Several of his closest radical friends, such as James Ashley, were following an alternative route by introducing the prohibition as an amendment to the U.S. Constitution.[79] Ashley believed that with Lincoln as president, a constitutional amendment was the safer legislative route to take while conservative Roger Brooke Taney was Chief Justice of the U.S. Supreme Court, for Taney might at any time find the Emancipation Proclamation unconstitutional. But an ailing Lovejoy feared that a constitutional amendment would take more months or years than he had, and indeed, he did not live to see it.

In the Senate, Lyman Trumbull, chairman of its Judiciary Committee, prepared the document for a constitutional amendment. Ashley introduced Trumbull's proposal in the House in April 1864, after Lovejoy's death. The House voted on it in June 1864 but failed to obtain the necessary two-thirds majority. Finally, on January 31, 1865—ten months after Lovejoy's death—the House approved the amendment.

After ratification, this act to prohibit slavery in the United States became the Thirteenth Amendment to the Constitution on December 18, 1865. Although Lovejoy died before its passage, scholars have assessed Lovejoy's impact upon it.

It prohibited slavery but said nothing about "the state of freedom that the absence of slavery implied"[80]—a vacuum Lovejoy had wanted filled. Historian Michael Vorenberg notes that the amendment's precise wording was a repudiation of radical Republican efforts to guarantee equal citizenship to freedmen.[81] Scholar Herman Belz recognizes that the radical Lovejoy fought for a much broader conception of rights, one that went beyond simple freedom from chattelism "that many Republicans came to identify with the Thirteenth Amendment."[82] Edward Magdol concludes that while Lovejoy was not present at the final passage, "Yet it was his cherished bill for universal emancipation in essence."[83]

Nevertheless, although the Thirteenth Amendment included a provision by which Congress could add punishments and penalties at some future time, such action to criminalize slavery was never taken. Congress never spelled out specific penalties for slaveholding. By contrast, it allowed old laws to remain on the books, specifically the law that anyone convicted of any crime could be exploited through forced labor. Unfortunately, by the 1880s, Southern white officials were arresting hundreds of thousands of blacks for standing on the corner, having no home, being in debt, lacking employment, talking back, or any imaginary misdemeanor in order to fill white businesses' requests for free labor in timber mills, factories, mines, and farms. African American men and women were sent in chains to provide forced labor—slavery by another name.[84]

Lovejoy had displayed perceptive foresight, predicting massive reenslavement and doing his best to prevent it. His brother's assassination had given him a painful and profound insight into the nature of human evil, and he had witnessed human beings who had succumbed to it. For a slaveholder to rid himself of the desire to control another, it would take a major religious reorientation that Lovejoy did not see happening. He believed that the law was the only recourse, but because of the timing of his death, he lost the opportunity to ensure that all necessary provisions were in place.

The End of the Illinois Black Laws

Nearly a year after Lovejoy's death, another of his goals was finally achieved. In the autumn of 1864, John Jones published the work for which he would be most remembered. On November 4, he composed and published, at his own expense, a sixteen-page argumentation titled "The Black Laws of Illinois and a few reasons why they should be repealed."[85] He especially targeted newly elected members of the state legislature and asked them "in the name of the Great God, who made us all," to "erase from your statute book that code of laws commonly called the Black laws." He incisively addressed each of the thirty sections of the revised Statutes of 1845, including sections of the Civil Code.[86] On January 25, 1865, the *New York Times* announced that the bill abolishing the Black Laws had passed the House and as of that date the Illinois Senate. On February 7, 1865, Governor Richard J. Oglesby signed the repeal of the state's Black Laws. Jones had thus confronted and challenged the white conscience of Illinois, capping off decades of effort by him, the black community, and the coalition for equality.

Historian Victoria Harrison doubts that Jones and his pamphlet were the deciding factors; she, along with the *Illinois State Journal* and the *Illinois State Register*, credits the military victory in Atlanta and Lincoln's reelection as changing the mood of the people.[87] Yet neither of these events pointed to eliminating the Black Laws as a necessary response. Was it political expediency? Was it deference to the memory of Lincoln? Was it the unceasing lobbying of state legislators by African Americans and their colleagues? Or was it the renewal of promised equality in a time of peaceful survival that pricked the people's goodwill? Regardless of which pressures were decisive, repeal of the Black Laws had been the major statewide goal of John Jones and the coalition for equality that Lovejoy had helped create.

A Gravely Ill Lovejoy Bids Farewell to Washington and Friends

For the first time since coming to Congress, in 1863 Lovejoy took a Christmas holiday to New York City with Eunice and their twenty-year-old daughter, Sarah. Then, from January through the third week in March 1864, Lovejoy struggled between bed rest and brief visits to the White House and capitol. He wrote a letter of thanks to William Lloyd Garrison for his early support of Lincoln's 1864 reelection and his lifelong witness that slavery was against the laws of God.

Lovejoy wrote an affectionate farewell to John Andrew and shared with him his vision for the religion of the future. Lovejoy described a simplified religion, far from the destructive theologies he had witnessed in his lifetime. It would expunge all claims that slavery was good and that God was white. It would disable the Slave Power that had contorted Christianity throughout the nation. Out of the travail of war and abolition of slavery, a refreshing vision presented itself to Lovejoy: "Do you know that I am hoping when slavery has been swept away, for a revival—of religion, pure and undefiled . . . and instead of expanding its energies on theologies and creeds and rubrics, it shall go around, like its divine author, healing the sick, cleansing lepers, giving eyes to the blind, ears to the deaf and charity to all.[88]

The extended family received the news through letters that for health reasons, Owen and Eunice were going to sail to Port Royal, on Hilton Head Island, the main town in the Sea Islands off South Carolina's coast.[89] Before the rebellion, Hilton

Head Island had been a celebrated health spa. Now it represented the great national debate raging over how life for blacks and whites should be structured in the future and what role the federal government should play. Lovejoy wanted to be there.

Owen wrote his children almost every day. For the first time among all his extant letters, he closed with a trace of the ageless prayer: "The Lord bless and keep you all. Aff. Yr. Father Owen Lovejoy." It was a phrase from the great prayer of the church, a benediction, the finale of worship—and the end of life.[90]

The day before the Lovejoys were to leave, Charles Sumner entered the bedroom of Owen and Eunice, whom he called beloved partners. Lovejoy's hollowed-out eyes told Sumner that now was the time to share whatever was in his heart.[91] When Lovejoy informed his old friend that he and Eunice were going to Brooklyn to sail to the Sea Islands, Sumner was startled. He looked at his colleague lying against pillows on the bed and concluded that only unyielding willpower would get him as far as the Washington train station.

In the hotel in Brooklyn, Lovejoy became so ill that friends moved him into their home. He lamented he would not live long enough to accomplish his mission of universal emancipation: "I do not know as I shall get beyond Pisgah."[92] Rev. George Cheever, who sat beside his bed, remembered, "At one point he raised himself up as if he could with an effort of the will shake off the disease, and said, 'I must go to my place in Congress and see that my bill is carried through.'"[93] It was his bill for universal emancipation prohibiting reenslavement.

Owen Lovejoy died on March 25, 1864, Good Friday. Eunice and their daughter Sarah were at his side. On March 26, 1864, the wires flashed across the country: "Owen Lovejoy died last night half-past eleven" in Brooklyn, New York.[94]

Four Services at Epicenters of the Antislavery Movement

The first funeral was held on Easter Monday, March 28, at Plymouth Congregational Church in Brooklyn, a nationally recognized advocate of emancipation. Lewis Tappan, William Cullen Bryant, John Howard Bryant, an African American man named Mr. Davis, and four others carried the coffin. The son of Eunice's cousin, Rev. Richard Salter Storrs of the nearby Church of the Pilgrim, was present. Rev. Henry Ward Beecher gave the invocation: "Lovejoy never preached a gospel that left out human rights and human liberties."[95] Rev. George Cheever delivered the sermon: "Lovejoy did not leave the Ministry, he never did. He continued its sacred labors in that one direction pointed out by God, preaching Christ and him crucified in behalf of those for whom Christ died."[96]

The second funeral was held at Hampshire Colony Congregational Church, an acclaimed Underground Railroad station. According to the *Bureau County*

Republican, "Every place that one could stand was occupied, yet multitudes remained without."[97] Rev. Edward Beecher gave the sermon and Illinois College president Julian Sturtevant led the line of dignitaries.

In the nation's capital, on April 13, the Washington Island United Literary Association of African American pastors prepared their own memorial service for Lovejoy. These AME men had preached to Lovejoy, listened to him, and worked and worshipped with him.[98] They gathered at the E Street Chapel in the District of Columbia, arriving, they said, in the spirit of joy for those in heaven and with the solemnity of friends who had lost a dear champion, colleague, and friend. After singing and praying, five spoke with profound sensibility and sad intelligence.

Beginning formally, Rev. John F. N. Wilkinson introduced a resolution on behalf of the association: "Resolved, That the sacrifices and efforts of this illustrious person in the cause of his country, and the affectionate interest which he has at all times manifested for the freedom of the down-trodden sons of Africa, claim for the government, the people of the United States, and more especially the colored people, an expression of condolence for his loss, veneration for his virtues, and gratitude for his services."[99]

The second speaker, Rev. J. T. Costin, praised "the eloquence of J. Q. Adams and Joshua R. Giddings that fell upon the ear, like the dew of heaven upon nature's garden." Yet he considered no one to have reached the heights of the Honorable Owen Lovejoy: "Owen Lovejoy stood steadfast and unmovable."[100]

Rev. John W. Lee listed the "fruits of the labors of this great man" that were available to blacks in the city now that they were emancipated. Blacks could enjoy the right to walk after ten o'clock at night without producing a pass. They could testify in all legal courts of justice, shoulder a musket, and send their children to free public schools. And they were waiting the day when they will be able to hand in a "little piece of paper" with the name of a candidate and vote. Rev. Thomas H. C. Hinton, associate pastor at a black church in Washington, said, "Lovejoy was the most eloquent humanitarian in this country. He was a man who was willing to stake everything . . . for African liberty and the freedom of our race in this country." Reverend James L. N. Bowen was the last to speak: "When we were reviled by the public press and scorned by the pulpit," and none of the people were with us, "Owen Lovejoy stood steadfast and unmovable. . . . When we groped in darkness like that of Egypt, he was with us, and like Moses, helped to lead us to the promised land—Owen Lovejoy. May he rest in peace."[101]

Nearly two months later, on June 1, 1864, representatives from the Illinois religious-political antislavery coalition for equality, gathered together in Princeton to build a Lovejoy monument. William T. Allan, Charles Kelsey, John Howard Bryant, and William Cullen Bryant spoke before an audience that had worked with

Lovejoy from the formation of the Illinois Anti-Slavery Society in 1837 through four successive antislavery political parties to the creation of a wide-flung interracial coalition for equality.

Ichabod Codding, abolitionist lecturer and Unitarian minister, explained that it was the antislavery movement that had saved American democracy. When Lovejoy began in 1837, the Slave Power had gained complete control by encroaching on all the nation's influential institutions. Its claim of "property in man" controlled the church, the state, the press, and the commerce of the country. It hovered supreme in all the high places, and any word of common humanity was considered offensive and impolite. But the word from Owen Lovejoy was the exception: "When it was statesmanlike, religious, human, a mark of social culture and position to curse and kick the negro, and spit upon and mob all his friends—He saw in him, the *negro*, a man and a brother, God's image and child." Lovejoy "saw from the beginning our *common human nature* and that in *his* rights were involved the rights of man, equality, the principle of popular government."[102]

Notes

Introduction

1. Dorrien, *The Making of American Liberal Theology*, 53; R. O. Johnson, *Liberty Party*, 252–53.

2. N. D. Harris, *History of Negro Servitude in Illinois*, 2–5, 15.

3. N. D. Harris, *History of Negro Servitude in Illinois*, 48.

4. Lincoln, *Collected Works*, 1: 75.

5. N. D. Harris, *History of Negro Servitude in Illinois*, 58.

6. Wilder, *Ebony and Ivory*, 29, 32, 70, 230.

7. Laurie, *Beyond Garrison*, 296

8. Walters, *American Reformers*.

9. John Majewski, "Why Did Northerners Oppose the Expansion of Slavery?," 298.

10. Weiner, *Race and Rights*, 237.

11. Campbell, *Fighting Slavery in Chicago*, 42.

12. Weiner, *Race and Rights*, 237.

13. Reed, "Early African American Settlement of Chicago," 230, 235–36, 238.

14. Schwalm, *Emancipation's Diaspora*, 263.

15. Salafia, *Slavery's Borderland*, 1–14.

16. Cha-Jua, *America's First Black Town*; LaRoche, *Free Black Communities and the Underground Railroad*; Parker, *His Promised Land*; Hagedorn, *Beyond the River*.

17. Middleton, *Black Laws in the Old Northwest*, 269–342; Winkle, "Paradox Though It May Seem," 11–20; Reed, "Early African American Settlement of Chicago," 219.

18. Reed, "Early African American Settlement of Chicago," 238.

19. H. R. Muelder, *Fighters for Freedom*, 84–116.

20. Weiner, *Race and Rights*, 237.

21. Spinka, *History of Illinois Congregational and Christian Churches*, 84–89.

22. Zaeske, *Signatures of Citizenship*, 160, 206n27.

23. Robertson, *Hearts Beating for Liberty*, 49. 51–52.

24. Robertson, *Hearts Beating for Liberty*, 174–75.

25. Reed, "Early African American Settlement of Chicago," 220.

26. Lasser and Robertson, *Antebellum Women*; Robertson, *Hearts Beating for Liberty*, 37–66.

27. Weiner, *Race and Rights*, 71–72; Reed, "Early African American Settlement of Chicago," 218.

28. Reed, "Early African American Settlement of Chicago," 223, 226; Dolinar, *Negro in Illinois*, 72.

29. Reed, "Early African American Settlement of Chicago," 223.

30. Reed, "Early African American Settlement of Chicago," 238.

31. Roberts, *Evangelicalism and the Politics of Reform*, 107.

32. *Freeport (Ill.) Journal*, Sept. 20, 1860; HBB, 222,

33. Robertson, *Hearts Beating for Liberty*, 167; R. O. Johnson, *Liberty Party*, 259.

34. Desmond and Moore, *Darwin's Sacred Cause*, 233–34.

35. Wilder, *Ebony and Ivory*, 190.

36. Weiner, *Race and Rights*, 3.

37. Sinha, *Slave's Cause*, 582.

38. Bellamy, *True Religion Delineated*.

39. *Western Citizen*, Jan. 20, 1843; HBB, 38.

40. Dorrien, *The Making of American Liberal Theology*, 116, 118, 119–20.

41. *Memoir*, 360; HBB, 14.

42. Dorrien, *The Making of American Liberal Theology*, 51–53.

43. *Western Citizen*, January 1843; HBB, 34.

44. Gossard, "New York City Congregational Cluster."

45. Dorrien, *The Making of American Liberal Theology*, 29–30. William Ellery Channing wrote, "We are in danger of extending to all times and places [a passage of scripture] what was of temporary and local application."

46. *Addresses on the Death of Hon. Owen Lovejoy*.

47. Accessible Archives, *Christian Recorder*, April 30, 1864.

48. *Congregational Herald*, April 1864.

49. Hoffmann, *Lincoln Hall at the University of Illinois*, 6, 66.

50. Ernest, *Liberation Historiography*, 156–57; Dillon, "The Abolitionists," 519.

51. Douglass, *Life and Writings*, 4:44; Douglass, *Papers*, 4:270.

52. W. E. B. Du Bois, *Black Reconstruction*, 152; scriptural reference: Isaiah 52:7.

53. Dolinar, *Negro in Illinois*, 18.

54. Magdol, *Owen Lovejoy*, 327–28.

55. Bennett, *Forced into Glory*, 200, 402.

Chapter 1. Becoming a Political Abolitionist: 1811–1842

1. Forbes, *Missouri Compromise*, 66, 76, 82.

2. Cushman, *Address to the People of Maine*, CC.

3. Remarks given by Owen Bryant Lovejoy, quoting Owen Lovejoy's sermon at the funeral for his mother, Betsey Lovejoy, 1857, presented at the dedication of the Lovejoy Homestead, a National Historic Landmark Site, Princeton, Illinois, September 14, 1997.

4. Sassi, *Republic of Righteousness*, 94; Fischer, *Albion's Seed*, 796. Five formal beliefs of early Congregationalists were total depravity, limited atonement, unconditional election, irresistible grace, and the final perseverance of the saints.

5. C. M. Clark, *History of the Congregational Churches in Maine*, 2:24; Letter from the Society for the Propagation of the Gospel among the Indians to Daniel Lovejoy, June 1, 1807, TT; June 13, 1816, TT; Letter from the Trustees of Maine Missionary Society to Daniel Lovejoy, July 1, 1820, TT; July 10, 1823, TT.

6. Betsey Lovejoy, undated manuscript, n.d., TT.

7. Burnsted, *Henry Alline*, 77–88; Mayer, *All on Fire*, 6, 10, 14–15.

8. Joseph Bellamy's colleague, Jonathan Edwards, was a renowned theologian and philosopher who brought together the Reformed theology of John Calvin and the Enlightenment view of science and Greek philosophy. See Dorrien, *The Making of American Liberal Theology*, 116, 120, 135.

9. Betsey Lovejoy, "Autobiography," n.d. TT.

10. Wiggin, *Albion on the Narrow Gauge*, 178.

11. Grow, *China, Maine*, 23; Price and Talbot, *Maine's Visible Black History*, 23, 164.

12. Betsey Lovejoy to Owen Lovejoy, March 30, 1831, Clements.

13. Dillon, *Elijah P. Lovejoy*, 29; Albert Barnes to Elijah Lovejoy, June 21, 1833, CC. Samuel Cornish, editor of the *Colored American*, called Reverend Barnes "America's unparalleled preacher," Nov. 25, 1837, quoted in Swift, *Black Prophets of Justice*, 94.

14. *Memoir*, 66–67.

15. *1834* and *1835 Catalogue of Ipswich Female Academy*, Mount Holyoke College Archives, South Hadley, Massachusetts.

16. Owen Lovejoy, Poem: "To Our Absent Brother," n.d., c. 1830, CC.

17. *Christian Freeman*, Sept. 17, 1843; *Western Citizen*, Sept. 14, 1843; HBB, 24, 59, 60.

18. Owen Lovejoy to James Birney, December 9, 1837, ALPLM.

19. Merton Dillon, in *Elijah P. Lovejoy*, ix, states, "But of all the abolitionists, only Lovejoy was murdered for his beliefs." John Quincy Adams, in his introduction to Elijah Lovejoy's *Memoir*, 12, describes Lovejoy as "the first American Martyr to THE FREEDOM OF THE PRESS, AND THE FREEDOM OF THE SLAVE."

20. Simon, *Freedom's Champion*, 158.

21. Simon, *Freedom's Champion*, 126–39.

22. Owen Lovejoy to Joshua Leavitt, December 14, 1837, CC; *Emancipator*, December 28, 1837, CC.

23. Betsey Lovejoy to Children, December 1837, n.d., TT.

24. *Western Citizen*, September 14, 1843; HBB, 14.

25. Joseph Lovejoy to Owen Lovejoy, November 25, 1837, CC.

26. Dillon, *Elijah P. Lovejoy*, 178.

27. Joseph Lovejoy to Owen Lovejoy, November 29, 1837, CC.

28. Barnes, *Antislavery Impulse*, 133–34.

29. Hambrick-Stowe, *Charles G. Finney*, 164, 176. Finney moved to Oberlin in May 1835 and returned to preach in New York City during the winters of 1836 and 1837; he resigned from the church in April 1837 (Swift, *Black Prophets of Justice*, 99).

30. H. R. Muelder, *Fighters for Freedom*, 7–15; Wyatt-Brown, *Lewis Tappan and the Evangelical War against Slavery*, 64–65.

31. Dumond, *Antislavery*, 161–62.

32. Dumond, *Antislavery*, 185.

33. Miller, *Arguing about Slavery*, 325–33.

34. Sarah Moody Lovejoy to Betsey Lovejoy, January 29, 1838, CC.

35. Swift, *Black Prophets of Justice*, 75; DeBoer, *Be Jubilant My Feet*, 52–53.

36. Swift, *Black Prophets of Justice*, 48–49, 166–67.

37. Sarah Moody Lovejoy to Joseph Lovejoy, February 24, 1838, CC; Sarah Moody Lovejoy to Sibyl Lovejoy, February 27, 1838, TT; Ripley, *Black Abolitionist Papers*, 1:82–83; 3:187–88.

38. "Thomas Holcombe of Connecticut: Person Page," entry for Hon. Warren Canfield Humphrey, *Holcombe Family Genealogy*, www.holcombegenealogy.com/data/p952htm.

39. J. B. Stewart, *Abolitionist Politics and the Coming of the Civil War*, 192; *Emancipator-Extra*, February 24, 1838, in Simpson Collection at Wadsworth Athenaeum, www.hartford-hwp.com/HBHP/exhibit/04/2.html.

40. Thomas, "Analysis of the Life and Work of James W. C. Pennington," 82–83.

41. Sarah Moody Lovejoy to Joseph Lovejoy, February 24, 1838, CC.

42. Richards, *Life and Times of Congressman John Quincy Adams*, 126; Barnes, *Antislavery Impulse*, 144, 266n35; Miller, *Arguing about Slavery*, 309–11. It is possible that Joseph Lovejoy delivered the petitions to Adams.

43. Zaeske, *Signatures of Citizenship*, 86, 119.

44. *Memoir*, 338–62.

45. Simon, *Freedom's Champion*, 163.

46. Magdol, 32. Six or seven thousand copies were available for New England, 2,000 for Ohio and 2,000 for Indiana.

47. Magdol, *Owen Lovejoy*, 34.

48. Hermann Muelder describes the colonies in Illinois in *Fighters for Freedom*, 62–114. Marilynn Robinson describes the West's development in *The Death of Adam*.

49. Melish, *Disowning Slavery*, 15, 18–19, 23, 25, 40–41.

50. Laurie, *Beyond Garrison*, 91.

51. Melish, *Disowning Slavery*, 190–92, 208–9.

52. Ella W. Harrison, "The Hampshire Colony Congregational Church—Its First Hundred Years" (Princeton, Illinois: mimeographed, 1931); Harrison, "A History of the First Congregational Church, Princeton, Illinois."

53. Bradsby, *History of Bureau County, Illinois*, 90, 125.

54. Sarah Cooper, "Black History in Bureau County," BCR, February 21, 2017.

55. Spinka, *History of Illinois Congregational and Christian Churches*, 19–21.

56. H. R. Muelder, *Fighters for Freedom*, 129–33.

57. *Illinois State Anti-Slavery Society Minute Book*, 1839, CHS; N. D. Harris, *History of Negro Servitude in Illinois*, 128.

58. Weiner, *Race and Rights*, 237.

59. *American Anti-Slavery Society Minutes*, 1838, Annual Meeting. Boston Public Library Archives.

60. *Illinois State Anti-Slavery Society Minute Book*, 1838, CHS; Dillon, *Benjamin Lundy*, 184–85, 214, 250–51.

61. Magdol, *Owen Lovejoy*, 36.

62. Bradsby, *History of Bureau County, Illinois*, 332–39; N. D. Harris, *History of Negro Servitude in Illinois*, 142.

63. Dillon, *Benjamin Lundy*, 251–52; Dobbert and Nelson, *Friends of Clear Creek*.

64. Betsey Lovejoy to Children, March 1839, TT.

65. H. Jones, *Mutiny on the Amistad*.

66. Owens, *Black Mutiny*, 263–77.

67. R. J. M. Blackett, "James W. C. Pennington," in *Beating Against Barriers: Biographical Essays in Nineteenth Century Afro-American History*, edited by Leon Litwack and August Meier (Baton Rouge: Louisiana State University Press, 1986), 22–26.

68. Quarles, *Black Abolitionists*, 79; Thomas, "Analysis of the Life and Work of James W. C. Pennington."

69. DeBoer, *Be Jubilant My Feet*, 26–41; *Hampshire Colony Congregational Church Minutes*, December 20, 1842, BCGS; Barnes, *Antislavery Impulse*, 165–70, 175–76.

70. Swift, *Black Prophets of Justice*, 223.

71. Owen Lovejoy to Lewis Tappan, Dec. 21, 1841, ARC; HBB, 36.

72. Guyatt, "A Peculiar Revolt," 31.

73. Richards, *Slave Power*, 1–27.

74. Richards, *Slave Power*, 35, 57, 71, 81, 90.

75. R. O. Johnson, *Liberty Party*, 373.

76. Dillon, *Antislavery Movement in Illinois*, 352–53.

77. Dillon, *Antislavery Movement in Illinois*, 352–53.

78. Dillon, *Antislavery Movement in Illinois*, 353.

79. Dugan, "Illinois Martyrdom," 111.

80. Dillon, *Antislavery Movement in Illinois*, 351–53.

81. *Memorial of Zebina Eastman.*

82. *Memorial of Zebina Eastman*, 282.

83. *Memorial of Zebina Eastman*, 355.

84. HBB, 48–49; Magdol, *Owen Lovejoy*, 60–61.

85. HBB, 49; Dumond, *Antislavery*, 296.

86. N. D. Harris, *History of Negro Servitude in Illinois*, 148.

87. Campbell, *Fighting Slavery in Chicago*, 48.

88. N. D. Harris, *History of Negro Servitude in Illinois*, 149.

89. Campbell, *Fighting Slavery in Chicago*, 22.

90. N. D. Harris, *History of Negro Servitude in Illinois*, 150

91. *Western Citizen*, Jan. 20, 1843; HBB, 34–43.

92. 2 Samuel 23:3.

93. Lovejoy held a view opposite to churches in the South that declared religion should be kept entirely separate from affairs of state. See Harlow, *Religion, Race, and the Making of Confederate Kentucky*, 4.

94. *Western Citizen*, Jan. 20, 1843; HBB, 36.

95. HBB, 37.

96. Heagle, *Great Anti-Slavery Agitator*, 13.

97. Middleton, *Black Laws in the Old Northwest*, 321.

98. H. R. Muelder, *Fighters for Freedom*, 196–97, 200–203; Magdol, *Owen Lovejoy*, 45.

99. Dillon, *Antislavery Movement in Illinois*, 318–19.

100. Dillon, *Antislavery Movement in Illinois*, 339–42; HBB, 19.

101. BCR, June 16, 1864.

102. W. Richard Scott, quoted in Hall, *Occupations and the Social Structure*, 92; D. M. Scott, *Office to Profession*, 155.

103. Owen Lovejoy to Betsey Lovejoy, November 3, 1842, TT.

104. C. Storrs, *Storrs Family*, AA.

105. C. Storrs, *Storrs Family*. Eunice's grandfather, Rev. John Storrs, 1735–1799, was a chaplain in the Continental Army and officiated at her wedding to Butler Denham. Eunice's uncle was Rev. Richard Salter Storrs (I), 1765–1819, of Longmeadow, Massachusetts. Her cousin was Rev. Richard Salter Storrs (II), 1787–1873, of Braintree, Massachusetts. His son was Rev. Richard Salter Storrs (III), 1821–1900, of Brooklyn, New York.

106. Marriage license, BCHS.

Chapter 2. Working against Slavery with Churchmen, Women, and Blacks: 1843-1846

1. Magdol, *Owen Lovejoy*, 227.
2. Dumond, *Antislavery*, 189; Abzug, *Passionate Liberator*, 124; Jeffrey, *Great Silent Army of Abolitionism*, 53.
3. Magdol, *Owen Lovejoy*, 65.
4. Spinka, *History of Illinois Congregational and Christian Churches*, 76, 85, 92.
5. Magdol, *Owen Lovejoy*, 43.
6. E. Foner, *Fiery Trial*, 24.
7. Ella W. Harrison, "Lovejoy, the Pastor," manuscript, ca. 1931, BCHS.
8. Bradsby, *History of Bureau County, Illinois*, 32-34; Magdol, *Owen Lovejoy*, 40-46.
9. *Western Citizen*, May 24, 1843.
10. From 1837 to 1842 Codding traveled in Vermont, Massachusetts, Maine, Connecticut, and New York lecturing and establishing antislavery newspapers, *Advocate of Freedom* in Maine and *Christian Freeman* in Connecticut.
11. Codding, "Ichabod Codding," 8.
12. Sarah Lovejoy to Joseph Lovejoy, February 24, 1838, CC.
13. Dillon, *Antislavery Movement in Illinois*, 309.
14. Dillon, *Antislavery Movement in Illinois*, 368-70.
15. Hochschild, *Bury the Chains*, 358.
16. Rael, *Black Identify and Black Protest*, 77.
17. Lange, "Owen Lovejoy vs. the Town of Princeton," 31-32; Magdol, *Owen Lovejoy*, 46-47.
18. *Western Citizen*, August 17, 1843.
19. H. R. Muelder, *Fighters for Freedom*, 18-24.
20. *Christian Freeman*, Sept. 28, 1843; HBB, 59.
21. Roberts, *Evangelicalism and the Politics of Reform*, 171.
22. Stuckey, "A Last Stern Struggle," 137.
23. Sernett, *Abolition's Axe*, 55, 71.
24. Martin, "Frederick Douglass," 70.
25. Swift, *Black Prophets of Justice*, 138.
26. Pease and Pease, *They Who Would Be Free*, 196-97.
27. Stuckey, "A Last Stern Struggle," 134.
28. HBB, 58-61.
29. Swift, *Black Prophets of Justice*, 119-20.
30. *Free West*, April 5, 1855; HBB, 108.
31. CG, 57th Cong., 2d Sess., Mar. 25, 1862, 1368-69; CG, 57th Cong., 2d Sess., Apr. 24, 1852, 1815-18; HBB, 302, 314, 323.
32. Roberts, *Evangelicalism and the Politics of Reform*, 107, 111.
33. Stuckey, "A Last Stern Struggle," 129-38.
34. Pasternak, "Rise Now and Fly to Arms," 58.
35. Sernett, *North Star Country*, 117, 94.
36. Ward, *Autobiography of a Fugitive Negro*, 84.
37. Swift, *Black Prophets of Justice*, 337.
38. Work, "Life of Charles B. Ray"; Quarles, *Black Abolitionists*, 184-85; Ripley, *Black Abolitionist Papers*, 1:74-75.
39. Roberts, *Evangelicalism and the Politics of Reform*, 107.
40. R. O. Johnson, *Liberty Party*, 194.

41. Pease and Pease, *They Who Would Be Free*, 196–97; *Western Citizen*, September 7, 1843.

42. Roberts, *Evangelicalism and the Politics of Reform*, 133, 137; Pease and Pease, *They Who Would Be Free*, 83; Stauffer, *Black Hearts of Men*, 205–6.

43. Swift, *Black Prophets of Justice*, 14

44. D. B. Davis, *Problem of Slavery in the Age of Emancipation*, 210.

45. Pease and Pease, *They Who Would Be Free*, 83.

46. Blackett, *Building an Antislavery Wall*, 23–26.

47. Stuckey, "A Last Stern Struggle," 134.

48. Dumond, *Antislavery*, 293–94.

49. Alvan Stewart, "Argument in the Case of State vs. Edward Van Buren," in *Writings and Speeches*, 339.

50. Blue, *No Taint of Compromise*, 30.

51. Magdol, *Owen Lovejoy*, 40.

52. E. Foner, *Free Soil, Free Labor, Free Men*, 79; Harrold, *Gamaliel Bailey*, 115.

53. Blue, *Salmon P. Chase*, 45–46, 51, 56–57; E. Foner, *Free Soil, Free Labor, Free Men*, 78–79.

54. Oakes, *Freedom National*, 27–28; R. O. Johnson, *Liberty Party*.

55. L. J. Friedman, *Gregarious Saints*, 90–92.

56. Wyatt-Brown, *Lewis Tappan and the Evangelical War against Slavery*, 264, 276; L. J. Friedman, *Gregarious Saints*, 92–94.

57. Joseph Lovejoy to Owen Lovejoy, September 8, 1843, TT.

58. Zebina Eastman Collection, Box 2, CHS.

59. *Western Citizen*, October 23, 1843.

60. Magdol, *Owen Lovejoy*, 44.

61. N. D. Harris, *History of Negro Servitude in Illinois*, 110–14. The judge in the next court case supported "slave in transit" for the final time in Illinois. See Finkelman, *Imperfect Union*, 99; W. F. Moore and J. A. Moore, *Collaborators for Emancipation*, 52.

62. Robertson, *Hearts Beating for Liberty*, 175.

63. Salerno, *Sister Societies*, 175. Salerno's lists place Elk Grove as the earliest female antislavery society in Illinois in 1841. Princeton is listed as beginning in either 1842 or 1843.

64. Betsey Lovejoy to Zebina Eastman, "Female Antislavery Society of Princeton, Illinois," n.d. 1843, TT; *Western Citizen*, November 9, 1843.

65. *Western Citizen*, November 9, 1843.

66. Carwardine, *Lincoln*, 81–82, 85.

67. Spinka, *History of Illinois Congregational and Christian Churches*, 85.

68. Magdol, *Owen Lovejoy*, 65.

69. Magdol, *Owen Lovejoy*, 65.

70. Spinka, *History of Illinois Congregational and Christian Churches*, 92

71. C. M. Clark, *American Slavery and Maine Congregationalists*, 114–15, 118–19.

72. Spinka, *History of Illinois Congregational and Christian Churches*, 93.

73. Howard, *Conscience and Slavery*, 35–39.

74. Spinka, *History of Illinois Congregational and Christian Churches*, 9–24, 70.

75. Spinka, *History of Illinois Congregational and Christian Churches*, 347n91. In his book *Conscience and Slavery*, 34–70, Victor Howard describes Badger's activities at length.

76. Spinka, *History of Illinois Congregational and Christian Churches*, 86.

77. W. Richard Scott, 92. "Professional employees are at least partially subordinated to an externally imposed administrative framework" (D. M. Scott, *Office to Profession*, 155).

78. D. M. Scott, *Office to Profession*, 104.

79. D. M. Scott, *Office to Profession*, 110.

80. D. M. Scott, *Office to Profession*, 103, 150.

81. Spinka, *History of Illinois Congregational and Christian Churches*, 86–87, 96.

82. Spinka, *History of Illinois Congregational and Christian Churches*, 357n5; Minutes of the General Congregational Association of Illinois, CTS.

83. Spinka, *History of Illinois Congregational and Christian Churches*, 155–56

84. Spinka, *History of Illinois Congregational and Christian Churches*, 87–88.

85. Spinka, *History of Illinois Congregational and Christian Churches*, 72.

86. Spinka, *History of Illinois Congregational and Christian Churches*, 136.

87. Swift, *Black Prophets of Justice*, 153–55, 168.

88. Pasternak, "Rise Now and Fly to Arms," 59; Burke, "Samuel Ringgold Ward," 52.

89. Frederick Irving Kuhns, "Rock River Congregational Association," unpublished manuscript, CTS; Wyatt-Brown, *Lewis Tappan and the Evangelical War against Slavery*, 320–21.

90. Howard, *Conscience and Slavery*, 40–55.

91. Kuhns, "The Rock River Congregational Association," 18; Kuhns, "The American Home Missionary Society in relation to the Antislavery Controversy in the Old Northwest," unpublished manuscript, CTS.

92. Owen Lovejoy Papers, William L. Clements Library, University of Michigan, Ann Arbor; HBB, 63–64.

93. Ward, *Autobiography of a Fugitive Negro*, 61–72; Hedrick, *Harriet Beecher Stowe*, 229–30. Proslavery sentiment among clergy was common in declarations by ecclesiastical bodies of most denominations.

94. Roberts, *Evangelicalism and the Politics of Reform*, 131, 143–45; Douglass, *Life and Writings*, 2:289.

95. Wilder, *Ebony and Ivy*, 190.

96. Martin, "Frederick Douglass," 234.

97. Douglass, *Life and Writings*, 2:295.

98. Dillon, *Antislavery Movement*, 367; Magdol, *Owen Lovejoy*, 68.

99. Ezra M. Prince, "Obituary of Ichabod Codding," *Pantagraph*, June 20, 1866, 1–3.

100. Codding, "Ichabod D. Codding," 13.

101. N. D. Harris, *History of Negro Servitude in Illinois*, 151, 154.

102. R. O. Johnson, *Liberty Party*, 201. Johnson concludes that the significance of the Illinois Liberty Party has been underrated.

103. Dixon, *Perfecting the Family*, 21, 44.

104. Zaeske, *Signatures of Citizenship*, 86; Salerno, *Sister Societies*, 130; E. C. DuBois, *Feminism and Suffrage*, 33.

105. R. O. Johnson, *Liberty Party*, 276; Robertson, *Hearts Beating for Liberty*, 7.

106. Salerno, *Sister Societies*, 172–73.

107. Weiner, *Race and Rights*, 81, 89; Robertson, *Hearts Beating for Liberty*, 44–45.

108. Dobbert and Nelson, *Friends of Clear Creek*; H. R. Muelder, *Fighters for Freedom*, 180.

109. Stoneburner and Stoneburner, *Influence of Quaker Women*, 19, 23.

110. Dixon, *Perfecting the Family*, 82.

111. Jeanne Humphreys (DeNovo), "Mary Brown Davis, Journalist, Feminist, and Social Reformer," Honors Paper, Knox College, May 23, 1939, Special Collections and Archives, Knox College Library, Galesburg, Illinois.

112. R. O. Johnson, *Liberty Party*, 283.

113. Robertson, *Hearts Beating for Liberty*, 51.

114. Betsey Lovejoy to Irene Ball (Mrs. William T.) Allan, May 27, 1844. TT.

115. H. R. Muelder, *Fighters for Freedom*, 182–83.

116. Hiram Kellogg served as president of Knox College from 1841 until 1845. He was a close associate of the abolitionists in Illinois. See "Knox College: Our History," https://www.knox.edu/about-knox/our-history/knox-presidents, and "Rev Hiram Huntington Kellogg," https://www.findagrave.com/memorial/5579973/hiram-huntington-kellogg.

117. Blanchard, *Discovery and Conquest*, 2:295–301.

118. Weiner, *Race and Rights*, 141.

119. Robertson, *Hearts Beating for Liberty*, 214–15; *Western Citizen*, September 5, 1844.

120. Robertson, *Hearts Beating for Liberty*, 169; *Western Citizen*, June 20, 1844.

121. Salerno, *Sister Societies*, 146.

122. *Western Citizen*, March 21, 1844; Robertson, *Hearts Beating for Liberty*, 46–49.

123. Weiner, *Race and Rights*, 94–95, 235.

124. Salerno, *Sister Societies*, 8.

125. Robertson, *Hearts Beating for Liberty*, 51.

126. *Western Citizen*, March 21, 1844.

127. *Western Citizen*, April 8, 1845.

128. Robertson, *Hearts Beating for Liberty*, 36, 160, 164.

129. Dumond, *Antislavery*, 163–64.

130. William T. Allan, Speech at the Monument Committee Meeting, June 9, 1864, BCR; R. O. Johnson, *Liberty Party*, 448n205. Johnson describes William Allan as taking "the leading role . . . that transformed that organization into a machine for the Liberty Party."

131. R. O. Johnson, *Liberty Party*, 51.

132. R. O. Johnson, *Liberty Party*, 51–53.

133. Blue, *Salmon P. Chase*, 51.

134. R. O. Johnson, *Liberty Party*, 54.

135. Quarles, *Black Abolitionists*, 166; Blue, *Salmon P. Chase*, 49–50.

136. Harrold, *Gamaliel Bailey*, 55–56; Dixon, *Perfecting the Family*, 33.

137. R. N. Scott, "What Price Freedom?"

138. Gliozzo, "John Jones: A Study of a Black Chicagoan," 177–78.

139. N. D. Harris, *History of Negro Servitude in Illinois*, 24, 234.

140. Campbell, *Fighting Slavery in Chicago*, 30.

141. R. O. Johnson, *Liberty Party*, 242, 245.

142. R. O. Johnson, *Liberty Party*, 197.

143. R. O. Johnson, *Liberty Party*, 252; *Western Citizen*, February 23, 1844.

144. Gliozzo, "John Jones: A Study of a Black Chicagoan," 177–188; R. N. Scott, "What Price Freedom?," 33.

145. Campbell, *Fighting Slavery in Chicago*, 30.

146. R. O. Johnson, *Liberty Party*, 198.

147. Robertson, *Hearts Beating for Liberty*, 52.

148. R. O. Johnson, *Liberty Party*, 242, 245.

149. *Western Citizen*, March 25, 1846.

150. R. O. Johnson, *Liberty Party*, 197.

151. Campbell, *Fighting Slavery in Chicago*, 77.

152. Zebina Eastman Collection, CHS; Codding, "Ichabod Codding," 185; *Western Citizen*, March 11, 1846; Magdol, *Owen Lovejoy*, 73–74.

153. Campbell, *Fighting Slavery in Chicago*, 51–55.

154. *Western Herald*, July 1, 1846, CTS.

155. R. O. Johnson, *Liberty Party*, 55.

156. *Liberty Tree*, June 1846; HBB, 66

157. HBB, 67.

158. HBB, 68.

159. HBB, 68.

160. Robertson, *Hearts Beating for Liberty*, 52.

161. *Western Citizen*, March 25, 1846.

162. Robertson, *Hearts Beating for Liberty*, 52.

163. Robertson, *Hearts Beating for Liberty*, 54.

164. Robertson, *Hearts Beating for Liberty*, 49; "Address of the Ladies' Anti-Slavery Association of Dundee," *Western Citizen*, March 25, 1846.

165. R. O. Johnson, *Liberty Party*, 200.

166. *Western Citizen*, June 30, 1846.

167. R. O. Johnson, *Liberty Party*, 198–202.

168. R. O. Johnson, *Liberty Party*, 197.

169. Howard, *Conscience and Slavery*, 54.

170. Jonathan Blanchard to Mary Blanchard, July 22/23, 1846, Wheaton College, Wheaton, Illinois.

171. Spinka, *History of Illinois Congregational and Christian Churches*, 81; H. R. Muelder, *Fighters for Freedom*, 293–95.

172. DeBoer, *Be Jubilant My Feet*, 82–83.

173. Blackett, *Beating against the Barriers*, 26.

174. Swift, *Black Prophets of Justice*, 1–11.

175. DeBoer, *Be Jubilant My Feet*, 84.

176. Clifton Johnson, "Illinois Northern Congregational Churches and Ministers," 63–66; United Church Board for Homeland Ministries, "150th Anniversary."

177. R. O. Johnson, *Liberty Party*, 197–202.

178. *Western Citizen*, Oct. 13, 1846 and Nov. 14, 1846.

179. R. O. Johnson, *Liberty Party*, 96.

180. *Western Citizen*, November 14, 1846.

181. *Western Citizen*, November 14, 1846.

182. *Lowell Daily Courant*, October 26, 1846.

183. *Lowell Daily Courant*, October 26, 1846; HBB, 73.

184. J. B. Stewart, "Emergence of Racial Modernity," 235.

185. Horton and Horton, *Black Bostonians*, 7–13, 86; Strangis, *Lewis Hayden and the War against Slavery*; Kantrowitz, *More Than Freedom*, 106, 112, 234.

186. *Lowell (Mass.) Daily Courier*, October 26, 1846; *Western Citizen*, November 24, 1846; HBB, 75.

187. David Todd to Charlotte Farnsworth, November 9, 1846, David Todd and Charlotte Farnsworth Letters, 1846–1874, MS 327, Illinois History and Lincoln Collections, University of Illinois at Urbana-Champaign Library.

188. David Todd to Charlotte Farnsworth, April 7, 1847, David Todd and Charlotte Farnsworth Letters, 1846–1874, MS 327, Illinois History and Lincoln Collections, University of Illinois at Urbana-Champaign Library.

Chapter 3. Responding to Legislative Maneuverings: 1847–1851

1. Meites, "The 1847 Illinois Constitutional Convention and Persons of Color," 274–75.

2. Middleton, *Black Laws in the Old Northwest*, 282.

3. Meites, "The 1847 Illinois Constitutional Convention and Persons of Color," 284; Bridges, "Antebellum Struggle for Citizenship," 317.

4. Middleton, *Black Laws in the Old Northwest*, 282.

5. *Western Citizen*, September 28, 1847.

6. Meites, "The 1847 Illinois Constitutional Convention and Persons of Color," 284; Bridges, "Antebellum Struggle for Citizenship," 298.

7. Blue, *Free Soilers*, 100–103.

8. E. Foner, *Free Soil, Free Labor, Free Men*, xxiv.

9. Blue, *Free Soilers*, x.

10. Oakes, *Scorpion's Sting*, 72–73.

11. E. Foner, *Free Soil, Free Labor, Free Men*, xv.

12. Volpe, *Forlorn Hope of Freedom*, 109, 129–30.

13. H. Davis, *Joshua Leavitt*, 235–36; Harrrold, *Gamaliel Bailey*, 113–15.

14. Blackett, *Building an Antislavery Wall*, 19–20.

15. Stauffer, *Black Hearts of Men*, 134–38.

16. Swift, *Black Prophets of Justice*, 143.

17. Sernett, *North Star Country*, 198–202.

18. Stauffer, *Black Hearts of Men*, 135–40.

19. Stuckey, "A Last Stern Struggle," 142.

20. The meeting was held July 8, 1847. Saunders, *Illinois Liberty Lines*.

21. Zaeske, *Signatures of Citizenship*, 174.

22. Miller, *Arguing about Slavery*, 312.

23. Miller, *Arguing about Slavery*, 103.

24. Lasser and Robertson, *Antebellum Women*, 77.

25. Zaeske, *Signatures of Citizenship*, 48; Miller, *Arguing About Slavery*, 65, 111, 277, 314, 321.

26. *National Era*, March 18, 1847; R. O. Johnson, *Liberty Party*, 199.

27. *Western Citizen*, December 7, 1847; HBB, 77.

28. Volpe, *Forlorn Hope of Freedom*, 134.

29. Blue, *Salmon P. Chase*, 56–57.

30. R. O. Johnson, *Liberty Party*, 201.

31. Salerno, *Sister Societies*, 41.

32. *Western Citizen*, May 2, 1848.

33. *Western Citizen*, March 28, 1848.

34. Magdol, *Owen Lovejoy*, 84.

35. *True Republican*, Sycamore, Illinois, on November 20, 1880, reprinted from the *Earlville Gazette*: "Rev. Mr. Lovejoy then borrowed a horse and buggy of Pierpont Edwards, now of Earlville, in which to ride home to Princeton; which he returned a fortnight later." Joiner room, DeKalb County Historical Society, Sycamore, Illinois.

36. James Collins to Owen Lovejoy, March 17, 1847, ALPL.

37. *Aurora Guardian*, July 18, 1848; HBB, 83–86.

38. Oakes, *Scorpion's Sting*, 13.

39. Magdol, *Owen Lovejoy*, 89.

40. R. O. Johnson, *Liberty Party*, 201–2.

41. Gliozzo, "John Jones: A Study of a Black Chicagoan," 179, 182; Gliozzo, "John Jones and the Black Convention Movement"; R. O. Johnson, *Liberty Party*, 338.

42. Blue, *Salmon P. Chase*, 63–65.

43. Pasternak, "Rise Now and Fly to Arms," 84–86.

44. Ginzberg, *Elizabeth Cady Stanton*, 59–60.

45. Philip S. Foner, introduction to Douglass, *Life and Writings*, 2:15–18.

46. Philip S. Foner, introduction to Douglass, *Life and Writings*, 2:15–18, 70–71.

47. Sernett, *North Star Country*, 126.

48. Pasternak, "Rise Now and Fly to Arms," 84.

49. *Western Citizen*, Aug. 22, 1848; HBB, 87.

50. Julian, *Political Recollections*, 72–73; J. B. Stewart, *Joshua R. Giddings*, 167; Blue, *Free Soilers*, appendix C, 302.

51. Miller, *Arguing about Slavery*, 406, 514.

52. Reed, "Early African American Settlement of Chicago," 223–26.

53. R. O. Johnson, *Liberty Party*, 338.

54. Gliozzo, "John Jones: A Study of a Black Chicagoan," 180.

55. Gliozzo, "John Jones: A Study of a Black Chicagoan," 181; Bridges, "Antebellum Struggle for Citizenship," 299–300.

56. Gliozzo, "John Jones: A Study of a Black Chicagoan," 180.

57. *Western Citizen*, September 19, 1848.

58. N. D. Harris, *History of Negro Servitude in Illinois*, 10, 24.

59. Bridges, "Antebellum Struggle for Citizenship," 299.

60. Ida Lovejoy to William Lloyd Garrison Jr., ca. 1879, Smith College Archives.

61. Elliott, "Owen Lovejoy," 231.

62. Wyatt-Brown, *Lewis Tappan and the Evangelical War against Slavery*, 278–79.

63. Miller, *Arguing about Slavery*, 339, 403, 461, 501, 514; H. Davis, *Joshua Leavitt*, 177–78.

64. Harrold, *Gamaliel Bailey*, 81–93.

65. Harrold, *Gamaliel Bailey*, 125.

66. Julian, *Political Reflections*, 72–74; Harrold, *Gamaliel Bailey*, 132–34.

67. Applegate, *The Most Famous Man in America*, 202.

68. BCR, June 9, 1864.

69. Gossard, "New York City Congregational Cluster." Gary Dorrien (*The Making of American Liberal Theology*, 191) writes that Henry Ward Beecher would put liberal Protestantism "on the map."

70. Gossard, "New York City Congregational Cluster," 54.

71. Gossard, "New York City Congregational Cluster," 58.

72. Gossard, "New York City Congregational Cluster," 34.

73. Gossard, "New York City Congregational Cluster," 60.

74. Marsden, *Fundamentalism and American Culture*, 22–23.

75. *Western Citizen*, December 4, 1849.

76. Johannsen, *Stephen A. Douglas*, 264.

77. Owen Lovejoy Papers, William L. Clements Library, University of Michigan, Ann Arbor; HBB, 89.

78. HBB, 89.

79. Lovejoy rejected Calvin's doctrine of predestination but embraced Calvin's emphasis on aiding the poor, as described by M. Robinson in *When I Was a Child*, 66–83, 174–75, 177–81.

80. E. Foner, "Inhuman Bondage," 30.

81. HBB, 89.

82. Roberts, *Evangelicalism and the Politics of Reform*, 146–47.

83. Bay, *White Image in the Black Mind*, 31.

84. Owen Lovejoy Papers, William L. Clements Library, University of Michigan, Ann Arbor; HBB, 89.

85. HBB, 91, 89; Achinstein, *Literature and Dissent in Milton's England*.

86. HBB, 90.

87. HBB, 91.

88. HBB, 36.

89. Dorrien, *The Making of American Liberal Theology*, 54.

90. Dorrien, *The Making of American Liberal Theology*, 53; HBB, 124.

91. Richards, *Slave Power*, 79; Forbes, *Missouri Compromise*, 147–48.

92. Blue, *Free Soilers*, 178; Magdol, *Owen Lovejoy*, 92.

93. Freehling, *Road to Disunion*, 1: 516.

94. Blackett, *Building an Antislavery Wall*, 147; E. Foner, *Story of American Freedom*, 87.

95. Many Christians in Illinois rejected the political involvement of "postmillennialist Yankee reformers" (Carwardine, *Lincoln*, 82).

96. Lewis Woodson was a minister, lecturer, and barber in Pittsburgh; John Vashon of Pittsburgh was elected to the Board of Managers of the American Anti-Slavery Society (Quarles, *Black Abolitionists*, 81, 20–32, 200; H. R. Muelder, *Fighters for Freedom*, 279; Howard, *Conscience and Slavery*, 92).

97. Blue, *Free Soiler*, 169n34.

98. *North Star*, June 27, 1850; *Western Citizen*, January 28, 1851; Blight, *Frederick Douglass' Civil War*, 7ff; Martin, *Mind of Frederick Douglass*, 178.

99. Stauffer, *Black Hearts of Men*, 156.

100. "Frederick Douglass—Abolitionist Leader," *America's Story from America's Library*, www.americaslibrary.gov/aa/douglass/aa_douglass_leader_3.html.

101. *Western Citizen*, January 28 and April 29, 1851.

102. McKivigan, *War against Proslavery Religion*, 135.

103. *Western Citizen*, April 23, 1850.

104. *Western Citizen*, June 11, 1850.

105. N. D. Harris, *History of Negro Servitude in Illinois*, 179–80.

106. *Western Citizen*, July 15, 1851.

107. Ward, *Autobiography of a Fugitive Negro*, 87.

108. Ernest, *Liberation Historiography*, 210–17.

109. Sernett, *North Star Country*, 157.

110. Baker, "Millard Fillmore."

111. Turner, *Underground Railroad in Illinois*, 24; Quarles, *Black Abolitionists*, 197–202; Campbell, *Fighting Slavery in Chicago*, 85–87; John Jones Scrapbook, CHS; Blanchard, *Discovery and Conquests*, 1:298.

112. Quarles, *Black Abolitionists*, 200.

113. Sernett, *North Star Country*, 149.

114. Philip S. Foner, introduction to Douglass, *Life and Writings*, 2:28–29.

115. Franklin, *From Slavery to Freedom*, 377; Philip S. Foner, introduction to Douglass, *Life and Writings*, 2:43.

116. *Western Citizen*, October 8, 1850; *Chicago Daily Journal*, October 8, 1850.

117. Gliozzo, "John Jones: A Study of a Black Chicagoan," 181.

118. *Western Citizen*, October 8, 1850.

119. Bridges, "Antebellum Struggle for Citizenship," 300.

120. Gliozzo, "John Jones: A Study of a Black Chicagoan," 182.

121. Gliozzo, "John Jones: A Study of a Black Chicagoan," 182.

122. Johannsen, *Stephen A. Douglas*, 301–3.

123. Campbell, *Fighting Slavery in Chicago*, 85–87.

124. Minutes, Committee for the Relief of Fugitives in Canada, November 11, 1850, Zebina Eastman Collection, CHS.

125. Magdol, *Owen Lovejoy*, 96–97.

126. Applegate, *The Most Famous Man in America*, 234–36, 258–59.

127. Gossard, "New York City Congregational Cluster," 54–58, 67, 71–72, 102–3, 258.

128. Bains, "An Anti-Slavery Church in Washington, D.C." The American Missionary Association made efforts to start the church in 1847, in 1850, in 1854, and each autumn thereafter, until it succeeded in 1865.

129. Payne, *Josiah Bushnell Grinnell*, 21–23.

130. Harrison, "Hampshire Colony Congregational Church," 29.

131. Samuel G. Wright, Journal, 1839–65, entry dated March 24, 1851, Knox College archives.

Chapter 4. Organizing a Christian Political Response to Win Elections: 1852–1854

1. *Western Citizen*, December 23, 1851.

2. Blue, *Free Soilers*, 234.

3. *Western Citizen*, March 9, 1852.

4. Blue, *Free Soilers*, 239–242.

5. *Western Citizen*, August 17, 1852; *National Era*, August 19, 1852; Quarles, *Black Abolitionists*, 186; Philip S. Foner, introduction to Douglass, *Life and Writings*, 2:75–76; Blue, *Free Soilers*, 248.

6. Magdol, *Owen Lovejoy*, 98–99.

7. Blue, *Free Soilers*, 243–44.

8. Blue, *Free Soilers*, 248–49.

9. Blue, *Free Soilers*, 242–43.

10. Blue, *Free Soilers*, 262–63.

11. *Western Citizen*, August 31, 1852.

12. During the first year after its publication, three hundred thousand copies were sold in the United States and one million in Britain. Foreman, *World on Fire*, 26.

13. Yeager, *Julian M. Sturtevan*, 194.

14. *Western Citizen*, August 31, 1852.; Magdol, *Owen Lovejoy*, 100.

15. R. L. Harris, "H. Ford Douglas"; Molyneaux, *African Americans in Early Rockford*, 24.

16. Blue, *Free Soilers*, 262.

17. Bridges, "Antebellum Struggle for Citizenship," 321n49.

18. Bridges, "Antebellum Struggle for Citizenship," 321n48.

19. Dolinar, *Negro in Illinois*, 46.

20. Weiner, *Race and Rights*, 114.

21. Bridges, "Antebellum Struggle for Citizenship," 300–302.

22. N. D. Harris, *History of Negro Servitude in Illinois*, 235–36; Meites, "The 1847 Illinois Constitutional Convention and Persons of Color," 285; J. P. Jones, "*Black Jack.*"

23. Gliozzo, "John Jones: A Study of a Black Chicagoan," 185.

24. N. D. Harris, *History of Negro Servitude in Illinois*, 235–36.

25. *JHR*, 1853, 442–43.

26. N. D. Harris, *History of Negro Servitude in Illinois*, 236; Middleton, *Black Laws in the Old Northwest*, 299–302.

27. E. Foner, *Free Soil, Free Labor, Free Men*, 281.

28. *Congregational Herald*, April 16, 1853, CTS.

29. Bridges, "Antebellum Struggle for Citizenship," 302–3.

30. *Western Citizen*, March 1, 1853.

31. N. D. Harris, *History of Negro Servitude in Illinois*, 236.

32. Elliott, "Owen Lovejoy," 233.

33. Ahlstrom, *Religious History of the American People*, 457–58.

34. Willey, *History of the Antislavery Cause in State and Nation*, 407.

35. Spinka, *History of Illinois Congregational and Christian Churches*, 123–24, 132.

36. Jeanne Humphreys (DeNovo), "Mary Brown Davis, Journalist, Feminist, and Social Reformer," Honors Paper, Knox College, May 23, 1939; *Oquawka Spectator* 6, no. 50 (January 18, 1854), Special Collections and Archives, Knox College Library, Galesburg, Illinois; Buechler, *Transformation of the Woman Suffrage Movement*, 57.

37. *Chicago Tribune*, September 12 and 19, 1853.

38. Kerr, *Lucy Stone*, 71.

39. Cazden, *Antoinette Brown Blackwell*, 82; Strong, *Perfectionist Politics*, 44–46.

40. *Chicago Tribune*, September 12 and 19, 1853; Cole, *Centennial History of Illinois*, 3:212.

41. Philip S. Foner, introduction to Douglass, *Life and Writings*, 2:28.

42. Blackett, *Beating against the Barriers*, 48; Blackett, *Building an Antislavery Wall*, 128.

43. Philip S. Foner, introduction to Douglass, *Life and Writings*, 2:29.

44. Gliozzo, "John Jones: A Study of a Black Chicagoan," 183–84.

45. The Corresponding Committee included William Johnson, Rev. Byrd Parker, Rev. J. A. Warren, and Joseph H. Barquet, secretary. See Bridges, "Antebellum Struggle for Citizenship," 305–6.

46. *Chicago Tribune*, December 18, 1852; *Chicago Daily Times*, December 29, 1852.

47. *Proceedings of the First Convention of the Colored Citizens of the State of Illinois . . . 1853*, 49–57, CHS; *Western Citizen*, May 3, 1853.

48. In Chicago, Byrd Parker, Lewis Isbell, Joseph H. Barquet, Edward Gordon, and Henry O. Wagner were elected (Bridges, "Antebellum Struggle for Citizenship," 306).

49. McCaul, *Black Struggle for Public Schooling*, 23–25.

50. Frederick Douglass's travels from October 10 to November 2, 1853, are listed in the itinerary compiled by Blassingame and McKivigan in Douglass, *Papers*, Series 1, vol. 2, *1847–54* (1991), xxxiv–xxxv; R. N. Scott, "What Price Freedom?," 71.

51. *Free West*, December 1, 1853.

52. Martin, *Mind of Frederick Douglass*, 177–78.

53. *Free West*, December 1, 1853.

54. Apocalyptic revelation disclosed doom for sinners, while millennialists believed Christ would rule on earth for a thousand years of justice and peace.

55. Blight, *Frederick Douglass' Civil War*, 102–3.

56. Ernest, *Liberation Historiography*, 100.

57. *Free West*, December 1, 1853.

58. Roberts, *Evangelicalism and the Politics of Reform*, 202; Rael, *Black Identity and Black Protest*, 175, 241.

59. Codding, "Ichabod D. Codding"; Johannsen, *Stephen A. Douglas*, 451, 457.

60. N. D. Harris, *History of Negro Servitude in Illinois*, 186–87.

61. Blue, *Free Soilers*, 274–75

62. Blue, *Salmon Chase*, 93–95; Blue, *Free Soilers*, 280–81; Forbes, *Missouri Compromise*, 278; J. B. Stewart, *Joshua R. Giddings*, 222–25.

63. Harrold, *Gamaliel Bailey*, 159–60.

64. Johannsen, *Stephen A. Douglas*, 443.

65. Kelsey, *Israel Washburn, Jr.*, 63; Harrold, *Gamaliel Bailey*, 161.

66. Blackett, *Building an Antislavery Wall*, 170.

67. Philip S. Foner, introduction to Douglass, *Life and Writings*, 2:35.

68. Harrison, "We Are Here Assembled," 329.

69. Staudenraus, *African Colonization Movement*, 241–44.

70. Kelsey, *Israel Washburn, Jr.*, 67–68.

71. *Racine Wisconsin Advocate*, May 22, June 5, 1854.

72. Howard, "Illinois Republican Party: Part I," 127.

73. Introduction to speech by Frederick Douglass, "Slavery, Freedom, and the Kansas-Nebraska Act: An Address Delivered in Chicago, Illinois, on 30 October 1854," in Douglass, *Papers*, Series 1: *Speeches, Debates, and Interviews, 1847–54*, 2:538.

74. Bradsby, *History of Bureau County, Illinois*, 161–69.

75. Howard, "The Illinois Republican Party: Part I," 136–39.

76. Selby, "Republican State Convention."

77. *Free West*, September 7, 1854.

78. Gienapp, *Origins of the Republican Party*, 123.

79. Howard, "The Illinois Republican Party: Part I"; Codding, "Ichabod Codding's Lecture Tour."

80. *Freeport [Ill.] Journal*, October 12, 1854.

81. *CW*, 2:266.

82. *Freeport [Ill.] Journal*, October 12, 1854.

83. *Illinois State Register*, October 6, 1854.

84. Cole, *Centennial History of Illinois*, 3:129.

85. Peter Bryant to Aunt Melissa Dawes, November 10, 1854, in Murray and Rodney, "Letters of Peter Bryant: First Installment," 325; HBB, 105–9.

86. Introduction to speech by Frederick Douglass, "Slavery, Freedom and the Kansas-Nebraska Act: An Address delivered in Chicago, Illinois, on 30 October 1854," in Douglass, *Papers*, Series 1, *Speeches, Debates, and Interviews, 1847–54*, 2:538.

87. Douglass, *Papers*, Series 1, *Speeches, Debates, and Interviews, 1847–54*, 2: x.

88. Owen Lovejoy to Lucy Denham, October 25, 1854; Clements.

89. Pinsker, "Senator Abraham Lincoln," 3. It refers to a "List of the Members Composing the Nineteenth General Assembly of the State of Illinois," printed by the State Register Office, 1855, Broadside Collection, ALPLM, Springfield, Illinois.

90. Owen Lovejoy to Joshua Giddings, November 10, 1854, OHS.

91. Robertson, *Hearts Beating for Liberty*, 188; Miller, *Arguing about Slavery*, 314.

92. Johannsen, *Stephen A. Douglas*, 259, 462–63.

93. Magdol, *Owen Lovejoy*, 120.

94. D. L. Wilson and R. O. Davis, *Herndon's Informants*, 467; King, *Lincoln's Manager*, 107.

95. *JHR*, 1855, 306–9.

96. Howard, "The Illinois Republican Party: Part I," 154.

97. R. N. Scott, "What Price Freedom?," 33; Gliozzo, "John Jones: A Study of a Black Chicagoan," 177–88.

Chapter 5. Achieving Political Fusion and Winning a Seat in Congress: 1855–November 1857

1. *Rockford Republican*, January 5, 1855, Rockford Public Library; Floyd S. Barringer, "A Walk through Oak Ridge Cemetery," 1985; revised 2010 by Kathie Nenaber and Susan Cull as *Faith of Our Founders: Celebrating 175 Years of Ministry*, Westminster Presbyterian Church, 533 South Walnut Street, Springfield, Illinois, May 26, 1835–May 26, 2010, Church Archives.

2. Jane Ann Moore, "Chipping Away at Racism in the 1855 Illinois Legislature," presented at the meeting of the Society of Historians of the Early American Republic, July 17, 2009, in Springfield, Illinois; IS.

3. Bridges, "Antebellum Struggle for Citizenship," 315.

4. Pinsker, "Senator Abraham Lincoln," 3. This officially printed list of 1855 representatives identified members as D (Democrat), A.N.D. (anti-Nebraska Democrat), W (Whig), K.N. (Know Nothing), or R (Republican). The authors have applied the term "early republican" to identify those who designated themselves Republican in 1854 before the party was formally organized in 1856. See Bateman and Selby, *Historical Encyclopedia of Illinois*, 189.

5. Monaghan, *Man Who Elected Lincoln*, 39–45.

6. *Free West*, January 11, 1855.

7. Matteson, "Message of the Governor"; JHR, 1855, 17–18.

8. Harrison, "A History of the First Congregational Church, Princeton, Illinois."

9. JHR, 1855, 20–21.

10. JHR, 1855, 24.

11. *Free West*, January 11, 1855; JHR, 1855, 23, 25.

12. *Free West*, January 11, 1855.

13. JHR, 1855, 95.

14. *Free West*, January 11, 1855; JHR, 1855, 105.

15. *Free West*, January 11 and 18, 1855; JHR, 1855, 75, 723.

16. *Free West*, February 1, 1855; HBB, 102–5.

17. *Free West*, February 1, 1855; *HBB*, 103.

18. *Free West*, February 1, 1855; JHR, 1855, 86.

19. *Free West*, February 1, 1855; HBB, 104.

20. JHR, 1855, 86.

21. *Alton Telegraph*, January 13, 1855.

22. The Illinois State Archives does not have this petition in its possession.

23. Guelzo, *Lincoln's Emancipation Proclamation*, 76. "No one in Civil War America . . . had a monopoly on racial self-interest."

24. Harrison, "We Are Here Assembled," 329–30. Harrison sees the petition as "dripping with sarcasm," based on an article in the *Alton Courier*, January 11 and 18, 1855.

25. Walker, *Rock in a Weary Land*, 90.

26. *Alton Telegraph*, January 12, 1855.

27. Bridges, "Antebellum Struggle for Citizenship," 315.

28. *Free West*, April 5, 1855; *HBB*, 108.

29. HBB, 113–14.

30. *Free West*, March 16, 1855; HBB, 120.

31. Oakes, *Freedom National*, 266–67.

32. D. B. Davis, "How They Stopped Slavery."

33. Oakes, *Scorpion's Sting*, describes a cornered poisonous scorpion that stings itself to death, a metaphor of the Republican policy to contain slavery to the Southern states in order to constrict it so that it kills itself.

34. JHR, 1855, 286.

35. JHR, 1855, 307.

36. JHR, 1855, 307–8.

37. JHR, 1855, 283–84.

38. JHR, 1855, 308–9.

39. Johannsen, *Stephen A. Douglas*, 460–64.

40. JHR, 1855, 348–60.

41. JHR, 1855, 358–60.

42. Trefousse, *Radical Republicans*, 10.

43. *Rockford Republican*, February 21, 1855.

44. McCaul, *Black Struggle for Public Schooling*, 29.

45. JHR, 1855, 168.

46. *Free West*, January 18 and February 1, 1855.

47. *Free West*, January 18 and February 1, 1855.

48. JHR, 1855, 338.

49. JHR, 1855, 266.

50. JHR, 1855, 385.

51. JHR, 1855, 385.

52. JHR, 1855, 599; *Free West*, February 13, 1855.

53. JHR, 1855, 620.

54. McCaul, *Black Struggle for Public Schooling*, 29.

55. McCaul, *Black Struggle for Public Schooling*, 30–31.

56. *Proceedings of the State Convention of Colored Citizens of the State of Illinois . . . 1856*, 76.

57. McCaul, *Black Struggle for Public Schooling*, 152.

58. Joshua Giddings to Owen Lovejoy, February 20, 1855, OHS.

59. Magdol, *Owen Lovejoy*, 126.

60. Haberkorn, "Owen Lovejoy in Princeton, Illinois," 288.

61. Ron Grossman, "Joseph Medill and His Vision," *Chicago Tribune*, 150th Anniversary Commemorative Edition, June 8, 1997.

62. Howard, "Illinois Republican Party: Part II," 288.

63. Ichabod Codding to Maria Preston, April 14, 1855, Ichabod Codding Papers, ALPLM.

64. Charles Henry Ray to Elihu Washburne, April 21, 1855, Library of Congress.

65. "Ichabod Codding's 1854 Lecture Tour in Behalf of a Fusion Party" compiled by Maria Preston Codding, a supplement to Howard, "Illinois Republican Party: Part I."

66. *Quincy Whig*, July 31, 1855.

67. Howard, "Illinois Republican Party: Part II," 291.

68. Gienapp, *Origins of the Republican Party*, 286–87.

69. Howard, "Illinois Republican Party: Part II," 292.

70. CW, 2:316–17.

71. Lyman Trumbull to Owen Lovejoy, August 23, 1855, ALPLM.

72. Howard, "Illinois Republican Party: Part II," 294.

73. Cole, *Centennial History of Illinois*, 3:129; Fuller, *Crusade against Slavery*, 276, wrote, "The effort of the Illinois abolitionists to organize was a failure"; William F. Gienapp, "Who Voted for Lincoln?," 124, agreed: "Lincoln's decline [to join the Republicans in 1854] symbolized the failure of the fusion movement . . . that doomed it to ineffectiveness."

74. E. Foner, *Fiery Trial*, 76–78.

75. Howard, "Illinois Republican Party: Part II," 291–94; Pinsker, "Senator Abraham Lincoln," 3.

76. Owen Lovejoy to Archibald Williams, August 6, 1855, Lilly Library Manuscript Collections, African-American-Related Collections, University of Indiana; W. F. Moore and J. A. Moore, *Collaborators for Emancipation*, 36.

77. Howard, "Illinois Republican Party: Part II," 298.

78. Selby, "Editorial Convention," 41.

79. Monaghan, *Man Who Elected Lincoln*, 60–61.

80. Selby, "Editorial Convention."

81. Selby, "Editorial Convention," 36. Blizzard conditions kept away editors from Oquawka, Danville, Vermont, Aurora, Freeport, Joliet, Lockport, Kankakee City, Peru, and Waukegan—many locations that were in the northern part of the state. Belleville was in the south.

82. See entry for Paul Selby in D. L. Wilson and R. O. Davis, *Herndon's Informants*, 770.

83. Gienapp, *Origins of the Republican Party*, 289.

84. Selby, "Editorial Convention," 38.

85. *Chicago Tribune*, May 17, 1856.

86. Gienapp, *Origins of the Republican Party*, 255; Magdol, *Owen Lovejoy*, 137, *New York Times*, February 23, 1856.

87. Gienapp, *Origins of the Republican Party*, 254–56; Harrold, *Gamaliel Bailey*, 176.

88. Julian, *Political Recollections*, 148.

89. Reprinted from *Proceedings of the First Three Republican National Conventions*; HBB, 124.

90. Philip S. Foner, introduction to Douglass, *Life and Writings*, 2:80–81; Stauffer, *Black Hearts of Men*, 8–9.

91. Martin, *Mind of Frederick Douglass*, 3.

92. *Chicago Tribune*, May 17, 1856.

93. Magdol, *Owen Lovejoy*, 143; Cunningham, "Bloomington Convention of 1856," 105; W. F. Moore and J. A. Moore, *Collaborators for Emancipation*, 41.

94. Crissey, *Lincoln's Lost Speech*, 133.

95. Crissey, *Lincoln's Lost Speech*, 297.

96. E. Foner, *Fiery Trial*, 45. Palmer and Browning had defended blacks held in long-term indentures who were seeking freedom pro bono.

97. Gienapp, *Origins of the Republican Party*, 294.

98. HBB, 127–28.

99. Prince, "Official Account of the Convention," 156, and "Unofficial Account of the Convention," 174; J. O. Cunningham, Address; Bateman and Selby, *Historical Encyclopedia of Illinois*, 791–92; Crissey, *Lincoln's Lost Speech*, 121; Church, *History of the Republican Party in Illinois*, 34.

100. Beveridge, *Abraham Lincoln*, 2:396; CW, 2:343.

101. Cole, *Centennial History of Illinois*, 3:129; Fuller, *Crusade against Slavery*, 276; Gienapp, "Who Voted for Lincoln?," 124.

102. Owen Lovejoy to Betsey Lovejoy, June 12, 1856, TT.

103. Magdol, *Owen Lovejoy*, 150–52.

104. Julian, *Life of Joshua R. Giddings*, 335–36.

105. Beveridge, *Abraham Lincoln*, 2:390.

106. Carwardine, *Evangelicals and Politics*, 253.

107. Carwardine, *Evangelicals and Politics*, 263.

108. Carwardine, *Evangelicals and Politics*, 254.

109. Carwardine, *Evangelicals and Politics*, 274.

110. BCR, June 16, 1864.

111. Magdol, *Owen Lovejoy*, 154–55.

112. *Ottawa Republican*, July 6, 1856.

113. *Pantagraph*, July 23, 1856.

114. *Weekly National Flag*, Bloomington, November 7, 1856.

115. Magdol, *Owen Lovejoy*, 158–59.

116. HBB, 132; Matthew 25:35.

117. HBB, 133.

118. HBB, 132; Elliott, "Owen Lovejoy," 229; Cunningham, *History of Champaign County*, 791–92.

119. Jesse Fell to Brs., October 10, 1856, Augusta Cowan Papers, ALPLM.

120. Magdol, *Owen Lovejoy*, 165.

121. Brown, *From Fugitive Slave to Free Man*, 34–35.

122. Walther, *Shuttering of the Union*, 91–92.

123. H. W. Allen and V. A. Lacey, *Illinois Elections, 1818–1990*; Magdol, *Owen Lovejoy*, 166.

124. *Democratic Press*, December 11, 1856, CHS.

125. Center for Range Voting, "Composition of Congress by Political Party, 1855–2007," http://rangevoting.org/CongParty.html.

126. "Election of 1856," United States History (website), http://www.u-s-history.com/pages/h85.html.

127. Bridges, "Antebellum Struggle for Citizenship," 309–10.

128. *Proceedings of the State Convention of Colored Citizens of the State of Illinois . . . 1856*.

129. Gienapp, *Origins of the Republican Party*, 431–32.

130. Applegate, *The Most Famous Man in America*, 285–88.

131. Carwardine, *Evangelicals and Politics*, 274.

132. Owen Lovejoy to Gerrit Smith, November 15 and December 21, 1856, and January 16, 1857, Gerrit Smith Papers, Syracuse University Library.

133. J. B. Stewart, *Joshua R. Giddings*, 247–49.

134. Calonius, *The Wanderer*, 43–44.

135. Calonius, *The Wanderer*, 2:119–20.

136. CG, 35th Cong., 2d Sess., Feb. 17, 1858, 752–54; HBB, 142, 146.

137. Freehling, *Road to Disunion*, 2:119–122.

138. E. Foner, *Fiery Trial*, 98.

139. Pasternak, "Rise Now and Fly to Arms," 142–43.

140. Douglass, *Life and Writings*, 2:412.

141. Magdol, *Owen Lovejoy*, 167.

142. "Hampshire Colony Congregational Church," 103.

Chapter 6. Confronting the Slave Power and Unifying Illinois Republicans: November 1857–November 1859

1. "Shooting in Illinois," *Chicago Press and Tribune*, August 4, 1857; "Two Negroes Burned Alive," *Chicago Press and Tribune*, October 30, 1857.

2. Johannsen, *Stephen A. Douglas*, 585–86, 632.

3. W. F. Moore and J. A. Moore, *Collaborators for Emancipation*, 66.

4. Trefousse, *Radical Republicans*, 106.

5. Owen Lovejoy to Lucy Storrs Denham, December 5, 1857, Clements; Magdol, *Owen Lovejoy*, 170.

6. Elihu Washburne added an "e" to his last name.

7. Washburne, *Biography*, 283.

8. Center for Range Voting, "Composition of Congress by Political Party, 1855–2007," http://rangevoting.org/CongParty.html.

9. *CG, 1857–1858*, December 14, 1857, 59.

10. *CG, 1857–1858*, December 14, 1857, 58.

11. Owen Lovejoy to Lucy Storrs Denham, n.d., Clements.

12. J. B. Stewart, *Joshua R. Giddings*, 248–50.

13. *HBB*, 140–41.

14. Trefousse, *Radical Republicans*, 14; U.S. Congress, *Biographical Directory of the United States Congress, 1774–Present*, http://bioguide.congress.gov.

15. "Morrill, Justin Smith," U.S. Congress, *Biographical Directory*, http://bioguide.congress.gov/scripts/biodisplay.pl?index=M000969.

16. Trefousse, *Radical Republicans*, 75; "Potter, John Fox," U.S. Congress, *Biographical Directory*, http://bioguide.congress.gov/scripts/biodisplay.pl?index=P000465.

17. *Harper's Weekly*, April 16, 1864.

18. Arnold, *Life of Abraham Lincoln*, 227.

19. Trefousse, *Radical Republicans*, 13–14.

20. *CG, 1857–1858*, December 14, 1857, 58; Kelsey, *Israel Washburn, Jr.*, 94.

21. J. B. Stewart, *Joshua R. Giddings*, 257.

22. Freehling, *Road to Disunion*, 2:132, 139–40, 255. In 1857 Lawrence M. Keitt raised a cane against Senator Sumner (Magdol, *Owen Lovejoy*, 189). Washburne knocked Mississippian Barksdale's wig off his head.

23. "Occasional Remarks during the 35th Congress," January 25, 1858, CG.

24. Kathryn Turner letter in the Owen Lovejoy Papers, Bowdoin College Archives and Katherine Turner Letters in the Carl Sandburg Papers, University of Illinois archives.

25. H. Davis, *Joshua Leavitt*, 188.

26. Harrold, *Subversives*, 170.

27. Harrold, *Subversives*, 44.

28. Harrold, *Subversives*, 43, 170–71. See Lovejoy's similar phrase, HBB, 222.

29. Harrold, *Subversives*, 170–71; Bains, "An Anti-Slavery church in Washington, D.C.," 34. The minister of the fashionable First Presbyterian Church preached against the Congregational Society.

30. d'Entremont, *Southern Emancipator*, 107.

31. Owen Lovejoy to Eunice Lovejoy, n.d., Clements. Lovejoy's "daughter" was his stepdaughter Lucy Denham.

32. HBB, 142–54.

33. HBB, 143.

34. HBB, 144.

35. HBB, 147.

36. HBB, 149.

37. HBB, 150.

214 *Notes to Chapter 6*

38. HBB, 151.

39. HBB, 146.

40. Owen Lovejoy to Lewis Tappan, March 15, 1858, ARC.

41. Fischer, *Albion's Seed*, 205, 411.

42. E. Foner, *Fiery Trial*, 94.

43. "Dred Scott in Practice," *Chicago Daily Tribune*, May 3, 1858.

44. Takaki, *Pro-Slavery Crusade*, 134–59.

45. Calonius, *The Wanderer*, 42–43.

46. Freehling, *Road to Disunion*, 2:173–182.

47. Abraham Smith to Abraham Lincoln, June 4, 1858, LC.

48. Josh Whitmore to General W. H. L. Wallace, June 5, 1858, in Wallace, *Life and Letters of General W. H. L. Wallace*, 82–83.

49. *CW*, 2:468.

50. Johannsen, *Stephen A. Douglas*, 653; W. F. Moore and J. A. Moore, *Collaborators for Emancipation*, 76.

51. "Only Lincoln could hold this rag-tag coalition together." *Dictionary of American Biography*, 2:435; CW, 2:112; Haberkorn, "Owen Lovejoy in Princeton, Illinois," 308; Curry, *Blueprint for Modern America*, 29

52. BCR, July 8, 1858 (extra edition); HBB, 159.

53. Sophia Lovejoy Dickinson, n.d., BCHS.

54. *BCR*, July 15, 1858.

55. *Bloomington Daily Pantagraph*, August 13, 1858.

56. *Bloomington Daily Pantagraph*, August 24, 1858.

57. Abraham Lincoln Association, *Collected Works of Abraham Lincoln*, University of Michigan Library Digital Collections, http://abrahamlincolnassociation.org/lincoln-repository/collected-works/.

58. CW, 3:6

59. Magdol, *Owen Lovejoy*, 211.

60. CW, 9

61. CW, 3:10.

62. HBB, 163; *Chicago Press and Tribune*, August 26, 1858.

63. *Chicago Press and Tribune*, August 26, 1858.

64. Shaw, "Lovejoy, the Abolitionists, and Republican Party," 71–72.

65. Shaw, "Lovejoy, the Abolitionists, and Republican Party," 43–44.

66. Shaw, "Lovejoy, the Abolitionists, and Republican Party," 72.

67. E. Foner, *Fiery Trial*, 107–10.

68. Refers to Matthew 25:35–36.

69. E. D. Jones, *Lincoln and the Preachers*, 65.

70. Magdol, *Owen Lovejoy*, 216.

71. *Weekly National Flag*, August 1 and November 7, 1858.

72. *Tribune Almanac and Political Register*, 61.

73. H. W. Allen and V. A. Lacey, *Illinois Elections, 1818–1990*, 142.

74. Guelzo, *Lincoln and Douglas*, 284–88; Guelzo, "Houses Divided."

75. Reed, "Early African American Settlement of Chicago," 216.

76. Harrold, *Gamaliel Bailey*, 195–96.

77. Harrold, *Gamaliel Bailey*, 170.

78. Harrold, *Gamaliel Bailey*, 195.

79. Harrold, *Gamaliel Bailey*, 195–96.

80. Harrold, *Gamaliel Bailey*, 195–96.

81. Owen Lovejoy to Mary Denham, January 22, 1859, Clements; French, *Witness to the Young Republic*, 307.

82. Gail Hamilton (pseudonym for Mary Abigail Dodge), "Obituary" for Owen Lovejoy, *Congregationalist*, April 1864, CTS.

83. "Obituary of Owen Lovejoy," *Congregationalist*, April 1864.

84. "Obituary of Owen Lovejoy," *Congregationalist*, April 1864.

85. Ginzberg, *Women and the Work of Benevolence*, 124.

86. Buechler, *Transformation of the Woman Suffrage Movement*, 58–59; Stowell, *In Tender Consideration*, 134, 155n20. The act allowed a married woman to own land she brought into a marriage and to acquire land during marriage.

87. John W. Blassingame, Partial Speaking Itinerary, in Douglass, *Papers*, 3:xxix–xxx; R. L. Harris, "H. Ford Douglas," 224.

88. Douglass, *Life and Writings*, 2:448.

89. Molyneaux, *African Americans in Early Rockford*, 60.

90. Douglass, *Life and Writings*, 2:448–50.

91. Douglass, *Life and Writings*, 2:448–50.

92. Julian, *Political Recollections*, 366.

93. CG, 35th Cong., 2d Sess., Feb. 22, 1859, 196–98; HBB, 166.

94. Trefousse, *Radical Republicans*, 126; Johannsen, *Stephen A. Douglas*, 692.

95. Kennedy, *Nigger*.

96. CG, 35th Cong., 2d Sess., Feb. 21, 1859, 196–98; HBB, 176.

97. Fischer, *Albion's Seed*, 300–307. Certain folkways permitted men to maintain a predatory attitude toward women: "The abolitionist indictment of slavery for its association with predatory sex had a solid foundation in historical fact."

98. CG, 35th Con., 2d sess., Feb. 21, 1859, 198; HBB, 178.

99. Julian, *Life of Joshua R. Giddings*, 363–64; J. B. Stewart, *Joshua R. Giddings*, 262.

100. Crofts, *Lincoln and the Politics of Slavery*, 15, 77–80. Crofts suggests James Bingham was Giddings's heir because he was as radical as Giddings and planned Giddings's farewell. Stevens, Ashley, Julian, and Lovejoy were also steadfast successors.

101. *National Era*, February, 1859.

102. Takaki, *Pro-Slavery Crusade*, 167, 176–84.

103. *Douglass' Monthly*, August 1858.

104. *New York Times*, April 22, 1859.

105. Jonathan Blanchard to Mary Blanchard, April 26, 1859, Wheaton College, Wheaton, Illinois.

106. *JHR*, 1855, 12.

107. McGiffert, *No Ivory Tower*, 14, 48, 51. Col. Charles G. Hammond was superintendent of the Michigan Central Railroad and later of the Chicago, Burlington and Quincy Railroad.

108. Drury, *Old Illinois Houses*, McLean County Historical Society, Bloomington, Illinois.

109. Harrold, *Gamaliel Bailey*, 193, 210.

110. Owen Lovejoy to Ozias Hatch, October 31, 1859, ALPL.

111. "An Agricultural Poem," BCR, July 5, 1860.

112. Campbell, *Fighting Slavery in Chicago*, 87, 138–39; Turner, "Mary Jones," in *Underground Railroad in Illinois*, 117–18; Blockson, *Underground Railroad*, 200.

113. Petrulionis, *To Set This World Right*, 127.

114. Philip S. Foner, introduction to Douglass, *Life and Writings*, 2:90–91.

115. Hohoff, *Ministry to Man*, 3.

116. Philip S. Foner, introduction to Douglass, *Life and Writings*, 2:91–93.

117. BCR, September 14, 1972 (anniversary edition; transcript first published April 19, 1860), citing the CG, 36th Cong., 1st Sess., Apr. 5, 1860, 202–6; HBB, 204.

118. Quarles, *Allies for Freedom*, 119, 124–25.

Chapter 7. Electing Lincoln and Holding the Party Together: December 1859–June 1861

1. Carr, *Belleville, Ottawa, and Galesburg*, 126–27.

2. "Another Case," *Chicago Press and Tribune*, November 26, 1859.

3. "Northwestern Christian Anti-Slavery Convention," *Chicago Press and Tribune*, October 22, 1859.

4. Myers, *Henry Wilson and the Coming of the Civil War*, 402.

5. Washburne, *Biography*, 368; Magdol, *Owen Lovejoy*, 229.

6. Center for Range Voting, "Composition of Congress by Political Party, 1855–2007," http://rangevoting.org/CongParty.html.

7. Trefousse, *Thaddeus Stevens*, 99.

8. Trefousse, *Radical Republicans*, 12–13.

9. "Ashley, James Mitchell," U.S. Congress, *Biographical Directory*, http://bioguide.congress.gov/scripts/biodisplay.pl?index=A000314; Horowitz, *Great Impeacher*.

10. Magdol, *Owen Lovejoy*, 231–32; Bailey, *Hinton Rowan Helper*, 34.

11. CW, 3:494.

12. Applegate, *The Most Famous Man in America*, 286.

13. Applegate, *The Most Famous Man in America*, 231.

14. Holzer, *Lincoln at Cooper Union*, 10–11, 15, 23–25, 73.

15. Holzer, *Lincoln at Cooper Union*, 74–76.

16. Applegate, *The Most Famous Man in America*, 321–23; Holzer, *Lincoln at Cooper Union*, 106; C. S. Johnson, *Politics and a Belly-Full*, 106.

17. Magdol, *Owen Lovejoy*, 231.

18. BCR, April 5, 1860, citing the CG, 36th Cong., 1st Sess., Mar. 26, 1860, appendix, 174; HBB, 186.

19. HBB, 187.

20. HBB, 188–89.

21. Richardson, "Abraham Lincoln and the Politics of Principle," 1390–91.

22. BCR, April 5, 1860, citing the CG, 36th Cong., 1st sess., Mar. 26, 1860, appendix, 174; HBB, 189.

23. HBB, 190.

24. Richardson, *Greatest Nation of the Earth*, 144.

25. Harrold, *Subversives*, 151, 157–58.

26. Douglass, *Life and Writings*, 2:483.

27. P. S. Foner, *Business and Slavery*, 164–68; Bilger, "Mystery on Pearl Street," 59–60.

28. Bohman, "Owen Lovejoy on 'The Barbarism of Slavery,'" 118.

29. Cox, *Union—Disunion—Reunion*, 75.

30. Bohman, "Owen Lovejoy on 'The Barbarism of Slavery,'" 114–32; CG, 36th Congress, 1st session, 2590–2603; HBB, 192–211.

31. Lovejoy speaks in the same vein as Hosea Easton's *Treatise*, commented on by Pease and Pease, *They Who Would Be Free*, 111.

32. CG, 36th Cong., 1st Sess., Apr. 5, 1860, 191–211; HBB, 192.

33. HBB, 193.

34. Fischer, *Albion's Seed*, 388, 412.

35. HBB, 194.

36. HBB, 197–200.

37. Finkelman, *Slavery and the Founders*, chapter 3.

38. HBB, 200.

39. HBB, 205.

40. HBB, 203.

41. HBB, 204–5.

42. HBB, 206.

43. HBB, 207.

44. HBB, 208.

45. HBB, 201, 207–8.

46. Miller, *Lincoln's Virtues*, 431.

47. Freehling, *Road to Disunion*, 2:288–91.

48. Bohman, "Owen Lovejoy on 'The Barbarism of Slavery,'" 130.

49. J. B. Stewart, *Abolitionist Politics and the Coming of the Civil War*, 115–16, 127–35.

50. LC, Microfiche 45/1213.

51. LC, Microfiche 45/1222.

52. LC, Microfiche 45/1226.

53. Owen Lovejoy to Lydia Maria Child, April 28, 1860. Bohman owns the letter. See Bohman, "Owen Lovejoy on 'The Barbarism of Slavery,'" 117.

54. H. Wilson, *History of Antislavery Measures*, 2: 671.

55. Johannsen, *Stephen A. Douglas*, 760.

56. Johannsen, *Stephen A. Douglas*, 772–73.

57. Republican Party Platform of 1860, Teaching American History, https://teaching americanhistory.org/library/document/republican-party-platform-1860.

58. W. F. and J. A. Moore, *Collaborators for Emancipation*, 96.

59. Owen Lovejoy to Dear Friend, June 15, 1860, Jesse Fell Papers, IS.

60. Owen Lovejoy to Jesse Fell, June 27, 1860, Jesse Fell Papers, IS.

61. *Bloomington Daily Telegraph*, May 28, 1900.

62. Arnold, *Life of Abraham Lincoln*, 7.

63. Elliott, "Owen Lovejoy," 229–30.

64. *Alton Courier*, July 23, 1860.

65. Elliott, "Owen Lovejoy," 231.

66. John Wycliffe lived from ca. 1330 to 1384. In 1428 the Bishop of Lincoln burned Wycliffe's remains. In "Ecclesiastical Sonnets," William Wordsworth envisions Wycliffe's ashes flowing to the sea, a metaphor for spreading his teachings onto the European continent. Similarly, Owen Lovejoy envisioned Elijah's ashes carrying the message of human freedom to the world. HBB, 211n51.

67. *New York Times*, September 19, 1860; Heinzel, "'To Protect the Rights of the White Race,'" 384. A second definition of *scout* is "to reject contemptuously."

68. Douglass, *Life and Writings*, 2:490–91.

69. W. F. Moore and J. A. Moore, *Collaborators for Emancipation*, 101.

70. *Freeport (Ill.) Journal*, September 20, 1860; HBB, 219.

71. *Salem Advocate*, October 25, 1860.

72. *Chicago Press and Tribune*, October 18, 1860; HBB, 227–28.

73. HBB, 230.

74. HBB, 220–21. Hinton Rowan Helper wrote *The Impending Crisis of the South*, a book endorsed by a long list of Republican congressmen. Southern congressmen refused to vote for any of the endorsees for Speaker.

75. *BCR*, November 1, 1860.

76. Grinspan, "'Young Men for War.'"

77. BCR, November 1, 1860.

78. *BCR*, November 1, 1860.

79. Magdol, *Owen Lovejoy*, 255.

80. HBB, 225.

81. Berwanger, *Frontier against Slavery*, 133.

82. Berwanger, *Frontier against Slavery*, 133.

83. E. Foner, *Free Soil, Free Labor, Free Men*, 265.

84. Berwanger, *Frontier against Slavery*, 133.

85. Mayer, *All on Fire*, 509.

86. Berwanger, *Frontier against Slavery*, 133. See also James, "Lincoln's Own State in the Election of 1860," and Cunningham, "Bloomington Convention of 1856," 106–7.

87. L. J. Friedman, *Gregarious Saints*, 240; Miller, *Lincoln's Virtues*, 362.

88. *Freeport (Ill.) Journal*, September 20, 1860; HBB, 218.

89. E. Foner, *Free Soil, Free Labor, Free Men*, 265; Berwanger, *Frontier against Slavery*, 133.

90. E. Foner, *Free Soil, Free Labor, Free Men*, 281, 284, 286.

91. Ashworth, "The Republican Triumph," 168–69.

92. E. Foner, *Fiery Trial*, xvii–xviii, 76, 174. Foner lists the "leading Radicals in Congress" as Ashley, Julian, Lovejoy, Stevens, and Sumner.

93. Oakes, *Freedom National*, 59.

94. Raboteau, "Ethiopia Shall Soon Stretch Forth Her Hands," 210.

95. Rael, "The Market Revolution and Market Values," 279.

96. Easton, *To Heal the Scourge of Prejudice*, 87–88; J. B. Stewart, *Abolitionist Politics*, 193.

97. *Freeport (Ill.) Journal*, September 20, 1860; HBB, 221.

98. HBB, 222.

99. HBB, 239–40; *Chicago Press and Tribune*, October 18, 1860 (italics added); HBB, 239–40.

100. BCR, December 5, 1860.

101. Arnold, *Life of Abraham Lincoln*, 170.

102. Goodwin, *Team of Rivals*, 274.

103. Stampp, *And the War Came*, 14.

104. "Dissatisfaction in Mississippi," Accessible Archives, *Christian Recorder*, March 9, 1861; "Union Sentiment in Maryland," Accessible Archives, *Christian Recorder*, March 30, 1861.

105. Fischer, *Albion's Seed*, 231, 241–43, 253–56, 341–43, 368.

106. Reed, "Early African American Settlement of Chicago," 240–41.

107. Ripley, *Black Abolitionist Papers*, 5:71–73.

108. Stampp, *And the War Came*, 63.

109. Freehling, *Road to Disunion*, 2:446.

110. Goodwin, *Team of Rivals*, 289–99.

111. Baker, "James Buchanan," 115.

112. Stampp, *And the War Came*, 189.

113. Magdol, *Owen Lovejoy*, 263–64.

114. Stampp, *And the War Came*, 137.

115. Freehling, *Road to Disunion*, 2:472.

116. Stampp, *And the War Came*, 130.

117. D. B. Davis, *Problem of Slavery in the Age of Emancipation*, 287.

118. Oakes, *Freedom National*, 73.

119. Goodwin, *Team of Rivals*, 296.

120. Sweeney, *Lincoln's Gift from Homer, New York*, 69–70; E. D. Leonard, *Lincoln's Forgotten Ally*, 127.

121. Joseph Medill to Abraham Lincoln, December 26, 1860, Lincoln Papers, LC.

122. CG, 36th Cong., 2d Sess., January 12, 1861, 341–44.

123. Goodwin, *Team of Rivals*, 299–303.

124. CG, 36th Cong., 2d Sess., January 31, 1861, appendix, 124–27; Stampp, *And the War Came*, 128.

125. Stampp, *And the War Came*, 143.

126. CG, 36th Cong., 2d Sess., January 21, 1861, 306–311.

127. Jefferson Davis would claim later in his 1881 book, *The Rise and Fall of the Confederate Government*, that slavery was not the central cause of the war. See David Von Drehle, "The Way We Were: The Civil War, 1861–1865," *Time Magazine*, April 16, 2011, 42.

128. CG, 36th Cong., 2d Sess., appendix, 84–87; HBB, 250–61.

129. HBB, 259.

130. Stampp, *And the War Came*, 137.

131. HBB, 260.

132. HBB, 257.

133. HBB, 251.

134. HBB, 260.

135. A. L. Robinson, *Bitter Fruits of Bondage*, 5–6. One-quarter of white families in the South owned slaves; half of these owned fewer than five slaves. The plantation elite (planters who owned twenty or more slaves) comprised only 3 percent of Southerners: "Only a tiny elite, in fact, controlled the plantations that dominated Southern society and economy."

136. *HBB*, 207.

137. BCR, June 9, 1864. Ichabod Codding reiterated Owen Lovejoy's argument when he reminded the Lovejoy Monument Association on June 1, 1864, that three hundred thousand slaveholders possessed a capital of $1,2 billion "in human bodies and human souls."

138. Stampp, *And the War Came*, 157; CG, 36th Cong., 2d Sess., appendix, 85–86.

139. Stampp, *And the War Came*, 148.

140. Oakes, *Freedom National*, 62.

141. Letter from Owen Lovejoy to My Dear Sir, February 4, 1861, Moorland-Spingarn Research Center, OG Collection, OG44, Howard University Library.

142. Ibid.

143. Masur, *Example for All the Land*, 8.

144. "Confederate States of America—Declaration of the Immediate Causes Which Induce and Justify the Secession of South Carolina from the Federal Union," Declarations of Secession:

South Carolina; December 24, 1860, in the Confederate States of America document collection in The Avalon Project: Documents in Law, History, and Diplomacy, Yale Law School Lillian Goldman Law Library, https://avalon.law.yale.edu/subject_menus/csapage.asp.

145. Alexander Stephens, "Cornerstone Speech," March 21, 1861, Teaching American History, https://teachingamericanhistory.org/library/document/cornerstone-speech.

146. A. L. Robinson, *Bitter Fruits of Bondage*, 4

147. Desmond and Moore, *Darwin's Sacred Cause*, 327, 332–33, 337, 413n36. Three members of the London Anthropological Society Council were on the Confederate payroll.

148. Blackett, *Divided Hearts*, 15, 37, 41.

149. Blight, *Frederick Douglass' Civil War*, 142–44; Douglass, *Life and Writings*, 2:289–309.

150. *BCR*, March 21, 1861.

151. Ripley, *Black Abolitionist Papers*, 5:112; *Chicago Tribune*, April 4 and 6, 1861.

152. *BCR*, April 11, 1861.

153. Foote, *The Civil War*; Holzman, *Adapt or Perish*, 49.

154. *HBB*, 263.

155. *BCR*, April 25, 1861; HBB, 264.

156. Magdol, *Owen Lovejoy*, 289.

157. Douglass, *Life and Writings*, 2:102, 3:11, 13.

158. Martin, "Frederick Douglass," 71, 74.

159. Reed, "Early African American Settlement of Chicago," 246–47.

160. Harrold, *Subversives*, 240–241; Douglass, *Life and Writings*, 3:14; Horton and Horton, *Black Bostonians*, 136.

161. Botume, *First Days among the Contrabands*.

162. Arnold, *Life of Abraham Lincoln*, 227–28.

163. E. Foner, *Fiery Trial*, 171.

164. Donald, *Lincoln*, 343; Goodwin, *Team of Rivals*, 369.

Chapter 8. Promoting Emancipation in the Thirty-Seventh Congress: July 1861–August 1862

1. Trefousse, *Radical Republicans*, 14.

2. Browne, *Abraham Lincoln and the Men of His Time*, 2:599.

3. Oakes, *Scorpion's Sting*, 49.

4. Center for Range Voting, "Composition of Congress by Political Party, 1855–2007," http://rangevoting.org/CongParty.html; Martis, *Historical Atlas of Political Parties*, 115.

5. Trefousse, "Owen Lovejoy and Abraham Lincoln," 21.

6. *Harper's Weekly*, April 16, 1864

7. Magdol, *Owen Lovejoy*, 280.

8. Bogue, *Congressman's Civil War*, 148.

9. Trefousse, *Thaddeus Stevens*, 141.

10. Richardson, "Abraham Lincoln and the Politics of Principle," 11.

11. Richardson, *Greatest Nation of the Earth*.

12. Trefousse, "Owen Lovejoy and Abraham Lincoln," 21.

13. E. Foner, *Fiery Trial*, 169–71.

14. Oakes, *Freedom National*, 112–13.

15. HBB, 270–71.

16. Arnold, *Life of Abraham Lincoln*, 228–29; E. Foner, *Fiery Trial*, 173; Oakes, *Freedom National*, 112–13.

17. LC, Microfiche 48/1318. Child was living in Wayland, Massachusetts, compiling the *Freedmen's Book* for former slaves and supplying materials to contraband. http://uudb.org/articles/lydiamariachild.html.

18. Oakes, *Freedom National*, 119.

19. Oakes, *Freedom National*, 174–75.

20. D. B. Davis, "How They Stopped Slavery," 60.

21. Oakes, *Freedom National*, 110.

22. *Douglass's Monthly*, August 1861; Douglass, *Life and Writings*, 3:126.

23. Quarles, *Negro in the Civil War*, 48.

24. Harbour, "I Earn by My Own Labor."

25. Livermore, *My Story of the War*, 146–47.

26. Reed, "Early African American Settlement of Chicago," 240.

27. O. M. Muelder, *Underground Railroad in Western Illinois*, 114.

28. Livermore, *My Story of the War*, 135–54.

29. Giesberg, *Civil War Sisterhood*.

30. Bradsby, *History of Bureau County, Illinois*, 186.

31. Körner, *Memoirs*, 2:182.

32. Oakes, *Freedom National*, 172, 177.

33. Owen Lovejoy to Sarah Lovejoy, October 24, 1861, Clements.

34. Owen Lovejoy to Eunice Lovejoy, November 8, 1861, Clements.

35. Oakes, *Freedom National*, 62.

36. HBB, 274; Oakes, *Scorpion's Sting*, 104–66; BCR, December 5, 1861; HBB, 274–75.

37. Magdol, *Owen Lovejoy*, 300.

38. Oakes, *Scorpion's Sting*, 159.

39. HBB, 275.

40. BCR, March 28, 1861.

41. Oakes, *Freedom National*, 186.

42. Magdol, *Owen Lovejoy*, 311.

43. "A Bill Making it a penal offence for any officer or private of the army or navy to capture or return, or aid in the capture or return, of fugitive slaves" (37th Congress, H.R. 110), https://memory.loc.gov/ammem/amlaw/browse/llhb_037_keyw.html; Curry, *Blueprint for Modern America*, 78–79.

44. Bogue, *Congressman's Civil War*, 136–37.

45. Frederick Douglass to Gerrit Smith, December 22, 1861, in Douglass, *Life and Writings*, 3:184.

46. CG, 37th Cong., 2d Sess., Dec. 1, 1861, 56; HBB, 281; Douglass, *Life and Writings*, 3:87.

47. Quarles, "Black History's Antebellum Origins," 86.

48. BCR, December 12, 1861.

49. Douglass, "What Shall be done with the Slaves if Emancipated?" in Douglass, *Life and Writings*, 3:189.

50. D. B. Davis, "How They Stopped Slavery," 206.

51. Accessible Archives, *Christian Recorder*, January 14 and 25, 1862.

52. Wayman, *My Recollections of African M. E. Ministers*, 82–83.

53. *Christian Recorder*, March 22, 1862.

54. CG, 37th Cong., 2d Sess., Apr. 24, 1862, 1815–18; HBB, 323.

55. CG, 37th Cong., 2d Sess., Apr. 24, 1862, 1815–18; HBB, 314.

56. Voegeli, *Free but Not Equal*, 19–20.

57. Merton Dillon quotes James McPherson in "The Abolitionists," 512.

58. Belz, *A New Birth of Freedom*, 69.

59. D. B. Davis, *Problem of Slavery in Western Culture*, 259–61.

60. Price and Talbot, *Maine's Visible Black History*, 23, 164, 346–48, 370.

61. CG, 37th Cong., 2d Sess., Mar. 25, 1862, 1368–69; HBB, 301–2.

62. Stuckey, "A Last Stern Struggle," 41–43. Garnet predicted that "blacks after slavery, under the yoke of monopolists, would still be grievously oppressed."

63. Magdol, *Owen Lovejoy*, 318.

64. Rose, *Rehearsal for Reconstruction*, 200–201.

65. "An Act to establish a Department of Agriculture" (37th Congress, H.R. 269), https://memory.loc.gov/ammem/amlaw/browse/llhb_037_keyw.html.

66. BCR, March 28, 1861.

67. "An Act to Secure Homesteads to Actual Settlers on the Public Domain" (37th Congress, H.R. 125), https://memory.loc.gov/ammem/amlaw/browse/llhb_037_keyw.html.

68. Magdol, *Owen Lovejoy*, 354.

69. In 1863 George W. Julian introduced a bill to extend the Homestead Act of 1862 to abandoned and confiscated estates of the South and to include blacks as eligible buyers. "These estates would be carved into 40 and 80 acre tracts and made available to Union soldiers, southern freedmen and loyal southern whites on the homestead principle of full ownership after five years' residence and cultivation." See McPherson, *Struggle for Equality*, 255.

70. Masur, *Example for All the Land*, 91.

71. Arnold's bill (37th Congress, H.R. 351) can be found at https://memory.loc.gov/ammem/amlaw/browse/llhb_037_keyw.html; see also Oakes, *Freedom National*, 273–74. The House finally passed the Senate version, S. 108, with a vote of ninety-two to thirty-eight; CG, 37th Cong., 2d Sess., Apr. 16, 1862.

72. CG, 37th Cong., 2d Sess., Apr. 11, 1862, 1646; HBB, 304.

73. CG, 37th Cong., 2d Sess., Apr. 11, 1862, 1646; HBB, 304.

74. Accessible Archives, *Christian Recorder*, April 30, 1864.

75. H. Wilson, *History of Antislavery Measures*, 39.

76. Magdol, *Owen Lovejoy*, 327.

77. Quarles, *Negro in the Civil War*, 141.

78. "Mass Meeting of the Colored People of Chicago," *Chicago Tribune*, n.d., IS.

79. "A bill [To render freedom national and slavery sectional]" (37th Congress, H.R. 374), https://memory.loc.gov/ammem/amlaw/browse/llhb_037_keyw.html. On May 9, 1862, Lovejoy offered a modification to the bill: to exclude federal territory on vessels on the high seas. On June 17 Lovejoy moved that the House concur in the Senate amendment, passage was assured, and the president signed the act on June 19. See also Oakes, *Freedom National*, 266–67.

80. Magdol, *Owen Lovejoy*, 332.

81. *Chicago Tribune*, June 29, 1862.

82. Greeley, *American Conflict*, 2:261.

83. Curry, *Blueprint for Modern America*, 55–56.

84. Magdol, *Owen Lovejoy*, 335.

85. *Chicago Tribune*, June 29, 1862; Magdol, *Owen Lovejoy*, 335.

86. "An Act relating to Schools for the Education of Colored Children in the Cities of Washington and Georgetown in the District of Columbia" (37th Congress, H.R. 543), https://memory.loc.gov/ammem/amlaw/browse/llhb_037_keyw.html.

87. Masur, *Example for All the Land*, 26.

88. Masur, *Example for All the Land*, 26.

89. E. Foner, *Fiery Trial*, 184–85, 223, 234, 258. Caleb B. Smith was a strong advocate of colonization.

90. Harrold, *Subversives*, 229–39.

91. H. Wilson, *History of Antislavery Measures*, 187.

92. Greeley, *American Conflict*, 2:262.

93. Oakes, *Freedom National*, 247.

94. Oakes, *Freedom National*, 128.

95. Oakes, *Freedom National*, 242.

96. Curry, *Blueprint for Modern America*, 78–79; Magdol, *Owen Lovejoy*, 309; Greeley, *American Conflict*, 2:262–64.

97. Crofts, *Lincoln and the Politics of Slavery*, 266.

98. Oakes, *Freedom National*, 229.

99. Curry, *Blueprint for Modern America*, 85.

100. CG, 37th Cong., 2d Sess., Apr. 24, 1862, 1815–18; HBB, 320–21.

101. *New York Times*, June 18, 1862; Bryant, *Letters*, 4:242.

102. HBB, 329–32.

103. HBB, 333.

104. HBB, 348.

105. Oakes, *Freedom National*, 231.

106. Magdol, *Owen Lovejoy*, 340.

107. Magdol, *Owen Lovejoy*, 398.

108. Oakes, *Freedom National*, 235.

109. Oakes, *Freedom National*, 237.

110. Randall, *Constitutional Problems under Lincoln*, 275–92; discussed in Oakes, *Freedom National*, 515n15.

111. Oakes, *Freedom National*, 515n15.

112. Oakes, *Freedom National*, 239.

113. Pinsker, *Lincoln's Sanctuary*, 30–40; CW, 5:223; Donald, *Lincoln*, 362, 182.

114. Arnold, *Life of Abraham Lincoln*, 251.

115. Browne, *Abraham Lincoln and the Men of His Time*, 2:673–75.

116. Browne, *Abraham Lincoln and the Men of His Time*, 2:679–81.

117. Browne, *Abraham Lincoln and the Men of His Time*, 2:681.

118. *Chicago Tribune*, August 2, 1862.

Chapter 9. Struggling to Enact Legal and Enduring Equality: Autumn 1862–March 25, 1864

1. BCR, August 7, 1862.

2. D. B. Davis, *Problem of Slavery in the Age of Emancipation*, 39, 52.

3. Murray and Rodney, "Letters of Peter Bryant: Concluded," 471.

4. Schwalm, *Emancipation's Diaspora*, 265–66.

5. Voegeli, *Free but Not Equal*, 52–72.

6. N. D. Harris, *History of Negro Servitude in Illinois*, 241.

7. Magdol, *Owen Lovejoy*, 369.

8. Quarles, *Negro in the Civil War*, 165–66; Douglass, *Life and Writings*, 3:27.

9. Joseph G. Cannon of Danville, Illinois, later the Speaker of the House of Representatives, described Lovejoy in "Address at the State Convention in Springfield" (unidentified newspaper, October 10, 1910), Owen Lovejoy Papers, Clements.

10. HBB, 354.

11. HBB, 355.

12. "Union and Patriotism vs. Partisans and Politics," campaign broadside, Union Congressional Convention, October, 1862, ALPLM.

13. HBB, 351.

14. *Peoria Daily Transcript*, November 1, 1862.

15. Magdol, *Owen Lovejoy*, 372.

16. *The Tribune Almanac and Political Register*; H. W. Allen and V. A. Lacey, *Illinois Elections, 1818–1990*, 150.

17. Center for Range Voting, "Composition of Congress by Political Party, 1855–2007," http://rangevoting.org/CongParty.html.

18. Reed, "Early African American Settlement of Chicago," 241, 244.

19. Reed, "Early African American Settlement of Chicago," 235.

20. Harbour, "I Earn by My Own Labor."

21. Reed, "Early African American Settlement of Chicago," 237.

22. Reed, "Early African American Settlement of Chicago," 235–36.

23. Abzug, *Passionate Liberator*, 286.

24. Dumond, *Antislavery*, 163–64.

25. Dorrien, *The Making of American Liberal Theology*, 102. The Twenty-Eighth Congregational Society was the most radical church in the Unitarian denomination. Theodore Parker was its pastor until his death in 1860.

26. Curry, *Blueprint for Modern America*, 72.

27. Quarles, *Negro in the Civil War*, 206; Douglass, *Life and Writings*, 3:372.

28. Douglass, "Day of Jubilee Comes: An Address Delivered in Rochester, New York, December 28, 1862," in Douglass, *Papers*, Series One: 3:546.

29. Masur, *Example for All the Land*, 41.

30. Reed, "Early African American Settlement of Chicago," 237, 241.

31. Reed, "Early African American Settlement of Chicago," 238.

32. Curry, *Blueprint for Modern America*, 64.

33. Douglass, *Life and Writings*, 3:31–33.

34. Strangis, *Lewis Hayden and the War against Slavery*, 117–18; Horton and Horton, *Black Bostonians*, 136–38.

35. E. Foner, *Fiery Trial*, 249.

36. HBB, 370–78; Curry, *Blueprint for Modern America*, 66–67.

37. HBB, 376.

38. "A bill to raise additional soldiers for the United States," CG, 37th Cong., 3d Sess., Jan. 29, 1863, 603–5; HBB, 375–76.

39. Voegeli, *Free but Not Equal*, 103–4. Voegeli interprets Lovejoy's words literally; HBB, 375.

40. McPherson, *Negro's Civil War*, 190–91.

41. Way, *History of the Thirty-Third Regiment*, 268.

42. Murray and Rodney, "Colonel Julian E. Bryant," 262–63.

43. Murray and Rodney, "Colonel Julian E. Bryant," 262–63.

44. Reed, "Early African American Settlement of Chicago," 248.

45. Sarah Cooper, "Record of Bureau County Civil War Soldiers," handwritten log compiled by J. H. Bryant, BCHS.

46. Escott, *Lincoln's Dilemma*, 242n13.

47. Magdol, *Owen Lovejoy*, 384.

48. BCR, March 12, 19, April 9, 16, 1863; *Peoria Daily Transcript*, March 17 and April 8, 1863.

49. H. Ford Douglas to Owen Lovejoy, February 3, 1863, described in R. L. Harris, "H. Ford Douglas," 229; Molyneaux, *African Americans in Early Rockford*, 60–66; Weiner, *Race and Rights*, 221.

50. Ahlstrom, *Religious History of the American People*, 711; Angell, *Bishop Henry McNeal Turner*, 51.

51. Fleischner, *Mrs. Lincoln and Mrs. Keckly*, 258.

52. Austin Wiswall to Rev. Henry Hammond, March 6, 1863, Austin Wiswall Papers, Wickett-Wiswall Papers, Southwest Collection, Special Collections, TT.

53. Douglass, *Life and Writings*, 3:40; Blight, *Frederick Douglass' Civil War*, 124.

54. Ochiai, "Port Royal Experiment Revisited."

55. Rose, *Rehearsal for Reconstruction*, 272.

56. Rose, *Rehearsal for Reconstruction*, 280

57. Rose, *Rehearsal for Reconstruction*, 290, 295–96; E. Foner, *Fiery Trial*, 287.

58. Livermore, *My Story of the War*, 411–12.

59. Harbour, "'I Earn by My Own Labor,'" 362, 372n66.

60. Harbour, "'I Earn by My Own Labor,'" 355–56, 361, 368, 371. Mary Jones was president; Mrs. James Blanks, vice president; Sallie Douglas, secretary; Mrs. George Lee, assistant secretary; and Mrs. Henry Bradford, treasurer.

61. Accessible Archives, *Christian Recorder*, April 30, 1864.

62. R. L. Harris, "H. Ford Douglas," 230–31.

63. Giesberg, *Civil War Sisterhood*, 105; Chang, *A Separate Battle*, 28.

64. BCR, Dec. 3, 1863; HBB, 394.

65. Magdol, *Owen Lovejoy*, 392.

66. Mayer, *All on Fire*, 559.

67. *Proceedings of the American Anti-Slavery Society . . . 1863*, 13; HBB, 391–93.

68. Magdol, *Owen Lovejoy*.

69. Magdol, *Owen Lovejoy*, 395.

70. Trefousse, *Radical Republicans*, 265.

71. Remarks concerning Lovejoy's bill making slaveholding a crime, CG, 38th Cong., 1st Sess., Dec. 14, 1863, 20.

72. Belz, *A New Birth of Freedom*, 119.

73. Oakes, *Freedom National*, 434.

74. Whiting, *War Powers of the President*, i–ii; E. Foner, *Fiery Trial*, 242, 244.

75. Belz, *A New Birth of Freedom*, 57.

76. Oakes, *Freedom National*, 426.

77. Oakes, *Freedom National*, 423.

78. Oakes, *Freedom National*, 354.

79. Magdol, *Owen Lovejoy*, 397.

80. Reidy, "Emancipation," 292.

81. Reidy, "Emancipation," 292; Vorenberg, *Emancipation Proclamation*, 133.

82. Belz, *A New Birth of Freedom*, 118–19.

83. Magdol, *Owen Lovejoy*, 398.

84. Blackmon, *Slavery by Another Name*.

85. John Jones, *Black Laws of Illinois*; Harrison, "We Are Here Assembled," 344n45.

86. Gliozzo, "John Jones: A Study of a Black Chicagoan," 185–88; Harrison, "We Are Here Assembled," 333.

87. Harrison, "We Are Here Assembled," 333, 344n46.

88. BCR, May 5, 1864; HBB, 410.

89. Edward Lovejoy to Austin Wiswall, March 11, 1864, Austin Wiswall Papers, Wickett-Wiswall Papers, Southwest Collections, Special Collections, TT. Edward was the son of Joseph and Sarah Lovejoy.

90. Edward Lovejoy to Austin Wiswall, March 11, 1864, Austin Wiswall Papers, Wickett-Wiswall Papers, Southwest Collections, Special Collections, TT.

91. Sumner's Eulogy, CG, 38th Cong., 1st Sess., Mar. 29, 1864, 1334.

92. Owen Lovejoy to Sarah Moody Lovejoy, March 15, 1864, Clements. In Deuteronomy 34:4, God tells Moses he shall not get to the Promised Land, but he shall get to see it from the top of Mount Pisgah.

93. *New York Tribune*, March 29, 1864.

94. "Obituary" by Abigail Dodge (Gail Hamilton), *The Congregationalist*, CTS.

95. *New York Tribune*, March 29, 1864.

96. *New York Tribune*, March 29, 1864.

97. BCR.

98. Accessible Archives, *Christian Recorder*, April 30, 1864.

99. Accessible Archives, *Christian Recorder*, April 30, 1864.

100. Accessible Archives, *Christian Recorder*, April 30, 1864.

101. Accessible Archives, *Christian Recorder*, April 30, 1864.

102. Ichabod Codding, Owen Lovejoy Monument Meeting, Princeton, Illinois, BCR, June 16, 1864.

Bibliography

Archival Materials

Abraham Lincoln Presidential Library and Museum, Springfield, Illinois

> Broadside Collection; Ichabod Codding Family Papers; Augustus W. Cowan Papers and Duff & Cowan Records; O. M. Hatch Papers; Thomas Jefferson Henderson Papers; Owen Lovejoy Papers; Hattie Wiswall Letters

Amistad Research Center, Tulane University, New Orleans

> American Missionary Association Archives

Boston Public Library, Special Collections

> Minutes of the Executive Committee of the American Anti-Slavery Society

Bureau County Historical Society, Princeton, Illinois

> John Howard Bryant Papers; Owen Lovejoy Papers

Chicago History Museum

> Zebina Eastman Papers; Illinois State Anti-Slavery Society Minute Book; John Jones Papers

Colby College, Waterville, Maine, Special Collections

> Elijah Parish Lovejoy Collection

Congregational Library, Boston

> Congregational Library and Archives Collection of the Congregational Conference of Illinois Records

Howard University Libraries, Washington, D.C., Moorland-Spingarn Research Center, Manuscript Division

> Omnium Gatherum Correspondence

Illinois State University, Normal, Milner Library, Special Collections

> Jesse Fell Papers

Knox College Library, Galesburg, Illinois, Special Collections and Archives
  Samuel Guild Wright Diary

Library of Congress, Washington, D.C.
  Abraham Lincoln Papers

Ohio Historical Society, Columbus
  Joshua R. Giddings Papers

Smith College Archives, Northampton, Massachusetts, Sophia Smith Collection
  Garrison Family Papers

Syracuse University Libraries, Syracuse, New York, Special Collections Research Center
  Gerrit Smith Papers

Texas Tech University, Lubbock, Southwest Collection/Special Collections Library
  Lovejoy Papers; Elijah Parish Lovejoy Papers; Austin Wiswall Papers

University of Illinois, Urbana-Champaign, Rare Book and Manuscript Library
  Carl Sandburg Papers

University of Illinois, Urbana-Champaign, University of Illinois Library, Illinois History and
  Lincoln Collections
  David Todd and Charlotte Farnsworth Letters; Lovejoy Society Papers

University of Indiana, Bloomington, Lilly Library, Manuscript Collections
  African American Related Collections

University of Michigan, Ann Arbor, Clements Library
  Owen Lovejoy Papers

Wheaton College, Wheaton Illinois, Archives and Special Collections
  Jonathan Blanchard Papers

Newspapers

Alton Telegraph
Bloomington Pantagraph
Bureau County Republican
Chicago Daily Tribune
Chicago Press and Tribune
Chicago Tribune
Christian Recorder
Congregational Herald
Congregationalist
Douglass' Monthly
Emancipator
Free West
Geneseo Union Advocate
McLean County Weekly National Flag

New York Evening Post
New York Herald
New York Observer
New York Times
New York Tribune
New Yorker
Western Citizen

Other Sources

Abzug, Robert H. *Passionate Liberator: Theodore Dwight Weld and the Dilemma of Reform.* New York: Oxford University Press, 1980.

Achinstein, Sharon. *Literature and Dissent in Milton's England.* New York: Cambridge University Press, 2003.

Adams, John Quincy. *Diary of John Quincy Adams, 1794–1845.* Ed. Allan Nevins. New York: Scribner's, 1951.

Addresses on the Death of Hon. Owen Lovejoy, March 18, 1864. Washington, D.C.: U.S. Government Printing Office, 1864.

Ahlstrom, Sydney E. *A Religious History of the American People.* New Haven: Yale University Press, 1972.

Allen, Ernest, Jr. "Afro-American Identity." In Rael, *African American Activism before the Civil War.*

Allen, Howard W., and Vincent A. Lacey, eds. *Illinois Elections, 1818–1990: Candidates and County Returns for President, Governor, Senate, and House of Representatives.* Carbondale: Southern Illinois University Press, 1992.

Andrews, Charles C. *History of the New York African Free-Schools.* New York: Negro Universities Press, 1969.

Angell, Stephen Ward. *Bishop Henry McNeal Turner.* Knoxville: University of Tennessee Press, 1992.

Applegate, Debby. *The Most Famous Man in America: The Biography of Henry Ward Beecher.* New York: Doubleday, 2006.

Arnold, Isaac N. *History of Abraham Lincoln, and the Overthrow of Slavery.* Chicago: Clark, 1866.
———. *The Life of Abraham Lincoln.* Lincoln: University of Nebraska Press, 1994.

Ashworth, John. "The Republican Triumph." In *Civil War and Reconstruction*, ed. Lacy K. Ford. Oxford: Wiley-Blackwell, 2011.

Bailey, Hugh C. *Hinton Rowan Helper: Abolitionist-Racist.* University: University of Alabama Press, 1965.

Bains, David R. "An Anti-Slavery Church in Washington, D.C." *Bulletin of the Congregational Library*, 2nd ser., 11 (2015): 1.

Baker, Jean Harvey. "James Buchanan." In *"To the Best of My Ability": The American Presidents*, ed. James M. McPherson and David Rubel. New York: Dorling Kindersley, 2000.
———. "Millard Fillmore." In *"To the Best of My Ability": The American Presidents*, ed. James M. McPherson and David Rubel. New York: Dorling Kindersley, 2000.

Barnes, Gilbert Hobbs. *The Antislavery Impulse, 1830–1844.* New York: Appleton-Century, 1933.

Bartlett, Irving H. *John C. Calhoun.* New York: Norton, 1993.

Barton, William E. *Joseph Edwin Roy, 1827–1908.* Oak Park, Ill.: Puritan, 1908.

Bateman, Newton, and Paul Selby, eds. *Historical Encyclopedia of Illinois.* Chicago: Munsell, 1901.

Bay, Mia. *The White Image in the Black Mind: African-American Ideas about White People, 1830–1925*. New York: Oxford University Press, 2000.

Beckert, Sven, and Seth Rockman, eds. *Slavery's Capitalism: A New History of American Economic Development*. Philadelphia: University of Pennsylvania Press, 2016.

Beecher, Edward. *Narrative of the Riots at Alton*. Alton, Ill.: Holton, 1838.

Bell, Howard Holman, ed. *Minutes of the Proceedings of the National Negro Conventions, 1830–1864*. New York: Arno, 1969.

Bellamy, Joseph. *True Religion Delineated; or, Experimental Religion*. Boston: Kneeland, 1750.

Belz, Herman. *A New Birth of Freedom: The Republican Party and Freedmen's Rights, 1861–1866*. New York: Fordham University Press, 2000.

Bender, Thomas. *New York Intellect*. New York: Knopf, 1987.

Bennett, Lerone, Jr. *Forced into Glory: Abraham Lincoln's White Dream*. Chicago: Johnson, 2007.

Berlin, Ira, et al., eds. *Free at Last: A Documentary History of Slavery, Freedom, and the Civil War*. New York: New Press, 1992.

Berwanger, Eugene H. *The Frontier against Slavery: Western Anti-Negro Prejudice and the Slavery Extension Controversy*. 1967; Urbana: University of Illinois Press, 2002.

Beveridge, Albert J. *Abraham Lincoln, 1809–1858*. Vol. 2. Boston: Houghton Mifflin, 1928.

Bilger, Burkhard. "Mystery on Pearl Street." *New Yorker*, January 7, 2008.

Biographical Sketches of the Leading Men of Chicago. Chicago: Wilson and St. Clair, 1868.

Blackett, R. J. M. *Building an Antislavery Wall: Black Americans in the Atlantic Abolitionist Movement, 1830–1860*. Ithaca: Cornell University Press, 1983.

———. *Divided Hearts: Britain and the American Civil War*. Baton Rouge: Louisiana State University Press, 2001.

———. "James W. C. Pennington." In *Beating against the Barriers: Biographical Essays in Nineteenth-Century Afro-American History*, ed. Leon Litwack and August Meier. Baton Rouge: Louisiana State University Press, 1986.

Blackmon, Douglas A. *Slavery by Another Name: The Re-Enslavement of Black People in America from the Civil War to World War II*. New York: Doubleday, 2008.

Blanchard, Rufus. *Discovery and Conquests of the North-West, with the History of Chicago*. 2 vols. Chicago: Blanchard, 1900.

Blight, David W. *Frederick Douglass' Civil War: Keeping Faith in Jubilee*. Baton Rouge: Louisiana State University Press, 1989.

———. *Race and Reunion: The Civil War in American Memory*. Cambridge: Harvard University Press, 2001.

Blockson, Charles L. *Underground Railroad: First-Person Narratives of Escapes to Freedom in the North*. New York: Prentice-Hall, 1987.

Blue, Frederick J. *Free Soilers: Third Party Politics, 1848–54*. Urbana: University of Illinois Press, 1973.

———. *No Taint of Compromise: Crusaders in Antislavery Politics*. Baton Rouge: Louisiana State University Press, 2005.

———. *Salmon P. Chase: A Life in Politics*. Kent, Ohio: Kent State University Press, 1984.

Bogue, Allan G. *The Congressman's Civil War*. New York: Cambridge University Press, 1989.

Bohman, George V. "Owen Lovejoy on 'The Barbarism of Slavery,' April 5, 1860." In *Antislavery and Disunion, 1858–1861: Studies in the Rhetoric of Compromise and Conflict*, ed. J. Jeffery Auer. New York: Harper and Row, 1963.

Botume, Elizabeth Hyde. *First Days among the Contrabands*. Boston: Lee and Shepard, 1893.

Bradsby, H. C., ed. *History of Bureau County, Illinois*. Chicago: World, 1885.

Breed, Gulielma. *Appeal of the National Association for the Relief of Colored Women and Children*. Washington, D.C.: Privately printed, 1863.

Bridges, Roger D. "Antebellum Struggle for Citizenship." *Journal of the Illinois State Historical Society* 108 (2015): 296–321.

Brown, William Wells. *From Fugitive Slave to Free Man: The Autobiographies of William Wells Brown*. Ed. and intro. William L. Andrews. New York: Penguin, 1993.

Browne, Robert H. *Abraham Lincoln and the Men of His Time*. 2 vols. Cincinnati: Jennings and Pye, 1901.

Bryant, William Cullen. *Letters of William Cullen Bryant*. Ed. William Cullen Bryant II and Thomas G. Voss. 5 vols. New York: Fordham University Press, 1975–92.

Buechler, Steven M. *The Transformation of the Woman Suffrage Movement: The Case of Illinois, 1850–1920*. New Brunswick, N.J.: Rutgers University Press, 1986.

Bumsted, J. M. *Henry Alline, 1748–1784*. Hantsport, N.S.: Lancelot, 1982.

Burke, Ronald Kevin. "Samuel Ringgold Ward: Christian Abolitionist." Ph.D. diss., Syracuse University, 1975.

Burlingame, Michael. *Abraham Lincoln: A Life*. Baltimore: Johns Hopkins University Press, 2008.

Calonius, Erik. *The Wanderer: The Last American Slave Ship and the Conspiracy That Set its Sails*. New York: St. Martin's, 2006.

Campbell, Tom. *Fighting Slavery in Chicago: Abolitionists, the Law of Slavery, and Lincoln*. Chicago: AMP&RSAND, 2009.

Carpenter, F. B. *Six Months at the White House*. New York: Hurd and Houghton, 1867.

Carr, Kay J. *Belleville, Ottawa, and Galesburg: Community and Democracy on the Illinois Frontier*. Carbondale: Southern Illinois University Press, 1996.

Carwardine, Richard J. *Evangelicals and Politics in Antebellum America*, Knoxville: University of Tennessee Press, 1997.

———. *Lincoln*. London: Longman, 2003.

Cazden, Elizabeth. *Antoinette Brown Blackwell: A Biography*. Old Westbury, N.Y.: Feminist Press, 1983.

Cha-Jua, Sundiata Keita. *America's First Black Town: Brooklyn, Illinois, 1830–1915*. Urbana: University of Illinois Press, 2000.

Chang, Ina. *A Separate Battle: Women and the Civil War*. New York: Dutton, 1991.

Child, Lydia Maria. *The Collected Correspondence of Lydia Maria Child, 1817–1880*. Comp. Patricia G. Holland and Milton Meltzer. Millwood, N.Y.: KTO Microform, 1979.

Church, Charles A. *History of the Republican Party in Illinois, 1854–1912*. Rockford, Ill.: Wilson, 1912.

Clark, Calvin Montague. *American Slavery and Maine Congregationalists*. Bangor, Maine: Clark, 1940.

———. *History of Bangor Theological Seminary*, Boston: Pilgrim, 1916.

———. *History of the Congregational Churches in Maine, 1600–1826*. Portland: Congregational Christian Conference of Maine, 1926.

———. *History of the Maine Missionary Society, 1807–1925*. Portland: Southworth, 1926.

Clark, Jerusha Whitmarsh. "Childhood Reminiscences of Princeton." *Journal of the Illinois State Historical Society* 49 (1956): 95–110.

Clinton, Catherine. *Mrs. Lincoln: A Life*. New York: Harper Collins, 2009.

Codding, Hannah Maria Preston. "Ichabod Codding." *Proceedings of the State Historical Society of Wisconsin* (1897): 171–96.

———, comp. "Ichabod Codding's 1854 Lecture Tour in Behalf of a Fusion Party." *Journal of the Illinois State Historical Society* 64, no. 2 (Summer 1971), 155–60.

Coffin, Robert P. Tristram. *Kennebec: Cradle of Americans*. Camden, Me.: Down East Book, 1965.

Cole, Arthur Charles. *Centennial History of Illinois*. Vol. 3, *Era of the Civil War, 1848–1870*. Springfield: Illinois Centennial Commission, 1919.

———, ed. and intro. *The Constitutional Debates of 1847*. Springfield: Illinois State Historical Library, 1919.

Cone, James H. *The Cross and the Lynching Tree*. Maryknoll, N.Y.: Orbis, 2011.

Conlin, Michael F. "The Smithsonian Abolition Lecture Controversy." *Civil War History* 46 (2000): 301–23.

Cornish, Dudley T. *The Sable Arm: Black Troops in the Union Army, 1861–1865*. 1956; Lawrence: University Press of Kansas, 1987.

Cott, Nancy F. *The Bonds of Womanhood: "Women's Sphere" in New England, 1780–1835*. 2nd ed. New Haven: Yale University Press, 1997.

Cox, S. S. *Union—Disunion—Reunion: Three Decades of Federal Legislation, 1855–1885*. Providence, R.I.: Reid, 1885.

Crissey, Elwell. *Lincoln's Lost Speech*. New York: Hawthorne, 1967.

Crofts, Daniel W. *Lincoln and the Politics of Slavery: The Other Thirteenth Amendment and the Struggle to Save the Nation*. Chapel Hill: University of North Carolina Press, 2016.

Cunningham, Joseph O. Address. In Prince, *Transactions*, 91–95.

———. "The Bloomington Convention of 1856 and Those Who Participated in It." *Transactions of the Illinois State Historical Society for the Year 1905*, 101–10. Springfield, Ill.: Illinois State Journal Company, 1906.

———. *History of Champaign County*. Chicago: Munsell, 1905.

Curry, Leonard P. *Blueprint for Modern America: Nonmilitary Legislation of the First Civil War Congress*. Nashville: Vanderbilt University Press, 1968.

Cushman, Joshua. *An Address to the People of Maine*. Washington, D.C.: Davis and Force, 1820.

David, Reuben. *Recollections of Mississippi and Mississippians*. Jackson: University Press of Mississippi, 1972.

Davis, David Brion. "How They Stopped Slavery" (review of James Oakes, *Freedom National*). *New York Review of Books*, June 6, 2013.

———. *In the Image of God: Religion, Moral Values, and Our Heritage of Slavery*. New Haven: Yale University Press, 2001.

———. *The Problem of Slavery in the Age of Emancipation*. New York: Knopf, 2014.

———. *The Problem of Slavery in Western Culture*. Ithaca: Cornell University Press, 1966.

Davis, Hugh. *Joshua Leavitt, Evangelical Abolitionist*. Baton Rouge: Louisiana State University Press, 1990.

Davis, Rodney O., and Douglas L. Wilson, eds. *The Lincoln-Douglas Debates*. Urbana: Knox College Lincoln Studies Center and the University of Illinois Press, 2008.

DeBoer, Clara Merritt. *Be Jubilant My Feet: African American Abolitionists in the American Missionary Association, 1839–1861*. New York: Garland, 1994.

d'Entremont, John. *Southern Emancipator: Moncure Conway: The American Years, 1832–1865*. New York: Oxford University Press, 1987.

Desmond, Adrian, and James Moore. *Darwin's Sacred Cause: Race, Slavery, and the Quest for Human Origins*. Chicago: University of Chicago Press, 2011.

Dew, Charles B. *Apostles of Disunion: Southern Secession Commissioners and the Causes of the Civil War*. Charlottesville: University of Virginia Press, 2001.

Dictionary of American Biography. New York: Scribner's, 1946.

Dillon, Merton L. "The Abolitionists: A Decade of Historiography, 1959–1969." *Journal of Southern History* 35 (1969): 500–522.

——. *Antislavery Movement in Illinois: 1809–1844*. Ann Arbor: University Microfilms International, 1951.

——. *Benjamin Lundy and the Struggle for Negro Freedom*. Urbana: University of Illinois Press, 1966.

——. *Elijah P. Lovejoy: Abolitionist Editor*. Urbana: University of Illinois Press, 1961.

Dixon, Chris. *Perfecting the Family: Antislavery Marriage in Nineteenth-Century America*. Amherst: University of Massachusetts Press, 1997.

Dobbert, Marion Lundy, and Helen Jean Nelson. *The Friends of Clear Creek, 1830–1930*. DeKalb, Ill.: Westland, 1975.

Dolinar, Brian. *The Negro in Illinois: The WPA Papers*. Urbana: University of Illinois Press, 2013.

Donald, David Herbert. *Lincoln*. New York: Simon and Schuster, 1995.

Dorrien, Gary. *The Making of American Liberal Theology*. Louisville: Westminster John Knox Press, 2001.

——. *The New Abolition: W. E. B. Du Bois and the Black Social Gospel*. New Haven: Yale University Press, 2015.

Douglass, Frederick. *The Frederick Douglass Papers*. Series 1, *Speeches, Debates, and Interviews*. 5 vols. Ed. John W. Blassingame et al. New Haven: Yale University Press, 1979–92.

——. *Life and Times of Frederick Douglass*. Hartford: Park, 1882.

——. *Life and Writings of Frederick Douglass*. Ed. Philip S. Foner. 5 vols. New York: International, 1950.

Drury, John. *Old Illinois Houses*. Springfield: State of Illinois, 1948.

DuBois, Ellen Carol. *Feminism and Suffrage: The Emergence of an Independent Women's Movement in America, 1848–1869*. Ithaca: Cornell University Press, 1978.

Du Bois, James T., and Gertrude S. Matthews. *Galusha A. Grow, Father of the Homestead Law*. Boston: Houghton Mifflin, 1917.

Du Bois, W. E. B. *Black Reconstruction*. 1835; New York: Simon and Schuster, 1999.

Dugan, Frank H. "Illinois Martyrdom." *Transactions of the Illinois State Historical Society* (1938): 111–57.

Dumond, Dwight. *Antislavery: The Crusade for Freedom in America*. Ann Arbor: University of Michigan Press, 1961.

Easton, Hosea. *To Heal the Scourge of Prejudice: The Life and Writings of Hosea Easton*. Ed. George R. Price and James Brewer Stewart. Amherst: University of Massachusetts Press, 1999.

Elliott, John Lovejoy. "Owen Lovejoy." *Cornell Magazine*, January 15, 1890.

Ernest, John. *Liberation Historiography: African American Writers and the Challenge of History, 1794–1861*. Chapel Hill: University of North Carolina Press, 2004.

Escott, Paul D. *Lincoln's Dilemma: Blair, Sumner, and the Republican Struggle over Racism and Equality in the Civil War Era*. Charlottesville: University of Virginia Press, 2014.

Filler, Louis. *Crusade against Slavery: Friends, Foes, and Reforms, 1820–1860*. Algonac, Mich.: Reference, 1986.

Findley, Paul. *A. Lincoln: The Crucible of Congress*. New York: Crown, 1979.

Finkelman, Paul. *An Imperfect Union: Slavery, Federalism, and Comity*. Union, N.J.: Lawbook Exchange, 2000.

———. *Slavery and the Founders: Race and Liberty in the Age of Jefferson*. Armonk, N.Y.: Sharpe, 2001.

Fischer, David Hackett. *Albion's Seed: Four British Folkways in America*. New York: Oxford University Press, 1989.

Fleischner, Jennifer. *Mrs. Lincoln and Mrs. Keckly: The Remarkable Story of the Friendship between a First Lady and a Former Slave*. New York: Broadway, 2003.

Fleming, Thomas. "James K. Polk." In *"To the Best of My Ability": The American Presidents*, ed. James M. McPherson and David Rubel. New York: Dorling Kindersley, 2000.

Foner, Eric. *The Fiery Trial: Abraham Lincoln and American Slavery*. New York: Norton, 2010.

———. *Free Soil, Free Labor, Free Men: The Ideology of the Republican Party before the Civil War*. 1970. Reprint, New York: Oxford University Press, 1995.

———. "Inhuman Bondage" (review of Robin Blackburn, *The American Crucible*). *The Nation*, August 19–September 5, 2011.

———. *The Story of American Freedom*. New York: Norton, 1998.

Foner, Philip S. *Business and Slavery: The New York Merchants and the Irrepressible Conflict*. Chapel Hill: University of North Carolina Press, 1941.

Foote, Shelby. *The Civil War, a Narrative*. 3 vols. New York: Random House, 1958–74.

Forbes, Robert Pierce. *The Missouri Compromise and Its Aftermath*. Chapel Hill: University of North Carolina Press, 2007.

Foreman, Amanda. *A World on Fire: Britain's Crucial Role in the American Civil War*. New York: Random House, 2012.

Franklin, John Hope. *From Slavery to Freedom*. New York: Knopf, 1967.

Fredrickson, George M. *The Black Image in the White Mind: The Debate on Afro-American Character and Destiny, 1817–1914*. New York: Harper and Row, 1971.

Freehling, William W. *Road to Disunion*. Vol. 1, *Secessionists at Bay, 1776–1854*. New York: Oxford University Press, 1990.

———. *Road to Disunion*. Vol. 2, *Secessionists Triumphant, 1854–1861*. New York: Oxford University Press, 2007.

French, Benjamin Brown. *Witness to the Young Republic: A Yankee's Journal, 1828–1870*. Ed. Donald B. Cole and John J. McDonough. Hanover, N.H.: University Press of New England, 1989.

Friedman, Jane M. *America's First Woman Lawyer: Biography of Myra Bradwell*. Buffalo, N.Y.: Prometheus, 1993.

Friedman, Lawrence J. *Gregarious Saints: Self and Community in American Abolitionism, 1830–1870*. New York: Cambridge University Press, 1982.

Fuller, Louis. *Crusade against Slavery*. Algonac, Mich.: Reference, 1986.

Gertz, Elmer. "The Black Laws of Illinois." *Journal of the Illinois State Historical Society* 56 (1963): 463–72.

Gienapp, William E. *The Origins of the Republican Party, 1852–1856*. New York: Oxford University Press, 1987.

———. "Who Voted for Lincoln?" In *Abraham Lincoln and the American Political Tradition*, ed. John L. Thomas. Amherst: University of Massachusetts Press, 1986.

Giesberg, Judith Ann. *Civil War Sisterhood: The U.S. Sanitary Commission and Women's Politics in Transition*. Boston: Northeastern University Press, 2000.

Ginzberg, Lori D. *Elizabeth Cady Stanton*. New York: Hill and Wang, 2009.

———. *Women and the Work of Benevolence: Morality, Politics, and Class in the Nineteenth Century United States*. New Haven: Yale University Press, 1990.

Gliozzo, Charles A. "John Jones: A Study of a Black Chicagoan." *Illinois Historical Journal* 80 (1987): 177–88.

———. "John Jones and the Black Convention Movement, 1848–1856." *Journal of Black Studies* 3 (1972): 227–36.

Goodwin, Doris Kearns. *Team of Rivals*. New York: Simon and Schuster, 2005.

Gossard, John Harvey. "The New York City Congregational Cluster, 1848–1871." Ph.D. diss., Bowling Green State University, 1986.

Granville, Illinois, 150th Anniversary, 1836–1986. Hennepin, Ill.: Putnam County Historical Society, 1986.

Greeley, Horace. *The American Conflict: History of the Great Rebellion*. Vol. 2. Hartford: Case, 1866.

Grimsley, Mark. *The Hard Hand of War: Union Military Policy toward Southern Civilians, 1861–1865*. New York: Cambridge University Press, 1995.

Grinspan, Jon. "'Young Men for War': The Wide Awakes and Lincoln's 1860 Presidential Campaign." *Journal of American History* 96 (2009): 357–78.

Griswold, Robert L. "Divorce and the Legal Redefinition of Victorian Manhood." In *Meanings for Manhood: Constructions of Masculinity in Victorian America*, ed. Mark C. Carnes and Clyde Griffen. Chicago: University of Chicago Press, 1990.

Grow, Mary M. *China, Maine, Bicentennial History*. Weeks Mills, Maine: Van Strein, 1975.

Guelzo, Allen C. "Houses Divided: Lincoln, Douglas and the Political Landscape of 1858." *Journal of American History* 94 (2007): 391–417. http://archive.oah.org/special-issues/teaching/2007_09/index.html.

———. *Lincoln and Douglas: The Debates That Defined America*. New York: Simon and Schuster, 2008.

———. *Lincoln's Emancipation Proclamation: The End of Slavery in America*. New York: Simon and Schuster, 2004.

Guyatt, Nicholas. "A Peculiar Revolt" (review of Marcus Rediker, *The Amistad Rebellion: the Atlantic Odyssey of Slavery and Freedom*). *The Nation*, November 26, 2012.

Haberkorn, Ruth E. "Owen Lovejoy in Princeton, Illinois." *Journal of the Illinois State Historical Society* 34 (1943): 284–315.

Hagedorn, Ann. *Beyond the River: The Untold Story of the Heroes of the Underground Railroad*. New York: Simon and Schuster, 2002.

Hall, Richard H. *Occupations and the Social Structure*. Englewood Cliffs, N.J.: Prentice Hall, 1969.

Hambrick-Stowe, Charles E. *Charles G. Finney and the Spirit of American Evangelicalism*. Grand Rapids, Mich.: Eerdmans, 1996.

Hamilton, Gail [Mary Abigail Dodge]. "Obituary for Owen Lovejoy." *Congregationalist*, April 1864.

The Hampshire Colony Congregational Church—Its First Hundred Years. Princeton, Ill.: Press of Bureau County Record, 1931.

Harbour, Jennifer. "'I Earn by My Own Labor from Day to Day': African American Women's Activism in the Wartime Midwest." *Journal of the Illinois State Historical Society* 108 (2015): 347–73.

Harlow, Luke E. *Religion, Race, and the Making of Confederate Kentucky, 1830–1880*. New York: Cambridge University Press, 2014.

Harris, N. Dwight. *The History of Negro Servitude in Illinois and the Slavery Agitation in That State, 1719–1864*. Chicago: McClurg, 1904.

Harris, Robert L. "H. Ford Douglas: Afro-American Antislavery Emigrationist." *Journal of Negro History* 67 (1977): 217–34.

Harrison, Ella W. "The Hampshire Colony Congregational Church—Its First Hundred Years." Princeton, Ill.: n.p., 1931.

———. "A History of the First Congregational Church, Princeton, Illinois." *Journal of the Illinois State Historical Society* 20 (1927): 103–11.

Harrison, Victoria L. "We Are Here Assembled: Illinois Colored Conventions, 1853–1873." *Journal of the Illinois State Historical Society* 108 (2015): 322–46.

Harrold, Stanley. *Gamaliel Bailey and Antislavery Union*. Kent, Ohio: Kent State University Press, 1986.

———. *Subversives: Antislavery Community in Washington, D.C., 1828–1865*. Baton Rouge: Louisiana State University Press, 2003.

Hart, Richard E. "Lincoln's Springfield, the Underground Railroad." *For the People: A Newsletter of the Abraham Lincoln Association* 8 (Summer 2006): 1–8.

Hay, John. *Inside Lincoln's White House: The Complete Civil War Diary of John Hay*. Ed. Michael Burlingame and John R. Turner Ettlinger. Carbondale: Southern Illinois University Press, 1999.

Heagle, David. *The Great Anti-Slavery Agitator, Hon. Owen Lovejoy, as a Gospel Minister*. Princeton, Ill.: Streeter, 1886.

Hedrick, Joan D. *Harriet Beecher Stowe: A Life*. New York: Oxford University Press, 1994.

Heinzel, Sally. "'To Protect the Rights of the White Race': Illinois Republican Racial Politics in the 1860 Campaign and the Twenty-Second General Assembly." *Journal of the Illinois State Historical Society* 108 (2015): 374–406.

Helper, Hinton Rowan. *The Impending Crisis of the South: How to Meet It*. 1857; New York: Capricorn, 1960.

Henderson, Thomas J. "Lincoln and the Campaign of 1856." In Prince, *Transactions*, 78–89.

Herman, Janet. *Joseph Davis, Pioneer Patriarch*. Jackson: University Press of Mississippi, 1990.

———. *Pursuit of a Dream*. Oxford: Oxford University Press, 1981.

Herr, Pamela. *Jessie Benton Fremont*. New York: Watts, 1987.

Hicken, Victor. "The Record of Illinois's Negro Soldiers in the Civil War." *Journal of the Illinois State Historical Society* 56 (1963): 529–51.

Hochschild, Adam. *Bury the Chains: Prophets and Rebels in the Fight to Free an Empire's Slaves*. Boston: Houghton Mifflin, 2005.

Hodges, Graham Russell Gao. *David Ruggles: A Radical Black Abolitionist and the Underground Railroad in New York City*. Chapel Hill: University of North Carolina Press, 2010.

Hoffmann, John. *Lincoln Hall at the University of Illinois*. Urbana: University of Illinois Press, 2010.

Hohoff, Tay. *A Ministry to Man: Life of John Lovejoy Elliott*. New York: Harper, 1959.

Holzer, Harold. *Lincoln at Cooper Union: The Speech That Made Abraham Lincoln President*. New York: Simon and Schuster, 2004.

Holzman, Robert S. *Adapt or Perish: The Life of General Roger A. Pryor, C.S.A.* Hamden, Conn.: Archon, 1976.

Horowitz, Robert F. *The Great Impeacher: A Political Biography of James M. Ashley*. New York: Brooklyn College Press, 1979.

Horton, James Oliver, and Lois E. Horton. *Black Bostonians: Family Life and Community Struggle in the Antebellum North*. New York: Holmes and Meier, 1999.

Howard, Victor. *Conscience and Slavery: The Evangelistic Calvinist Domestic Missions, 1837–1861.* Kent, Ohio: Kent State University Press, 1990.

———. "The Illinois Republican Party: Part I: A Party Organizer for the Republicans in 1854." *Journal of the Illinois State Historical Society* 64 (1971): 125–60.

———. "The Illinois Republican Party: Part II: The Party Becomes Conservative, 1855–1856." *Journal of the Illinois State Historical Society* 64 (1971): 285–311.

———. *Religion and the Radical Republican Movement, 1860–1870.* Lexington: University Press of Kentucky, 1990.

James, Harold Preston. "Lincoln's Own State in the Election of 1860." Ph.D. diss., University of Illinois, 1943.

Jeffrey, Julie Roy. *The Great Silent Army of Abolitionism: Ordinary Women in the Antislavery Movement.* Chapel Hill: University of North Carolina Press, 1998.

Johannsen, Robert W. *Stephen A. Douglas.* Urbana: University of Illinois Press, 1997.

Johnson, Clifton. "Illinois Northern Congregational Churches and Ministers Supported by the AMA, 1846–1865." *New Conversations,* Winter–Spring 1989, 63–66.

Johnson, Curtiss S. *Politics and a Belly-Full: The Journalistic Career of William Cullen Bryant.* Westport, Conn.: Greenwood, 1974.

Johnson, Reinhard O. *The Liberty Party, 1840–1848: Anti-Slavery Third-Party Politics in the United States.* Baton Rouge: Louisiana State University Press, 2009.

Jones, Edgar DeWitt. *Lincoln and the Preachers.* New York: Harper, 1948.

Jones, Howard. *Mutiny on the Amistad.* New York: Oxford University Press, 1987.

Jones, James P. *"Black Jack": John A. Logan and Southern Illinois in the Civil War Era.* Carbondale: Southern Illinois University Press, 1995.

Jones, John. *The Black Laws of Illinois and a Few Reasons Why They Should Be Repealed.* Chicago: Chicago Tribune, 1864.

Journal of the Convention, Assembled at Springfield, June 7, 1847, in Pursuance of an Act of the General Assembly of the State of Illinois, Approved, February 20, 1847, for the Purpose of Altering, Amending, or Revising the Constitution of the State of Illinois. Springfield: Lanphier and Walker, 1847.

Julian, George Washington. *Life of Joshua R. Giddings.* Chicago: McClurg, 1892.

———. *Political Recollections, 1840 to 1872.* 1884; New York: Negro Universities Press, 1970.

Kantrowitz, Stephen. *More Than Freedom: Fighting for Black Citizenship in a White Republic, 1829–1889.* New York: Penguin, 2012.

Kelsey, Kerck. *Israel Washburn, Jr.* Rockport, Maine: Picton, 2004.

Kennedy, Randall. *Nigger: The Strange Career of a Troublesome Word.* New York: Random House, 2002.

Kerr, Andrea Moore. *Lucy Stone: Speaking Out for Equality.* New Brunswick: Rutgers University Press, 1992.

King, Willard L. *Lincoln's Manager: David Davis.* Cambridge: Harvard University Press, 1960.

Kingsbury, Henry D., and S. L. Deyo. "Town of Albion." In *Illustrated History of Kennebec County, Maine, 1625–1799–1892.* New York: Blake, 1892.

Körner, Gustave. *Memoirs of Gustave Koerner, 1809–1896.* Ed. Thomas J. McCormack. 2 vols. Cedar Rapids, Iowa: Torch, 1909.

Kuhns, Frederick Irving. *The American Home Missionary Society in Relation to the Antislavery Controversy in the Old Northwest.* Billings, Mont.: n.p., 1959.

Kyle, Otto R. *Abraham Lincoln in Decatur.* New York: Vantage, 1957.

Lange, Pamela Larson. "Owen Lovejoy vs. the Town of Princeton." Master's thesis, Western Illinois University, 1984.

LaRoche, Cheryl Janifer. *Free Black Communities and the Underground Railroad: The Geography of Resistance*. Urbana: University of Illinois Press, 2014.

Lasser, Carol, and Stacey Robertson. *Antebellum Women: Private, Public, Partisan*. Lanham, Md.: Rowman and Littlefield, 2010.

Laurie, Bruce. *Beyond Garrison: Antislavery and Social Reform*. New York: Cambridge University Press, 2005.

Leonard, Angela M., ed. *Antislavery Materials at Bowdoin College: A Finding Aid*. Brunswick, Maine: Bowdoin College, 1992.

Leonard, Doris Parr. *Big Bureau and Bright Prairies: A History of Bureau County, Illinois*. Moline, Ill.: Bureau County Board of Supervisors, 1968.

Leonard, Elizabeth D. *Lincoln's Forgotten Ally: Judge Advocate General Joseph Holt of Kentucky*. Chapel Hill: University of North Carolina Press, 2011.

Lerner, Gerda. *The Grimké Sisters from South Carolina*. Chapel Hill: University of North Carolina Press, 2004.

Levine, Bruce. *The Spirit of 1848: German Immigrants, Labor Conflict, and the Coming of the Civil War*. Urbana: University of Illinois Press, 1992.

Lincoln, Abraham. *Collected Works of Abraham Lincoln*. Ed. Roy P. Basler. 8 vols. New Brunswick, N.J.: Rutgers University Press, 1953–55.

Litwack, Leon. *North of Slavery*. Urbana: University of Illinois Press, 1961.

Litwack, Leon, and August Meier, eds. *Black Leaders of the Nineteenth Century*. Urbana: University of Illinois Press, 1988.

Livermore, Mary A. *My Story of the War*. Hartford, Conn.: Worthington, 1889.

Lovejoy, Clarence Earle. *The Lovejoy Genealogy, with Biographies and History, 1460–1930*. New York: Lovejoy, 1930.

Lovejoy, Joseph C. *The North and the South! Letter from J. C. Lovejoy, Esq., to His Brother, Hon. Owen Lovejoy, M.C.* N.p., 1859.

Lovejoy, Joseph C., and Owen Lovejoy. *Memoir of the Rev. Elijah P. Lovejoy, Who Was Murdered in Defence of the Liberty of the Press at Alton, Illinois, Nov. 7, 1837*. New York: John S. Taylor, 1838.

Lovejoy, Owen. *His Brother's Blood: Speeches and Writings, 1838–1864*. Ed. William F. Moore and Jane Ann Moore. Urbana: University of Illinois Press, 2004.

Magdol, Edward. *Owen Lovejoy: Abolitionist in Congress*. New Brunswick, N.J.: Rutgers University Press, 1967.

Magliocca, Gerald M. *American Founding Son: John Bingham and the Invention of the Fourteenth Amendment*. New York: New York University Press, 2015.

Majewski, John. "Why Did Northerners Oppose the Expansion of Slavery?" In *Slavery's Capitalism: A New History of American Economic Development*, ed. Sven Beckert and Seth Rockman. Philadelphia: University of Pennsylvania, 2016.

Mann, N. M. "Mrs. Cordelia A. P. Harvey." In L. P. Brockett and Mary C. Vaughan, *Woman's Work in the Civil War*. Philadelphia: Zeigler, McCurdy, 1867.

Marriner, Ernest Cummings. *The History of Colby College*, Waterville, Maine: Colby College Press, 1963.

Marsden, George M. *Fundamentalism and American Culture*. New York: Oxford University Press, 1980.

Martin, Waldo E., Jr. "Frederick Douglass: Humanist as Race Leader." In *Black Leaders of the Nineteenth Century*, ed. Leon Litwack and August Meier. Urbana: University of Illinois Press, 1988.

——. *The Mind of Frederick Douglass*. Chapel Hill: University of North Carolina Press, 1984.

Martis, Kenneth C. *The Historical Atlas of Political Parties in the United States Congress, 1789–1989*. New York: Macmillan, 1989.

Masur, Kate. *An Example for All the Land: Emancipation and the Struggle over Equality in Washington, D.C.* Chapel Hill: University of North Carolina Press, 2010.

Matteson, Joel A. "Message of the Governor of the State of Illinois to the Nineteenth General Assembly." Springfield, Ill.: 1855. Abraham Lincoln Presidential Library and Museum, Springfield.

Mayer, Henry. *All on Fire: William Lloyd Garrison and the Abolition of Slavery*. New York: St. Martin's, 1998.

McCarthy, Timothy Patrick, and John Stauffer. *Prophets of Protest: Reconsidering the History of American Abolitionism*. New York: New Press, 2006.

McCaul, Robert L. *The Black Struggle for Public Schooling in Nineteenth-Century Illinois*. Carbondale: Southern Illinois University Press, 1987.

McGiffert, Arthur Cushman, Jr. *No Ivory Tower: The Story of the Chicago Theological Seminary*. Chicago: Chicago Theological Seminary, 1965.

McKivigan, John R. *The War against Proslavery Religion: Abolitionism and the Northern Churches, 1830–1865*. Ithaca: Cornell University Press, 1984.

McPherson, James. *The Struggle for Equality: Abolitionists and the Negro in the Civil War and Reconstruction*. Princeton: Princeton University Press, 1964.

——. *The Negro's Civil War*. New York: Ballantine, 1965.

Meites, Jerome B. "The 1847 Illinois Constitutional Convention and Persons of Color." *Journal of the Illinois State Historical Society* 108 (2015): 266–95.

Melish, Joanne Pope. *Disowning Slavery: Gradual Emancipation and "Race" in New England, 1780–1860*. Ithaca: Cornell University Press, 1998.

A Memorial of Zebina Eastman by His Family. Chicago: N.p., 1883.

Meyer, Douglas K. *Making the Heartland Quilt: A Geographical History of Settlement and Migration in Early Nineteenth-Century Illinois*. Carbondale: Southern Illinois University Press, 2000.

Middleton, Stephen. *The Black Laws in the Old Northwest: A Documentary History*. Westport, Conn.: Greenwood, 1993.

Miller, William Lee. *Arguing about Slavery: The Great Battle in the United States Congress*. New York: Knopf, 1996.

——. *Lincoln's Virtues: An Ethical Biography*. New York: Knopf, 2002.

Molyneaux, John L. *African Americans in Early Rockford, 1834–1871*. Rockford, Ill.: Rockford Public Library, 2000.

Monaghan, Jay. *The Man Who Elected Lincoln*. Indianapolis: Bobbs-Merrill, 1956.

Moore, Jane Ann, and William F. Moore. "Ruling Justly in the Fear of God." *Bulletin of the Congregational Library and Archives*, 2nd ser., 11 (2015): 3–16.

Moore, William F. "Betsey Lovejoy." *Illinois Heritage*, May–June 2007.

Moore, William F., and Jane Ann Moore. *Collaborators for Emancipation: Abraham Lincoln and Owen Lovejoy*. Urbana: University of Illinois Press, 2014.

Muelder, Hermann R. *Fighters for Freedom*. New York: Columbia University Press, 1959.

Muelder, Owen M. *The Underground Railroad in Western Illinois.* Jefferson, N.C.: McFarland, 2008.

Murray, Donald M., and Robert M. Rodney. "Colonel Julian E. Bryant: Champion of the Negro Soldier." *Journal of the Illinois State Historical Society* 56 (1963): 257–81.

———. "The Letters of Peter Bryant, Jackson County Pioneer: First Installment, 1854–1861." *Kansas Historical Quarterly* 27 (1961): 320–52.

———. "The Letters of Peter Bryant, Jackson County Pioneer: Concluded, Final Installment, 1862–1906." *Kansas Historical Quarterly* 27 (1961): 469–96.

Myers, John L. *Henry Wilson and the Coming of the Civil War.* New York: University Press of America, 2005.

Nason, Emma Huntington. *Old Hallowell on the Kennebec.* Augusta, Maine: Burleigh and Flynt, 1909.

Newberry, J. S. *The Sanitary Commission in the Valley of the Mississippi during the War of the Rebellion, 1861–1866.* Cleveland: Fairbanks, Benedict, 1871.

Newman, Richard. *Freedom's Prophet: Bishop Richard Allen, the AME Church, and the Black Founding Fathers.* New York: New York University Press, 2008.

Noll, Mark A. *The Civil War as a Theological Crisis.* Chapel Hill: University of North Carolina Press, 2006.

Norton, A. T. *History of the Presbyterian Church in the State of Illinois.* St. Louis: Bryant, 1879.

Nye, Russel B. *Fettered Freedom: Civil Liberties and the Slavery Controversy, 1830–1860.* East Lansing, Michigan State College Press, 1949.

Oakes, James. *Freedom National: The Destruction of Slavery in the United States, 1861–1865.* New York: Norton, 2013.

———. *The Radical and the Republican: Frederick Douglass, Abraham Lincoln, and the Triumph of Antislavery Politics.* New York: Norton, 2007.

———. *The Scorpion's Sting: Antislavery and the Coming of the Civil War.* New York: Norton, 2014.

Oates, Stephen. *The Whirlwind of War: Voices of the Storm, 1861–1865.* New York: Harper Collins, 1998.

Ochiai, Akiko. "The Port Royal Experiment Revisited: Northern Visions of Reconstruction and the Land Question." *New England Quarterly* 74 (2001): 94–117.

Olson, Roger E. *History of Evangelical Theology.* Downers Grove, Ill.: Intervarsity Press, 2007.

Owens, William A. *Black Mutiny: Revolt on the Schooner Amistad.* Baltimore: Black Classic, 1953.

Parker, John P. *His Promised Land: The Autobiography of John P. Parker, Former Slave and Conductor on the Underground Railroad.* Ed. Stuart Seely Sprague. New York: Norton, 1996.

Pasternak, Martin B. "Rise Now and Fly to Arms: The Life of Henry Highland Garnet." Ph.D. diss., University of Massachusetts, Amherst, 1981.

Payne, Charles E. *Josiah Bushnell Grinnell.* Iowa City: State Historical Society, 1938.

Pease, Jane H., and William H. Pease. *They Who Would Be Free: Blacks' Search for Freedom, 1830–1861.* Urbana: University of Illinois Press, 1974.

Pennington, James W. C. *The Fugitive Blacksmith; or, Events in the History of James W. C. Pennington.* 1850; Miami: Hard Press, 2010.

Petrulionis, Sandra Harbert. *To Set This World Right: The Antislavery Movement in Thoreau's Concord.* Ithaca: Cornell University Press, 2006.

Pierce, Edward L. "The Freedmen at Port Royal." *Atlantic Monthly*, September 1863.

Pierson, Michael B. *Free Hearts and Free Homes: Gender and American Antislavery Politics.* Chapel Hill: University of North Carolina Press, 2003.

Pinsker, Matthew. *Lincoln's Sanctuary: Abraham Lincoln and the Soldier's Home*. New York: Oxford University Press, 2003.

———. "Senator Abraham Lincoln." *Journal of the Abraham Lincoln Association* 14 (1993): 1–21.

Price, H. H., and Gerald E. Talbot. *Maine's Visible Black History: The First Chronicle of Its People*. Gardiner, Maine: Tilbury House, 2006.

Prince, Ezra M. "Official Account of the Convention." In Prince, *Transactions*, 148–65.

———, ed. *Transactions of the McLean County Historical Society*. Vol. 3, *Meeting of May 29, 1900, Commemorative of the Convention of May 28, 1856, That Organized the Republican Party in the State of Illinois*. Bloomington, Ill.: McLean County Historical Society, 1900.

———. "Unofficial Account of the Convention." In Prince, *Transactions*, 66–80.

Proceedings of the American Anti-Slavery Society, at Its Third Decade, Held in the City of Philadelphia, December 3rd and 4th, 1863. 1864; New York: Negro Universities Press, 1969.

Proceedings of the First Convention of the Colored Citizens of the State of Illinois Convened at the City of Chicago, Thursday, Friday, and Saturday, October 6th, 7th, and 8th, 1853. Chicago: Langdon and Rounds, 1853.

Proceedings of the First Three Republican National Conventions of 1856, 1860, and 1864. Minneapolis: Johnson, 1893.

Proceedings of the General Convention of Congregational Ministers and Delegates in the United States, Held at Albany, New York, . . . October 1852. New York: Benedict, 1852.

Proceedings of the State Convention of Colored Citizens of the State of Illinois Held in the City of Alton, Nov. 13th, 14th, and 15th, 1856. Chicago: Hays and Thompson, 1856.

Quarles, Benjamin. *Allies for Freedom: Blacks on John Brown*. 1974; New York: Da Capo, 2001.

———. *Black Abolitionists*. New York: Oxford University Press, 1969.

———. "Black History's Antebellum Origins." In Rael, *African-American Activism before the Civil War*.

———. *The Negro in the Civil War*. Boston: Little, Brown, 1953.

Raboteau, Albert J. "Ethiopia Shall Soon Stretch Forth Her Hands." In Rael, *African-American Activism before the Civil War*.

Rael, Patrick, ed. *African-American Activism before the Civil War*. New York: Routledge, 2008.

———. *Black Identity and Black Protest in the Antebellum North*. Chapel Hill: University of North Carolina Press, 2002.

———. "The Market Revolution and Market Values." In Rael, *African-American Activism before the Civil War*.

Randall, James Garfield. *Constitutional Problems under Lincoln*. New York: Appleton, 1926.

Rawley, James A. "Franklin Pierce." In *"To the Best of My Ability": The American Presidents*, ed. James M. McPherson and David Rubel. New York: Dorling Kindersley, 2000.

Reed, Christopher Robert. "The Early African American Settlement of Chicago, 1833–1870." *Journal of the Illinois State Historical Society* 108 (2015): 211–65.

Reidy, Joseph P. "Emancipation." In *A Companion to the Civil War and Reconstruction*, ed. Lacy K. Ford. Oxford: Wiley-Blackwell, 2011.

Report of the Proceedings of the Colored National Convention Held at Cleveland, Ohio, on Wednesday, September 6, 1848. Rochester, N.Y.: Dick, 1848. http://coloredconventions.org/items/show/280.

Richards, Leonard L. *Gentlemen of Property and Standing*. New York: Oxford University Press, 1970.

———. *Life and Times of Congressman John Quincy Adams*. New York: Oxford University Press, 1986.

———. *Slave Power: The Free North and Southern Domination, 1780–1860*. Baton Rouge: Louisiana State University Press, 2000.

Richardson, Heather Cox. "Abraham Lincoln and the Politics of Principle." *Marquette Law Review* 93 (2010): 1383–98.

———. *The Greatest Nation of the Earth: Republican Economic Policies during the Civil War*. Cambridge: Harvard University Press, 1997.

Ripley, C. Peter, et al. *The Black Abolitionist Papers*. 5 vols. Chapel Hill: University of North Carolina Press, 1985–92.

Roberts, Rita. *Evangelicalism and the Politics of Reform in Northern Black Thought, 1776–1863*. Baton Rouge: Louisiana State University Press, 2010.

Robertson, Stacey M. *Hearts Beating for Liberty: Women Abolitionists in the Old Northwest*. Chapel Hill: University of North Carolina Press, 2010.

Robinson, Armstead L. *Bitter Fruits of Bondage: The Demise of Slavery and the Collapse of the Confederacy, 1861–1865*. Charlottesville: University of Virginia Press, 2005.

Robinson, Marilynne. *The Death of Adam: Essays on Modern Thought*. New York: Picador, 2003.

———. *When I Was a Child I Read Books: Essays*. New York: Farrar, Straus, and Giroux, 2013.

Rose, Willie Lee. *Rehearsal for Reconstruction: The Port Royal Experiment*. New York: Vintage, 1964.

Roy, Joseph E. *Pilgrim's Letters: Bits of Current History*. Boston: Congregational Sunday-School and Publishing Society, 1888.

Salafia, Matthew. *Slavery's Borderland: Freedom and Bondage along the Ohio River*. Philadelphia: University of Pennsylvania Press, 2013.

Salerno, Beth A. *Sister Societies: Women's Organizations in Antebellum America*. DeKalb: Northern Illinois University Press, 2005.

Sassi, Jonathan D. *A Republic of Righteousness: The Public Christianity of the Post-Revolutionary New England Clergy*. New York: Oxford University Press, 2001.

Saunders, Delores T. *Illinois Liberty Lines: The History of the Underground Railroad*. Farmington, Ill.: Saunders, 1982.

Schneider, Carl E. *The German Church on the American Frontier: A Study in the Rise of Religion among the Germans of the West Based on the History of the Evangelical Church Society of the West, 1840–1866*. St. Louis: Eden, 1939.

Schriver, Edward O. *Go Free: The Antislavery Impulse in Maine, 1833–1855*. Orono: University of Maine Press, 1970.

Schwalm, Leslie A. *Emancipation's Diaspora: Race and Reconstruction in the Upper Midwest*. Chapel Hill: University of North Carolina Press, 2009.

Scott, Donald M. *Office to Profession: The New England Ministry, 1750–1850*. Philadelphia: University of Pennsylvania Press, 1978.

Scott, R. Nathaniel. "What Price Freedom? John Jones, a Search for Negro Equality." Master's thesis, Southern Illinois University, 1971.

Selby, Paul. "The Editorial Convention, February 22, 1856." In Prince, *Transactions*, 30–42.

———. "Republican State Convention, Springfield, Ill., Oct. 4–5, 1854." In Prince, *Transactions*, 43–47.

Sernett, Milton C. *Abolition's Axe: Beriah Green, Oneida Institute, and the Black Freedom Struggle*. Syracuse: Syracuse University Press, 1986.

———. *North Star Country: Upstate New York and the Crusade for African American Freedom*. Syracuse: Syracuse University Press, 2002.

Shaw, Benjamin F. "Lovejoy, the Abolitionists, and Republican Party." In Prince, *Transactions*, 59–74.

Simon, Paul. *Freedom's Champion: Elijah Lovejoy*. Carbondale: Southern Illinois University Press, 1994.

Sinha, Manisha. "The Coming of Age: The Historiography of Black Abolitionism." In *Prophets of Protest: Reconsidering the History of American Abolitionism*, ed. Timothy Patrick McCarthy and John Stauffer, 23–40. New York: New Press, 2006.

———. *The Slave's Cause: A History of Abolition*. New Haven: Yale University Press, 2015.

Smith, Asa P. *History of the Congregational Church of Litchfield, Maine*. N.p., 1911.

Smith, George Owen. *The Lovejoy Shrine, Home of Owen Lovejoy*. Tiskilwa, Ill.: Bureau Valley Chief, 1987.

Spinka, Matthew. *A History of Illinois Congregational and Christian Churches*. Chicago: Congregational and Christian Conference of Illinois, 1944.

Stampp, Kenneth M. *And the War Came: The North and the Secession Crisis, 1860–1861*. Baton Rouge: Louisiana State University Press, 1950.

Staudenraus, P. J. *The African Colonization Movement, 1816–1865*. New York: Columbia University Press, 1961.

Stauffer, John. *The Black Hearts of Men*. Cambridge: Harvard University Press, 2001.

Sterling, Dorothy, ed. *Speak Out in Thunder Tones: Letters and Other Writings by Black Northerners, 1787–1865*. Garden City, N.Y.: Doubleday, 1973.

Stewart, Alvan. *Writings and Speeches of Alvan Stewart on Slavery*. Ed. Luther R. Marsh. New York: Burdick, 1860.

Stewart, James Brewer. *Abolitionist Politics and the Coming of the Civil War*. Amherst: University of Massachusetts Press, 2008.

———. "The Emergence of Racial Modernity." In Rael, *African-American Activism before the Civil War*.

———. *Holy Warriors: The Abolitionists and American Slavery*. New York: Hill and Wang, 1976.

———. *Joshua R. Giddings and the Tactics of Radical Politics*. Cleveland: Press of Case Western Reserve, 1970.

———. *Wendell Phillips: Liberty's Hero*. Baton Rouge: Louisiana State University Press, 1986.

———. *William Lloyd Garrison and the Challenge of Emancipation*. Arlington Heights, Ill.: Harlan Davidson, 1992.

Stewart, James H., and James H. Moorhead, eds. *Charles Hodge Revisited*. Grand Rapids, Mich.: Eerdmans, 2002.

Stone, Lucy. *Friends and Sisters: Letters between Lucy Stone and Antoinette Brown Blackwell, 1846–93*. Ed. Carol Lasser and Marlene Deahl Merrill. Urbana: University of Illinois Press, 1987.

Stoneburner, Carol, and John Stoneburner, eds. *The Influence of Quaker Women on American History: Biographical Studies*. Lewiston, N.Y.: Mellen, 1986.

Storrs, Charles, comp. *Storrs Family: Genealogical and Other Memoranda*. New York:, 1886.

Storrs, Richard Salter. *American Slavery and the Means of Its Removal: A Sermon Preached in the First Congregational Church, Braintree, Annual State Fast, April 4, 1844*. Boston: Marvin, 1844.

Stowell, Daniel W., ed. *In Tender Consideration: Women, Families, and the Law in Abraham Lincoln's Illinois*. Urbana: University of Illinois Press, 2002.

Strangis, Joel. *Lewis Hayden and the War against Slavery*. North Haven, Conn.: Linnet, 1999.

Strong, Douglas M. *Perfectionist Politics: Abolitionism and the Religious Tensions of American Democracy*. Syracuse: Syracuse University Press, 1999.

Stuckey, Sterling. "A Last Stern Struggle: Henry Highland Garnet and Liberation Theory." In *Black Leaders of the Nineteenth Century*, ed. Leon Litwack and August Meier. Urbana: University of Illinois Press, 1988.

Study, Guy. *History of St. Paul's Episcopal Church, Alton, Illinois*. St. Louis: Mound City, 1943.

Sweeney, Martin A. *Lincoln's Gift from Homer, New York: A Painter, an Editor, and a Detective*. Jefferson, N.C.: McFarland, 2011.

Sweet, William Warren, ed. *His Religion on the American Frontier*. Vol. 2, *Presbyterians: A Collection of Source Materials*. 1936; New York: Cooper Square, 1964.

Swift, David E. *Black Prophets of Justice: Activist Clergy before the Civil War*. Baton Rouge: Louisiana State University Press, 1989.

Takaki, Ronald R. *A Pro-Slavery Crusade: Agitation to Reopen the African Slave Trade*. New York: Free Press, 1971.

Thomas, Herman Edward. "An Analysis of the Life and Work of James W. C. Pennington, a Black Churchman and Abolitionist." Ph.D. diss., Hartford Seminary Foundation, 1978.

Trefousse, Hans L. *Benjamin Franklin Wade: Radical Republican from Ohio*. New York: Twayne, 1963.

———. "Owen Lovejoy and Abraham Lincoln during the Civil War." *Abraham Lincoln Journal* 22 (2001): 16–32.

———. *The Radical Republicans: Lincoln's Vanguard for Racial Justice*. New York: Knopf, 1968.

———. *Thaddeus Stevens, Nineteenth-Century Egalitarian*. Chapel Hill: University of North Carolina Press, 1997.

The Tribune Almanac and Political Register for 1865. New York: The Tribune Association, 1865.

Turner, Glennette Tilley. *The Underground Railroad in Illinois*. Glen Ellyn, Ill.: Newman Educational, 2001.

United Church Board for Homeland Ministries. "150th Anniversary of the American Missionary Association." *New Conversations*, Winter–Spring, 1989.

Venet, Wendy Hamand. *Neither Ballots nor Bullets: Women Abolitionists and the Civil War*. Charlottesville: University Press of Virginia, 1991.

Voegeli, V. Jacque. *Free but Not Equal: The Midwest and the Negro during the Civil War*. Chicago: University of Chicago Press, 1967.

Volpe, Vernon L. *Forlorn Hope of Freedom: The Liberty Party in the Old Northwest, 1838–1848*. Kent, Ohio: Kent State University Press, 1990.

Vorenberg, Michael. *The Emancipation Proclamation: A Brief History with Documents*. Boston: Bedford/St. Martin's, 2010.

Walker, Clarence E. *A Rock in a Weary Land: The A.M.E. Church during the Civil War and Reconstruction*. Baton Rouge: Louisiana State University Press, 1982.

Wallace, Isabel. *Life and Letters of General W. H. L. Wallace*. Chicago: Donnelley, 1909.

Walters, Ronald G. *American Reformers, 1815–1860*. New York: Hill and Wang, 1978.

———. *The Antislavery Appeal: American Abolitionism after 1830*. Baltimore: Johns Hopkins University Press, 1976.

Walther, Eric H. *The Shuttering of the Union: America in the 1850s*. Lanham, Md.: Rowman and Littlefield, 2004.

Ward, Samuel Ringgold. *Autobiography of a Fugitive Negro*. 1855; Eugene, Ore.: Wipf and Stock, 2000.

Washburne, Mark. *A Biography: Elihu Benjamin Washburne: Congressman, Secretary of State, Envoy Extraordinary*. 6 vols. Philadelphia: Xlibris, 2000–2016.

Way, Virgil G., comp. *History of the Thirty-Third Regiment Illinois Veteran Volunteer Infantry in the Civil War*. Gibson City, Ill.: Regimental Association, 1902.

Wayman, Alexander Walker. *My Recollections of African M.E. Ministers; or, Forty Years' Experience in the African Methodist Episcopal Church*. Philadelphia: A.M.E. Book Rooms, 1881.

Weiner, Dana Elizabeth. *Race and Rights: Fighting Slavery and Prejudice in the Old Northwest, 1830–1870*. DeKalb: Northern Illinois University Press, 2015.

Weld, Theodore Dwight. *American Slavery as It Is: Testimony of a Thousand Witnesses*. 1839; New York: Arno, 1969.

Whiting, William. *The War Powers of the President, and the Legislative Powers of Congress in Relation to Rebellion, Treason, and Slavery*. 2nd ed. Boston: Shorey, 1862.

Whittemore, Edwin Carey. *The Centennial History of Waterville*. Waterville, Maine: Executive Committee of the Centennial Celebration, 1902.

Wiggin, Ruby Crosby. *Albion on the Narrow Gauge*. Auburn, Maine: Little Guy, 1964.

Wilder, Craig Steven. *Ebony and Ivy: Race, Slavery, and the Troubled History of American Universities*. New York: Bloomsbury, 2013.

Willey, Austin. *History of the Antislavery Cause in State and Nation*. 1860; New York: Negro Universities Press, 1969.

Wilson, Douglas L., and Rodney O. Davis, eds. *Herndon's Informants: Letters, Interviews, and Statements about Abraham Lincoln*. Urbana: University of Illinois Press, 1998.

Wilson, Henry. *History of Antislavery Measures of the 37th and 38th Congresses, 1861–1864*. Boston: Walter, Wise, 1864.

———. *Rise and Fall of the Slave Power in America*. 3 vols. Boston: Osgood, 1875–77.

Winger, Stewart. *Lincoln, Religion, and Romantic Cultural Politics*. DeKalb: Northern Illinois University Press, 2003.

Winkle, Kenneth J. "Paradox Though It May Seem." In *Lincoln Emancipated: The President and the Politics of Race*, ed. Brian R. Dirick. DeKalb: Northern Illinois University Press, 2007.

Wiswall, J. M. *The Wiswall Descendants of Leofwine the Saxon*. Freehold Township, N.J.: Wiswall, 1978.

Work, Monroe N. "Life of Charles B. Ray." *Journal of Negro History* 4 (1919): 361–71.

Wright, Theodore S. "The Progress of the Antislavery Cause." In *God Ordained this War: Sermons on the Sectional Crisis, 1830–1865*, ed. David O. Chesebrough. Columbia: University of South Carolina Press, 1991.

Wyatt-Brown, Bertram. *Lewis Tappan and the Evangelical War against Slavery*. Cleveland: Press of Case Western Reserve University, 1969.

Wyman, Mark. *Immigrants in the Valley: Irish, Germans, and Americans in the Upper Mississippi Country, 1830–1860*. Chicago: Nelson-Hall, 1984.

Yeager, Ivor. *Julian M. Sturtevant, 1805–1886*. Jacksonville, Ill.: Trustees of Illinois College, 1999.

Yellin, Jean Fagan, and John C. Van Horne, eds. *The Abolitionist Sisterhood: Women's Political Culture in Antebellum America*. Ithaca: Cornell University Press, 1994.

Zaeske, Susan. *Signatures of Citizenship: Petitioning, Antislavery, and Women's Political Identity*. Chapel Hill: University of North Carolina Press, 2003.

Index

Congregational associations: Illinois General Association, 40–42, 54; Rock River Association, 23, 30, 39, 41, 42, 92

Congregational Herald, 10, 82

Conkling, Roscoe, 158

Connecticut State Anti-Slavery Society, 20

Constitutional Union Party, 140

containment of slavery, 9, 63, 100, 152, 156. *See also* nonextension of slavery

contraband: as label applied to former slaves, 6, 155–56; policies on, 160

Conway, Moncure, 119

Cook, Chauncey, 25

Cooper, Richard S., 74

Cooper Union (New York City), x, 135, 172–73

Copperhead Democrats, 178

Costin, J. T., 190

Cox, Samuel S., 137, 170

Crittenden, John, 172

Cross, John, 26, 31, 32, 40, 41, 64

Crummell, Alexander, 73

Cunningham, Joseph O., 107

Cushman, Joshua, 13, 14

Cutler, Hannah, 93, 126

Dana, Charles, 181

Davis, David, 94, 110, 121, 129, 144

Davis, Mary Brown, 44–46, 60, 84

Davis, Reuben, 118

Davis, Samuel, 44

Declaration of Independence, 2, 13, 35, 138, 147; opposition to, 37, 123

democracy, 2, 120, 136; antislavery's impact on, 191; and colonization, 90; majority vs. minority rule in, 138, 151; and middle class, 136; Ward on, 73

Democratic Party, 112, 158; and confiscation, 171; and emancipation, 172; and expansion of slavery, 43, 89, 113, 170; and homestead bills, 136, 142–43; Lovejoy criticizes, 128; racism and Black Laws, 57, 98, 122, 125, 128, 145, 179, 180–81; splintered, 140. *See also* secession and secessionism

Democrats: antislavery, 55, 91, 93, 95, 106; Copperhead, 178; Free, 81; and fusion, 104, 107, 121, 177; in Illinois legislature, 57, 60, 92, 94, 96, 102, 112, 124; Jacksonian, 54; in U.S. Congress, 93, 117, 134, 150–51, 158, 178; War, 177

Denham, Butler, 28, 29, 31, 127

Denham, Elizabeth (Libbie, stepdaughter), 28

Denham, Eunice. *See* Lovejoy, Eunice Storrs Denham

Denham, Lucy (stepdaughter), 44, 92

Denham, Mary (stepdaughter), 28

DeWolf, Calvin, 74

Dickey, James H., 23, 28, 47

Dickey, T. Lyle, 110, 121

District of Columbia: antislavery churches in, 68, 119, 171; black army volunteers from, 155; black churches in, 93, 118, 129, 152, 153, 165, 169, 190; and education of black children, 168, 170, 175, 183; and emancipation of slaves, 11, 51, 133, 152, 158, 168, 169; *National Era* in, 67, 68; power of Congress over, 23, 48, 63; regulations affecting slaves in, 190; social season in, 119, 129; society in, 68, 112, 129; Underground Railroad in, 141

disunionists, 150, 151. *See also* secession and secessionism

Disunion Vigilance Committee, 150

Divine Spirit, 15, 71

Dixon Telegraph, 123

Dodge, Mary Abigail (pen name Gail Hamilton), 10, 125, 126, 226n94

Doolittle, James R., 125

Douglas, H. Ford: and black troops, 181, 182; and Lincoln campaign, 148; marriage of, 184; touring, 81, 86, 88, 127

Douglas, Sattira, 184

Douglas, Stephen A., 69, 116, 118, 124, 140; and Chicago Common Council, 74; debates with Lincoln, 123; debate with Lovejoy, 92; Nebraska bill, 88–90

Douglass, Frederick, 34, 60, 63, 73, 87–88, 165; as army recruiter, 180; on blacks' human and civil rights, 84–85, 90, 166; and colonialism vs. interracial democracy, 89–90, 155, 183; at Colored Conventions, 66, 85–86; Stephen Douglas and, 122, 123–24; on *Dred Scott* decision, 114; on emancipation, 177, 179–80; and Free Democratic Party, 80, 87–88, 94; and Free Soilers, 64; and fugitive slaves, 72, 74, 137, 160; in Illinois, 72, 85, 86, 87–88, 91–92, 127; John Jones and, 66, 85–86, 94, 127–28; Lovejoy and, 11, 72–73, 80, 87–89, 106, 142, 160–61; newspaper, 79, 99, 129, 131, 160–61; opinions of Lincoln, 142, 164; on race theory, 43, 154; at Radical Abolition Party convention, 106; warrant for arrest, 131

Dred Scott decision (*Dred Scott v. Sandford*), 41, 114, 115, 117, 137

Dubois, Jesse, 107

Durkee, Charles, 119

Dyer, Charles V.: as antislavery organizer, 26, 27, 32, 49; as host, 127; John Brown and, 130; at Liberty Convention, 50–52, 63 64; and refugees, 75

Dyer, Louisa M. Gifford, 46, 52, 62

Lovejoy as minister, 22, 23, 56; and Lovejoy's
antislavery positions, 32, 42–43, 70, 83; after
Lovejoy's resignation, 103, 114, 184, 189; and
Lovejoy's salary, 28–29; Ebenezer Phelps
as president, 96; rejects AHMS subsidy, 41;
David Todd as substitute minister, 55; and
Underground Railroad, 67, 69, 76
Hatch, Ozias, 130
Hayden, Lewis, 7, 55, 131, 180
Henderson, Thomas J., 178
Hewitt, J. G., 118, 122, 163, 167, 169
Higbee, Chauncey, 101, 102
Higginson, T. W., 131
Hinton, Thomas H. C., 190
human rights, 17–18, 26, 70–71, 94, 147, 173; Dou-
glass on blacks', 84–85, 90, 166; education,
101; petitions, 161
Hurlbut, Mrs. T. C., 46
Hurlbut, Thaddeus B., 17, 20

Illinois Anti-Slavery Society, 5, 17, 25, 73, 191
Illinois Convention of Colored People. *See* Colored Conventions: in Illinois
Illinois Female Anti-Slavery Society, 6, 45–48,
50–52, 60, 62
Illinois General Assembly: and Black Laws, 57,
60, 66, 82, 86, 187; on colonization, 97; Demo-
crats lose and regain majority, 93, 96, 99, 102;
election of U.S. senator, 100; Lovejoy and,
86, 98, 101–2, 123; and public education, 112;
redraws congressional districts, 176; slavery
resolutions by, 94, 96, 99, 115
Illinois General Congregational Association,
40–42, 54
Illinois Staat-Zeitung (newspaper), 105
Illinois State Journal, 103, 188
Illinois State Register, 92, 103, 188
Ingersoll, Ebon C., 177
Ipswich Seminary or Academy, 16, 93
Isbell, Luis, 74, 169, 182

Jay, John, 185
Johnson, William, 49
Jones, John, 6, 48–50, 67, 180; and Black Exclusion law, 57–58, 67, 82; and Black Laws, 57,
60, 66–67, 82, 86, 96–99, 112, 187–88; Chicago
response to D.C. Emancipation, 169; and
colonization, 89, 90, 97, 98, 125; at Colored
People's Conventions, 66, 85, 86, 102, 112; and
Douglass, 66, 85, 86, 88, 94, 127–28; and Fugitive Slave Law, 74–75, 154; and Liberty Party,
49–52; petitions by, 82–83, 98–99; recruits
soldiers, 182; and Repeal Association, 125, 178;
and Republican Party, 103, 124, 147 154–55;

tours Illinois with Douglass and H. Ford
Douglas, 86, 88, 127; and Underground Rail-
road, 67, 74, 75, 130, 137, 154
Jones, Mary, 6, 48, 49, 52, 86, 130
Jubilee, 179
Judd, Norman, 82, 109
Julian, George W.: and Free Democratic Party,
79, 80; and Free Soil Party, 65; and Republi-
can Party, 106, 145, 163

Kansas: statehood, 105, 116, 118
Kansas-Nebraska Act, 9, 41, 89–90, 94, 114. *See
also* anti-Nebraska movement; anti-Nebraskans
Kansas Territory, 88–89, 107, 115
Keckly, Elizabeth, 182
Keitt, Lawrence M., 118
Kellogg, William P., 112, 116, 150
Kelsey, Charles L., 47, 79, 90, 105, 190
King, Preston, 125
Kingdom of God, 9, 14, 61, 76
Know-Nothing Party, 103, 107–8
Knox, James, 81
Knox College, 45, 48
Koerner, Gustave, 161

Ladies Loyal League, 184
Lamar, Lucius Q. C., 118
La Moille, Ill., 31, 33, 39
Lamphier, Charles H., 92
Leavitt, Joshua, 18, 65, 118; and American Anti-
Slavery Society, 19–20; and *Emancipator*, 18,
37–38; and Liberty Party, 59; and Mendian
Committee, 24; research by, 20, 68
Lecompton Constitution, 116, 118
Lee, G., 169
Lee, John W., 169, 190
Lewis, Lydia S., 44
Lewis, M. L., 169
Liberator (newspaper), 55, 90, 144. *See also* Gar-
rison, William Lloyd
Liberty Party, 2, 3, 31, 40, 42; campaigns, 43, 54,
62; in Chicago, 49–50; conventions, 33–37,
47, 50–52, 56; and Free Soil Party, 58, 59, 60,
61; nominee for Electoral College, 47; "Old
Liberty Party men," 78, 80; "one idea," 51;
and Underground Railroad, 49; women's
participation, 44, 52
Lincoln, Abraham: antislavery view, 92, 94, 103;
Cooper Union speech, 134–36; debates with
S. Douglas, 122–23; and Fugitive Slave Law,
154, 159, 164; and "Illinois friends," 157–58;
Lovejoy and, 110, 113, 157, 172, 173–74, 182, 185;
and nonextension of slavery into territories,
145, 149

JANE ANN MOORE and WILLIAM F. MOORE are co-directors of the Lovejoy Society. They are the authors of *Collaborators for Emancipation: Abraham Lincoln and Owen Lovejoy* and the editors of Owen's Lovejoy's *His Brother's Blood: Speeches and Writings, 1838–64*. They manage the website www.increaserespect.com, which applies the concepts of this book.

The University of Illinois Press
is a founding member of the
Association of University Presses.

Composed in 10.75/13.5 Bulmer Std
by Kirsten Dennison
at the University of Illinois Press
Cover designed by Jim Proefrock
Cover illustration: Owen Lovejoy when he was in Congress,
photographed by Julian Vannerson, ca. 1859 (Library of Congress,
Prints and Photographs Division)

University of Illinois Press
1325 South Oak Street
Champaign, IL 61820-6903
www.press.uillinois.edu